42.09

Meeting the Needs of People with Disabilities:
A Guide for Librarians, Educators, and Other Service Professionals

by Ruth A. Velleman

ORYX PRESS
1990

Copyright © 1990 by
The Oryx Press
2214 North Central at Encanto
Phoenix, AZ 85004-1483

Published simultaneously in Canada

Printed and Bound in the United States of America

∞ The paper used in this publication meets the minimum requirements of American National Standard for Information Science—Permanence of Paper for Printed Library Materials, ANSI Z39.48, 1984.

Library of Congress Cataloging-in-Publication Data

Velleman, Ruth A.
  Meeting the needs of people with disabilities: a guide for librarians, educators, and other service professionals / by Ruth A. Velleman.
      p.   cm.
Bibliography: p.
Includes index.
ISBN 0-89774-521-3
1. Libraries and the handicapped.   2. Handicapped—Books and reading.   3. Handicapped—Services for.   4. Handicapped—Education.
5. Rehabilitation.   I. Title.
Z711.92.H3V44   1990
025.5′27663—dc20   89-8570
                                                                          CIP

Contents

For My Grandsons
Daniel, David, and Evan

Foreword

by Mary Roatch
Special Needs Center Supervisor
Phoenix Public Library

The challenge to identify, collect, and organize the vast amount of information regarding people with disabilities is made more difficult by the variety of credible resources available. Ruth A. Velleman has effectively approached the task of dealing with such variable topics as attitudes, emotional and social problems, advocacy, and resources and services related to people with disabilities by dividing her book into four major parts: Part I-People with Disabilities: An Overview; Part II-Consumer Information; Part III-Rehabilitation and Special Education: Information for Professionals; and Part IV-Library Applications. Such an arrangement makes information collection and application much easier, and the index and five appendices allow quick retrieval of needed information.

The comprehensive range of data collected in this volume provides an encyclopedic handbook for information and service providers. However this book will also be helpful to individuals with disabilities by providing answers to their questions concerning available community resources and accessibility issues.

In 1979, Velleman's original book, *Serving Physically Disabled People: An Information Handbook for All Libraries,* heralded the beginning of a new awareness of people with disabilities. In the years following publication of that first edition, many major events and pieces of legislation related to disabilities have unfolded. Nineteen eighty-one was declared "International Year of the Disabled"; the 1980s were designated the "Decade of the Disabled." These are examples of events that have been instrumental in increasing awareness and thus encouraging better service to people with disabilities. The printing of this revised edition is a necessary and timely event.

The most dramatic change in services to this special population is the development of technology which can be used to organize, search, access, and communicate information. Velleman has devoted a chapter to the new technology that enables people to function with disabilities by using computers with synthetic speech output, voice recognition input, and adaptive switches. This equipment allows communication and print production, literacy instruction, and game playing to stimulate the perceptual/motor process. Electronic access to information has allowed people with disabilities to capitalize on their abilities.

Computer access to information is not only a benefit to blind, deaf, physically challenged, and developmentally disabled persons, but it provides librarians, educators, and other service professionals with a powerful tool for organizing the multiplicity of resources available. This aspect of service to the disabled is addressed in Part III; Rehabilitation and Special Education: Information for Professionals, in which Velleman discusses several national databases of disability information and addresses the real need for a revised and second edition of her 1979 book.

Part IV of this book is dedicated to "Library Applications," in which the author recognizes the role of libraries as society's information centers. Within their framework of classifying, cataloging, and structuring for quick retrieval, libraries become structures which can touch the information needs of all those with disabilities as they relate to individuals, families, friends, and the professionals serving them. Resources and accessibility issues of public, school, university, and rehabilitation libraries are clearly illustrated.

Libraries are the catalytic agents that provide information access and organize the proliferation of currently available data. For the past five years, I have been in charge of the Phoenix Public Library Special Needs Center, where I have consolidated services, materials, and programs for people with disabilities and provided specially trained staff, so that people who previously had difficulty using a public library now have complete accessibility to its resources. The Center has a Computer Workplace for People with Disabilities that provides for blind and physically handicapped library users electronic access to print and computer information via synthetic speech and braille output. Through this Center, we have demonstrated that public libraries can be more accessible for people with disabilities. A resource guide such as Ruth Velleman's book will provide a condensed format for quick information retrieval to assist our library users in the Phoenix Public Library Special Needs Center. It is an effective, easy-to-use tool and will surely find a prominent place on the desks of librarians, educators, rehabilitators, and service providers working with people with disabilities.

In using the phrase "person with disabilities" to identify people who are limited in their ability to function, Velleman has emphasized the "ability" segment of the word. Now the emphasis of the phrase denotes a "person with disABILITIES" as an individual who has the ability to effectively reach beyond a sensory, physical, or mental limitation. This has real significance as an indicator of the political, emotional, and philosophical attitude change toward and among persons with disabilities as this Decade of the Disabled draws to a close. With legislative support to allow persons with disabilities equal access in the areas of education, employment, public services, and transportation, their quality of life is improving. The task of this book is to encourage society, through service providers, to address the needs of this special population and build on the increased knowledge and awareness of the 1980s, through the 1990s, and into the twenty-first century.

Foreword

by Jay Rochlin
Executive Director
President's Committee on Employment of People
with Disabilities

In order to be employable, people with disabilities must become as independent as possible. Being able to function independently in activities of daily living, to travel to and from a job, to live as independently as possible in adapted housing, are all prerequisites to successful employment. Yet a Harris Poll, conducted in 1986 under the auspices of the National Council on Disability and the International Center for the Disabled, indicated that most people with disabilities are not familiar with services that exist to assist them to gain independence.

It is for the above reasons that this book is so important to the field of rehabilitation, and to people with disabilities. In her book, Ruth A. Velleman has addressed the problems of attitudes toward people with disabilities. Most importantly, she has supplied answers to where to obtain essential services that will enable people with disabilities to live and work to their potential.

An important chapter on new technology recognizes that today's technology can enable persons with severe disabilities to work competitively, once properly trained. Chapters on the fields of rehabilitation and special education delineate the important issues confronting professionals working in these fields today.

The entire rehabilitation community, including vocational rehabilitation counselors, rehabilitation centers, hospitals with rehabilitation facilities, and information providers who work with people with disabilities should benefit from this valuable work. It should be on the shelves of personnel directors in corporations which are being called upon to make greater efforts to employ people with disabilities. And it should serve as a text for university programs in Rehabilitation Counseling and Special Education.

Preface

As the decade of the 1980s draws to a close the progress that has been made in the lives of people with disabilities has been enormous. And yet much remains to be accomplished.

In this work, I have attempted to document these changes, with the ever-present knowledge that even as I wrote the picture was shifting. A book can do no more than offer one moment in time. Legislation continues to be written, new organizations formed, and old ones relocated. Most important, advances in technology, notably the advent of computer use for people with disabilities, have necessitated that a chapter be devoted to this exciting development.

Although I have worked primarily with people with physical disabilities, in this book I offer some definitions and services in some areas of developmental disabilities and mental retardation, as well as in the field of learning disabilities.

The designation "people with disabilities" is now being employed in the names of organizations such as the President's Committee on Employment of People with Disabilities. I applaud this change as a positive one, and I have made an attempt to use it in this text. Many of the organizations quoted, however, still use the alternate descriptive titles such as disabled or handicapped people.

Throughout the text I have deliberately omitted telephone numbers, except for 800 numbers. I have found that local numbers change continually and it is best to check these with directory assistance. Similarly, I have omitted prices of publications since these also change over time.

Many persons have been of help as I gathered the information I needed. In particular I would like to thank Alice Hagemeyer, librarian for the deaf community of the Martin Luther King Public Library in Washington, DC, for supplying up-to-date information about library service to the hearing impaired. My appreciation goes to Lenore Roseman, executive director of the Dysautonomia Foundation; Ann Scherer, director of information and education, Epilepsy Foundation of America; and Allison H. Borrows, administrative assistant, community education department, Helen Keller National Center for Deaf-Blind Individuals, for reviewing the sections of my manuscript devoted to each of these disabilities and updating and making corrections to the definitions.

My thanks to Jack Victor, formerly director of grants management at Human Resources Center, for delineating the important areas in the rehabilitation field today; Dale Brown, employment advisor for the President's Committee for Employment of People with Disabilities, for the very helpful materials she supplied in the field of learning disabilities; and Craig Michaels, senior coordinator for learning disabilities programs and projects at Human Resources Center, for his account of the programs at his Center.

I am grateful to Shirley Everett Clark, director of training, education and video production at Planned Parenthood in Cincinnati, Ohio, for information about programs in the area of sexuality for people with mental disabilities. Inez Storck, program specialist at the National Institute on Disability and Rehabilitation Research (NIDRR) has provided continuing support, advice and information for which I express my heartfelt thanks.

June C. Holt, director of the Massachusetts Rehabilitation Commission Library, and Joan Appel, coordinator of reference services at the Moss Rehabilitation Hospital Library, were gracious in sharing information with me about their programs, for which I thank them very much. And special thanks goes to The IBM National Support Center for Persons with Disabilities and the Apple Inc., Office of Special Education, both of which supplied extensive information about their programs.

My research was ably supported by Amnon Tishler, research librarian of the Human Resources Center Research Library, who has maintained the collection most impressively, producing much of the rehabilitation material I needed. I thank him for his work on my behalf. I am grateful also to the many other persons who responded to my requests for information and sent literature. They are too numerous to name here. Special thanks to Susan Slesinger for her very able editing of the manuscript and to editor Jan Krygier for overseeing its publication. My sons, Paul, David, and Daniel Velleman, performed valiant service as instructors and coaches, helping me master the intricacies of my Macintosh Word Processing program. As always, my husband Moritz Velleman supplied moral support throughout the project. My gratitude and love to them all.

Introduction

In the early 1970s two significant laws were enacted to mandate equal rights and appropriate educational opportunity for all people with disabilities: Public Law 93-112, The Rehabilitation Act of 1973, and Public Law 94-142, The Education of All Handicapped Children Act. It was hoped that these two pieces of legislation, as well as several subsequent ones, would lead to very great changes.

In some instances these positive changes have occurred. However, in many cases they have not gone far enough, and in some cases partial efforts without appropriate follow-through have had disastrous results for those people with disabilities as well as for the community at large. An example is de-institutionalization, in which people are left in need of a supportive living environment. The Independent Living movement, propelled by hopeful ideas during the 1970s, is still not able to serve people with severe physical disabilities, and while some group homes have been established for those people with mental handicaps, community resistance has hampered the development of the needed numbers.

The library profession has attempted to serve the disabled population by developing many outreach programs nationwide. However, the results of a Harris Poll conducted under the auspices of the International Center for the Disabled, New York, NY, with the cooperation of the National Council on Disability, Washington, DC, in March 1986 disclosed that most people with disabilities are not familiar with some widely available services and, in fact, a 53 percent majority feel that it is difficult to find out about these services. A minority of disabled persons is familiar with medical and rehabilitation services (44 percent), Section 8 or other housing for disabled persons (31 percent), and independent living centers (25 percent). These findings leave no doubt that much could be done to better inform persons with disabilities about the most important services available to them, a remaining priority for information providers.

Many libraries in hospital settings have begun, in this decade, to provide information concerning daily living skills for patients returning to their homes, but this is not universally true. Unfortunately, most rehabilitation facilities do not yet have trained librarians on their staffs.

For a period of about 10 years, beginning in the early 1970s, many library schools and other educational facilities sponsored workshops in the field of library service to people with disabilities; however, federal funding has been harder to come by in recent years, and these workshops have been fewer. At the same time I have found a greater need on the part of school librarians for information regarding how to deal with the special needs of the many disabled students now being mainstreamed into their schools and libraries and how to provide information to teachers, administrators, therapists, nurses and other professional personnel, as well as to parents. Some library schools have incorporated this information into their course work or have created special courses. I fear, however, that many still need to do so and all must keep their information updated.

This book is offered in the hope that it will serve as a current guide to working librarians, to professors and students in library schools and schools of education, as well as to schools offering course work in the area of rehabilitation counseling and to information providers in rehabilitation settings. Because librarians have the opportunity to assume leadership roles in the community in helping to shape attitudes and convey understanding about the special problems and needs of the disparate groups that form their public, the first chapter of the book offers them some background to help them develop their own perspectives.

PART I

People with Disabilities: An Overview

Chapter 1
Attitudes about Disabilities

It is estimated that 36 to 40 million Americans are disabled in some way, either physically, mentally, or emotionally. About one in six physically disabled Americans was born with his or her disability; the others become disabled through injury or accident or by contracting debilitating diseases such as multiple sclerosis or by developing visual or hearing impairments.

In 1980 the Carnegie Council on Children published its fifth and final report, a book entitled *The Unexpected Minority: Handicapped Children in America* by John Gliedman and William Roth. Written by a psychologist and a political scientist, this important and innovative study opened the decade of the 1980s. Their conclusion was that Americans with disabilities are the targets of social and political oppression that is often more damaging to their lives than are their physical disabilities. Social stereotypes cause society to perceive people with disabilities in terms of disease, blaming biology for social inferiority and treating disability as a kind of deviance or departure from the biological and behavioral norms of the able-bodied world. The authors state that "of all America's oppressed groups, only the handicapped have been so fully disenfranchised in the name of health."

In his book *Handicapping America* (1978), Frank Bowe points out that we have designed the United States for the average able-bodied majority, without realizing the barriers we have placed in the way of the millions of our citizens with disabilities. Many of these barriers are, of course, architectural, but a teenager with whom I once worked said "You know, the real barriers are not architectural, they are attitudinal." Because of the standards that have become indigenous to American culture—youth and beauty and economic success—and our perception of the image of perfection—the biggest, the tallest, and the prettiest as the most desirable measures of social acceptance—these barriers are in truth largely attitudinal.

Before we can deal with our roles as service providers to the segment of our population that we identify as having disabilities, it is necessary to examine our own attitudes in terms of how we perceive our fellow human beings. How has society looked at the less than physically perfect? What are the effects of labeling? How have the media contributed to a negative portrayal of disabled people? And conversely, how do people with disabilities perceive themselves? What are their similarities to and differences from able-bodied people and how are these individuals the same or different from each other? In terms of emotional problems, what are some of their very real difficulties and the difficulties of their families as they grow up in American society?

Beatrice Wright, in her book *Physical Disability—A Psychosocial Approach* (1983), places importance on the use of terminology as it influences the way we perceive people. She deplores the fact that the structure of our language makes it difficult for us to subordinate consistently the condition of disability to the personhood of the individual. It is easier to refer to "the disabled" than to the person with a disability. Wright also distinguishes between the terms disability and handicap. A disability refers to limitation of function that results directly from an impairment at the level of a specific organ or a body system while a handicap refers to the actual obstacles the person encounters in the pursuit of goals in real life, no matter what their source. Most recently the term physically challenged has emerged. Used originally in the sports field, it has now begun to permeate other fields and is a positive word. Persons with physical disabilities may also be referred to as mobility impaired. The term "emotionally disabled" is now used to describe a person with a mental illness or one receiving psychiatric or psychological care. Another term increasing in use is "hidden disability," which describes a condition for which there are no outward manifestations. Those who do not have disabilities are able-bodied. This term is infinitely preferable to the use of the word normal, which is generally accompanied by quotation marks executed in the air, seeming to indicate that there is something abnormal about someone who has a disability. Another term is "alternative media" when it is used to refer to tape recordings, braille or other non-print materials. "Alternative media" are used by people with vision impairments, or physical or learning disabilities which make it impossible to use print materials.

Society has developed certain myths that surround our perceptions of people with disabilities. Stories are told by many disabled people, usually about being ignored in a restaurant as the waiter or waitress asks his (or her) companion, "What does he (or she) want to eat?" One friend who uses a wheelchair commented that often when he waits for an elevator, the operator will call out, "Let the wheelchair on first." He receives an instant image of his chair proceeding without him, as the comment effectively obliterates him as a person.

There are two concepts involved here. One, which Beatrice Wright calls the concept of "spread," is the practice of assuming that if a person has one disability, he or she is totally incapacitated in all physical and mental areas. For example, long after becoming adults, many people in wheelchairs are still treated as children, and "overprotecting" disabled people extends to organizations for blind people, selecting reading materials for taping or brailling that do not represent a full range of what adults might choose to read.

The other and even more deeply significant concept is one of total depersonalization, as if having a disability makes a person less than a whole human being. This is perhaps the cruelest degradation of all, because it not only excludes disabled people from society but also totally obliterates them from the minds of others, thereby denying their existence.

Two more attitudes, seemingly opposites, are actually two sides of the same coin. One is that people with disabilities are to be pitied and the other is that the person, because of a disability, is somehow more courageous than other people. This latter attitude, one of overromanticizing, has led to the acceptance of disabled students into educational and vocational programs for which they are not legitimately qualified. Related to it is the phenomenon of "identification." Because people such as Franklin D. Roosevelt and Helen Keller or other less well-known, severely physically disabled, highly motivated people attain outstanding success in some way, others with similar disabilities should be able to do the same thing. This feeling is met, justifiably, with resentment. And the fact that these accomplishments are considered more laudable than accomplishments by similarly gifted, able-bodied people, and the extent to which they may be publicized by the media, put further undue emphasis on the disabilities and serve to set people with disabilities farther apart from their able-bodied peers.

The emotion of fear pervades our world—fear of the unknown, fear of the different, fear of the unusual. Able-bodied people sometimes exhibit fear in the presence of people with disabilities. Perhaps there is a fear of contagion, but more likely there is a fear of undue involvement, as if the disabled person is going to ask for help, requiring more time or emotional involvement than the able-bodied person is willing to give. Because our society places undue emphasis on the way people look, the aspect of a disabled person, less than physically perfect, often engenders a feeling of repulsion in the able-bodied. Viewing a person who is physically different sometimes creates anxiety because it negates our mental expectation of a well-ordered body image. The viewer's own body image is being threatened (Livneh 1980). When the Human Resources School for physically disabled children was first built in Albertson, Long Island, the neighbors objected to the sight of children in wheelchairs when they looked out their windows far more than they did added traffic from school buses.

The use of image-loaded words connotes social attitudes toward disabled people. People are referred to as "afflicted" with a disability. Those who use wheelchairs are often said to be "condemned" or "confined" to their chairs. In the nineteenth century, people with developmental disabilities were called "mentally defective" and physically disabled people were described as "crippled" or "maimed." All of these words are certainly loaded with many different emotions—the notion that a disability has been visited upon someone in payment for sinful behavior, the image of a less than perfect person, the image of the childlike person (as in Dostoevski's concept in *The Idiot*) somehow imbued with supernatural powers or with a purity beyond the ordinary.

If we are to mainstream many disabled children in response to the mandate of PL 94-142 (the Education of All Handicapped Children Act), all of the above attitudes will need to be dealt with by parents and teachers. Placing students who are severely disabled into regular school settings without preparation in terms of attitudes may be courting failure. Often the disabled students are isolated socially, and this isolation is exacerbated by the fact that they are generally excluded from such special school programs and areas as physical education, science laboratories, cafeterias, field trips, and extracurricular activities. Thus differences rather than similarities are emphasized, making children with disabilities feel devalued as human beings. In addition, after school physically disabled children are often confined to their homes and have little contact with neighborhood youngsters and little opportunity to socialize and to develop friends in their neighborhoods.

In order to deal positively with this problem, during the school year of 1974–1975, an interesting experiment with interaction between able-bodied children and those with disabilities was conceived by Dr. Ronald S. Friedman, the psychologist at the Human Resources School. Called the Peer-Peer program, its objectives and curriculum, as well as an attitude test and report of resultant attitudinal changes, have been described in a monograph entitled *The Peer-Peer Program: A Model Project for the Integration of Severely Physically Handicapped Youngsters with Nondisabled Peers*. Copies of the monograph are available free of charge for as long as the supply lasts from Dr. Friedman at the Human Resources School. The objectives of the program were to:

1. help re-educate the community to the abilities as well as realistic limitations of disabled people;
2. help develop positive social attitudes toward the disabled;
3. provide a rewarding experience for youngsters with disabilities, thus encouraging further contact with able-bodied people;
4. develop cooperative projects that would utilize the skills and talents of each child with disabilities and able-bodied; and
5. provide a mechanism by which disabled children would feel a part of the larger community setting.

Groups of students from a local elementary school for able-bodied children were matched with a group from the Human Resources School, and joint activities were planned under the overall supervision of Dr. Friedman, with the cooperation of teachers from both schools. An evening meeting featured presentations by each group to all parents. Results of attitude tests conducted during this first year showed positive attitude changes among the children, as well as great enthusiasm among the parents of both groups. A similar activity with the Human Resources Junior High School group in cooperation with a local junior high school for able-bodied students was equally successful.

In April 1980, after the Peer-Peer experiment had been in place for several years, an interesting article appeared in *Exceptional Children* magazine in which the author, Joy Donaldson (1980), analyzed research that had taken place during the 1970s. Two basic conclusions emerged that were born out by the success of the Peer-Peer program. One was that the most successful intervention takes place through planned experiences where the disabled persons have equal status in age and education, and the other that game-type disability simulations, where able-bodied people use wheelchairs or blindfolds, have little effect in helping nondisabled people see disabled people in less stereotypical ways.

Further research on attitudes was published in *Exceptional Children* magazine in 1981 and 1986. The 1981 study (Thomas W. Jones et al.) indicated that young childrens' perceptions of people with disabilities could be altered by a relatively short period of training. However, in 1986 Beverly Esposito and Thomas Reed II stated that no research had measured the long-term effects on attitudes which their study was designed to do. They reported that young children who had contact with persons with disabilities, whether in the present or the past, have significantly more favorable attitudes than children without that contact.

ATTITUDES TOWARD BLINDNESS

Blindness has always engendered stereotyped attitudes among sighted people. Certain "mannerisms"—habits of rubbing or poking the eyes, holding the head rigidly, not looking toward the speaker, and maintaining a blank facial expression—are in reality the absence of sighted mannerisms, and they can cause sighted people to be uncomfortable. The education of children who are blind and the rehabilitation of adventiously blind (meaning adults or young adults who were born with sight) include training in how to avoid these mannerisms.

Two sensitively written autobiographies graphically portray the experiences of growing up blind in a sighted world. *To Catch an Angel: Adventures in a World I Cannot See* by Robert Russell and *To Race the Wind* by Harold Krents are the life stories of men who became blind in early childhood. Russell was educated in a school for blind children, while Krents was educated with sighted children in public schools. Their higher education, in Ivy League colleges and at Oxford University, and success in later life indicate that both are intellectually gifted and must not be considered typical of all people with disabilities. However, had they not been gifted, they could not have portrayed their childhood years so well. Both speak about loneliness, the lack of friends, the cruelty of other children and the sensitivity of a few, the rare understanding teacher, and the fact that they were looked upon as "blind boys" rather than as "boys who are blind."

ATTITUDES TOWARD DEAFNESS

Deafness is frequently misunderstood. As with other groups of people who are disabled, much has happened during the 1980s in attitudes toward individuals who are deaf and hearing impaired. First, the philosophy of teaching only lip reading to deaf children, espoused by the Alexander Graham Bell Society and used in most schools for deaf children until the 1970s, has continued to give way in many schools to the use of "total communication," the employment of all techniques of communication to enable people who are deaf to learn language and speech. American sign language, known as Ameslan, finger spelling, lip reading, writing, or any other method of communication can be used to allow people who are deaf to express themselves and to develop language skills.

Deafness is a problem of communication through spoken language and has nothing to do with intelligence or ambition; people who are hearing impaired do not want to be shut off from society, but often, through fear of rejection, they isolate themselves from hearing people. They have normal vocal organs and nearly all of them can speak, but because they are unable to modulate their voices, they may speak with what seems like a speech impediment. Sometimes listeners may find their speech unintelligible, and as a result, many people who are deaf choose not to use their voices in public. Many read lips, but even an adept deaf listener can only understand 30 to 40 percent of spoken sounds by watching the lips of the speaker.

Because medical advances have succeeded in keeping more premature infants alive, there are now more children who are prelingually deaf than there were and many with multiple handicapping conditions.

An excellent book for developing a general awareness of the feelings of deaf people is Leo Jacob's *A Deaf Adult Speaks Out.* (Jacobs 1981). Jacobs explains that people who are deaf enjoy being together and have their own community. But it is also important that attitudes of the hearing population toward people with any degree or type of deafness be radically changed and that real attempts be made to learn the language of the deaf or at least be ready to attempt communication in whatever way possible—body language, pantomime and gestures of all kinds, written communication, and lip reading.

ATTITUDES TOWARD HIDDEN DISABILITIES

A student at the Human Resources School who had hemophilia felt that his peers, who had visible physical disabilities, might have had less difficulty accepting their own limitations and might have achieved greater acceptance by able-bodied peers than he whose disability was not visible. He himself felt ambivalent as he stood between the able-bodied and the disabled community. In explaining this phenomenon, Beatrice Wright cautions that psychological processes do not add up in a simple way. One might assume that the greater the disability the more difficult it is for the person to accept it, or to achieve a good adjustment. However, it may be postulated that persons with mild disabilities may, because they are almost normal, have a greater need to hide and deny the disability, thereby thwarting adjustment.

PORTRAYAL OF PEOPLE WITH DISABILITIES IN THE MEDIA

According to Shari Thurer (1980) people with disabilities have been portrayed badly in literature. Physical infirmities are reserved for the evil and malevolent. In *Handicapping America*, Frank Bowe cites as examples the evil Captain Hook in *Peter Pan*, the monster Frankenstein, and the classic good and evil example in the *Strange Case of Dr. Jekyll and Mr. Hyde* (Bowe 1976, 109). Thurer states that there is also the tendency to portray people who are disabled as better than average, perhaps because they have been tempered by suffering. Quasimodo, the Hunchback of Notre Dame, and Cyrano de Bergerac are noteworthy, because they are both deformed and good.

Sometimes people with disabilities are portrayed as humorous, often as a burden to be taken care of and almost always as nonsexual or totally incapable of sexual activity. In the latter case, a successful departure from this was the paraplegic Vietnam War veteran portrayed by Jon Voight, for which he won an Academy Award in the 1978 film *Coming Home*.

Indeed, the nonprint media have made a good deal of progress during the 1970s and 1980s. The popular children's television show "Sesame Street" has since 1974 included children with disabilities among the population at the show, and a regular member of the adult cast is Linda Bova, a deaf actress who signs on the program. "Sesame Street" has also created a disabled puppet, a concept which has been popularized by the "Kids on the Block," traveling shows of life size puppets with various types of disabilities who perform at meetings to portray positive attitudes toward people with disabilities. Headquarters for the program is at 9385-C Gerwig Lane, Columbia, MD 21046 (1-800-368-KIDS).

Disabled actors and actresses have fought a hard battle to get jobs. Whereas in the past able-bodied actors portrayed people with disabilities, performers with disabilities, after much effort to bring attention to their situation, now have roles in theater, television and films, as well as television commercials. Their story is told in an article in the final issue of *Disabled USA*, a publication of the President's Committee on Employment of People with Disabilities (Somers 1987).

In the play *Children of a Lesser God*, actress Phyllis Frelich, who is deaf, won a Tony Award, while the movie gave actress Marlee Matlin, also deaf, an Academy Award for the same role. In "Love Is Never Silent," a television drama based on Joanne Greenberg's book *In This Sign*, the roles of deaf parents who raise a hearing daughter were played by Phyllis Frelich and Ed Waterstreet, both deaf graduates of Gallaudet University. Commercials now depict people who are disabled: McDonald's, Levi Strauss Jeans, and Coca Cola, to name a few. Beyond Sound is a film and production company run by and for the deaf to help actors who are deaf get jobs; of course the National

Theatre of the Deaf is well-known. Many television stations are now signing news programs and commercials for the hearing impaired (see also Chapter 9). On radio programs for the blind in many areas of the country newspapers and magazine selections are read. Organizations that have had a part in this encouraging development are the Media Office of the Governor's Committee for Employment of the Handicapped (California), the Council of Disabled Artists, and the Media Office of the California Foundation on Employment and Disability.

In June 1982 a United Nations Seminar was held in Vienna, Austria, and guidelines were developed to assist media personnel in improving public perception of people with disabilities. The resulting monograph urges that people with disabilities be depicted in a variety of ordinary social and physical situations, be included as part of the general population in media products in addition to those in which their story is the primary focus, and avoid all the stereotypes mentioned above. It is to be hoped that in the decade of the 1990s the print media will follow the lead of the nonprint media in this effort. To further all of these efforts a pamphlet called "Guidelines for Reporting and Writing about People with Disabilities," written by the Research and Training Center on Independent Living, is now in its second edition (1987). For copies write Media Project, RTC/IL, BCR/3111 Haworth, University of Kansas, Lawrence, KS 66045.

ATTITUDES OF PEOPLE WITH DISABILITIES

In May 1977, a White House Conference on Handicapped Individuals was held in Washington, DC, attended by people with disabilities as well as by members of the helping professions. It reflected all of the major concerns that people with disabilities share as they work toward economic and social independence. Crosscutting all other concerns, however, was the great need for campaigns that emphasize the abilities rather than the disabilities of this group of people, as well as their diversity.

In the area of attitudes, one concern was that blanket legislation, recommendations, and approaches toward issues affecting all groups of people with disabilities lack specificity. It was resolved that consideration be given to recommendations from special groups, particularly from those consumer organizations that are under the leadership of individuals who are disabled. The older, more traditional groups continue to emphasize pleas for contributions for medical research or rehabilitation programs, but the newer groups have become more assertive, insisting on recognition of their basic civil rights and access to all of the privileges and rights enjoyed by able-bodied people.

Many people with disabilities are ambivalent about joining in activism with other people who are disabled, believing that such action will tend to cut them off from associating with the able-bodied. The development of diverse independent living projects that include people with disabilities in their management but allow them to live among the able-bodied may be a partial solution to this problem (see also Chapter 4).

EMOTIONAL AND SOCIAL PROBLEMS OF PEOPLE WITH DISABILITIES

Certain principles of human behavior apply to all individuals. Usually, however, the strengths and weaknesses in the individual are intensified in persons with physical disabilities. Young adults, for example, go through a painful growing-up period. A large nose or a pimple to a teenager may seem as disabling as a serious facial disfigurement for a person who is disabled. Conformity to the norm among young adults is terribly important. How difficult, then, is it for a young adult who is physically disabled, undersized, or in some other way nonconforming to the norm for his or her age?

Sexual development for the teenager with disabilities holds all of the struggles that confront the able-bodied teenager, but they are magnified. Usually the female with a disability has her menstrual period, and often she can bear children, but the American macho image of maleness can cause disaster for a male in a wheelchair, who must look up to women. The professional's role is to help the disabled male achieve a strong self-image in the face of these disadvantages. The topic of sexuality is an important one and sources of information in this area are found in Chapter 4.

Individual concepts of self-worth—how we perceive ourselves—depend on how we were handled by our parents, our teachers and society. Differing concepts of self-worth in those with disabilities do not always depend upon the degrees of disability. Some people with disabilities feel very handicapped indeed, while others do not perceive themselves as particularly disabled, but rarely does the physical condition determine this perception.

The question often asked is whether the congenitally disabled are better adjusted than those who are disabled later in life; there is evidence to support both positions. The child who is born disabled has a much longer time to be influenced by overprotected parents, or conversely, to learn to cope with his or her disability, helped by wise and supportive parents. The newly disabled adult, however, brings to the experience all the emotional strengths and weaknesses that were a part of his or her able-bodied personality.

One student entered the Human Resources School after experiencing a stroke, and he exhibited socially objectionable and hostile personality traits. Upon conferring with the psychologist at the school he attended before the stroke, it was determined that testing done when he was eight years old showed the same characteristics. It would have been easy to blame brain damage for the behavioral pattern, but this youngster was the same person before and after his disability (Meier 1976).

The person who has had an accident or develops a sudden disability experiences many personality changes, and generally goes through a series of stages—first denial, then hostility, then depression which Wright calls the "period of mourning" for the lost healthy body (p. 166). Most people, after a period of time, which may be months or even years, become the same people they were before. Some people who have had accidents actually show intensification of strength and very great courage.

The Role of the Family

Can the psychological limitations of a disabled person be traced back to the way he or she was handled as a child? Yes, of course, in the same way that any parent has influence on a child's development, with perhaps a little bit extra. Because children are seen as extensions of the parent, bearing a child who is less than physically perfect can be taken by the parent as a personal failure. The parent must then deal with feelings of grief at the loss of the anticipated healthy child and go through a period of mourning for that child (Poznanski 1973). This period is similar to that experienced by the young adult or adult who has an accident. Time for adjustment cannot be estimated but depends on individual cases. Parents' reactions to handicapping conditions in an older child are similar to the response at the birth of a disabled child, with one major difference. When the child becomes handicapped later in life, the parents have already formed a strong attachment. With the newborn, the attachment is not yet formed and is more easily interfered with (Poznanski 1973). Lack of contact at birth, because of prolonged medical treatment in the hospital, for example, further disrupts the formation of this attachment.

Some parents respond to the birth of a disabled child by rejection. This withdrawal may be temporary or it may result in the disabled baby's being placed in an institution. A visible disability is harder to deny than an invisible one and consequently will engender the greater reaction from both parents and the rest of society. One stage in a parent's adjustment to what may be a life-long disability is denial that it will be permanent. Parents comment that they tried to place a child in a regular school program, whether or not it was the most advantageous placement for the child, simply to be able to say to themselves and to their friends that the child was in a regular school and thus not really disabled. Denial over a long period of time can, of course, interfere with proper medical management, as well as appropriate school placement and education or vocational plans for the future.

All parents face the occasional wish that their children—able-bodied or disabled—did not exist. But parents of disabled children feel this way more often because these children make so many more demands on their time. The feelings of anger and resentment at the extra burden can produce guilt feelings, all of which the disabled child may perceive and use to pressure the parent and make more demands. The result is very often overprotection, a common reaction of parents, many of whose children need a certain amount of physical protection and care. Overprotection is caused by the parents' need to feel less guilty about their negative feelings. It also allows the parents to atone to the child for the disability, a need that comes in part from the parents' sense of guilt at having "given" the child a defective endowment.

Overprotection is also emphasized in the isolation that parents of chronically ill children sometimes experience as they retreat from relationships with their neighbors, hesitate to take their handicapped children on vacations, and often discourage socializing by the disabled son or daughter. However, this is not always the case. Many parents have encouraged their severely disabled children to attend sleep-away summer camps or, in the case of disabled teenagers, go on trips, thus forcibly breaking the protective ties and enabling the children to develop into socially and emotionally independent individuals, even though they might always need a certain amount of physical care.

One serious problem affecting families of disabled children is a lack of communication between husbands and wives. There is a high rate of disrupted marriages in families with handicapped children, usually, but not always, with the father leaving a situation he cannot tolerate and the mother remaining isolated with the children. However, sometimes the mother will leave the child with the father because he can cope more effectively.

One way in which parents can deal positively with the fact of having a disabled child is to inform themselves fully about the disability and work within parent organizations that have been formed to encourage educational opportunities and research. Addresses for some of these organizations can be found in Chapter 2.

Problems of adolescence can be heightened by parental attitudes. Most of the time the parents' overprotective attitude serves to help keep the adolescent asexual. Most disabled adolescents, in their own group discussions, move far more quickly into issues of sexuality than do their parents.

Parents for the most part are now encouraged to care for disabled children at home rather than to place them in institutions. There are now more educational and respite care services to help ease the very real burdens that fall upon the parents of severely disabled children. Moreover, the effects of PL 94-142, The Education of All Handicapped Children Act, which requires that parents act as advocates for their children with school districts, have been to bring professionals and parents into greater partnership. Dorothy Kerzner Lipsky, Ph.D., is both the parent of a disabled teenager and a social science researcher. In an article in the *American Journal of Orthopsychiatry* (October 1985) she states that the team approach is essential to correct the negative assumptions concerning family stress and coping (p. 614). Many parents show great resilience, and do well in spite of the stress which carries a substantial risk of adverse outcome. Lipsky states that when professionals treat parents as valued and contributing members of the team parents will view professionals as a source of support. Stress will be viewed not as a factor of psychological dysfunction but rather the absence of a sympathetic social or economic support system.

Siblings

Poznanski (1973) stated that as a child psychiatrist she frequently saw siblings of disabled children with emotional problems more severe than those of the disabled children themselves. In the early 1970s many professional people and parents were aware that this was so, but there was very little literature to back up these personal observations, and no programs geared to helping the families. In the early 1980s Dr. Ronald Friedman, the psychologist at Human Resources School, initiated an innovative sibling program during the summer school session. Its purpose was to allow able-bodied brothers and sisters of Human Resources School students to join the program and meet other children who had disabled siblings. The siblings were integrated with age-appropriate peers who were disabled, interacting in areas of sports, music, art and educational activities. The program was open to children from first grade through high school. They were also divided into two large groups (elementary and secondary) for special activities which included rap sessions with the psychologist or discussions on parent attitudes, sibling rivalry, social pressures, and expectations and limitations imposed by a disabled family member. Information sessions provided information about medical and physical aspects of disabilities. This program proved very successful and with the enthusiastic support of the parents it continues to this day.

At around the same time, Dr. Thomas H. Powell and Dr. Peggy Ahrenhold Ogle founded the Sibling Information Network at the University of Connecticut at Storrs, and began to publish a newsletter. It continues to be published twice a year and is available on subscription. The Sibling Information Network

Program of Connecticut's University Affiliated Program on Developmental Disabilities is now located at 991 Main Street, Suite 3A, East Hartford, CT 06108. In 1985 Powell and Ogle published a book entitled *Brothers and Sisters—A Special Part of Exceptional Families.* In it they state that siblings of brothers and sisters with disabilities experience a number of special concerns and have special needs. They offer concrete suggestions to families and describe strategies parents can use to provide emotional support. Their suggestions include making information about the brother's or sister's disability readily accessible, being careful not to put an undo burden of helping on the able-bodied sibling, discussing what the future will hold, how to handle the reactions of friends, concerns about genetic implications for their future lives, etc. Powell and Ogle point out that siblings have a unique relationship which is longer lasting than that of children with their parents.

Adults who are siblings of persons with disabilities face unique concerns and challenges. Adults with disabled siblings need to balance their own family responsibilities with some responsibility toward their disabled siblings as parents pass away. Information about trusts and guardianship will be important (see Chapter 3).

HELPFUL ADVICE WHEN MEETING A PERSON WITH DISABILITIES

Despite the attitude of a person who is disabled, and regardless of the severity of his or her disability, when an occasion for interaction between you and this person presents itself, sensitivity, combined with the following helpful pieces of advice, may be of great assistance in creating a more comfortable and successful situation for both parties.

1. Offer assistance as you would to anyone else, for example, to push a wheelchair or to guide a person who is blind. The person will indicate whether or not the help is needed, and a "no thank you" must be respected. Most people will not hesitate to ask for needed help and will be specific as to how it should be given; for example, the person who is blind usually prefers to take your arm rather than to have you grab his or hers.

2. Noticing an obvious disability is not rude; however, asking personal questions about it is inappropriate.

3. Always talk directly to a person who is disabled rather than to the person who may be accompanying him or her. Never talk about a person with disabilities to the person he or she is with as if the former did not exist, including an interpreter for a person who is deaf.

4. Do not be concerned if you use the words "walking" or "running" when talking to a person in a wheelchair, or "Do you see?" when talking to a person who is blind. People who are disabled use these words themselves and think nothing of it.

5. Do not avoid using words such as blind or deaf when associating with people with these disabilities. These people know that they have disabilities and do not need to be shielded from the facts.

6. When talking with a person in a wheelchair for any length of time it is better to sit down in order to be at the same eye level. It is very tiring for a person to look up for a long time. Never touch a wheelchair or a crutch, unless you are in a relationship where you would touch the person.

7. Be sensitive to architectural barriers in your workplace; by law they should be removed. Everyone must be concerned and alert to this very real problem.
8. Remember that if a person does not turn around in response to a call, it may be that he or she is deaf. A light tap on the shoulder to get a person's attention makes sense.
9. Never gesture about a blind person to someone else who may be present. This will inevitably be picked up and make the person who is blind feel that you are "talking behind his or her back."
10. Lip reading by deaf persons can be aided by being sure that the light is on your face and not behind you, and by taking all obstructions, such as pipes, cigarettes, or gum out of the mouth, keeping the lips flexible, and speaking slowly. Additional communication could include body language, pantomime and gestures of all kinds, and written communication if necessary.

The July 1988 issue of the *Handicapped Requirements Handbook* (Supplement No. 116), published an article entitled "Practical Perspectives on Attitudinal Barriers" which points out that major breakthroughs have occurred in recent years. One of the clearest examples was the hiring of a new president by Gallaudet University, in Washington, DC, in the spring of 1988. The students rebelled against the appointment of a college administrator with normal hearing rather than a qualified person with a hearing disability. After the students had shut down the college, all of their demands were met including the one for a deaf president, the first in the 120-year history of the university. What follows is a list of misconceptions which appeared in the same article and which may be helpful in addition to the list of suggestions mentioned above.

1. People with disabilities cannot speak for themselves. The events at Gallaudet clearly dispelled this.
2. Mental retardation (or other conditions) is easily catchable and a clear and present danger to the neighborhood. Actually mental retardation is an organic condition and is not contagious. Most disabling conditions are not.
3. No one uses parking for disabled. Too often, able-bodied people use the wide parking spaces designated for people with disabilities, forcing those who are disabled to park far from their destination. Accessible parking near a facility sometimes makes a difference in whether or not a person with a disability can obtain access to a structure. People who are disabled do use the spaces—when others have not usurped the parking (*Handicapped Requirements Handbook* 1988).

REFERENCES

Bowe, Frank. 1978. *Handicapping America.* New York: Harper & Row, Introduction, 4.

Donaldson, Joy. 1980. "Changing Attitudes Toward Handicapped Persons: A Review and Analysis of Research." *Exceptional Children* 46 (7): 504–14.

Donaldson, Joy. 1981. "The Visibility and Image of Handicapped People on Television." *Exceptional Children* 47 (6): 413–16.

Esposito, Beverly G., and Reed, Thomas M. II. 1986. "The Effects of Contact with Handicapped Persons on Young Children's Attitudes." *Exceptional Children* 53 (3): 224–29.

Friedman, Ronald S. 1975. *The Peer-Peer Program: A Model Project for the Integration of Severely Physically Handicapped Youngsters with Nondisabled Peers.* Albertson, NY: Human Resources School.

Friedman, Ronald S. *Summer Sibling Program.* Albertson, NY: Human Resources School, unpublished.

Gliedman, John, and Roth, William. 1980. *The Unexpected Minority: Handicapped Children in America.* Carnegie Council on Children. New York and London: Harcourt Brace Jovanovich, 303.

Handicapped Requirements Handbook, Federal Programs Advisory Service, Thompson Publishing Group, Washington, DC 20006, with monthly supplements.

Improving Communications about People with Disabilities. Recommendations of a United Nations Seminar, Vienna, Austria, June 8–10, 1982. New York: United Nations, Division for Economic and Social Information, Department of Public Information.

Jacobs, Leo M. 1981. *A Deaf Adult Speaks Out.* Second Edition. Washington, DC: Gallaudet University Press.

Jones, Thomas W., Sowell, Virginia M., Jones, Julie K., and Butler, Lester G. 1981. "Changing Children's Perceptions of Handicapped People." *Exceptional Children* 47 (5): 365–68.

Krents, Harold. 1972. *To Race the Wind.* New York: Putnam.

Lipsky, Dorothy Kerzner, Ph.D. 1985. "A Parental Perspective on Stress and Coping." *American Journal of Orthopsychiatry* 55(4): 617.

Livneh, Hanoch. 1980. "Disability and Monstrosity: Further Comments." *Rehabilitation Literature* 41 (11–12): 280.

Meier, Marie M. "The Psychology of Disability." Speech, Greenvale, New York, Palmer Graduate Library School, C. W. Post Center of Long Island University, August 3, 1976.

Powell, Thomas H., and Ogle, Peggy Ahrenhold. 1985. *Brothers and Sisters—A Special Part of Exceptional Families.* Baltimore/London: Paul H. Brooks Publishing Company, 43, 172.

Power, Paul and Dell Orto, Arthur E. 1980. *Role of the Family in the Rehabilitation of the Physically Disabled.* Baltimore: University Park Press.

Poznanski, Elva O. 1973. "Emotional Issues in Raising Handicapped Children." *Rehabilitation Literature* 34 (11): 322–26.

Russell, Robert. 1962. *To Catch an Angel: Adventures in a World I Cannot See.* New York: Vanguard Press.

Somers, Clair. 1987, December. "Employment of Disabled Actors and Actresses in Commercials, Televisions and Films." Washington, DC: Disabled USA, President's Committee on Employment of the Handicapped, 26–27.

Thurer, Shari. 1980. "Disability and Monstrosity: A Look at Literary Distortions of Handicapping Conditions." *Rehabilitation Literature* 41 (1–2): 12–15.

White House Conference on Handicapped Individuals. 1977. *Summary, Final Report.* Washington, DC: Office of Handicapped Individuals, DHEW pub. no. (OHD) 78-22003, 119.

Wright, Beatrice A. 1983. *Physical Disability—A Psychosocial Approach.* Second Edition. New York: Harper & Row, 8, 11, 32, 152.

Chapter 2
Defining Disabilities

We live in a society in which everyone is expected to conform to certain physical standards. How one looks often influences how one is treated. It takes some time before an individual's personality emerges, takes over, and creates an impression on the observer that is closer to the truth. The truth about each individual lies somewhere among his or her innate capacities, how well these capacities have been developed with the assistance of family and professionals, and the degree of emotional strength the person brings to his or her life experiences.

One tends to think of those who are disabled as a cohesive group, with certain similar characteristics. To some extent this is true, and some of these similarities have been explored. There are, however, many differences among the population of disabled people. All persons in wheelchairs or using crutches or braces do not have the same kinds of physical problems.

Physical disabilities fall into three basic anatomical categories: those involving the skeletal structure, the muscular system, and the neuromuscular system. The major skeletal disabilities include various forms of dwarfism, osteogenesis imperfecta, amputees (congenital and traumatic), arthrogryposis, and rheumatoid arthritis. The major muscular disability is muscular dystrophy; other major muscular disorders are inter-related and included under this heading. Neuromuscular disabilities include cerebral palsy, postpolio, and multiple sclerosis. Some disabilities may involve more than one basic anatomical category. Spina bifida, for instance, affects both the skeletal structure and the neuromuscular system. Other special health problems include hemophilia, sickle cell anemia and cystic fibrosis, and syndromes such as Tourette's and Marfan's. The effects of these syndromes have been discovered and publicized only in the last few years.

In November 1978 Public Law 95-502 was signed. Known as the Rehabilitation, Comprehensive Services and Developmental Disabilities Amendments of 1978, it provided a new definition of developmentally disabled people as follows: "A severe, chronic disability of a person which (a) is attributable to a mental or physical impairment or combination of mental and physical impairments; (b) is manifested before the person attains age twenty-two, (c) is likely to continue indefinitely; (d) results in substantial functional limitations in three or more of the following areas of major life activity: 1. self-care, 2. receptive and expressive language, 3. learning, 4. mobility, 5. self-direction, 6. capacity for independent living, and 7. economic self-sufficiency; and reflects the person's need for a combination and sequence of special, interdisciplinary or generic care, treatment, or other services which are of lifelong or extended duration and are individually planned and coordinated."

Five groups of individuals were identified as making up the majority of those who fall within the classification of "developmentally disabled": people with mental retardation, autism, cerebral palsy, epilepsy and neurological impairment. Thus the lines were blurred, as many people who were considered to have physical disabilities could now be considered also to have developmental disabilities. Definitions of two major groups of developmental disabilities, autism and Down's Syndrome, have been included here.

Some of these disabilities are well known and a great deal has been written about them. Others are fairly rare and it has not been easy in the past to acquire information about them. This chapter discusses some of the well-known disabilities as well as some of the rarer types probably being encountered for the first time by the general public. Many of the parent organizations have published pamphlets dealing with disabilities in lay terms that are often free of charge. Fortunately, there is an excellent source for both public and school libraries that offers definitions of many of these disabilities using simplified medical terminology—*Physically Handicapped Children: A Medical Atlas for Teachers*, by Eugene E. Bleck and Donald A. Nagel (1982). This volume makes a fine addition to reference and teacher information collections.

AMPUTATION

A missing limb is the result of acquired or congenital amputation. In acquired amputation, the person was born able-bodied, but through accident or surgery (most often for a malignant tumor), a limb was removed. Congenital amputation means that the child was born without the limb, in part or in total.

The cause of total or partial congenital limb absence is a failure of fetal limb bud development in the first three months of pregnancy. Artificial limbs (prostheses) and training in their use is the treatment for this condition. Absence of both upper or lower limbs presents obvious problems which must be solved on an individual basis, in some cases with special electric prostheses and devices. With total loss of upper limbs, children sometimes become adept at using feet or toes. In our cosmetically oriented society this can prove disturbing and in some cases children are restricted from doing this. Generally the intellectual capabilities of children with amputations do not differ from those found in the general population and the advent of new technology has changed attitudes and made it more acceptable to encourage use of all residual assets (Setoguchi 1982, 17).

ARTHRITIS

The word arthritis means inflammation of a joint but it is widely used to cover almost one hundred different conditions that cause aching and pain in the joints and connective tissues throughout the body. There are five kinds of arthritis:

1. Rheumatoid arthritis is the most serious and painful type. It is inflammatory and chronic and can affect the whole body. It primarily attacks the joints and can flare up unpredictably causing progressive damage to the tissues. Crippling can result. Women are affected three times more often than men. When occurring in children, it is known as juvenile rheumatoid arthritis.

2. Juvenile Rheumatoid Arthritis may occur in children as early as six weeks of age. The greatest number have a type called Polyarticular Arthritis, with severely involved joints. These children are usually in pain and will tend to sit very still so as not to feel it, with a subsequent loss of range of motion and contractures. Treatment consists of medication (aspirin), rest, appropriate exercise, and in some cases surgery. Classroom attendance may be poor. High aspirin dose may cause temporary loss of high tones in hearing and vision problems may be detected (Miller 1982, 423).
3. Osteoarthritis is principally a wear-and-tear disease of the joints which occurs with age. It is usually mild and not inflammatory.
4. Ankylosing spondylitis is a chronic, inflammatory arthritis of the spine which affects men ten times more often than women, usually beginning in the teens or early twenties.
5. Rheumatic fever: A disease that follows a streptococcus infection, frequently damages the heart and also causes arthritis in the joints, which subsides quickly and does not cause disability.
6. Gout, also called gouty arthritis, is an inherited disease which most often attacks small joints, especially the big toe. It usually attacks men and is very painful.

The purposes of treatment programs are to relieve pain, reduce inflammation, prevent damage to joints or deformities, and retain mobility. Treatment involves medication, exercise, splints, heat, walking aids, surgery, and rehabilitation therapy. Since there is no cure (except for remissions), treatment must continue. Most of the time arthritis does not prevent people from functioning in employment and other daily activities. Informational pamphlets may be obtained from the national headquarters of the Arthritis Foundation, 115 East 18th Street, New York, NY 10003.

ARTHROGRYPOSIS MULTIPLEX CONGENITA

From the Greek words arthro (joints) and gryposis (curved), this congenital disease begins in utero. It involves the muscles, or more accurately the spinal cord cells that control muscle contraction, resulting in failure of muscle function. This causes lack of movement in the joints and consequent stiffness and deformity. Children born with this disability usually have their arms fixed in a straight twisted position. Surgery may sometimes allow the arms to bend so that hands can be used, however, once in a bent position the arms often cannot be straightened. Some children walk with a stiff legged gait, while others are in wheelchairs. There is often hip dislocation. Surgery is often needed to correct knee and/or foot deformities. Scoliosis (spinal curvature), which sometimes occurs, is corrected by surgery and spinal fusion.

Children with arthrogryposis have normal intelligence and speech, but physical rehabilitation is limited. Educationally, children with this condition should be given the opportunity for academic achievement (Bleck, 27). Accommodations will need to be made in the areas of mobility and handwriting, and new technological developments, such as special computer switches can help (see Chapter 5).

During the 1970s the parents of children with this disability formed a national association. Although there is not an extensive pamphlet literature there are medical articles published about this disability. The association is now publishing a newsletter entitled *Avenues*, which comes out twice a year. For subscriptions contact Mrs. Mary Ann Schmidt, PO Box 5192, Sonora, CA 95370.

AUTISM

A severe, incapacitating, lifelong condition, autism usually appears during the first three years of life. It occurs in about five out of every ten thousand births, and is four times more common in boys than in girls. In most cases, the cause, or causes, are still unknown, but most scientists believe the cause is physical and parents are being reassured that they cannot have caused this condition. There appear to be several types of autism, each with a distinct neurological basis. No known factors in the psychological environment of a child have been proven to cause autism.

People with autism are slow to develop and may lack physical, social, and learning skills. They have immature speech patterns, are limited in understanding ideas, and may use words without attaching the usual meaning to them. They may also have abnormal ways of relating to people, objects, and events. They typically do not respond to other people. In its severest forms, autism may cause behaviors which are self-injurious, repetitive, highly unusual, and aggressive.

Highly structured educational programs, tailored to each individual's needs and emphasizing learning social and language skills, have proven most helpful. Some medications have also been successful in controlling symptoms of autism. Some people with autism can lead very productive lives but most will require supervised living and working situations (Wilson 1978). Further information can be obtained from the National Society for Children and Adults with Autism, 1234 Massachusetts Avenue NW, Washington, DC 20005.

CEREBRAL PALSY

Cerebral palsy results from damage to the brain, usually at birth. Cerebral refers to the brain and palsy to lack of control over the muscles. It is a nonprogressive condition that remains throughout life. In addition to lack of motor control, there may be seizures, spasms, mental retardation, abnormal sensation and perception, or impairment of sight, hearing, or speech, all in varying degrees. Teeth often require special attention. When the tongue muscle is involved, eating and talking are affected. Sometimes involvement of the facial muscles can cause grimaces, which can alter the perception of the personality of someone with cerebral palsy. Medication usually plays a minor part in treatment, but experimental surgery on the brain has been performed and neurosurgeons hope to be successful in finding a procedure to end spasticity or uncontrolled movement.

Cerebral palsy is caused by defective development, injury, or disease. Chief among its causes is an insufficient amount of oxygen reaching the fetal or newborn brain. Other causes may be premature birth, Rh or A-B-O blood type incompatibility between parents, German measles in the mother, or other viruses or bacteria.

There are three main types of cerebral palsy: spastic, the largest group, causing tense, contracted muscles; athetoid, causing constant uncontrolled motion; and ataxic, causing a poor sense of balance that may result in falling. Some people with cerebral palsy exhibit a combination of spasticity and athetosis. Preventive programs include better testing during pregnancy to try to prevent the causes.

Management of children with cerebral palsy consists of trying to help them achieve maximum potential growth and development. Programs utilize physicians, therapists, educators, nurses, and social workers. In some cases surgery and braces are used. Children range in mental ability from mentally retarded to extremely bright, with no correlation between the severity of physical impairment and the mental condition.

School programs must be highly individualized, requiring a great deal of attendant care for the most severely disabled children. When a child with cerebral palsy is bright, it is imperative that adequate schooling is offered. New college programs, geared to acceptance of the severely physically disabled, now make it possible for bright cerebral palsied individuals to go on to higher education. Support services for the cerebral palsied young adult must include psychological counseling, special living accommodations, and a realistic understanding of possible life goals. To date, most people with cerebral palsy have found little success in the employment field and have been the objects of much prejudice on the part of the able-bodied community, as well as on the part of the community of people with other disabilities.

The United Cerebral Palsy Association, Inc., the national organization to help parents and children with cerebral palsy, was formed in 1949. At the local level, direct services are provided by affiliates, including medical diagnosis, evaluation and treatment, special education, career development, social and recreation programs, parent counseling, adapted housing, advocacy, and community education. The National Easter Seal Society also has information about available services. Persons with cerebral palsy who cannot turn book pages may borrow talking books under the program of the National Library Service for the Blind and Physically Handicapped of the Library of Congress. For pamphlets on cerebral palsy and further information contact the United Cerebral Palsy Association, Inc., 66 East 34th Street, New York, NY 10016. A very detailed description of the clinical aspects of cerebral palsy can be found in Bleck and Nagel (1982, 59ff).

CYSTIC FIBROSIS

First described in 1936, this is the most common chronic lung disease in Caucasian children, usually resulting in early death. When first reported almost all deaths occurred before the age of 1 year. With improvement in treatment, the average life expectancy is now 14 years, with an upward trend so that a large percentage of children reach adulthood and function well.

It is estimated that 1 in 1,500 children is born with this hereditary disorder. Approximately 1 in every 25 Caucasians carries the gene. The disease occurs much less frequently in Black youngsters and is very rarely reported in Oriental children.

Originally thought to be a disease involving only the pancreas and the lungs, cystic fibrosis is now known to be caused by an abnormal mucus secreted in these and other organs as well. The basic reason for the abnormality has not been found. Cystic fibrosis is a simple recessive genetic disorder; when two parents carrying the gene produce a child, there is a one in four chance that the baby will have cystic fibrosis, two in four that he or she will be a carrier, and one in four that he or she will not carry the gene. Recent research may soon become the basis for a method to identify carriers (Harvey 1982, 256).

The primary treatment for this disease involves keeping the lungs clear of mucus and free of infection as much as possible. The use of antibiotics has slowed the course of cystic fibrosis somewhat (Harvey 1982). Literature on cystic fibrosis is available from the National Cystic Fibrosis Research Foundation, 6000 Executive Building, Suite 309, Rockville, MD 20852.

DEAFNESS AND HEARING IMPAIRMENT

Hearing impairment is a generic term referring to the whole audiologic continuum of hearing loss without specific regard to the manner or age of onset of the impairment (Luterman 1986). One simple and effective division for describing hearing losses is as follows (Dalton 1985):

Prelingual: Persons who were deaf at birth or very early in infancy. The person has been deprived of the opportunity to acquire normal speech and language patterns, thus the problem in communication is linguistic as well as aural.

Postlingual or adventitiously deaf: These people sustain a hearing impairment after the acquisition of normal speech and language patterns. Included in this group are those whose hearing loss is the result of injury, illness, or old age. Problem in communication is aural rather than linguistic.

Hearing tests measure the amplitude level and frequency range of the many different degrees of hearing loss and a chart is developed showing the relationship at various coordinate points. By connecting these points an audiogram is developed which indicates the hearing range of the individual and may also indicate the pockets of hearing. Scores (in decibels) are as follows (Dalton 1985):

.0-20 normal
.20-60 mild to moderate loss
60-90 severe loss
90-100 profound loss (Dalton 1985)

Hagemeyer (1979) paraphrases Jacobs (1980) in further describing types of deaf and hearing-impaired individuals. She notes differences based on the age when deafness occurred as well as on the person's language environment, i.e., children who are deaf raised by parents who are deaf, or children who are deaf born into hearing families; differences stemming from educational programs; deafened adults who lost their hearing after they were through their educational programs; and adults who are hard of hearing, who have residual hearing which is functional. Hagemeyer thus identifies eight groups in the community of the deaf:

- American Sign Language Users
- Users of ASL and English (Bilingual)
- Oralists
- Deafened Adults
- Hearing-Impaired Elderly
- Minimal Language Users
- Hard of Hearing Individuals
- Family Members with Normal Hearing

Hagemeyer also states the main causes of deafness as heredity, illnesses, accidents, modern living and the aging process (Hagemeyer 1988). She further points out that nearly all people who are deaf can speak, but because of their inability to hear their own voices and because they are aware that their unusual sound characteristics and speech are not intelligible to the general public, most do not want to use their voices at all.

The controversy over oral programs vs. total communication in the education of children who are deaf has become less confrontational. During the 1980s a great deal of progress was made by the proponents of total communication, the use of sign language and/or finger spelling, as well as gestures, written communication, mime, and lip reading, toward the goal of using all possible means to develop communication.

Organizations offering further information include the National Association of the Deaf, 814 Thayer Avenue, Silver Spring, MD 20910, Alexander Graham Bell Association for the Deaf, Inc., 3411 Volta Place NW, Washington, DC 20007, the National Information Center on Deafness, Gallaudet University, 7th and Florida Avenue NE, Washington, DC 20002, and Self Help for Hard of Hearing (SHHH), PO Box 34889, Bethesda, MD 20817.

DOWN'S SYNDROME

Down's Syndrome is a form of mental retardation resulting from a genetic defect. It occurs in about 1 in every 640 births, and it affects all races and economic levels equally. The incidence of Down's Syndrome is strongly dependent on maternal age, with the rate climbing steeply after maternal age of 35 (Diamond 1982). The most common kind of Down's Syndrome, Trisomy 21, results when either the egg or the sperm contributes an extra chromosome at conception. As a result, there is an additional chromosome in every cell of the child's body and this extra 21st chromosome produces the mental and physical characteristics of Down's Syndrome: flatness of back of the head and of the face; oriental looking eyes, with an extra skin fold in many babies at the inside corner of the eyes; small ears, with the top rim often folded over; protruding tongue and open mouth; a shortened neck with extra skin; often webbing between fingers and toes; and a single crease across the palm. Loose muscle tone causes general flabbiness and increased range of motion in joints. Health problems may include heart defects, immature digestive tracts, ear infections leading to mild hearing defects and dental infections. Down's Syndrome adults age faster than their peers and their life expectancy is about 50.

There is a wide variation of mental retardation among children with Down's Syndrome with most falling within the mild to moderate range. Early intervention and continuing education, good medical care, and a stimulating home environment have proven very effective in improving social and intellectual performance. National and local groups are now working to improve information about Down's Syndrome and obtain appropriate educational facilities. The National Down's Syndrome Society was established in 1979 to deal with the multifaceted questions relating to the disability. It disseminates information to new parents and can furnish information packets on request (146 East 57th Street, New York, NY 10022). The National Down's Syndrome Congress (NDSC), 1800 Dempster Street, Park Ridge, IL 60068-1146, was established in 1973 by a group of parents and professionals, and now includes more than 500 chapters of volunteers in the United States and around the world. It offers publications, an annual convention, adoption facilitation, advocacy for adolescents and adults with Down's Syndrome, educational guidelines for pre-school and elementary school, and extended family support.

DWARFISM

An individual who is smaller than others to a marked degree is considered to be a dwarf. Either his or her rate of growth, the length of time for which growth continues, or both have been inadequate. Early diagnosis is critical because once a certain stage of growth has been reached, nothing can be done to accelerate it. There are many different types of dwarfism, and only simple definitions are given here. Very extensive information about human growth can be found in the chapter "Short Stature and Growth" by William A. Horton and David L. Rimoin in *Physically Handicapped Children, A Medical Atlas for Teachers* (Bleck and Nagel 1982).

Hypopituitarism, a condition of unknown cause, begins early in life. Height, weight, and bone age are symmetrically depressed. Pituitary hormones are affected, and thyroid and adrenal functions are mildly or severely impaired.

Primordial dwarfism refers to the individual who is unusually small at birth, although born at full term. Growth is slow from earliest infancy. Bone age generally keeps pace with chronological age. Sexual maturation is normal and at the usual time. The child develops into a miniature adult, comparatively normal in every way save size.

Nutritional dwarfism means short stature that may result from inadequate intake of calories, proteins, or certain vitamins.

Chondrodystrophy is a group of conditions, of which achondroplasia is a major disorder. The slightly enlarged skull and disproportionately shorter extremities typical of this disease generally can be seen at birth and are due to a major defect in chondrogenesis (the function of cartilage). A bone lengthening technique for children with achondroplasia was developed in the Soviet Union 30 years ago by Dr. Gavriel A. Ilizarov of Siberia and is now being practiced in several hospitals in the United States, including the Hospital for Joint Diseases in New York, NY. Children between the ages of 11 and 14 are eligible for the program, which involves cracking the bones of the legs, and ultimately of the arms as well, and gradually stretching them over a period of time, thereby gaining approximately one foot in height, and corresponding arm length.

Dr. Victor H. Frankel at the Hospital for Joint Diseases performs this operation and can be reached there for information (Frankel, Gold and Golyakhovsky 1988). An information release entitled "A Guide to the Remarkable New Ilizarov Method of Orthopaedic Reconstruction" is available from the Department of Orthopaedics, Hospital for Joint Diseases Orthopaedic Institute, Bernard Aronson Plaza, 301 East 17th Street, New York, NY 10003. It must be stated that the organization Little People of America does not endorse this procedure because of medical complications that may occur, as well as the pain involved. Little People of America, Inc., Box 633, San Bruno, CA 94066, is a society in which a condition of membership is dwarfed stature, with a maximum allowable height of five feet. Also opposed to the procedure is Dr. Steven E. Kopits, director of the International Center for Skeletal Dysplasia (a congenital growth disorder) at St. Joseph Hospital in Towson, MD (Gately 1988).

There is a group of miscellaneous disorders associated with short stature in which the mechanisms of defective growth are not established. One of these is

Turner's Syndrome, in which short stature is associated with many abnormalities in glandular functions, chromosomal abnormalities, and other congenital defects.

It is possible to diagnose dwarfism, using such information as height of parents and siblings, birth height and weight, current height and weight, roentgenograms of the hands and the lateral skull to exclude the possibility of certain types of tumors, and X rays of the knees to detect chondroplasia. Research, sponsored by the National Institute of Arthritis and Metabolic Diseases, the National Pituitary Agency (210 West Fayette Street, Suite 503-7, Baltimore, MD 21201), and the Human Growth Foundation (601 Light Street, Baltimore, MD 21230) is ongoing. Earlier use of pituitary glands to stimulate growth has been discontinued. The Human Growth Foundation now advocates the use of a bio-synthetic hormone which is readily available (as pituitary glands were not), and is injected three times per week. This is only done, however, when it is determined by a doctor that it might be beneficial. Pediatricians should be consulted first to rule out possibilities of the presence of medical reasons for the lack of growth.

All dwarfs are capable of having a regular sex life, the biggest problem being to find an appropriate partner. Many dwarfs are able to have children, who may or may not be dwarfs. Schooling for this group of young people should be commensurate with intellectual ability. Some architectural problems will exist and must be overcome. Vocational training, if suitable, can lead to successful employment and a satisfactory life adjustment. Information is available from all of the above-mentioned organizations.

EPILEPSY

The term epilepsy comes from the Greek word for seizure. It describes a disorder of the central nervous system, which causes recurring seizures or convulsions resulting from uncontrolled electric discharges in the brain. Seizures vary in type and severity; about 20 individual seizure disorders are included under the umbrella term "epilepsy." Until quite recently, epilepsy has been surrounded by myth and distorted ideas. One percent of the population, or about two million Americans, have some form of epilepsy, although accurate statistics are not easy to obtain, since many people still hide the fact that they have the disorder.

Generalized tonic clonic seizures (formerly called grand mal) cause loss of consciousness, violent shaking of the entire body, accompanied by irregular breathing. Sometimes there is a pale blue color in the face, fingernails, or lips. A warning, called an "aura," is sometimes experienced before a seizure in the form of odd feelings or distortions of sound or vision. After the seizure, the patient may seem confused or feel tired and may fall asleep.

Generalized absence seizures (formerly known as petit mal) usually start to occur between the ages of 6 and 14. They cause a person to look as if he or she is staring blankly and may be mistaken for daydreaming spells or behavior or learning problems in children. They may also include rapid eye blinking or twitching movements. These seizures may occur as often as 100 times a day, usually lasting less than a minute.

Generalized myoclonic and akinetic seizures affect muscle control and movement, causing abrupt jerking movements of all or part of the body. They have been nicknamed "lightning seizures" because they may occur from 5 to 300 times a day. This disorder should be suspected in infants who seem apathetic or in 6- to 18-month-old children with colic, poor eating habits, or slow motor development. A baby may exhibit muscle jerks or twitching, may draw his or her body into a ball, and the facial color may change to pale or red or blue. The older child or adult may suddenly fall to the ground, sustaining frequent bumps and bruises.

Complex partial seizures (sometimes called psychomotor or temporal lobe seizures) arise from a specific area in the brain and may occur at any age. They produce brief periods of automatic behavior and clouded consciousness. They take many forms, including lip smacking, staring, headache and stomachaches, buzzing or ringing in the ears, dizziness, or feelings of strong emotions such as fear or rage. There is no memory of actions during the seizure once full consciousness returns.

Simple partial seizures affect single areas of the brain without changing consciousness. If an area controlling muscle activity is involved, involuntary movements or weakness may occur. If other areas of the brain are affected there may be distortions of the senses, changes in feelings, and even pain.

It is possible for a patient with epilepsy to have more than one type of seizure, and careful diagnosis and individual treatment are very important. Epilepsy that can be traced to a specific brain injury is called symptomatic. It may sometimes be caused by faulty development of brain tissue before birth, injury during birth, tumors, abscesses, or blood clots in the brain, severe head injury, or brain infections such as meningitis or encephalitis. Epilepsy with no determinable cause is called idiopathic. Heredity seems to play some role in this type of epilepsy, which usually does not appear until after the age of five. As persons grow older, the incidence of the onset of seizures diminishes, except among the elderly. There are now many drugs available to control most epilepsies, enabling most people with this disorder to enjoy normal lives.

Parents of children with epilepsy are encouraged to allow them to be active. With understanding and support, children can meet with academic success. People with epilepsy exhibit the same wide range of intellect as the population in general, and most children with epilepsy are able to attend regular classes. It is imperative that all teachers and support staff be provided with general information about epilepsy so as to forestall hostility or teasing on the part of other children. The School Alert program of the Epilepsy Foundation of America (EFA) provides materials to enhance understanding of the disorder as well as explanations of emergency aid techniques.

Adolescents with epilepsy experience the same problems as other adolescents, sometimes magnified by the medical and social problems connected with the disorder. Local organizations affiliated with EFA often provide special services for these adolescents and sponsor support groups for parents and for adults as well. Students often go on to college. In any case, all persons with epilepsy should consider training for future employment. Prejudice, which used to exist against their employment, has been combatted successfully through educational campaigns by EFA and through an employment program called the Training and Placement Service (TAPS) which EFA runs to help those who are having difficulty finding jobs. The Office of Vocational Rehabilitation or a local EFA affiliate can also be of assistance. In addition, the Epilepsy Foundation of America has a toll-free telephone information service (1-800-EFA-1000) and will provide referral and written information on request. A research study entitled "Plan for Nationwide Action on Epilepsy: Vol. I," published by the Commission for the Control of Epilepsy and Its Consequences (US Department of

HEW, PHS, NIH, Pub. No. (NIH) 78-0276, Washington, DC, August 1977) remains a useful and comprehensive source of information.

FAMILIAL DYSAUTONOMIA

Originally described in 1949, Familial dysautonomia (FD) is a recessive genetic birth defect, with both parents carrying the gene, although they are normal. There is at present no prenatal test. All cases reported to date have been in Jewish families of Eastern European extraction (Ashkenazim) and have included an equal number of males and females.

Familial dysautonomia is a disorder of that part of the nervous system controlling sensation and autonomic functions. The severity of symptoms varies among individuals and at different ages in any one individual; however, early symptoms generally include difficulty in sucking (in the infant) and swallowing and drooling. Vomiting is common, and blood pressure and temperature fluctuate widely. Blood does not circulate oxygen to the brain sufficiently, and as a result dizziness or an actual cessation of breathing sometimes occurs in the slightly older child. Skin blotches come and go with excitement and sweating is profuse, but both decrease with age.

Lack of overflow tears with crying is one of the most distinctive signs of familial dysautonomia, and eye dryness, combined with decreased sensation in the cornea, leaves these children particularly prone to corneal abrasion or ulcers. To supplement eye moisture, methyl cellulose eyedrops or a similar eye lubricant must be used about four times a day.

Lack of sensation causes lack of taste, lack of sensitivity to hot and cold, and loss of feeling; thus care must be taken to avoid any injuries or burns. The pitch of the voice is also affected, and speech will appear immature. Coordination problems occur in areas of gross motor movement, and gait will often be awkward.

There is an overall slower growth rate and weight gain, and the average height is usually less than that of the shorter parent. Spinal curvatures occur in almost all children with dysautonomia and can be aided by bracing. For all of these reasons, these children may appear somewhat younger than their actual age and may also show emotional immaturity. Sexual maturation is delayed in both males and females, commonly occurring in the late teens. The oldest known dysautonomic to date is 47. There have been 11 marriages reported of those with this disability, and the first FD mother was reported to have borne a child in 1975. Since then there have been 10 babies born to 3 FD mothers, and 1 FD father (Axelrod 1988).

Individuals with dysautonomia will be carriers of the disease, and so genetic counseling is advisable. Some older dysautonomics should be able to work depending on stamina and educational level. Travel can be a problem and driving a car may not be feasible, since perception and coordination are poor for many dysautonomics.

The school-age child with dysautonomia is somewhat delayed in verbal intelligence, but with careful educational planning, many can perform at an average or above-average level. Children who have been followed have been able to complete high school, and several have gone on to college.

Parents of these children are usually very knowledgeable and should be consulted by school districts and medical and nursing personnel. Because of the serious nature of the physical problems, early special education is often advisable.

Excellent literature about this disease is available from the Dysautonomia Foundation, Inc., 20 East 46th Street, New York, NY 10017. The major medical research in dysautonomia is conducted by Felicia B. Axelrod, MD, Departments of Pediatrics, and Obstetrics and Gynecology, at the Dysautonomia Treatment & Evaluation Center, New York University Medical Center, 530 First Avenue, New York, NY 10016.

HEMOPHILIA

The term hemophilia is used to describe a hereditary condition in which the blood has difficulty in clotting. Descriptions of this disease date back almost two thousand years, and the royal families of Russia and England figure in its history. There are many bleeding disorders. Blood clots are formed by chemical reactions aided by clotting proteins, which are molecules that circulate in the blood. There are 12 different clotting substances represented by I through XIII. (For some reason, the number VI has never been assigned.) A deficiency of any one of these substances can cause a serious bleeding disorder. Factor VIII (classic hemophilia) and Factor IX (parahemophilia) are the causes of the most common and most severe forms of hemophilia, accounting for over 90 percent of serious bleeding disorders.

Both Factor VIII and Factor IX are transmitted through sex-linked recessive genes, meaning that the abnormality is carried by the female, who has a 50 percent chance of passing it on to her son. A female carrier also has a 50 percent chance of passing on the disorder to her daughter, who will then become a carrier. A male hemophiliac will pass the disorder on to all his female offspring, who will become carriers. Males do not inherit hemophilia from their fathers. Children born to female carriers of hemophilia, therefore, have a 50 percent chance of being completely free of the disease (Berberich 1982).

One of the major physical problems in children with hemophilia is recurrent joint bleeding, which causes thickening of the joint lining and finally extensive destruction of the whole cartilage lining. Degenerative arthritis then sets in and can cause crippling joint disease in early adult life. Braces may be necessary for children who have this problem.

Children with hemophilia can bleed from minor cuts or lacerations, and trauma to the head and neck can cause life-threatening bleeding into vital areas. Neurological symptoms such as headache, sleepiness, nausea, and vomiting should be recognized as serious. Even more serious are unequal pupil size of the eyes, slurred speech, disorientation or muscle weakness, or dark brown urine, of which school nurses, teachers and others working with hemophiliacs should be aware.

Children with hemophilia usually have average to above-average intelligence and may be educated in either public or special school situations, depending on the severity of their condition and the willingness of the school to take the reponsibility for maintaining the child on a modified physical program. They should not be involved in any contact sports, but exercise is important for maintaining strong muscles and well-functioning joints.

Swimming is an excellent exercise. Adults who handle children with hemophilia should be cautioned against overprotection. A hemophiliac will not bleed to death from a cut finger, and often spontaneous internal bleeding occurs, which cannot be avoided.

In the 1970s medical progress was made to enable hemophiliacs to maintain themselves in good condition. Factor concentrates to replace the deficient

VIII and IX are now available, although costly, and patients can infuse themselves at home with these concentrates whenever clotting is needed. This is a tremendous step forward for parents and children who had to spend so much of their time in emergency visits to the hospital (Massie 1975). However, ideally, hemophiliacs should always live fairly near a large hospital that has facilities for treating hemophilia and is familiar with all of the problems.

Marriage for the adult hemophiliac should involve genetic counseling. Wives must be willing to provide supportive assistance during bleeding episodes, and the couple must understand that if they have female children, who will become carriers, any male grandchildren may have hemophilia. Information can be obtained from the National Hemophilia Foundation, The Soho Bldg., 110 Greene Street, Room 406, New York, NY 10012.

LEGG-CALVE-PERTHES

Early in the 1900s, the development of X-ray examinations of the hip enabled doctors to see changes in children between the ages of four and five years who complained of pain in the knee, thigh, or occasionally in the hip joint and who started to walk with a limp indicating this temporary orthopedic disability, also called Legg-Calve-Perthes disease. This disease should not be ignored. Boys are more frequently affected than girls with this disease which consists of the destruction of the growth center (epiphysis) at the hip end of the thigh bone (femur). Over a period of two to three years, there is a repair of the growth, consisting of resorption of the dead bone and laying down of new bone. Treatment during this period of healing involves absolute rest, usually by immobilizing the leg or legs of the affected hip(s) with a special brace. In some cases, surgical repair is indicated.

In most cases the child must receive special attention for two to three years during the time of elementary education, necessitating special architectural accommodations for braces or wheelchair use in schools and classrooms (Nagel 1982).

MARFAN SYNDROME

The Marfan Syndrome is a hereditary disorder of the connective tissue that affects many organ systems, including the skeleton, the lungs, the eyes, and the heart and blood vessels. A single abnormal gene causes the condition, most of the time inherited from a parent who is also affected. About one-quarter of the cases occur when the abnormal gene arises in the egg or sperm (a "new mutation") of an unaffected parent. Someone with the Marfan Syndrome has a 50-50 chance that any offspring will inherit the condition.

Marfan Syndrome can affect both men and women of any race or ethnic group. In general, it is diagnosed after a careful physical examination, including tests, such as the echocardiogram (a sound-wave picture of the heart) or X-rays. Symptoms may be severe or mild and may be present at birth or show up in adult life. The disorder sometimes causes sudden death in adults who were unaware that they had it.

The most serious problems associated with the Marfan Syndrome involve the cardiovascular system. The two leaflets of the mitral valve may billow backward when the heart contracts, a condition called "mitral valve prolapse."

This feature may lead to blockage of the mitral valve or be associated with irregularities of the heart rhythm. The aorta (the main artery carrying blood away from the heart) is generally wider and more fragile in these patients. This deterioration is progressive and may result in leakage of the aortic valve or the development of tears in the wall of the aorta, sometimes requiring surgical repair when severe. Since a sudden split in the aorta can cause sudden death Marfan patients are warned to avoid heavy exercise, contact sports, and lifting heavy objects.

Involvement of the skeleton includes curvature of the spine (scoliosis), abnormally shaped chest, tall stature, and loose jointedness. Arms and legs may be unusually long in proportion to the torso. The face may be long and narrow, with a high roof of the mouth and crowded teeth. People with the Marfan Syndrome are generally near-sighted and about half have dislocation of the ocular lens.

Treatment may consist of implanting an artificial heart valve to replace a weakened valve, anticlotting medication and braces or surgery to correct spinal curvature. Early diagnosis and careful management of the condition can help affected persons lead a much longer, reasonably comfortable life (*Marfan Syndrome Fact Sheet,* and Marfan Syndrome, Genetic Series, March of Dimes).

The National Marfan Foundation supports and fosters research, provides accurate and timely information to patients, family members and physicians, organizes conferences and will send information upon request (382 Main Street, Port Washington, NY 11050). The Foundation publishes the bi-monthly newsletter *Connective Issues.*

MULTIPLE SCLEROSIS

Multiple sclerosis is a disability that affects the central nervous system. It usually attacks adults in the 20- to 40-year age bracket. Onset before the age of 18 or after 45 is uncommon. It is caused by the destruction of patches of the myelin with which many nerve fibers are coated. This destruction causes difficulty when nerve impulses travel past the damaged areas. Why this happens has not yet been discovered. Symptoms of multiple sclerosis include:

- numbness in parts of the body
- prickling sensation in parts of the body
- double or otherwise defective vision, such as involuntary movements of eyeballs
- extreme weakness or fatigue
- loss of coordination
- tremors of hands
- noticeable dragging of one or both feet
- speech difficulties, such as slurring
- severe bladder/bowel trouble (loss of control)
- partial or complete paralysis of parts of the body

The combination of three or more of these symptoms signals danger and should not be ignored. Sometimes symptoms disappear for periods of several years, and occasionally they never return. Multiple sclerosis is usually progressive, proceeding in a series of attacks, each one causing further disability; however, many patients remain at a constant level or plateau of capability with no noticeable increase in disability.

There is no cure for multiple sclerosis and no definitive diagnostic test. No treatment will halt or alter its progress. Many drugs have been tried without long-term success. Treatment can and should be given for prevention of upper respiratory and other infections. Physical therapy and braces can be prescribed for stabilizing limbs and keeping the patient as active as possible. A variety of nursing needs of long duration, as well as architectural modification of living facilities, must be anticipated.

The National Multiple Sclerosis Society has 178 chapters and branches in the 50 states and the District of Columbia, all staffed by volunteers. The society offers patients equipment, aids to daily living, nursing services, counseling, and physical and occupational therapy. Its research programs operate in cooperation with the National Institute of Neurological and Communicative Disorders and Stroke, a branch of the federal government. The aim is to find the cause, prevention, and cure of multiple sclerosis. Literature on this disease is available from the National Multiple Sclerosis Society, 205 East 42nd Street, New York, NY 10036.

MUSCULAR DYSTROPHY

Muscular dystrophy is a general designation for a group of chronic diseases whose most prominent characteristic is the progressive degeneration of the skeletal or voluntary musculature. The age of onset and the muscles affected, as well as the rate of progression, vary according to the type of dystrophy. These diseases are, for the most part, hereditary, although spontaneous occurrences as the result of genetic mutation are not uncommon. The cause is some as yet undertermined error in the hereditary materials that brings about a metabolic defect. It is not yet known whether the primary lesion is in the muscles themselves or in some other part of the body.

There are seven types of muscular dystrophy as well as two muscle diseases classified as myotomas. In addition, polymyositis and dermatomyositis, five myophathies, and six disorders classified as neurogenic atropies, the neuromuscular disease myasthenia gravis and Friedrich's ataxia are listed in this grouping. A chart available from the Muscular Dystrophy Association (MDA) Headquarters (810 Seventh Avenue, New York, NY 10019) lists all of these disorders and their types of inheritance, clinical onset, progression, and treatment.

There is no cure for any of the dystrophies. Medical management is limited to relieving symptoms of the disease. Orthopedic devices may be prescribed at appropriate stages in the progression. Because muscular dystrophy is not a reportable disease, there is no way to determine accurately the number of people who have it.

The principal type of muscular dystrophy that occurs in childhood, and that educators are most likely to encounter, is muscular dystrophy-Duchenne type. This disease predominantly affects boys, and it is an inherited form due to a gene carried by the mother and transmitted to her sons. Early symptoms, usually appearing around age three include an awkward gait with tiptoeing, and swayback posture. By the time children enter kindergarten, they are sometimes diagnosed as learning disabled or having minimal brain damage. In reality the children are of average intelligence, although low energy levels and frequent absences generally place them in the IQ range of 80.

Batteries of tests are in order at this time to identify the disease. In time, with the progression of the disease, children will fall a great deal and need to stand up by "walking up their lower limbs" with their hands. Eventually a wheelchair will be indicated, usually by the time the child is in the fourth to seventh grade. If a regular school is architecturally accessible, the child may be mainstreamed. Otherwise a special school equipped to handle orthopedically disabled children will be necessary. With the progression of the disease, a good deal of nursing care is needed. Children may be obese because of flabby musculature, or else become excessively thin. This causes posture problems (scoliosis), sometimes necessitating braces. Pain can occur when the child is seated in one position for too long. Upper extremity weakness is progressive, rendering the child very disabled by early teens. Cause of death, usually in the late teens, is from heart failure, as the heart muscle weakens, or lung infection due to weakened breathing muscles.

Relatives of people with these disabilities have an extremely active organization working to provide services and information, and to fund and encourage the research that will bring the hoped-for breakthrough to a cure. There are 227 chapters of the MDA in 50 states, the District of Columbia, Puerto Rico, and Guam, providing a full range of medical services, orthopedic aids, transportation, and 92 summer camps in 36 states. Many services are provided to patients and their families free of charge.

Association chapters have established a national network of hospital-affiliated outpatient clinics providing medical and counseling services. These are described and locations of chapters and clinics are listed in the booklet "Muscular Dystrophy Association Services to the Patient, the Family and the Community," available from the Association. Additional literature, including pamphlets on individual dystrophies, is also available. Literature is also available on Amyotrophic Lateral Sclerosis (ALS) or Lou Gehrig's disease as well as Friedrich's ataxia. Both the National Multiple Sclerosis Society and the MDA provide services for persons with ALS, and MDA also provides services for persons with Friedrich's ataxia. In addition there are individual associations for both ALS and Friedrich's ataxia (National ALS Foundation, 185 Madison Avenue, New York, NY 10016 and Friedrich's Ataxia Group in America, PO Box 11116, Oakland CA 94611).

OSTEOGENESIS IMPERFECTA

Osteogenesis imperfecta (OI) is a skeletal disease that affects about 1 out of 50 thousand babies born in the United States. A deficiency in the manner in which the protein fibers in the bone are arranged causes a reduction in bone salts (calcium and phosphorus) and a consequent weakening of structure. The resultant breaking of bones has given this condition the name of "brittle bone disease," although this popular term is an oversimplification (Bleck and Nagel 1982).

Osteogenesis imperfecta is classified in two major categories: congenita and tarda. The tarda group is further divided into tarda I and tarda II. Children with osteogenesis are born with numerous fractures, some appearing in utero, and sustain repeated fractures in childhood, which result in skeletal deformities such as malfunctioning joints, stunted growth, barrel chest, and often scoliosis. Eventual deafness is a possibility. A characteristic facial appearance includes bulging forehead and temples and a triangular shape, blue discoloration of the whites of the eyes, and poorly formed teeth. The disease is the result of a spontaneous change in the genes (mutation). The tarda children show milder symptoms, usually not at birth but within the first year of life. In both tarda groups there has been a family history of OI and proper genetic counseling is advisable.

Since the cause of the disease is unknown, treatment is directed toward the symptoms. To prevent deformities and reduce the number of fractures, metal rods are threaded through the bones of the legs in a surgical procedure. This allows some ambulation, although children with the congenita type use wheelchairs most of the time. Often a person with OI who uses a wheelchair is able to walk limited distances. New research has developed telescoping rods designed to "grow" with the bone and there are new improved techniques for insertion. However, research into drug therapy has proven nonproductive. Physical therapy is an important form of treatment to prevent the wasting away of muscles and ultimately of bones, and swimming is an ideal exercise.

Proper schooling is important, as there is a prevalence of average and above-average intelligence among children with OI. Early stimulation at home and proper school placement will enable these children to benefit from a normal education.

In April 1970, parents of OI children formed the Osteogenesis Imperfecta Foundation, Inc., a voluntary national organization which has area representatives in most states and active chapters in many. The national address is Osteogenesis Imperfecta Foundation, PO Box 148071, Clearwater, Fl 34629-4807. The organization distributes literature and publishes the newsletter *Breakthrough.*

PARAPLEGIA AND QUADRIPLEGIA

Paraplegia means paralysis of the legs, affecting both motion and sensation. Quadriplegia means a degree of paralysis of all four limbs. Weakness of the upper limbs may range from limited use to total paralysis, depending upon the level of injury to the spinal cord. Paraplegia and quadriplegia are caused by injury, either at birth or in accidents such as automobile, motorcycle, diving, and other types of sports injuries or bullet wounds. Often it is the most active young people who sustain injuries, making adjustment to the disability difficult.

Paralysis is caused by damage to the spinal cord or, in some cases, a fracture of the spine. Interruption of the nerve connection between the brain and the limbs causes the disability and pressure on the cord from bone fragments or other damage causes the injury. Some repair techniques now exist and much research is being done to improve them so as to repair more of these injuries.

Emergency measures are very important in spinal cord injuries. The way in which the patient is moved after an accident, the need for emergency hospital treatment, and the fact that rehabilitation must begin as soon as possible after injury are all important to the success of the treatment. Morale is, of course, of primary importance (see Chapter 1).

Problems involved with paraplegics and quadriplegics include loss of bowel and bladder control and skin breakdowns, called decubitus (Nagel 1982). Physical limitations will range from use of crutches and braces to wheelchair use. When the patient returns home, steps must be taken for return to school, employment if possible, and, in general, an active life. Many people who become adventitiously disabled (disabled later in life) have been active in sports. For these, there are wheelchair sports of all kinds in which they can participate. Upon returning home, the patient should make contact with his or her office of vocational rehabilitation for the assignment of a rehabilitation counselor who will help guide the person's future.

Information about pariplegia and quadraplegia is available from the National Spinal Cord Injury Foundation, 600 West Comming Park, Suite 6000, Woburn, MA 01801, which publishes a national resource directory as well as the magazine *Spinal Cord Injury Life.* Paralyzed Veterans of America, Inc., 4330 East West Highway, Suite 300, Washington, DC 20014, publishes the Magazine *Paraplegia News. Accent on Living Magazine* (Cheever Publishing, Inc., PO Box 700, Gillum Road and High Drive, Bloomington, IN 61701) also carries many advertisements for commercial products useful to paraplegics and quadriplegics. Spinal cord injury research is being carried on in 13 model spinal cord injury research and demonstration centers under the auspices of the National Institute on Disability and Rehabilitation Research.

SICKLE CELL ANEMIA

Sickle cell anemia is an inherited disease found in Black people or individuals of Black heritage. It occurs when an altered type of hemoglobin present in the red blood cells takes on a sickle-shaped form, which gives the disease its name. General symptoms include weakness, jaundice, leg ulcers, malfunction of certain organs, and a lowered resistance to infectious disease. Most patients die before their thirtieth year. No treatment has yet been discovered.

Sickle cell anemia is inherited from parents, and between 8 and 13 percent of American Blacks are carriers. The disease seems to have developed as a protective mechanism against malaria in Africa and the Mediterranean area but in the United States it constitutes a serious health problem. To date, the only prevention is genetic counseling, although research is in progress to determine the basic nature of the disease.

Children with sickle cell anemia may be able to attend school but face the dangers of bad weather and coming in contact with contagious diseases. Limiting sweets and carbohydrates in diet is indicated. Adults with sickle cell anemia should refrain from physical labor (Berberich 1982).

Information on the disease is available from the National Institutes of Health (Public Health Service Information Office, National Institute of Arthritis and Metabolic Diseases, Bethesda, MD 20014).

SPINA BIFIDA WITH MYELOMENINGOCELE

This is one of the most serious handicapping conditions that affect children at birth. Until the 1940s very few of these babies survived beyond infancy. However, treatments developed in recent years have improved conditions so that these children are able to live into adulthood. Many of them are able to pursue active, productive lives.

In spina bifida, some of the vertebrae that normally cover the spinal cord fail to develop fully. In one type called spina bifida occulta, the spinal cord and the skin covering it are normal, and this condition occurs in more than 30 percent of all births. Most adults who have this condition are unaware of it unless a low back problem with subsequent X-rays uncover this mild structural abnormality. Spina bifida with myelomeningocele describes a condition in which the spinal cord protrudes from the surface of the body in some area of the back and is covered only with the membranes that normally cover it when it lies within the vertebrae. This condition is called spina bifida manifesta.

The term myelomeningocele describes the spinal cord when it takes the shape of a flat plate, as it does in this condition, rather than exhibiting its normal tubular shape. In spina bifida myelomeningocele, one part of the nervous system has not developed as it should, and a baby with the condition may not be able to move the muscles in his or her legs. The lower extremities may also be insensitive to pressure, friction, pin pricks, heat, and cold. Paralysis and insensitivity only occur below the point where the protrusion exists. The arms, shoulders, and chest can become very strong with training. A less severe condition is called spina bifida with meningocele, where the spinal cord does not bulge out and paralysis is not usual, although other aspects of the disability may be present.

A major problem for children with spina bifida is the lack of voluntary muscle action for bowel and bladder control. Older children can have special surgical procedures done to allow them to handle their own bladder and bowel problems. Since the bladder is never completely empty, however, odor is often a problem unless very careful hygienic measures are used. Care must always be taken to avoid urinary tract infections, and a urologist is very often a member of the team of specialists caring for people with this disability. Constant medication is often used to prevent infection.

Persons with spinal cord injury often have similar problems of incontinence. Also similar is the problem of decubitus ulcers, raw skin openings resulting from constant wetness and poor skin care and circulation. Buttocks and feet must be checked constantly for this condition. These skin sores may, on occasion, become so deep as to require plastic surgery.

Sometimes fluid, which originates normally inside the brain and is absorbed at a regular rate, leaks into the myelomeningocele sac, allowing for possible infection. Also, in about 75 percent of spina bifida cases, there is interference with the circulation and absorption of the fluid and pressure can increase beyond normal levels, causing hydrocephalus, an abnormally rapid and excessive enlargement of the head, with resultant brain damage. Neurosurgeons have developed a procedure called shunting to prevent this occurrence. Shunts must be constantly watched and changed as the child grows.

Physical therapy is an important aspect in the early care of spina bifida. Gentle exercise of the legs, performed by the parent even with young babies, will help prevent joint deformities. Most of these children need wheelchairs, but some are able to ambulate with braces and crutches. Often trunk muscle weakness will cause scoliosis, dislocation of hips, club feet, or other deformities. Orthopedic surgical procedures are used to prevent these problems. A team of specialists is needed to cope with the considerable physical problems of spina bifida (Bleck and Nagel 1982).

Except where mild hydrocephalus has caused minimal brain damage, many spina bifida children have normal intelligence and may do acceptable schoolwork. Until recently, incontinence in childhood, plus a high level of school absence, has not made it possible for these children to be mainstreamed, and special education programs or home instruction were indicated. More sophisticated bladder management has enabled some children as young as first grade level to be able to function independently in this area and consequently to attend regular school. This is successful only where the nursing, physical therapy, and other professional staff have been prepared to handle the considerable medical problems. Many adults with spina bifida, now in their thirties, are holding responsible positions in the working world, and living independently.

In September 1959 the first spina bifida parent group was organized. In 1972 the Spina Bifida Association of America was formed, which sponsors research, monitors legislation, publishes pamphlets, and holds an annual conference in June. The national organization maintains a listing of local spina bifida groups (1700 Rockville Pike, Suite 540, Rockville, MD 20852, 1-800-621-3141).

TOURETTE SYNDROME

Tourette Syndrome is a little known neurological disorder, characterized by multiple tics due to an organic dysfunction of the central nervous system. It is named after Gilles de la Tourette, the French doctor who described it in 1885. Too often it is undiagnosed or misdiagnosed as a passing tic or a psychological illness.

Tourette Syndrome usually begins between the ages of 2 and 16 with tic-like muscular movements such as eye twitching and facial grimaces, head and shoulder jerking, and throat noises. Over time these become worse, and involuntary utterances of sounds or words, sometimes obscene (coprolalia), may occur. Some patients may touch other people excessively, repeat actions obsessively, or constantly repeat the words of other people (echolalia). A few bite their lips and cheeks, bang their heads against hard objects, and develop other self-destructive behavior. Tics become worse during periods of stress. About 50 percent of children with this disability may have minimal brain damage resulting in some learning disabilities.

Physicians have had some success treating Tourette Syndrome patients with the drug haloperidol (also known as Haldol) which suppresses symptoms but does not cure the condition. Psychotherapy may help the patient cope with his or her disorder and deal with the social and emotional problems that sometimes accompany it. Teachers often have problems dealing with students with Tourette Syndrome who require a tolerant and compassionate setting to accommodate their special needs.

Research is being supported at major medical institutions throughout the country and by the National Institute of Neurological and Communicative Disorders and Stroke, the National Institute of Child Health and Human Development and the National Institute of Mental Health. It is believed that there may be a familial form of Tourette Syndrome since some families have more than one member suffering from the disorder, or with a higher incidence of tics (Fact sheet, Tourette Syndrome 1983).

The Tourette Syndrome Association, Inc., a voluntary nonprofit organization of patients, their families and friends, and health care professionals, is located at 41-02 Bell Boulevard, Bayside, NY 11361. They stimulate and support research on Tourette Syndrome and offer information about the disorder.

NORD (National Organization for Rare Disorders, Inc.)

Tourette Syndrome and Marfan Syndrome are two of the more than 5,000 "orphan diseases" monitored by NORD, a nonprofit, voluntary agency composed of national health organizations, scientific researchers, physicians, and individuals who are dedicated to the identification, control and cure of rare debilitating disorders. NORD was formed in 1983 to help pass the Orphan Drug Act, legislation that made important new orphan drugs and devices available. Many of these drugs had not been manufactured because they were unprofitable. NORD acts as a clearinghouse for information, networks families with similar disorders, fosters communication among agencies, government bodies, industry, scientific researchers, academic institutions and concerned individuals and encourages research. It maintains the Rare Disease Database, accessible to the public and professionals through CompuServe, and publishes the newsletter *Orphan Disease Update*. Reprints from the NORD database are available for $2.50 each and take about two to six weeks to arrive. For a free publications list, a listing of the articles in the database, or any other information, write NORD at PO Box 89231, New Fairfield, CT 06812.

VISUAL IMPAIRMENTS

There are many types and degrees of visual impairment. The government definition of legal blindness, which governs the provision of services to individuals who are blind, bases its definition on visual acuity and visual field. However, this definition fails to cover many other types of vision impairment or causes of blindness. Persons may be legally blind and still have some vision; one is legally blind with acuity of 20/200 or less in the better corrected eye or a visual field (peripheral vision) of no greater than 20 degrees.

Other common visual impairments are:

- **Albinism**: a hereditary condition in which there is a lack of pigment throughout the body, including the eyes. It is usually accompanied by a nystagmus condition (see below). People with albinism are very sensitive to light and sometimes wear tinted glasses.
- **Astigmatism**: blurred vision caused by defective curvature of the refractive surfaces of the eye, as a result of which light rays are not sharply focused on the retina.
- **Cataract**: a condition in which the normally transparent lens of the eye becomes cloudy or opaque.
- **Glaucoma**: a condition in which pressure of the fluid inside the eye is too high. Depending upon the type of glaucoma, visual loss may be gradual, sudden, or present at birth. When visual loss is gradual, it begins with decreasing peripheral vision.
- **Hyperopia**: a condition in which the eyeball is too short from front to back, causing farsightedness.
- **Myopia**: a condition in which the eyeball is too long from front to back, causing nearsightedness.
- **Nystagmus**: involuntary, rapid movement of the eyeballs from side to side, up and down, in a rotary motion, or a combination of these.
- **Retinitis pigmentosa**: a hereditary degeneration of the retina beginning with night blindness and producing a gradual loss of peripheral vision. Though some persons witnn this disease lose all of their vision, many do retain some central vision.
- **Retrolental fibroplasia (RLF)**: visual impairment caused by oxygen given to incubated premature babies.
- **Strabismus**: eyes not simultaneously directed to the same object as a result of an imbalance of the muscles of the eyeball (Corn and Martinez 1986, 23).

Additional information may be obtained from the American Foundation for the Blind, 15 West 16th Street, New York, NY 10011, which publishes a catalog of devices, the *Journal of Visual Impairment*, conference proceedings, films for purchase or rental and pamphlet information. Other organizations for the blind will be listed in later chapters.

CONCLUSION

The disabilities described in this chapter were included in some detail because until very recently it was difficult to find information about many of them that was not entirely medical in nature. The emergence of individuals with these physical disabilities into the mainstream of life, schools, and the workplace makes it imperative that graduate library school courses and courses in schools of education incorporate some knowledge of these disabilities into their curricula. Some better known disabilities have been mentioned only briefly in order to provide definitions and addresses for further information. Choices are arbitrary according to the perception of the author. Many syndromes and other rare and lesser known (orphan) diseases have not been included. For additional help in dealing with the topic of birth defects and genetic counseling, the March of Dimes, Birth Defects Foundation at 1275 Mamaroneck Avenue, White Plains, NY 10605, has published two pamphlets, available from the main office or local chapters. The titles are "Genetic Counseling" and "Birth Defects: Tragedy and Hope."

REFERENCES

Axelrod, Relicia B., and Sein, Mary Ellen. 1982. *Caring for the Child with Familial Dysautonomia*. New York: Dysautonomia Treatment & Evaluation Center, New York University Medical Center.

Berberich, F. Ralph. 1982. "Sickle Cell Disease." In Bleck, Eugene E., and Nagel, Donald A., eds. *Physically Handicapped Children: A Medical Atlas for Teachers*. Second Edition. Orlando, FL: Grune & Stratton, Inc., 469–76.

Bleck, Eugene E. 1982. "Arthrogryposis." In Bleck, Eugene E., and Nagel, Donald A., eds. *Physically Handicapped Children: A Medical Atlas for Teachers*. Second Edition. Orlando, FL: Grune & Stratton, Inc., 27–30.

Bleck, Eugene E. 1982. "Muscular Dystrophy." In Bleck, Eugene E., and Nagel, Donald A., eds. *Physically Handicapped Children: A Medical Atlas for Teachers*. Second Edition. Orlando, FL: Grune & Stratton, Inc., 385–94.

Bleck, Eugene E. 1982. "Myelomeningocele, Meningocele, and Spina Bifida." In Bleck, Eugene E., and Nagel, Donald A., eds. *Physically Handicapped Children: A Medical Atlas for Teachers*. Second Edition. Orlando, FL: Grune & Stratton, Inc., 345–62.

Bleck, Eugene E. 1982. "Osteogenesis Imperfecta." In Bleck, Eugene E., and Nagel, Donald A., eds. *Physically Handicapped Children: A Medical Atlas for Teachers*. Second Edition. Orlando, FL: Grune & Stratton, Inc., 405–12.

Corn, Anne Lesley, and Martinez, Iris. 1986. *When You Have a Visually Handicapped Child in Your Classroom: Suggestions for Teachers*. New York: American Foundation for the Blind, 23.

Dalton, Phyllis I. 1985. *Library Service to the Deaf and Hearing Impaired*. Phoenix, AZ: Oryx Press, 25–26.

Diamond, Liebe S. 1982. "Down Syndrome." In Bleck, Eugene E., and Nagel, Donald A., eds. *Physically Handicapped Children: A Medical Atlas for Teachers*. Orlando, FL: Grune & Stratton, Inc., 279–92.

Frankel, Victor, Gold, Stuart, and Golyakhovsky, Vladimir. 1988. "The Ilizarov Technique." *Bulletin of the Hospital for Joint Diseases Orthopaedic Institute* 48 (1): 17–27.

Gately, *Gary. New York Times.* December 11, 1988, 70.

Hagemeyer, Alice. 1979. "Special Needs of the Deaf Patron." In Velleman, Ruth A. *Serving Physically Disabled People: An Information Handbook for All Libraries.* New York: Bowker, 140–61.

Hagemeyer, Alice. 1988, November. "The Deaf Community," District of Columbia Public Library Flier.

Harvey, Birt. 1982. "Cystic Fibrosis." In Bleck, Eugene E., and Nagel Donald A., eds. *Physically Handicapped Children: A Medical Atlas for Teachers.* Second Edition. Orlando, FL: Grune & Stratton, Inc. 255–64.

Horton, William A., and Rimoin, David L. 1982. "Short Stature and Growth." In Bleck, Eugene E., and Nagel, Donald A., eds. *Physically Handicapped Children: A Medical Atlas for Teachers.* Second Edition. Orlando, FL: Grune & Stratton, Inc., 451–68.

Luterman, David M. 1986. *Deafness in Perspective.* San Diego: College Hill Press, 58.

March of Dimes Birth Defects Foundation. 1985. "Marfan Syndrome," Public Health Education Information Sheet, Genetic Series.

"Marfan Syndrome," National Marfan Foundation Fact Sheet.

Massie, Robert, and Massie, Suzanne. *Journey.* New York, Knopf, 1975.

Miller, John J. III. 1982. "Juvenile, Rheumatoid Arthritis." In Bleck, Eugene E., and Nagel, Donald A., eds. *Physically Handicapped Children: A Medical Atlas for Teachers.* Second Edition. Orlando, FL: Grune & Stratton, Inc., 423–30.

Nagel, Donald A. 1982. "Temporary Orthopedic Disabilities in Children." In Bleck, Eugene E., and Nagel, Donald A., eds. *Physically Handicapped Children: A Medical Atlas for Teachers.* Second Edition. Orlando, FL: Grune & Stratton, Inc., 413–18.

Nagel, Donald A., 1982. "Traumatic Paraplegia and Quadraplegia." In Bleck, Eugene E., and Nagel, Donald A., eds. *Physically Handicapped Children: A Medical Atlas for Teachers.* Second Edition. Orlando, FL: Grune & Stratton, Inc., 395–404.

Setoguchi, Yoshio. 1982. "Amputations in Children." In Bleck, Eugene E., and Nagel, Donald A. eds. *Physically Handicapped Children: A Medical Atlas for Teachers.* Second Edition. Orlando, FL: Grune & Stratton, 17–26.

"Tourette Syndrome," Tourette Syndrome Association Fact Sheet.

Wilson, Nancy O. 1978. *Childhood Autism.* Cincinnati: Pamphlet Publications Division RMA.

PART II

Consumer Information

Chapter 3
Benefits under the Law

People with disabilities have certain rights guaranteed by law: rights to education, employment, health care, and any other public or private services provided by federal assistance. It is the responsibility of the Office of Civil Rights in the Department of Education, through its local offices (see Appendix A) to enforce federal laws prohibiting discrimination because of disabilities and to investigate discrimination complaints brought by individuals under these laws. Most advocacy organizations for the disabled monitor legal rights. In addition, several organizations deal exclusively with legal rights.

Disabled in Action, an organization started in New York City in 1970, has grown into a national civil rights organization, Disabled in Action National, consisting of eight city, county, and state chapters. It consists primarily of and is directed by people with disabilities, and works to raise consciousness concerning paternalism and derogatory attitudes, laws and customs that handicap individuals who are disabled. Disabled in Action is concerned with the implementation and enforcement of legislation to promote equal access to all areas of living. Disabled in Action of Metropolitan New York publishes a monthly newspaper, the *DIA Activist*, Box 30954, New York, NY 10011-0109.

Disability Rights Education and Defense Fund, Inc. (DREDF), 2212 6th Street, Berkeley, CA 94710, was founded in 1979 as a national nonprofit organization run primarily by persons with disabilities to monitor legislative efforts and conduct training and research programs. In 1981 DREDF opened a Washington, DC, office at 1616 P Street NW, Suite 100, Washington, DC 20036. It offers up-to-date information on civil rights of disabled persons to attorneys, federal agencies, legislators and their staffs. It publishes the *Disability Rights Review*, a free quarterly newsletter distributed to people with disabilities, their parents, concerned organizations, attorneys and legislators. While independent living centers and social agencies provide services to disabled individuals, DREDF works on laws and policies that challenge the discrimination which has prevented them from being integrated into schools, jobs, and community life. The fund has 12 staff members who are primarily either disabled or the parents of disabled children.

The National Center for Law and the Deaf, 800 Florida Avenue NW, Washington, DC 20002, is a project of Gallaudet University. The center publishes information in the field of law and the deaf and hearing-impaired community. Recently, the center has taken a leading role in providing information concerning the legal rights of people with disabilities as they become in any way involved in the law enforcement, justice, or correctional system (*Rehab Brief* Vol. X, No. 5, 1988).

Over the past few years a number of studies have been done to investigate whether disabled offenders receive equal treatment under the law and what the psychological, economic, social, and legal experiences of people with disabilities are—victim or accused—in law enforcement, judical, or correctional systems. Also, what information is known about the attitudes or behavior of those in law enforcement toward people with disabilities? And what can be done to improve the treatment of people with disabilities when they come in contact with the law enforcement and justice systems (*Rehab Brief*, 1988)? The newsletter *First Dibs* (Vol. 2, No. 6, May-June, 1988) has published a bibliography of references dealing with the disabled offender, including the mentally retarded and learning disabled, offering many sources of information in this relatively new field of investigation. The same issue carries a book review of the book *Special Education in the Criminal Justice System* by C. Michael Nelson, Robert B. Rutherford, Jr., and Bruce I. Wolford (eds.), Merrill Publishing Co., PO Box 508, Columbus, OH 43216-0508. This seems to be the first book on the topic of educating the handicapped offender.

The American Bar Association publishes a periodical called *Mental and Physical Disability Law Reporter*. In Volume 12 Number 2, a survey was published as one component of the American Bar Association's Life Services Planning Project, funded by the US Department of Health and Human Services, Office of Human Development Services (Grant No. 90-OJ-1035/02). The project designed and tested a local demonstration model to train volunteers to assist elderly and developmentally disabled people and their families with long-range legal, financial, health, and social services planning and published a training module for volunteers and practitioners and a manual for replicating and adapting the model program. These publications are available from the Commission on the Mentally Disabled, 1800 M Street NW, Washington, DC 20036. The survey "Support Services and Alternatives to Guardianship" lists addresses of State Associations of Retarded Citizens, State Units on Aging, and Protection and Advocacy Agencies by state, offering information on services, goals, eligibility, fees, funding, and staff. Reprints of this survey are available from the Commission on the Mentally Disabled.

Certainly a basic right of all Americans is the right to vote, and this right should be exercised by people who are disabled, and who need to be informed about the laws that affect them. They must make their legislators aware of how they feel. Many states have had laws for some time requiring that polling places be made accessible. On December 31, 1985, Public Law 98-935 "The Voting Accessibility for the Elderly and Handicapped Act" was passed, making accessibility to polling places a federal law. In addition, the Act mandates that instructions printed in large type and information by telecommunications devices for the deaf be made available at each polling place. All people who find it difficult to leave their homes are entitled to absentee ballots, which can be obtained from the local board of elections. In addition, in 1988, the National Organization on Disability began a national public service campaign to teach people with disabilities how, when, and where to register to vote. The organization is publicizing its toll-free number (1-800-248-2254) and distributing a series of public service television spots to 400 outlets across the country. Former presidential press secretary James Brady and former Texas Congresswoman Barbara Jordan have appeared in newspaper and magazine advertisements on behalf of the campaign (New York State Advocate 1988).

An extremely valuable newsletter in the field of rights and regulations is the *Report on Disability Programs* (formerly the *Handicapped Americans Report*), published biweekly by Business Publishers, Inc., 951 Pershing Drive, Silver Spring, MD 20910-4464. Passage of all laws concerning the disabled and news about pending legislation are reported in this newsletter.

THE BIG TEN—CIVIL RIGHTS OF PEOPLE WITH DISABILITIES

I. The Right to Live in a Barrier-Free Environment

Federal and state laws providing for the accessibility of public buildings to disabled people have existed since the late 1960s. Public Law 90-480, the Architectural Barriers Act of 1968, states that "any building constructed or leased whole or in part with federal funds must be made accessible to and usable by the physically handicapped" (US Code, Title 42, Section 4151.56). Public Law 93-87, the Federal Highway Act of 1973, states that the secretary of transportation may not approve any state highway program that does not provide for curb cuts on all curbs constructed or replaced at pedestrian crossways on or after July 1, 1976 (US Code, Title 23, Section 402). Many state laws make similar provisions where state and local public funds are used.

For several years, PL 90-480 was not enforced with determination. Then the Architectural and Transportation Barriers Compliance Board (ATBCB) was established to ensure compliance with the standards (US Code, Title 29, Section 792, PL 93-112, Section 502, and PL 93-516, Section 111, Rehabilitation Act Amendments of 1974). This legislation does not affect buildings erected without government money. However, disabled and able-bodied people alike are trying to make communities aware of their responsibility to make churches, museums, parks, theaters and certainly libraries architecturally accessible.

The ATBCB is composed of members representing 11 federal agencies, including the 4 standard setting agencies (the General Services Administration, the Department of Defense, the Department of Housing and Urban Development, and the US Postal Service), plus the departments of Education, Health, and Human Services; Interior; Justice; Labor and Transportation; and the Veterans Administration. Another 11 members are appointed by the president from the general public. The board is responsible for handling complaints about inaccessible facilities, and may conduct investigations, hold public hearings, and issue orders to comply with PL 90-480. The board also plans for accessible transportation and housing in cooperation with other agencies, organizations, and individuals. It publishes the quarterly *Access America*, free on request, and answers technical information questions through its technical services division. Complaints should be put in writing to ATBCB, 1111 18th Street NW, Washington, DC 20036.

In 1985, the ATBCB published a document, with updates, which originally appeared in the *Federal Register* on August 7, 1984 (49 FR 31528), entitled "Uniform Federal Accessibility Standards" (available from the US Government Printing Office (1985-494-187). This very complete and informative monograph presents uniform standards for design, construction, and alteration of buildings, and embodies an agreement to minimize the differences between the standards previously used by the four standard setting agencies (see above). It includes standards for designs of bathrooms, ramps, elevators, telephones, drinking fountains, tables, counters, and much more. Also, the American National

Standards Institute publishes *American National Standards: Specifications for Making Buildings and Facilities Accessible to and Usable by, the Physically Handicapped.* Known as ANSI A117.1, the latest edition now available is the 1986 edition. Chapter 12 suggests barrier-free designs for libraries.

Access for Persons Who Are Blind

Access for blind individuals means mobility, the ability to get around, as well as access to information. For the ways in which blind people can access information, see chapters 4, 5, and 9. Blind persons are eligible for rehabilitation and training as outlined in Chapter 6. Mobility training, supplied by agencies serving the blind may mean training in using a long cane, while some blind persons may choose training with a seeing eye dog. To find out about seeing eye dogs, write to The Seeing Eye, Inc., Morristown, NJ 07960, for an application form. Travel expenses to the place of training are paid by The Seeing Eye (Lunt 1984).

Training can also be supplied by agencies serving the blind in the use of the technology and equipment that are available to them. According to Dr. Hannan Selvin, learning to become proficient in braille is difficult for adventitiously blind persons, and using tape recorders is much easier, but the use of elementary braille is helpful. Training can also be supplied in the use of handling coins, paper money, dialing telephone numbers and sewing buttons, as well as learning to handle ordinary tools safely to make household repairs, and developing kitchen skills (Selvin 1979).

Access for Persons with Low Vision

Low vision has been defined as "reduced central acuity or visual field loss which even with the best optical correction provided by regular lenses still results in visual impairment from a performance standpoint" (Klauber and Covino 1981). Most of these people are not classified as legally blind and are not served by the national and local agencies comprising the "blindness system." But many of these people can be helped with proper knowledge. For those persons with low vision, or in the process of losing vision, the department of ophthalmology at the nearest medical school or school of optometry can supply information about the nearest low-vision clinic.

In an interesting article in the *Journal of Visual Impairment and Blindness* (December 1987) Richard Mettler points out that just as there is a visual order and reasonableness about the world, there is an order and reasonableness which can be experienced nonvisually (Mettler 1987). Mettler also lists the ANSI standards for blind persons that include warning textures at curbs, stairs, and doors to hazardous areas, and protection of pools by railings, walls, curbs, or detectable warnings. Many elevators now announce floors vocally, in addition to labeling them in braille. For additional architectural standards see the *ANSI Standards*, 1986 edition, and the "Uniform Federal Accessibility Standards" mentioned above.

Access for Persons Who Are Deaf

Access to deaf individuals means communication. The provision of interpreter services at public functions and in educational institutions is now the law under Section 504 of PL 93-112. Deaf people communicate with other people if both have TDD's, telecommunication devices that permit communication over regular telephone lines. As a matter of law, all federal agencies and institutions receiving federal funding must have TDD numbers.

Deaf people are usually not able to comprehend much of what they see on television. In 1972, the Public Broadcasting System began testing the use of closed captions on television programs which could only be seen on the screen by the use of a decoder. In the spring of 1979, two of the major networks, NBC and ABC, announced that they would begin using closed captions on their stations and that a national captioning institute would be established to coordinate the project. (CBS is also captioning programs for the deaf.) Since that time a tremendous amount of progress can be reported.

The National Captioning Institute, Inc. (NCI), at 5203 Leesburg Pike, Suite 1500, Falls Church, VA 22041, is in existence as a nonprofit organization, financed by federal funding, network contributions and corporate sponsorship. It has two 800 numbers, 1-800-533-WORDS (for voice) and 1-800-533-TDDS. NCI captions television programs for the Public Broadcasting Service (PBS), ABC, CBS, NBC and independent producers. ABC and PBS played major roles in developing the captioning system. As of July 1988, over 175 hours on regular networks and an additional 100 hours on cable TV were being broadcast with closed captions. NCI has also put into effect a unique service. Publishers of videocassette movies are approached for permission to equip some of their new productions with closed captions. These are then sent to distributors who can copy the master tape. The captions are only seen by those persons who have decoders, and the sound is not affected. While NCI does not have any control over the design of the packaging, there is a small logo somewhere on the package to indicate that a particular movie cassette has been closed captioned. Certainly video stores should be made aware of this in order to respond to customers requesting such films and the service should be publicized within the community of deaf people. Over 1,100 movie cassettes have been closed captioned so far, with 15 to 20 being produced each month. The Institute has two publications: *CAPTIONS*, a newsletter for viewers, and the "NCI MARKETING MEMO," an update sheet for producers and sponsors.

The equipment needed to receive closed captions is sold by Sears, Roebuck and Co. (catalog only), Service Merchandise, and hearing-aid dispensers through audiologists, as well as in 900 retail locations. They now cost under $200.

Access to deaf persons can also include such adaptations as warning lights for doorbells and telephones, and trained dogs. Persons desiring information about dogs to alert people to sounds, such as doorbells and telephones and babies crying, should contact Hearing Dog Program, American Humane Association, 5351 South Roslyn Street, Englewood, CO 80110, and Canine Companions for Independence, PO Box 446, Santa Rosa, CA 95402 (Lunt 1984), or Dogs for the Deaf, 13260 Highway 238, Jacksonville, OR 97530.

II. The Right to Appropriate Housing and Independent Living

Since 1937, the federal government has been attempting to provide suitable housing for its citizens. Attempts at assisting the private housing industry to meet these requirements proved inadequate, whereupon the government assumed greater responsibility for meeting the housing needs of the low-income population, especially the elderly. In the late 1950s and early 1960s, recognition .

was also given to the special needs of the physically disabled. Legislation from 1964 through the next 10 years attempted to make suitable housing available to them. It was not until 1974 that the Housing and Community Development Act included the developmentally disabled and mentally handicapped among the special user groups eligible for federally assisted housing (Thompson 1976).

PL 93-383, the Housing and Community Development Act, which was passed in 1974, is a comprehensive piece of legislation that encourages the building of housing suitable for the disabled and elderly by providing federal dollars for this purpose to private builders. Under Section 8 of this act, the Department of Housing and Urban Development's (HUD) housing assistance program attempts to provide decent housing for families that had not been able to afford such housing in the past by assisting in the renovation for accessibility of existing housing and the building of new, accessible housing units.

Section 202 of PL 93-383, the direct loan program, stimulates private builders to build accessible housing for physically and developmentally disabled and mentally handicapped people by making loans for this purpose. Builders are permitted to develop either independent living complexes or group homes. The section interprets "accessibility" as meaning the provision, in addition to architectural modifications, of a whole range of support services, including health, continuing education, and homemaking counseling, as well as transportation to these services. This provision reflects the independent living philosophy, which people with disabilities are now espousing in great numbers, as opposed to institutional living.

Under the act's rent subsidy program, low-income families with disabled or elderly members may be eligible for housing assistance payments from HUD, which are made directly to the owners of rental units to make up the difference between the HUD-approved rental amount and the amount the tenant is required to pay. Tenants pay an average of 30 percent of their adjusted income. A family is defined as one or more single-elderly or handicapped individuals living together; one or more such individuals living with an attendant; or a family of two people or more. The Housing Authority Act of 1976 prohibited rent subsidies provided under PL 93-383 from being considered income for persons receiving Supplementary Security Income support.

An individual with disabilities who wishes to adapt a private home to meet certain needs may be eligible for a Title I Home Improvement Loan, insured by the Federal Housing Administration (a part of HUD), which can be used to remove architectural barriers, hazards, or inconvenient features. The loans are applied for through banks or other lending institutions. To repair a home on a farm in a rural area, low-income disabled people may be eligible for loans from Farmers Home Administration, Department of Agriculture, Washington, DC 20250.

The Department of Housing and Urban Development has created the Office of the Special Advisor for Disability Issues, which is responsible for developing policy initiatives that concern the disabled community. This office works closely with all other agencies concerned with disability issues, as well as the HUD Office of Fair Housing and Equal Opportunity, to process complaints about discrimination in HUD programs on the basis of disability. The special advisor also acts as liaison between the department and public and private groups representing disability concerns. For a kit outlining all of this information, as well as listing addresses of local HUD offices, contact the Office of the Special Advisor for Disability Issues, US Department of Housing and Urban

Development, Office of the Deputy Under Secretary for Intergovernmental Relations, Suite 10140, 451 Seventh Street SW, Washington, DC 20410. This office also publishes a newsletter called *Dateline on Disability.*

Asking architects to design adapted housing that could be used by people who are able-bodied as well as disabled has been difficult, because confusion has existed among federal, local, and state codes as to architectural requirements. According to a January 1987 article in *Architecture,* "there will probably be, in the near future, uniform design standards for accessibility in this country." Margaret Milner, executive director of the ATBCB, says, "Now the challenge is to use those standards creatively in design" (Greer 1987). Her words were prophetic.

One architect who has been working in this field for many years is Ron Mace, President of Barrier Free Environments, Inc. (BFE), of Raleigh, North Carolina. BFE has received a three-year research and demonstration grant from the National Institute on Disability and Rehabilitation Research to develop materials describing design guidelines, methods of providing accessibility features, and sources of technical information on designing and building accessible housing (*Rehab Brief* 1988). Many publications may be ordered from: Barrier Free Environments, Inc., PO Box 30634, Raleigh, NC 27622. For information about other publications write to Less Restrictive Housing, Barrier Free Environments, Inc., PO Box 30634, Raleigh, NC 27622.

For all those working for many years toward the ideal of accessible housing a major event occurred September 13, 1988, when President Reagan signed the Fair Housing Amendments Act of 1988 (PL 100-430) (Handicapped Americans Report 1988). The act takes a step toward bringing to fruition the idea of universal design. It puts teeth into laws prohibiting the sale or rental of housing to individuals with disabilities or to individuals residing or associated with individuals with disabilities, by changing the legal method by which fair housing suits may be brought. For purposes of the legislation, discrimination includes preventing an individual with disabilities from making reasonable modifications to the premises, at the tenant's expense, so as to permit the individual full enjoyment of the premises. Refusing to make reasonable modifications of existing building rules so that individuals with disabilities can enjoy the premises would also constitute discrimination.

Pertinent to our discussion about universal design is the provision that new multi-family dwellings designed or constructed beginning 30 months after passage of the legislation require the following elements:

1. The public use and common use portions be readily accessible to and usable by individuals with handicaps.
2. All the doors be wide enough to allow passage into and within the premises by handicapped persons in wheelchairs.
3. All premises contain an accessible route into and through the building.
4. Light switches, electrical outlets, and other environmental controls be placed in accessible locations.
5. Reinforcements be built into bathroom walls to allow later installations of grab bars.
6. Kitchens and bathrooms be usable by individuals in wheelchairs.

These requirements do not pre-empt state legislation with stricter requirements than provided in the federal legislation (*Handicapped Requirements Handbook* 1988).

III. The Right to Transportation and Travel

Mobility is of primary importance to everyone because it means freedom. The ability to get around—to go to a job, to school, to shop, and travel—is basic to a way of life that ensures maximum independence. People with physical disabilities often are unable to use conventional transportation and consequently remain homebound.

Responsibility for encouraging accessibility of mass transit for people with disabilities rests with the US Department of Transportation, 400 Seventh Street SW, Washington, DC 20590. Inquiries about present status of federal laws may be addressed to the Office of Transportation Regulatory Affairs at the department. In brief, federal policies during the 1970s were set forth in PL 91-453, the Urban Mass Transportation Act of 1970; PL 93-87, the Highway Safety Act of 1973; and PL 93-503, the Mass Transit Act of 1974, all of which encouraged special efforts in the planning and design of mass transportation for accessibility, especially where federally funded projects were involved. PL 93-503 also stated that rates charged to the elderly and disabled will, during nonpeak hours, be one-half the rate for other persons traveling during peak hours (Velleman 1979). The department also issued three regulations in response to Section 504 of the Rehabilitation Act of 1973 (PL 93-112) as amended. A regulation issued in 1979 covered aviation, intercity rail, highways, commuter rail, and mass transit, but the mass transit provisions were found to require costly efforts to modify existing mass transit systems (Canny 1988). A new rule was published in May 1986 which conformed to the requirements of section 317(C) of the "Surface Transportation Assistance Act of 1982" (PL 97-424) and required each transit agency, after consultation with persons with disabilities and other interested members of the public, to select the type of service it would provide, using on-call accessible buses, paratransit vans subsidies for taxi fares, or other combinations of these services.

The Urban Mass Transportation Administration (UMTA) is the lead agency in an interdepartmental working relationship between the Department of Transportation (DOT) and the Department of Health and Human Services (DHHS). In the late 1980s a staff working group and an executive level Transportation Coordination Council were formed with membership from both departments. Federal, state, and local efforts are being encouraged to coordinate funding for specialized transportation services (Canny 1988).

Transportation concerns were addressed by The Third International Conference on Mobility and Transport of Elderly and Handicapped Persons, held in Orlando, Florida, in 1984. Conference proceedings, produced and distributed by Technology Sharing Program, Office of the Secretary of Transportation, Washington, DC 20590, detailed progress and programs in all participating countries. In the United States, new subway systems must be accessible if developed with federal funds. Prototypes are MARTA in Atlanta, METRO in Washington, and BART in San Francisco. Other cities have addressed the problem by providing buses equipped with wheelchair ramps (Seattle), paratransit facilities (The Ride, Boston), or cooperative taxi services (rural areas). After experiencing difficulties with ramped buses (breakdowns, loading time, etc.) cities in Pennsylvania have instituted other types of paratransit (Fix 1984). Intercity transit by bus and rail has made great progress in accessibility. AMTRAK has a system-wide policy of offering the disabled and elderly a 25 percent discount on one-way purchases with the exception of certain peak travel days, as well as other special services. Many train cars and stations are now accessible. For a free brochure entitled "Access Amtrak: A Guide to Amtrak Services for Elderly and Handicapped Travelers," contact Amtrak, PO Box 7717, 1549 West Glenlake Avenue, Itasca, IL, or use 800-523-6950 or 6951 TTY.

The Greyhound Lines established a program in 1975 called "Helping Hands," allowing a person with disabilities to travel with a companion on a single adult-fare ticket. A doctor's statement must be presented. Wheelchairs (nonmotorized) and other aids are carried without cost. Greyhound issues the free brochures "A Traveler's Guide for the Handicapped" and "Reach for Greyhound's Helping Hand," available from Greyhound Lines, Inc., Section S, Greyhound Tower, Phoenix, AZ 85077. Trailways also offers free transportation for the attendant of a person with disabilities and free baggage accommodation for wheelchairs. Call local offices or write Trailways, Inc., 1500 Jackson Street, Dallas, TX 75201.

The history of airlines transportation for people with disabilities has been a troublesome one, and many of these passengers have objected to airline policies, finding them discriminatory and inconsistent from one airline to the next or even from one terminal or flight crew to the next on the same airline. In 1982 the Civil Aeronautics Board (CAB) promulgated a regulation to prohibit discrimination on the basis of handicap by major airlines and commuter air carriers; however, specific enforcement provisions applied only to those few smaller carriers that received direct federal subsidy. In response to a court challenge, Congress enacted the Air Carrier Access Act of 1986 (PL 99-435, October 2, 1986), which restores Congressional intent that all departments within an institution receiving federal funds must comply with Section 504 of PL 93-112 and other civil rights laws. Airlines do use federal air controllers. (Watch for regulations on this law which are not yet completed; see also Chapter 4).

Airports have long been accessible. The publication *Access Travel: Airports,* a publication of the Airport Operators Council International is in its fifth edition and lists facilities and services at 519 airport terminals in 62 countries which are important to people with disabilities. For single, free copies of this publication, write: Access America, Washington, DC 20202, or Consumer Information Center, Pueblo, CO 81009.

IV. The Right to Financial Assistance

There are two basic federal programs that provide financial assistance to persons with disabilities. The acronyms for these programs sometimes cause confusion: Social Security Disability Benefits (SSDB) and Supplemental Security Income (SSI).

Social Security Disability Benefits

The purpose of SSDB is to provide continuing income for families or persons whose incomes have been reduced because of disability. Disability is defined as a physical or mental impairment that prevents a person from working, is expected to last or has lasted for at least 12 months, or is expected to result in death (US Code, Title 42, Section 423). This protection against loss of earnings because of disability became part of Social Security benefits in 1954. Benefits are available to persons disabled since childhood if parents or guardians have paid into Social Security during their working years, and to persons disabled as adults, available through their own Social Security contributions paid when they were in the work-force. A person disabled before the age of 31 may need 18 months of Social Security credit to receive assistance. Blindness is included under the law, according to definitions described in Chapter 2. Monthly benefits will be paid to:

1. Disabled workers under age 65 and their families.
2. Disabled spouses, disabled dependent spouses, and (under some conditions) disabled surviving divorced spouses of workers who were insured at death. Benefits may be payable at age 50 in these instances.
3. Persons disabled before age 22 who continue to be disabled; if the disability is permanent, benefits will last a lifetime and will continue after the death of parents.

It is important to apply for Social Security benefits soon after a disability is incurred, since payments generally do not begin until the sixth full month of the disability. A person disabled for more than 6 months before applying may receive some benefits for the months before the application. Back payments are limited to the 12 months preceding the date of application. A person disabled in childhood may be eligible for benefits as soon as one parent begins receiving retirement or disability benefits or dies. A worker who is disabled or a person disabled in childhood who returns to work in spite of the disability may continue to receive disability benefits for up to 12 months. When applying for Social Security benefits, it is helpful to bring along a Social Security number or card, the date of last working period, date of injury or illness, the date or recovery or return to work, and if no longer disabled, dates of treatments for disability, proof of age, name of illness or sickness, names and addresses of doctors, hospitals, or clinics, and names of jobs held before becoming disabled.

Supplemental Security Income

An individual who is blind or disabled and whose income and resources are very limited may be eligible for SSI benefits. SSI came into effect in January 1974 as an amendment to the Social Security Act, which provided that the federal government take over state programs of assistance to people with disabilities and those aged 65 and over. SSI is designed to provide a minimum monthly income for those whose disability prevents them from gainful employment and who, because of disability, may not have been able to contribute to the regular social security system. Excluded from benefits are persons in public institutions, drug addicts, and alcoholics, unless they are undergoing appropriate treatment.

SSI is available to children with disabilities, defined as unmarried persons under 18 years of age. Responding to a congressional mandate, on December 31, 1976, the Social Security Administration issued proposed criteria for making SSI disability determinations among children under the age of 18. Under previous regulations, a single list of impairments was applied to both children and adults. This section was retained, but a new subdivision was added to deal with the evaluation of disabling conditions peculiar to childhood. Criteria for this evaluation are as follows: (1) children with IQs of 59 or below would be considered disabled, rather than the adult standard of 49; (2) children with IQs of 60 to 69 must have a physical or other mental impairment that restricts their functional or developmental progress or must have chromosomally proven Down's Syndrome in order to be found disabled. Additional regulations govern epileptic and cerebral palsied children (Department of HEW 1979). Full-time students are eligible for SSI until the age of 22.

Up until 1980 a person could only have minimal income and still be eligible for SSI. In 1980, work incentive provisions of Section 1619 of the Social Security Act were originally enacted as a three-year demonstration project, extended temporarily through June 30, 1987, and finally incorporated into Public Law 99-643, the Employment Opportunities for Disabled Americans Act (Rocklin 1987).

The act (a) allows cash benefits and Medicaid coverage to certain SSI recipients who wish to work despite their impairments and (b) also continues SSI recipient status for Medicaid purposes to disabled and blind individuals whose earnings preclude SSI or 1619(a) cash payments. The law thus removes disincentives to work by continuing to provide income, until earned income reaches a certain amount. It also provides automatic reinstatement of SSI benefits should a disabled person lose employment.

In both the SSDB and SSI programs, vocational counseling, rehabilitation and training, and possible job referral are mandatory for all applicants. To avoid having SSDB and SSI checks stolen from mailboxes, or for persons who have difficulty getting around, recipients should arrange to have their checks deposited directly into their bank accounts. Notices from the Social Security Administration are available in braille upon request, accompanied by a written letter (also available in Spanish) should the blind person wish someone to read the notice. Requests should be sent to the Department of Health and Human Services, Social Security Administration, Baltimore, MD 21235. There are many publications available from local Social Security offices, or from the US Government Printing Office, about Social Security benefits such as "How We Decide If You are Still Disabled" (August 1987), "If You Become Disabled" (January 1987), and "Disability" (January 1988). These are updated continually to reflect changes in the law.

Legal and Financial Planning for Children with Disabilities

A topic that has received much attention during the 1980s has been legal and financial planning; how parents of children with mental disabilities and severe physical disabilities can provide for their long-term futures. Estate planning, regardless of size of the estate, should be the concern for all parents of these groups of children. It is possible to plan for supplementary income without jeopardizing government funding if done correctly. *Alternatives: A Family Guide to Legal and Financial Planning for the Disabled*, by L. Mark Russell covers wills, guardianship, trusts, government benefits, taxes and insurance, and financial planning. Although a certain amount of updating will be necessary due to changes in tax laws, the book will serve to alert parents to the various aspects of future care that they should be concerned about for their children (Russell 1983).

Another informative book, *A New Look at Guardianship*, edited by Tony Apolloni and Thomas P. Cooke, is based on the premise that certain people with developmental disabilities will always need protective care, and it was written to acquaint parents and professionals with emerging options for improving the security and continuity of services for dependent persons. It deals with both public and private guardianship programs and legal considerations affecting them.

Protection and advocacy organizations and parent groups can refer parents to lawyers who specialize in planning for the financial security of their children.

V. The Right to Health Care

The primary sources of federal medical assistance for persons with disabilities are Medicare and Medicaid, Crippled Children's Services, and the Early Periodic Screening, Diagnosis, and Treatment Program (EPSDT). Medicare and Medicaid are two different programs administered in different ways: Medicare is run by the Bureau of Health Insurance of the Social Security Administration, Department of Health and Human Services, and is made up of two parts: (1) hospital insurance and related health services after the patient leaves the hospital, such as nursing care or other home health visits, at no cost; (2) medical insurance to help pay doctor bills and other approved medical services, for which there is a small monthly charge. This part is voluntary.

Eligible for Medicare are people 65 years or older, people with disabilities who have had Social Security or Railroad Retirement disability annuities for two years or more, and people who are insured by Social Security or Railroad Retirement and are in need of dialysis treatment or kidney transplant because of permanent kidney failure. Wives, husbands, and children of insured people may also be eligible if they need maintenance dialysis or a transplant (Bruck 1978). Insurance benefits cover a wide range of services, including outpatient clinic or emergency room, home health visits under specified conditions, outpatient physical therapy and speech pathology services, X-rays, casts, braces, artificial limbs or eyes, wheelchairs or medical equipment, ambulance services, and anything else prescribed by a physician. Medicare can be applied for at local Social Security offices. Further information may be obtained from the Health Care Financing Administration, Inquiries Staff, Room GF-3, East Lowrise Bldg., Baltimore, MD 21207.

Medicaid is a joint federal and state medical assistance program. It is financed by the federal government on a sliding scale, from 50 percent in the wealthiest states to 78 percent in the states with the lowest per capita income. Forty-nine states participate in the program as well as the District of Columbia, Guam, Puerto Rico, and the Virgin Islands. (Arizona does not have a Medicaid program, because, I am told, there are few people on welfare and very little demand. They do have an alternate state program.) The program is run by state governments with federal guidelines.

Medicaid provides physical and related health care services to persons with low incomes. The payments do not go directly to the individual, but to the service provider. Since Medicaid is administered by the states, eligibility is determined by state social services programs on the basis of broad federal guidelines. Persons eligible for Medicaid are those on welfare, those receiving SSI benefits, the medically needy, the blind, and the disabled. Individuals with higher incomes or their children may be eligible if medical expenses exceed a given percentage of annual income (*Pocket Guide* 1987).

Medicaid services include necessary medical, dental, and other medically related care, nursing services in all institutions, outpatient or clinic services, home health care services, drugs, sickroom supplies, eyeglasses, and prostheses. When applying, the individual should have such information as name, address, age, Social Security number, annual income and income of persons in the family, amount of savings, cash value of insurance, and market value of any stocks, bonds, or other investments. Information on Medicaid and how to apply is available from local or state departments of social services or the Health Care Financing Administration, Inquiries Staff, Room GF-3, East Lowrise Bldg., Baltimore, MD 21207 (*Pocket Guide* 1987).

A recent law (PL 100-360) prohibits the Health Care Financing Administration (HCFA) from denying schools Medicaid reimbursement just because a service is part of a handicapped child's Individualized Education Program (IEP) (*Education of the Handicapped* 1988). At the present writing, some state and local officials are being cautious because officials are not sure what services HCFA will cover and because state rules may need to be changed before districts can be reimbursed for services such as speech, and physical and occupational therapy. The Health and Human Services Department, of which HCFA is an arm, states that claims should be filed. This seems, therefore, to be one of those policies that must evolve and of which school districts should be aware.

A full explanation of both financial and health benefits may be found in *Summary of Existing Legislation Affecting Persons with Disabilities* (August 1988).

VI. The Right to Insurance

Workmen's Compensation

This insurance provides payments in lieu of salary to those who become disabled as a result of injury or disease related to employment as well as payments for necessary medical services. Types of benefits and amounts paid vary from state to state. The second injury clause limits the liability of the employer who hires a disabled worker. Contrary to the belief of many prospective employers, workmen's compensation insurance rates are not higher for an employee who is disabled than for a non-disabled person. If a worker who is disabled has an accident on the job, under the second injury clause the employer is only liable for the percentage of disability that results from the second injury, not for any part of the disability that existed before the injury.

Salary Continuance

This form of insurance can be purchased by an individual or by a company for its employees. Such a policy provides the worker with an income while wages are discontinued due to an accident or illness that occurs during the policy period. Amounts of payments vary with the type of policy.

Tax Benefits

In the computation of income tax, the Internal Revenue Service allows many medical and dental expenses to be deducted from income, provided deductions are itemized on Schedule A. Because of recent changes in tax laws, only the amount of the totel medical expenses that exceeds 7.5 percent of the adjusted gross income may be deducted (in this case, of the individual with disabilities or his/her parents). Deductible items include special equipment such as a motorized wheelchair, a specially equipped automobile, a TDD for deaf persons, the cost and repair of special telephone equipment, artificial teeth or limbs, eyeglasses, hearing aids, crutches, and dogs for the blind, deaf, or physically disabled. Also included are payments for installation of special equipment in the home such as ramps or elevators, and capital expenditures for the removal of structural barriers in private residences necessary to accommodate the disability. Also deductible are payments to a special school for an individual with a mental or physical disability if the reason for attending is the ability of the institution to alleviate the handicap.

Under the new tax law, there will no longer be an additional personal exemption for the blind; however, a blind individual will be entitled to a higher standard deduction amount in 1987 and later years. In addition, the IRS allows tax credits for the cost of the care of a dependent or spouse who is disabled if this enables the taxpayer to be involved in gainful employment. Payment to relatives who provide this care can be included if the relative is not your dependent or your child under age 19 (*Pocket Guide* 1987).

IRS offers the following free publications that give more information on deductions, credits, and provisions of the new tax law: "Pub. 502: Medical and Dental Expenses"; "Pub. 503: Child and Dependent Care Credit, and Employment Taxes for Household Employees"; "Pub. 920: Explanation of the Tax Reform Act of 1986 for Individuals." To order copies, call the "Federal Tax Information and Forms" number listed under "IRS" in your telephone directory.

Veterans' Benefits

Veterans should apply to regional veterans administration offices to ascertain benefits available to them. For all veterans disabled by injury, accident, or disease, or permanently and totally disabled for reasons not traceable to service, there are many benefits, including partial payment on automobiles and automobile adaptations, mechanical aids and guide dogs for the blind, monthly disability payments, clothing and prosthetic and orthotic appliance payments, educational assistance, money for home remodeling, hospitalization, life insurance, and attendant care. Find address in the telephone directory under Veterans Affairs, Division of.

VII. The Right to Certain Social Services

Crippled Children's Services is a joint federal/state program to provide medical and related services to handicapped children from birth to age 21. All states must provide medical diagnosis and evaluation free for all children without the requirement of a state residency period. The range and cost of additional treatment or hospital care services vary from state to state. All programs accept third-party payments such as Medicaid, Blue Cross and Blue Shield, and other medical insurance. For further information on what is available contact local, county or state health department (*Pocket Guide* 1987).

The Early Periodic Screening, Diagnosis, and Treatment Program (EPSDT) screens children from poor families to find out if health care or related services may be necessary. Children receiving state Aid to Families of Dependent Children and children whose parents or guardians receive Medicaid and/or local or state public assistance benefits are eligible. Programs vary from state to state and are administered by state public assistance (welfare) or health departments (*Pocket Guide* 1987).

VIII. The Right to Work

Many people with disabilities would like to be able to work as productive members of society if at all possible. Through the vocational rehabilitation network and the Rehabilitation Act of 1973, plus subsequent laws, these disabled people have been assured counseling, testing, training, and placement in appropriate fields of work. Chapters 6 and 7 have outlined the structure of the rehabilitation field.

For blind and visually impaired individuals, the Commission for the Visually Handicapped provides training and placing for work, as well as services such as eye examinations, general examinations, training in mobility and homemaking, and information about recording devices, college and training fees, specific small business equipment, transportation costs, and small business enterprise aid programs. The commission can also supply up-to-date information on the current regulations concerning the Randolph Sheppard Amendments (PL 94-516) which deal with licensing blind vending facility and cafeteria operators and the Wagner O'Day Act (PL 92-28, PL 93-358) concerning sheltered workshop regulations.

A **Rehabilitation Research and Training Center on Blindness and Low Vision** is located at PO Drawer 6189, Mississippi State University, Mississippi State, MS 39762. Its focus is to identify, assess, and augment services intended to facilitate the employment and career development of blind and severely visually impaired persons. It is funded by the National Institute on Disability and Rehabilitation Research, the Rehabilitation Services Administration, state rehabilitation agencies serving blind persons, and the Helen Keller National Center for Deaf-Blind Youth and Adults. The center offers a university-based curriculum for the Vocational Specialist for the Visually Impaired, Counselor Education program; investigates the impact of sensory aids on the employability and career development of blind and severely visually impaired persons as well as deaf-blind individuals; develops materials for use in vocational evaluation centers; develops national training conferences on placement and career development; and offers in-service training for six state vocational rehabilitation agencies serving blind persons.

Rehabilitation for hearing-impaired persons is conducted through the State Offices of Vocational Rehabilitation. In addition, a liaison staff person in deafness rehabilitation is available in each of the 10 Rehabilitation Services Administration regional offices. For information contact the Deafness and Communicative Disorders Branch, Switzer Bldg., M/S 2312, Washington, DC 20202 (*Pocket Guide* 1987).

Organized labor supports the right of disabled people to work through the AFL-CIO Human Resources Development Institute's (HRDI) handicapped placement program. Through local projects in Baltimore, MD; Houston, TX; St. Louis, MO; and St. Paul, MN, the HRDI program provides counseling, job development, placement, and follow-up services, supported by grants from the US Department of Education Rehabilitation Services Administration's Projects with Industry program and by matching funds from the national labor federation (Smedley 1985). (See also Projects with Industry, Industry-Labor Council, and Job Accommodation Network in Chapter 7.)

Small-Business Loans

The Small Business Administration (SBA) makes business loans on reasonable terms to any disabled individual who wishes to establish, acquire, or operate a small business. SBA also assists certain businesses that employ disabled individuals. For further information contact the Small Business Administration, Director, Office of Business Loans, 1441 L Street NW, Washington, DC 20416.

Additional Sources of Information

Many states have a Governor's Committee on Employment of the Disabled which works with employers to open up job opportunities. The Job Training Partnership Program was created to prepare youth and unskilled adults for entry into the labor force and to afford job training to those economically disadvantaged individuals and other individuals facing serious barriers to employment, who are in special need of training to obtain productive employment (*Pocket Guide* 1987). State Employment Services or Offices of Vocational Rehabilitation will be able to provide information about this program. For obtaining a federal job, contact your local federal employment center. State employment offices are also required to help people with disabilities find jobs, and these offices are listed in the local telephone directory.

A magazine called *Careers and the Handicapped* is published twice a year by Equal Opportunity Publications, Inc., 44 Broadway, Greenlawn, NY 11740, and carries many informative articles. There is a special section in braille. A section called The Affirmative Action Career Directory lists companies that seek the talents of people with disabilities, scholarship offerings, etc.

IX. The Right to Education

In Chapter 8 we have outlined the developments that have taken place during the 1970s and 1980s in response to the laws passed that bear on the education of exceptional children. Today, no child with disabilities in the United States should be without the opportunity to receive an appropriate education.

Higher education is now being made available to a greater extent than ever before to those young adults eligible for college programs. These may be funded by vocational rehabilitation services if higher education is considered realistic. All college campuses receiving federal funds were required, by 1980, to be made accessible to persons with disabilities. Refer to Chapter 8 for information concerning services.

X. The Rights of Consumers with Disabilities

An important book in the area of consumerism was Lilly Bruck's *Access: The Guide to a Better Life for Disabled Americans*. This book is now out of print, but much of the information in it is still pertinent. Unique to her book was the thesis that the person with disabilities is a consumer of goods who spends money in the marketplace but is often restricted by environmental and transportation barriers. Often products needed to overcome the effects of disability are expensive and unreliable (Bruck 1978). Discussing catalog shopping by mail by the homebound, Bruck suggests that complaints about mail orders, including fraudulent advertising, be addressed to (1) Direct Mail Marketing Association, 6 East 43rd Street, New York, NY 10017, (2) local consumer affairs offices, and/or (3) Federal Trade Commission, Washington, DC 20580. The Consumer Information Center, Pueblo, CO 81009, has pamphlets about shopping by mail and mail fraud laws.

Bruck speaks about the importance of establishing a credit rating, which would apply to the able-bodied as well as to the disabled. She points out that persons receiving Social Security and SSI benefits may be eligible to participate in food stamp programs and may use food stamps, if disabled and elderly, to purchase meals from home delivery services. Local senior citizens' centers or food stamp offices can provide information about this. In certain instances, with a letter from a doctor, special diets may be listed as a medical expense.

Ideas mentioned by Bruck include electric and heating bills written in braille, a service instituted by Con Edison in New York City at the request of a blind user, and TTD communications for deaf subscribers to services; this last idea was mentioned by Bruck as a future possibility but is now being carried out in many parts of the country.

REFERENCES

Apolloni, Tony, and Cooke, Thomas P. 1984. *A New Look at Guardianship*. Baltimore and London: Paul H. Brookes Publishing Co.

Bruck, Lilly. 1978. *Access: The Guide to a Better Life for Disabled Americans*. New York: Random House.

Canny, Joseph. Director, Office of Transportation Regulatory Affairs, Washington, DC, letter, May 24, 1988.

"Congress Clears Housing Discrimination Bill." *Handicapped Requirements Handbook*. Supplement No. 118, September 1988, 2–3.

Education of the Handicapped, August 31, 1988, p. 5.

Everett, Carol T. 1984. "A Comparison of Five Exemplary Transportation Services for the Disabled." In Bell, William G. Third International Conference on Mobility and Transport of Elderly and Handicapped Persons, Conference Proceedings, Final Report, October 1984. Washington, DC: Technology Sharing Program, Office of the Secretary of Transportation, 6-96 to 6-101.

First Dibs. 1988, May/June. "Computers and Technology." 3–5.

Fix, Michael. 1984. "The Evolution of Transportation Programs for the Disabled in Three Pennsylvania Cities." In Bell, William G. Third International Conference on Mobility and Transport of Elderly and Handicapped Persons, Conference Proceedings, Final Report, October 1984. Washington, DC: Technology Sharing Program, Office of the Secretary of Transportation, 6-102 to 6-109.

Greer, Nora Richter. 1987. "The State of the Art of Design for Accessibility." *Architecture*, 58–61.

Handicapped Requirements Handbook, Federal Programs Advisory Service, Thompson Publishing Group, Washington, DC 20006, with monthly supplements.

Klauber, Julie, and Covino, Joseph. 1981, Fall. "The Partially Sighted: Low Vision and the Library." *The Bookmark* 40 (1): 40.

Lunt, Suzanne. *A Handbook for the Disabled: Ideas for Easier Living*. New York: Charles Scribner's Sons, 1984, 105.

Mettler, Richard, 1987, December. "Blindness and Managing the Environment." *Journal of Visual Impairment and Blindness*, 476–81.

Neustadt-Noy, Cory D. 1988, May. "A New Approach to Recreational Rehabilitation." *Journal of Visual Impairment and Blindness*, 195, 196.

New York State Advocate 11 (7), July 1988.

"News in Brief." *Handicapped Americans Report*. September 22, 1988, 177.

Pocket Guide for Federal Help for Individuals with Disabilities. 1987, September. U.S. Clearinghouse on the Handicapped, Department of Education, Publication E-87-22002, 4, 12–17, 24, 25.

Rehab Brief, 1988. Department of Education, Washington, DC 20202. "Design for the Life Span of all People? Spotlight on Adaptable Housing," Vol. 10, No. 12.

Rehab Brief, 1988. Department of Education, Washington, DC 20202, "Law Enforcement, Justice, and People with Disabilities," Vol. 10, No. 5.

Rocklin, Sarah G., and Mathson, David R. 1987, May. "The Employment Opportunities for Disabled Americans Act: Legislative History and Summary of Provisions," *Social Security Bulletin*, Vol 50, No. 3, U.S. Department of Health & Human Services, Social Security Administration, Washington, DC 20008.

Smedley, Lawrence T. 1984, July/August. "Labor's Role Job Placement of the Disabled." *Business and Health*, 43–45.

Summary of Existing Legislation Affecting Persons with Disabilities. 1988, August. Washington, DC: Clearinghouse on the Handicapped, Office of Special Education and Rehabilitative Services, U.S. Department of Education, Publication E-88-22014.

"Support Services and Alternatives to Guardianship." 1988, March/April. *Mental and Physical Disability Law Reporter* 12 (2): 202–27.

Thompson, Marie McGuire. 1976. Housing & Handicapped People. The President's Committee on Employment of the Handicapped, Washington, DC, 5.

Velleman, Ruth A. 1979. *Serving Physically Disabled People: An Information Handbook for All Libraries*. New York: Bowker, 60.

The Voice of the Physically Challenged. 1988, June. Rockville Center, NY: Long Island Family Publications.

Chapter 4
Information for Living

Human beings have certain basic needs, which, when fulfilled, enable them to function as active members of society. Good health, as well as appropriate clothing, housing, transportation, and recreation and a satisfactory adjustment as sexual human beings are taken for granted by most of us. But for the disabled segment of the population, fulfillment of these basic needs sometimes presents seemingly insurmountable problems. Today there are advocacy and government organizations that deal with all aspects of life for people with disabilities. A complete listing of these agencies and organizations may be found in the Directory of National Information Sources on Handicapping Conditions and Related Services, prepared by Harold Russell Associates for the Office of Special Education and Rehabilitative Services, US Department of Education, Washington, DC, 1986 plus supplement (or current edition).

LIVING WITH A DISABILITY

People with physical disabilities must make accommodations to live comfortably within their environment. This requires, first of all, proper prostheses (devices attached to the body, such as an artificial arm or leg) and orthotics (devices used by the disabled, such as a wheelchair, cane, or crutch). These items should be prescribed by a medical rehabilitation team at a rehabilitation hospital, or by a physician.

For the person who uses a wheelchair, the chair becomes an extension of his or her own body, somewhat as a prosthesis does for someone with an amputation. Wheelchairs vary in many respects—chair size, wheel size, reclining or straight-backed, with or without armrests, collapsible or not, electric and battery-powered as opposed to hand operated. The Training and Education Department of Everest Jennings Company (1803 Portius Avenue, Los Angeles, CA 90025), a major producer of wheelchairs, has issued several excellent booklets in its "Wheelchair Prescription" series, available free of charge. The titles and stock numbers are: "Measuring the Patient" Stock #1027; "Wheelchair Selection" Stock #1342; "Safety and Handling" Stock #1343; and "Care and Service" Stock #1344. *Accent on Living Magazine*, PO Box 700, Bloomington, IL 61702, publishes several books at affordable prices, including *Wheelchairs and Accessories, Ideas for Making Your Home Accessible, Single Handed: A Book for Persons with the Use of Only One Hand,* and *Easy Cooking* (97 recipes).

An extremely useful and informative book on activities for daily living is Suzanne Lunt's *Handbook for the Disabled: Ideas & Inventions for Easier Living* with up-to-date coverage of a whole range of information, including working around the house and the kitchen, suggestions for working with one hand or one leg, dressing, bathing and grooming aids, hints for parents of children with disabilities, speech and hearing aids, and equipment for persons with impaired vision. Lunt also covers travel and transportation information; reading, writing, and telephone aids; sports and recreation; walkers, standers, wheelchairs, wheelchair accessories, ramps, lifts, and elevators; financial aid information; and how to make your own furniture or other items. The appendix lists sources of equipment and information (Lunt 1984).

Many suppliers change addresses and new ones are added constantly. For this reason the database ABLEDATA was created and originally brought under the umbrella of NARIC. (See Chapter 6 for description of other services of NARIC.) ABLEDATA is the largest single source for information on consumer-related products, with over 15,000 commercially available products listed from over 1,800 manufacturers. Products are included from 15 categories of assistive technology, including personal care, communication, transportation and recreation. A custom search of the database helps to locate and compare similar products for the consumer or the professional working with a client.

In 1987 NARIC's ABLEDATA contract was not continued and ABLEDATA was awarded to its original creator, Marion Hall, in December 1988, at the Adaptive Equipment Center, Newington Children's Hospital, 181 East Cedar Street, Newington, CT 06111. For information or to request an ABLEDATA search call 1-800-344-5405. ABLEDATA is also available to search directly through BRS Information Technologies.

Since it is over one year since ABLEDATA has been updated, a major effort is underway to update existing information and add new products. A significant undertaking under the new contract will occur in cooperation with the TRACE Center at the University of Wisconsin–Madison. TRACE will be distributing copies of the entire database to those who wish to install ABLEDATA on personal computers. Initially the distributed version of ABLEDATA will be available for Macintosh computers only, but other Apple and IBM versions will be developed in the future (ABLEDATA Fact Sheet January, 1989).

The *National Resource Directory: An Information Guide for Persons with Spinal Cord Injury and Other Physical Disabilities*, by Barry Corbelt (ed.), is published by the National Spinal Cord Injury Association, 600 W. Cumming Park, Suite 2000, Woburn, MA 01801 (1985). The first section covers sources of medical and rehabilitation services, as well as instructions for personal care at home. Addresses of comprehensive care facilities for the spinal cord injured are listed by state, and a supplement updates this list as of 1986. A section on emotional adjustment explains the feelings that people have when they first become disabled, as well as the problems encountered by families, and details the kinds of professional psychological services available to help deal with them. There is a good bibliography of books, films and addresses of ongoing seminars on the topic of sexuality for the spinal cord injured. A section on independent living offers addresses of where to obtain information. The rest of the directory contains valuable and concrete information about such important aspects of living as financial assistance, legal rights, education, employment, transportation, sports and recreation, travel, and addresses of assistive oraganizations and other information sources.

During the decade of the 1980s a great deal of progress has been made in the area of universal design of products. This concept accepts the fact that products which are designed to be easily used by the elderly and physically disabled can be attractive and of benefit to everyone (Brown 1988). Companies such as the Whirlpool Corporation began to design appliances with this end in mind. Whirlpool introduced a model with large black lettering on a non-reflective white background, and enlarged dials and buttons. The response was so positive that these features were added to all models. In the spring of 1988, at the Museum of Modern Art in New York City, product designs for independent living were on display. Many of the 45 items were from Europe, and included lightweight wheelchairs, a nonslip cutting board with a knife guard, a button fastener, a portable electronic magnifying device and lightweight crutches of anodized aluminum. Sweden is notable for its pioneering designs, and the Lumex/Swedish Rehab Company represents five Swedish manufacturers whose designs were developed by the Swedish Institute for the Disabled, a nonprofit organization subsidized by the Swedish Government.

Although there are many commercially available aids and devices for people with disabilities they are usually obtained only through occupational therapists, doctors, medical supply houses or specialized mail-order catalogs. Many people with disabilities do not know that these devices exist. The following sources of information are free unless indicated:

Lumex/Swedish Rehab
100 Spence Street
Bayshore, NY 11706

'Comfortably Yours
61 West Hunter Avenue
Maywood, NJ 07607

Maneuverability
4015 Avenue U (Coleman St.)
Brooklyn, NY 11234 (Catalog $3.00)

Ways and Means
28001 Citrin Drive
Romulus, MI 48174 (*The Capability Collection Catalog* $3.50, refundable with order of $30)

Enrichments Inc.
145 Tower Drive
PO Box 32
Hinsdale, IL 60521

The American Association of Retired Persons publishes several books of interest, including *The Gadget Book* and *The Doable, Renewable House*. For a catalog write to: A.A.R.P. Fulfillment, PO Box 2240, Long Beach, CA 90801.

Other references are:

Chrysler Corporation
Physically Challenged Resource
  Center
PO Box 159
Detroit, MI 48288-0159
1-800-255-9877

Whirlpool Corporation
Appliance Information Service
2000 M-63 North
Benton Harbor, MI 49022

TELEPHONE SERVICES

The telephone is one of the most important devices for aiding people with disabilities to lead self-supporting lives. The development and distribution of specialized telecommunications equipment during recent decades was of inestimable value, and until January 1, 1984, the distribution of such equipment was regulated by state public services commissions. After the divestiture by AT&T of the Bell Operating Companies, rulings have, for the most part, eliminated this regulation and have opened the telecommunications industry to competition. The effect of this process on individuals with disabilities was discussed in *Rehab Brief* (Vol. X, No. 3, 1987). Suddenly there are now many companies that may supply special equipment and services and there is a trend to deregulate specialized customer premises equipment (SCPE) for people with disabilities and to sell it competitively.

In order to try to help consumers who are disabled to obtain information and services, the AT&T National Special Needs Center (NSNC) was established. The center attempts to standardize products and procedures and offers uniform prices and trained personnel who can respond to the needs of this group. Inevitably, equipment costs are now considerably higher, causing hardship for those consumers with limited resources. Some items available for lease prior to January 1, 1984, now can only be purchased. A catalog of available equipment is available from the American Telephone & Telegraph Company, National Special Needs Center, 2001 Route 46, Suite 310, Parsippany, NJ 07054-1315. The equipment catalog includes handsets for hearing and speech amplification, portable telephone amplifiers, signaling devices, a new line of TDD's, closed caption decoders, and speaker phones adapted for persons with all types of motor impairments. Toll-free telephone numbers are (800) 233-1222 for all persons including speech impaired. TDD users call (800) 833-3232.

CLOTHING

Many people with disabilities are faced with looking for information sources on inexpensive and attractive clothing adapted to their physical needs. People who are disabled generally need garments that are easily put on and removed, soil and crease resistant, with concealed zippers where necessary to suit orthopedic needs, and with elasticized waistbands. Underarm reinforcements are necessary for crutch users, and extra knee width in pants accommodates the wheelchair user. Women in wheelchairs need to avoid narrow skirts and look best in full, longer skirts or pants. Well-placed pockets are helpful for carrying small necessities (May, Waggoner, and Boettke 1974). If a person has a problem of incontinence and uses a collecting device under clothing, the right kind of clothes will make it possible for him or her to be in public without embarrassment.

The mail-order houses Fashion-Able, Rocky Hill, NJ 08553, and Wings of VGRS (Vocational Guidance and Rehabilitation Services), 2239 East 55th Street, Cleveland, OH 44103, supply much of the clothing that will meet these needs and it would be worthwhile to send for their catalogs. Additional information may be obtained from the following:

For a catalog of very feminine fashions write to:

Irwin Taylor: Designs for the
Physically Challenged
80 Superior Road
Rochester, NY 14625

For their catalog, *Facile Fashions*, write to:

Exceptionally Yours: Designer
Casualwear for Special Needs
Children & Adults
22 Prescott Street
Newtonville, MA 02160

Also for clothes for children write to:

Special Clothes for Special Children
PO Box 4220
Alexandria, VA 22303

To locate just one shoe instead of a pair, or for unusual sizes, write to:

Handicappers of America
R.R. 2 Box 58, Camby, IN

The National Odd-Shoe Exchange
1415 Ocean Front
Santa Monica, CA 90401 (Lunt
1984).

INDEPENDENT LIVING

The independent living movement was developed during the 1970s, primarily by young adults with disabilities wishing to live independent lives and avoid institutional living or living as shut-ins. This new kind of living arrangement required architectural adaptations plus some support services and, when necessary, the availability of full-time attendant services. Support services had to comprise household chore help, counseling, equipment repair, legal and medical services, adapted transportation, and vocational and educational services. For those who were severely disabled and could not be gainfully employed, appropriate government subsidies were needed to make all of these services economically feasible. And to protect them from exploitation and control by individuals who did not depend on them, these programs had to include those who were severely disabled in their planning and management (Pfleuger 1977).

The concept of housing for people with disabilities changed, therefore, from large institutional-type projects to a range of housing alternatives and a selection of support services based on individual needs. Many concepts have been developed, including group homes and cooperative residences, such as the Cheshire Homes project in England, now replicated in New Jersey. These homes, dependent on the funds available to the individual members, are discussed in terms of numbers of "beds." Individuals are restricted as to the amount of time they can spend away from the residence. Many people with physical disabilities wish for more of a sense of independence, even when the severity of their disabilities requires a great deal of attendant service. Regrettably, in spite of all the progress that has been made, the direction taken by the independent living movement during the 1980s has fallen short of the objective of providing appropriate housing for the severely physically disabled who wish to live independently.

There are now over 330 Independent Living Centers around the United States which can be located through state Office of Vocational Rehabilitation (OVR), protection and advocacy offices, or under social services in the local telephone directory. However, these so-called Independent Living Centers seldom, if ever, provide any form of residential living. Services provided include information and referral on availability of accessible housing; transportation; employment opportunities; rosters of persons available to serve as personal care attendants; interpreters for hearing-impaired people; or readers for visually impaired people. Training courses are provided to help people with disabilities gain skills that would enable them to live more independently.

The earliest center was formed in 1972 in Berkeley, California. Run from its inception by disabled students and former students, the **Berkeley Center for Independent Living (CIL)** was set up to demonstrate that people who are physically disabled can live within the able-bodied community with appropriate support services. CIL now operates the World Institute on Disability, 1720 Oregon Street, Suite 4, Berkeley, CA 94703, which is continuing research begun in 1983 focusing on cost, need, and demand for personal assistance services (see World Institute on Disability).

The **Boston Center for Independent Living (BCIL)**, 50 New Edgerly Road, Boston, MA 02115, was established in 1976. It includes a transitional living program in which persons with physical disabilities can live in adapted apartments which are serviced by attendants according to need. During the duration of the program (9 or 10 months), they are taught how to manage their money, how to function in the community, and how to supervise an attendant. Unfortunately, many persons with severe disabilities are unable to graduate to living on their own at the end of the program and often return to their former living arrangements, usually with parents or in institutions.

One of the two Research and Training Centers on Independent Living in the United States is at BCR 3111 Haworth, University of Kansas, Lawrence, KS 66045. The emphasis of the center is on "developing and evaluating, packaging and disseminating practical procedures for use by ILCs and their disabled consumers to promote opportunities for independence" (National Association of Rehabilitation Research and Training Centers 1986). Other research projects include improvement of portrayal in the media, investigation of the feasibility of extending ILC services to mentally retarded persons, and training of future design professionals in creating accessible designs. The center publishes a newsletter, *Independent Living Forum*; sponsors an annual national conference on independent living issues; and has published several monographs.

The Research and Training Center on Independent Living, **Independent Living Research Utilization (ILRU)**, at the Institute for Rehabilitation and Research, 3233 Weslayan, Suite 100, Houston, TX 77027, develops materials and sponsors studies relating to general issues in independent living, with an additional emphasis on independent living in rural areas. It publishes a newsletter called *ILRU Insights*, and operates an electronic bulletin board to facilitate networking among individuals and organizations in the independent living field. Locations of the over 330 independent living centers in the US are updated continually in their database. Of 164 centers questioned, only 18 reported on the operation of residential centers. The center will send a packet of information on request detailing information on its many publications which include: a printed *Registry of Independent Living Programs*, 1989 edition, vol 11, with supplements. *The New Options Project* (similar to the one at BCIL); *Independent Living with Attendant Care* (Board, Mary Ann et al.); a color video tape called "Ball Bearings and Bent Spokes: A Consumer's Guide to Wheelchair Repair & Maintenance"; "Independent Living and Rural America," and "Independent Living and Policy Changes", both in the *Issues in Independent Living* technical report series. Also in this series, "Independent Living and Mental Retardation: The Role of Independent Living Programs," develops the concept of independent living for retarded persons.

The **National Council on Independent Living (NCIL)**, 310 South Peoria Street, Suite 210, Chicago, IL 60607, was founded in 1982 as an advocacy center for the independent living movement when a group of Independent

Living Center directors met to discuss national and regional issues. NCIL works on eliminating discrimination on a national level and coordinates the national advocacy efforts of the independent living movement. Through provision of technical assistance and public education it attempts to strengthen local centers, and it lobbies in Washington for legislation concerning people with disabilities. It is governed by persons with various types of disabilities, and has member representatives in the 10 regions of the country.

Much work has been done and money spent in this field; however, the major problems remain to be solved. These are affordable and adapted housing of all kinds, accessible transportation, and attendant services. The Office of Mental Retardation and Developmental Disability (OMRDD), which can be reached on state and local levels, has the federal funding needed to develop group homes for the retarded and others who are developmentally disabled. United Cerebral Palsy also has the funds to develop residential facilities. More than 1,500 group homes, supervised apartment programs, community-based residential facilities, and institutions, all located in the US and its possessions and territories, are listed in the *Directory of Residential Centers for Adults with Developmental Disabilities*, published by Oryx Press, 2214 North Central, Phoenix, AZ 85004-1483. The facilities are indexed by the characteristics of clients accepted and the types of programs offered.

Shortages still exist, and for the person who is severely physically disabled and who needs physical care but wishes to live as independently as possible, there are few facilities that provide the backup 24-hour service required. Indeed, the lack of adequate attendant services is among the most important problems facing the severely disabled in the United States today.

PERSONAL ASSISTANCE SERVICES

In this country at the present time, an estimated 3.8 million people need personal assistance services, but only approximately 850,000 people currently receive such services. Therefore, almost 3 million people in need are going unserved, either receiving inadequate attendant services or no (publicly funded) services at all (*Rehab Brief* 1988). The National Institute on Disability and Rehabilitation Research (NIDRR) has funded three separate but coordinated efforts to study personal assistance services.

The Human Services Research Institute (HSR) in Cambridge, MA, working with United Cerebral Palsy Associations, Inc. (UCPA), is exploring methods for providing personal assistance services to people with severe mobility impairments, sensory impairments, and/or cognitive impairments. The ILRU (Independent Living Research Utilization) program at TIRR (Texas Institute of Rehabilitation Research) in Houston, TX, focuses on developing and testing a program evaluation instrument. The World Institute on Disability (WID) at Berkeley, CA, is focusing on cost, need and demand, and includes a national survey of spinal cord injury. The directors of all three projects have coordinated activities to avoid duplication and build on each other's work. WID's *Attendant Services Network* newsletter and the *UCPA Bulletin* report activities on all three projects.

WID (The World Institute on Disability) deserves some mention. Located at 1720 Oregon Street, Suite 4, Berkeley, CA 94703, WID is a private, nonprofit corporation, focusing on major policy issues from the perspective of the disabled community. Located in the San Francisco Bay area of California, the site of the first Center for Independent Living (CID) at Berkeley, it was founded in 1983 by three of the pioneers of CID: Edward V. Roberts, Judy Heumann, and Joan Leon. The center provides information and training to help people with disabilities around the world to meet their needs in their own communities, always drawing on the fundamental tenets of the independent living philosophy (WID 1988).

"Attending to America, Personal Assistance for Independent Living" authored by Simi Litvak et al, was a detailed 50-state study of the use of attendant services by all disabled populations, published by WID in April 1987. The Appendix lists addresses by state of sources of attendant services. WID is also collaborating on a national representative survey of the use of personal assistance services by persons with spinal cord injuries conducted by Monroe Bekowitz of the Bureau of Economic Research, Rutgers University, NJ, and is continuing with its analysis of national databases to determine the incidence of functional limitations requiring personal assistance in the US and prevalence by age group.

WID has also received a grant from the National Institute on Disability and Rehabilitation Research to develop four policy bulletins on health insurance and disability issues from a consumer perspective (WID 1988). They will cover comparison of different approaches to health insurance in the US as well as characteristics of persons with disabilities or chronic illness, limitations of existing systems for financing and delivery of health care to persons with disabilities or chronic illness, and international comparisons of health care systems as they affect persons with disabilities or chronic illness. WID has also embarked on a three-year federally funded program to advance cooperation and information exchange between US and foreign disability researchers. A listing of their publications is available from WID, as well as their newsletter, *Attendant Services Network*, published quarterly.

At the present writing, no comprehensive system for providing personal attendant services exists in the United States. Some mention is made in policies established by Congress such as Medicaid and the Older Americans Act. Existing service programs are funded by sources including Medicaid, Social Services block grant (Title XX), Older Americans Act (Title III), state and locally funded programs, and veterans' aid and attendance allowance (*Rehab Brief* 1988).

Services are fragmented and differ from state to state. Most programs foster dependency in that users may not participate in decision making on which services they need and may not hire their own providers. The provision of attendant services has not been seen as a public responsibility in the United States, while in countries such as England and Sweden, attendant services are made available at no cost to those who need them. Advocates are now working toward the institution of a National Personal Assistance Service Program, to include 24-hour, 7-day-a-week service (not now available in most instances) (*Rehab Brief* 1988).

THE USE OF PETS

Pets are being used more and more in nursing homes and mental hospitals for their therapeutic effect. Practical help can be obtained for blind and deaf people by acquiring seeing eye and hearing dogs. Dogs are also now available for adults with physical disabilities, as well as for children, who perform a variety of services in the fetching and carrying areas. **Canine Companions for**

Independence, PO Box 446, Santa Rosa CA 95402, and **Handi-Dog Inc.,** 5332 East Rosewood Avenue, Tucson, AZ 85711, are nonprofit organizations that train dogs to perform these services. Work has also been done with Capuchin monkeys at the Tufts New England Medical Center in Boston, to teach them to turn pages, play records, turn lights on and off, take food from refrigerators, and the like; however, they are temperamental, can be destructive, and not everyone can learn to handle them (Lunt, 1984).

TRAVEL FOR PEOPLE WITH DISABILITIES

Drivers with Disabilities

The design of the collapsible wheelchair made it possible for people who are disabled to travel. It was some years later, however, before automobiles were adapted with special controls, enabling these people to drive themselves. Persons whose legs are paralyzed but who have sufficient hand control, or someone with only leg control, can be taught to operate an automobile using special equipment. The American Automobile Association (AAA) has published a booklet entitled "The Handicapped Driver's Mobility Guide" (1984 edition), with descriptions of transportation services available to the disabled through a variety of organizations. Among the services listed are driving schools in the United States that can work with drivers with disabilities and manufacturers of adaptive equipment, with names, addresses, and telephone numbers for each listing. Contact any AAA office for an up-to-date copy or write AAA Traffic Safety Department, National Headquarters, Falls Church, VA. The *Accent on Living Buyers Guide* lists commercial companies that supply special driving controls and companies that do custom van conversions. For persons who cannot shift from a wheelchair to a driver's seat in a car, or even travel as a passenger, a van, with wheelchair lift can be the answer to mobility (*Accent on Living Buyers Guide* 1988).

Travel Accommodations for People with Disabilities

There are many travel guides for persons with disabilities which list accessible accommodations, restaurants, churches, museums, and other public buildings in many cities in the United States and abroad and are available from chambers of commerce. In addition, there are many tour groups organized for travelers with disabilities and travel agencies that specialize in helping these travelers plan a trip.

An organization which can give information about these groups is the Society for the Advancement of Travel for the Handicapped (SATH), a nonprofit association made up of many persons and organizations associated in some way with travel for the disabled. Information is offered on publications and listings of tour operators who specialize in tours and travel arrangements for the disabled traveler throughout the United States and abroad. They may be reached at 26 Court Street, Brooklyn, NY 11242. The association issues a newsletter called *SATH News,* which is extremely informative and available to members. Membership in the organization is on a calendar-year basis. SATH has published a listing of tour operators for the disabled and updates this list periodically.

Also, the Moss Rehabilitation Hospital at 12th Street and Tabor Road, Philadelphia, PA 19141, has a reference library and specializes in providing information about travel (see also Chapter 11).

An excellent reference guide is *The Physically Disabled Traveler's Guide* by Rod W. Durgin and Norene Lindsay, which provides information about accessible transportation, including rental cars and vans with hand controls, airlines, buses, trains, and cruises. It lists those hotel and motel chains with accessible accommodations, and travel agencies which serve clients who are disabled in the US and Canada and abroad. It offers a directory of resorts, camps and hard-to-find wilderness camps with facilities for the disabled, and lists national and international access guides. Information is supplied for visually or hearing impaired as well as speech and mobility-impaired persons. Addresses and telephone numbers are supplied.

Another handy information resource is *Travel for the Disabled: A Handbook of Travel Resources and 500 Worldwide Access Guides*, by Helen Hecker, R.N. (Twin Peaks Press, PO Box 8097, Portland, OR 97207, 1984). This book lists addresses for travel clubs, travel agencies, hints about travel by automobile, bus, train, air, and ship; hotel and motel information; camps; travel books and magazines; and addresses for obtaining access guides in the United States and abroad.

Louise Weiss's *Access to the World: A Travel Guide for the Handicapped* (new edition) is an informative book that will help the traveler who is disabled to plan a trip. Weiss describes current airlines regulations (now under change) and tips for bus, train, and ship travel. Toll-free numbers are given to call for car rentals with hand controls from Avis, Hertz, and National. Recreational vehicles or vans that can be adapted to carry wheelchairs are described, and addresses of manufacturers supplied. Weiss supplies listings of access guides for many cities in the US and abroad and names of special tour agencies for those wishing to travel with a group, but SATH might have more up-to-date information. Finally there is advice about how to cope with health problems, tips on handling luggage, packing, special clothing, and other hints that will contribute greatly to the comfort of the traveler with disabilities.

The Spring 1988 issue of *Accent on Living* carries an article about accessible bed and breakfast inns in the United States and supplies names and addresses as well as accessibility features for 17 inns in California, New Mexico, Texas, Colorado, South Carolina, Utah, and Stonybrook, New York.

The Library of Congress National Library Service for the Blind and Physically Handicapped has issued a reference circular, No. 87-3, July 1987, listing books on travel (including braille and recorded titles), travel agencies, travel information centers, and transportation services.

Travel Aids for the Blind is one of the few organizations in the US to provide technologically advanced travel devices to blind people who could otherwise not afford them which enable travel with increased confidence. For information contact: Travel Aids for the Blind, 175 Strafford Avenue, Wayne, PA 19087 (*The Voice* 1988).

The July/August/September 1988 issue of the *Journal of Rehabilitation* published an article on accessible vacations (Weiss 1988), highlighting advice from Robert and Elizabeth Zywicki, who run *Whole Person Tours*, and publish the magazine entitled *The Itinerary Magazine: The Magazine for Travelers with Physical Disabilities*, PO Box 1084, Bayonne, NJ 07002-1084.

Some of the other organizations running tours for the disabled (by no means all inclusive) are:

Handi-cap Horizons, Inc.
3250 Loretta Drive
Indianapolis, IN 46227

Mobility Tours
26 Court Street
Brooklyn, NY 11242

Flying Wheels Travel
143 West Bridge Sreet
P.O. Box 382
Owatonna, MI 55060

Wings on Wheels Tours
Evergreen Travel Service
19505 L 44th Avenue West
Lynnwood, WA 98036

MIUSA (Mobility International
USA)
PO Box 3551
Eugene, OR 97403

Canwee Travel
553 Broadway
Massapequa, NY 11758

Also available is the newsletter *Diabetic Traveler* (PO Box 8223 RW, Stanford, CT 06905). Each copy features information on cruises, rail travel, destinations, and useful foreign tips for diabetics, including insulin adjustments for travel.

Air Travel

In October of 1986, the Air Carrier Access Act became law (PL 99-435), amending a section of the Federal Aviation Act specifically to prohibit air carriers from discriminating against people with disabilities (EPVA 1988). During 1987 and early 1988, regulatory negotiations took place involving affected disability groups and US airline industry association representatives. But final regulations are still pending, to be issued by the Department of Transportation some time before the end of 1989. Meanwhile, available from the Eastern Paralyzed Veterans Association, 75-20 Astoria Boulevard, Jackson Heights, NY 11370-1178 is a pamphlet entitled "Ten Questions and Answers About Air Travel for Wheelchair Users." It cautions, however, in the preface, that some of the information may change once the final regulations are issued, and suggests that persons wishing to travel by air contact EPVA or a local disability group to find out about this. Complaints about discrimination may be filed to: Director, Office for Civil Rights, US Department of Transportation, 400 Seventh Street SW, Washington, DC 20590.

SEXUALITY

The obvious fact that people with disabilities have sexual feelings like everyone else was ignored for a long time. Now it is understood that all people are sexual beings, and human sexuality can be expressed in many ways. Body image—how we perceive ourselves—is important to all people, and no less so to people with disabilities. Males, whether congenitally disabled, or paraplegic or quadriplegic because of injury or illness, face difficulties because it is believed, often mistakenly, that they are impotent. Women may feel that their bodies do not conform to the stereotyped female standards for beauty. Research in the very important area of sex and the disabled was carried out during the 1970s, and a good deal of information is now available.

Sexual Adjustment: A Guide for the Spinal Cord Injured by Martha Ferguson Gregory is available from Accent on Living Publications (PO Box 700, Bloomington, IL 61710). It was written by a rehabilitation counselor whose husband is a quadriplegic as a result of an automobile accident. Gregory's book offers an overview of paraplegia and quadriplegia that is very informative and explains that, contrary to popular belief, most types of spinal cord injuries do not preclude some form of sexual activity. It is important for the psychological well-being of the paraplegic male that he not consider himself to be sexually impotent and that he find some accommodation in this area. Gregory also details typical psychological stages that most persons who have accidents and become paraplegic or quadriplegic pass through on their way to emotional recovery (see Chapter 1).

Two excellent pamphlets were developed by Planned Parenthood of Snohomish County, Inc.: "Toward Intimacy," and a companion pamphlet "Within Reach," which is a guide for health care personnel who would like a greater understanding of their clients with disabilities, can be obtained from Human Sciences Press, Order Department, 72 Fifth Avenue, New York, NY 10011. "Toward Intimacy" was written for women who are disabled and the professionals who counsel them. It is based on interviews with women who shared their experiences, women with a wide range of disabilities, both congenital and acquired, including cerebral palsy, rheumatoid arthritis, spinal cord injury, burns, and strokes. "Toward Intimacy" includes such topics as body image, how people feel about their bodies, alternate sexual methods, and ways of expressing affection. It also includes information on family planning and a chart which indicates some sexual problems for each of several physical disabilities; however, the range of degree of disability and physical capability is so varied that this attempt is not as successful as the rest of the booklet. Also available from the Human Sciences Press is the quarterly journal *Sexuality and Disability*.

A book that seeks to dispel some of the myths generally surrounding the sexual ability of people with disabilities is *Sexual Options for Paraplegics and Quadriplegics* by T. O. Mooney et al. (Boston, Little Brown 1979). It contains very explicit photographs and high school librarians may be wary of placing it on open shelves. It should certainly be made available to counselors working with adolescents who are disabled and to librarians in institutions and public libraries who wish to provide such materials for patrons.

Mooney makes the point that when impotence is present there are alternate ways of giving and receiving sexual pleasure and offers specific methods that have been used by disabled people and their partners and found to be satisfying.

The Coalition on Sexuality and Disability, Inc., 380 Second Avenue, 4th Floor, New York, NY 10010, was founded in 1978 for the purpose of advancing the full social integration of people with disabilities. A coalition of persons is maintained to improve the quality and delivery of sexual health services by promoting the professional training and ethical practice of health and human service workers who provide sexuality education, counseling, and therapy to persons with disabilities. The coalition also develops resources, promotes research in the field of sexuality and disability, and works with social, rehabilitation, and health care agencies to enrich their programs and services so that they are more responsive to the sexual needs and rights of persons with disabilities. Workshops and forums are conducted and a newsletter is published which focuses on current issues and developments in the area of sexuality and disability, including a listing of publications, conferences, and other events that may be of interest to the membership. Individual and organization memberships are available.

Finally, an excellent source of information on sexuality and disability is SIECUS, the Sex Information and Education Council of the US at New York University, 32 Washington Place, New York, NY 10003. Materials listed in their bibliography are available from the publishers indicated. Among them is *Who Cares? A Handbook on Sex Education and Counseling Services for Disabled People*, second edition. It was developed by the Sex and Disability Project at George Washington University and was originally a series of manuals involving sex education and counseling services in the areas of mental retardation, blindness, deafness, and spinal cord injury. The manuals' target audiences were disabled consumer groups, rehabilitation counselors, state vocational rehabilitation policymakers, and community resource agencies (e.g., Planned Parenthood). The second edition of this outstanding resource is available from Pro-Ed, 5351 Industrial Oaks Boulevard, Austin, TX 78734 (1982).

Sex Education Materials for Young People Who Are Learning Disabled and Developmentally Disabled

The need for sexual education for high school students who are learning disabled was described in a 1986 article in the *Journal of Learning Disabilities* (Haight and Fachting 1986). The authors determined that very little material existed on simple enough reading levels and developed their own unit, "Sexuality, Love and Maturity," to present students with the major philosophical aspects of human sexuality. However, a good deal of material has been developed for the purpose of presenting sex education to children and young adults who are developmentally disabled and these materials might also be used with learning-disabled students where the concepts presented are adult enough. The Resource Center of Planned Parenthood Southeastern Pennsylvania, 1144 Locust Street, Philadelphia, PA 19107, has available the following publications:

Love, Sex and Birth Control for Mentally Handicapped People: A Guide for Parents, rev. ed. by Winifred Kempton, Medora S. Bass and Sol Gordon, a Planned Parenthood S.E. PA Publication.

Sex Education for Persons with Disabilities That Hinder Learning—A Teacher's Guide by Winifred Kempton and Frank Caparulo, Amity Road Press, covers physical, sensory and developmental disabilities and current teaching concepts.

Also available are:

The Need to Know: Sexuality and the Disabled Child, by Phil Way, including perspectives on the special needs of people with physical, sensory or developmental disabilities, is available directly from Planned Parenthood Association of Humboldt County, 2316 Harrison Avenue, Eureka, CA 95501.

An Easy Guide for Caring Parents: A Book for Parents of People with Mental Handicaps; Sexuality and Socialization, 3rd printing, 1986 (c. 1981), is published by Network Publications, ETR Associates, PO Box 1830, Santa Cruz, CA 95061.

Ednick Communications, PO Box 3612, Portland, OR 97208, lists in their current catalog videos and publications to aid in working with persons with developmental disabilities and other special needs, including learning disabilities. In addition to training manuals for vocational and social learning, decision making, community living and functional language (this latter a video tape presenting a communication enhancement program for adults with mental retardation, living in a group home), Ednick has available a number of publications in the "Being Me" program. They include videos by Dr. Jean Edwards on social/sexual training, sex education slides, a teacher's guidebook by Jean Edwards and Suzan Wapnick, and assessment scale and photo cards appropriate for verbal and nonverbal students.

Planned Parenthood Association of Cincinnati has developed "The Sexual Abuse Prevention Videotape for Children Who Are Physically Handicapped." To find out about this tape contact Planned Parenthood Association of Cincinnati: Education/Training & Video Production Department, 2314 Auburn Avenue, Cincinnati, OH 45219.

Also developed by Planned Parenthood Association of Cincinnati is "Sexual Abuse Prevention: Five Safety Rules for Persons Who Are Mentally Handicapped." This tape is being rented or marketed by the Agency for Instructional Technology, Box A, Bloomington, IN 47402-0120 (800-457-4509).

Sex Information for Visually and Hearing-Impaired People

The materials published by Ednick include a guide by Jean Edwards et al, *Feeling Free: A Social/Sexual Training Guide,* for those who work with the hearing and visually impaired. Other publications include:

"For Boys: A Book about Girls," a braille booklet explaining menstruation includes braille diagrams of the female reproductive system; and "Growing up and Liking It," "a booklet explaining menstruation to girls, available in braille both from Personal Products, Co. (Milltown, NJ 08850, 1985).

Also, for deaf/blind students are teaching units developed by Ellen Cadigan and Roslye Roberts Geuss, "Sex Education for Deaf-Blind Students" (Perkins School for the Blind, Office of Public Relations and Publications, 175 North Beacon Street, Watertown, MA 02172, 1981).

Signs for Sexuality: A Resource Manual by Susan D. Doughten, Marlyn B. Minkin, and Laurie E. Rosen contains over 600 photographs illustrating 300 signed words and phrases associated with human sexuality. (Published by Planned Parenthood of Seattle/King County, 2211 East Madison, Seattle, WA 98122, 1978).

Growing up Sexually by Angela M. Bednarczyk consists of a booklet for parents, one for teachers and one for students (published by Kendall Demonstration Elementary School, Gallaudet University, Kendall Green, Washington, DC 20002, 1982).

Viewpoints: Sex Education and Deafness by Della Fitz-Gerald and Max Fitz-Gerald (eds), is a compilation of 10 articles on the need for and methods of sexuality education for hearing-impaired children and adolescents (Gallaudet University Bookstore, Outreach Products, PO Box 10-D, Kendall Green, Washington, DC 12002, 1985).

Many publications dealing with sexuality and disabilities such as spina bifida, spinal cord injury, multiple sclerosis, ostomy, kidney disease and cancer, are listed on the SIECUS bibliography.

RECREATION

Sports

Wheelchair sports actually began toward the end of World War II. Before then, there had not been a very significant paraplegic population because people with spinal cord injuries seldom survived. In the 1940s Harry C. Jennings, an engineer, had a friend, Herbert A. Everest, also an engineer, who was paralyzed with a broken back and rendered virtually immobile in a wooden, noncollapsible wheelchair. Jennings designed the first lightweight collapsible metal chair, and together the two men founded the Everest Jennings Company, the largest producer of wheelchairs in the United States (Savitz 1978). The first wheelchair games were held at the Spinal Injuries Centre at Stoke-Mandeville Hospital in Aylesbury, England.

Since that time, wheelchair design has evolved in response to consumer demand for an ultralight sport wheelchair. The Quickie, a wheelchair produced by Motion Designs Inc., of Fresno, California, came about as the result of a hang-gliding accident 10 years ago in which Marilyn Hamilton, co-founder of the company, was injured (Brown 1988). Lightweight wheelchairs are now produced by 21 companies, according to a recent survey by *Sports 'N Spokes* magazine (1988).

Wheelchair games are now held in all areas of the United States, governed by the National Wheelchair Athletic Association. From the national competition the United States team is chosen to compete internationally in the Paralympics, which are held annually in England, with the exception of every fourth year when they are held in the country that hosts the Olympics.

The Directory of National Information Sources on Handicapping Conditions and Related Services now lists 30 national sports organizations organized by and for people with disabilities. These include wheelchair basketball, bowling, golf, tennis, scuba diving and motorcycle associations; associations for blind skiing, and bowling; associations for deaf bowling, and sports; organizations serving all disabilities in archery; as well as the Special Olympics. Horseback riding for people with disabilities was a new concept that developed in America during the 1970s, although the sport had been popular in Europe and Great Britain for some time. **The North American Riding for the Handicapped Association, Inc. (NARHA),** PO Box 100, Ashburn, VA 22011, was founded in 1969 and now has many centers in the United States and Canada. NARHA has films, guidebooks, and training available for groups considering establishing riding programs for persons with disabilities. It sets standards for ensuring the safety of the riders. A newsletter called the **Winslow News** is published by the Winslow Riding for the Handicapped Foundation (RD 1 Box 245, Warwick NY 10990). There is also a Wheelchair Pilots Association which can advise on special controls for flying (2252 Barbara Drive, Clearwater, FL 33546).

Paralyzed Veterans of America (PVA) has published the brochure "Wheelchair Sports: Competitive and Recreational," which lists and describes competitive wheelchair sports as well as recreational activities, lists names and addresses of sports organizations, PVA chapters nationwide, addresses for manufacturers of adaptive equipment and apparel, and a resource guide that lists books, journals and video tapes. *Sports 'N Spokes* is the sports magazine published by PVA.

Outdoor Recreation

In 1974 the President's Committee on Employment of People with Disabilities and the National Recreation and Park Association cosponsored a national forum on meeting the recreational and park needs of people with disabilities. In October 1976 the Architectural and Transportation Barriers Compliance Board (ATBCB) held a national hearing in Boston, Massachusetts, at which the same needs were reiterated. Major problems facing the disabled in the area of recreation were listed as (1) inaccessibility of facilities and transportation; (2) public attitude; (3) failure of recreation professionals to be ambitious in creating programs; and (4) failure of politicians to commit themselves fully and to follow through (Fay et al. 1976). During the 1977 White House Conference, the topic of leisure fulfillment for the disabled was given a great deal of attention. Some gains have now been made in accessibility of parks, beaches, cabins, camps, trails for the blind and physically disabled, and the use of interpreters for the deaf on guided tours.

In 1978 the National Park Service, Department of the Interior, Washington, DC, published a guide, for a nominal price, called *Access National Parks: A Guide for Handicapped Visitors.* It described in detail the accessibility of parks or monuments with information about overnight accommodations, restroom adaptations, special outdoor trails, availability of medical services, and telephone numbers. This guide has not been republished. Instead the park service only has available a map entitled the "National Park System Map & Guide." On the back are indications of accessible parks and facilities (National Park Service, Public Inquiries Office, PO Box 37127, Washington, DC 20013).

The complete information contained in the original guide, plus additional features such as grading and surfacing of roads and pathways, availability of telecommunication devices, proximity of hospitals and medical support services, and special park programs, are now available for a much higher price from the Northern Cartographic Publishers (PO Box 133, Burlington, VT 05402). Unfortunately, this new guide, a 464-page book, ring-bound and in large type, will cost $89.95 plus $5.00 for shipping. Nonprofit organizations and people ordering the book for personal use get a 25 percent discount, making the price $67.45; the AARP states that this discount price is now $72.45 (*Modern Maturity* August/September 1988). Individual guides are being prepared, and the first one, *Access Yosemite,* is already available for $7.95 from the Northern Cartographic Publishers. Most of the park areas at high elevations have oxygen and first-aid equipment available. Some have clinics staffed by doctors and nurses. Many have wheelchairs, some electric. Improved exhibits now include contour maps, and many parks have sensory trails and interpreters for deaf visitors. The Publications and Information Service of the American Foundation for the Blind, 15 West 16th Street, New York, NY 10011, has available *Creative Recreation for Blind and Visually Impaired Adults,* which describes a wide variety of sports, hobbies, and other activities open to the visually impaired and their families, for a nominal fee (*Modern Maturity* August/ September 1988).

The March 1988 issue of *Exceptional Parent Magazine* (pp. 42–46) offers a listing of recreational organizations that include sports organizations in the US and Canada, as well as associations for art therapy, music therapy, and dance therapy, camping, handicapped scuba association, and many more.

Wilderness Inquiry II (Suite 327, Fifth Street SE, Minneapolis, MN 55414) is a nonprofit organization that provides wilderness adventures that integrate people with varying levels of disability with able-bodied people. Trips run from May to December, ranging from 3-day canoe trips to a 30-day adventure in the Yukon Territories (*The Voice* 1988).

The American Camping Association (43 West 23rd Street, New York, NY) publishes a yearly "Parents Guide to Accredited Camps," which has a section on residential and day camps for exceptional children that have been examined and approved by the association. The Easter Seal Society, United Cerebral Palsy, and other organizations run day camps for children with disabilities in many areas, and Easter Seal runs a sleep-away camp in New York State. The first camp for blind children, Camp Wapanacki, in northeastern Vermont, began 50 years ago and remains one of only a handful nationwide.

Resources for Children with Special Needs (200 Park Ave. South, Suite 816, New York, NY 10003) publishes a special camping guide entitled *Camps and Summer Programs for Children with Special Needs*, 5th edition, 1989.

The *International Directory of Recreation-Oriented Assistive Device Sources* is a compilation of devices specifically designed for the person with a disability. The directory lists devices to help with anything from scuba diving to writing for the person with just about any disability. Each entry lists the recreation, disability, problem and solution and it is cross-indexed by recreation, disability, and function. The appendix of the book gives the address of each company listed. For information call 1-800-872-8787 or write Lifeboat Press, PO Box 11782, Marina Del Rey, CA 90295 (*The Voice* 1988).

THE ARTS

Many people with disabilities do not visit museums because of inaccessibility. Museums wishing to make their facilities accessible should refer to the ANSI Standards. Also available is *Disabled Museum Visitors: Part of Your General Public*, a book and video set produced by the Office of Museum Programs of the Smithsonian Institution, Washington, DC 20560. It offers techniques for making tours accessible to visitors with disabilities. Emphasis is on general tours with both disabled and nondisabled participants. Order from: Audiovisual Program, Office of Museum Programs, Smithsonian Institution, Arts and Industries Building, Room 2235, Washington, DC 20560.

In New York City, the Lincoln Center for the Performing Arts, Inc., comprises four halls for philharmonic and chamber music concerts, ballet, and opera, two theatres, and the arts section of the New York Public Library. The Office of Programs and Services for Disabled People, a part of the community relations department, is a full-time office for outreach to persons with disabilities, located at 140 West 65th Street, New York, NY 10023. The coordinator, Ms. Bette Knapp, is disabled and uses a wheelchair (Witter 1988). The center is accessible and includes removable auditorium seats for wheelchair users; accessible telephones; modified restroom facilities; curb ramps at all major access routes; Sennheiser infrared listening devices; and special parking arrangements. Plans for additional accessibility at Lincoln Center include braille signage in elevators; an elevator to connect the Plaza and Concourse levels, accessible directly on the plaza; automated doors for Avery Fisher Hall; and increased wheelchair seating capacity. The Allegro Cafe in Avery Fisher Hall and the Fountain Cafe on the Plaza during the summer have braille menus. Now available are braille, large-type and audio-cassette house programs for all concerts by the New York Philharmonic, the Chamber Music Society of Lincoln Center, and selected concerts presented by Great Performers at Lincoln Center.

A volunteer program called VAPA (Volunteers for Access to the Performing Arts), has been developed by Ms. Knapp to assist in the dissemination of information about accessibility and services, greeting people with disabilities and helping to escort groups of people or individuals with disabilities who visit Lincoln Center. A cadre of bilingual volunteers is also being organized within this group, as the number of disabled visitors from abroad is increasing.

Most people are familiar with the wonderful work of the National Theatre of the Deaf (NTD), now located at the Hazel E. Stark Center, Chester, CT 06412. Early history of the NTD program goes back to the former Department of Health, Education and Welfare's Vocational Rehabilitation Administration which, jointly with the Office of Education, awarded a three-year grant to the Eugene O'Neill Center to establish the National Theatre of the Deaf. Another grant financed a five-week school for actors with hearing impairments at the O'Neill Center's Waterford, Connecticut, headquarters. The NTD continues to receive support from the Office of Special Education Programs (OSEP) in the Office of Special Education and Rehabilitative Services (OSERS). The National Theatre of the Deaf performs on an annual professional tour, and in addition performs for a variety of organizations (disabled and non-disabled), provides theatre arts instruction to school programs, conducts summer school sessions, and works with other persons with disabilities to provide them with training in theatre arts suggestions, and a referral directory for the local community (Dalton 1985). Other performing theatres for people with disabilities are the Performing Arts Theater of the Handicapped (PATH), PO Box 9050, Carlsbad, CA 92208, and the National Theatre Workshop of the Handicapped, at 106 West 56th Street, New York, NY 10019. The latter states in its brochure that it helps people with disabilities to qualify for work on the legitimate stage by offering training and the opportunity to learn how to perform.

A very old organization is **Rehabilitation through Photography (RTP),** 1133 Broadway, New York, NY 10010, which began as a group of volunteers trained to teach photography primarily to disabled veterans. It is a nonprofit organization, founded in 1941 to serve the chronically ill and physically and mentally handicapped. Since then, it has been providing recreation and training toward careers for all ages in hospitals, community centers, mental institutions, and drug rehabilitation centers in the New York City area.

The May 1988 issue of the *Journal of Visual Impairment and Blindness* published an article entitled "A New Approach to Recreational Rehabilitation" by Cory N. Neustadt-Noy, which explores the importance of recreation in rehabilitation programs for visually impaired adults. The program described took place in West Germany. Neustadt-Noy states that leisure time activity training works best if it takes place in unconventional settings such as resort hotels. His program takes place in a small hotel, allowing interaction with other hotel guests and village residents (Neustadt-Noy 1988).

SOURCES OF INFORMATION

The **American Alliance for Health, Physical Education, Recreation and Dance (AAHPERD),** at 1900 Association Drive, Reston, VA 22091, is a nonprofit association of professionals concerned with improving programs in schools and communities in the areas of physical education, sports, health and safety education, recreation, and dance. It issues numerous publications including the newsletter *Able Bodies*, the *Journal of Physical Education, Recreation and Dance, Health Education*, and *Research Quarterly for Exercise and Sport*. The organization sponsors a national convention (Russell 1986).

Special Recreation, Inc., at 362 Koser Avenue, Iowa City, IA 52240, publishes *Special Recreation Digest*, a quarterly publication that offers information on special recreation.

Sports 'N Spokes: The Magazine for Wheelchair Sports and Recreation is owned by Paralyzed Veterans of America, and is published in Phoenix, AZ 85015.

A Positive Approach is at Municipal Airport, a national magazine for the physically challenged, carries articles about all aspects of active life for people with disabilities, including sports, recreation, articles on family life, and an exercise column by Richard Simmons. Richard Simmons wrote *Reach for Fitness*, the first book of exercise, nutrition, and fun for people who are physically and/or medically challenged. He recently moved his Reach Foundation to the Carondelet Rehabilitation Centers of America and Daniel Freeman Hospitals in order to provide community-based exercise opportunities for adults and children with special physical needs (*A Positive Approach is at Municipal Airport* May/June, 1988). *A Positive Approach is at Municipal Airport* is published at 1600 Malone St., Municipal Airport, Millville, NJ 08332.

The *Journal of Expanding Horizons in Therapeutic Recreation* is published by Recreation Extension, 613 Clark Hall, University of Missouri, Columbia MO 65211.

REFERENCES

Accent on Living Buyers Guide. 1988. "Automobile Controls," 6–9.

Brown, Patricia Leigh. "For the Aging and Disabled, Products They Can Use." April 21, 1988, *New York Times*. Section C, pp. 1 and 12.

Directory of National Information Sources on Handicapping Conditions and Related Services. 1986. Winchester, MA: Harold Russell Associates, Inc., 195.

Durgin, Rod W., and Lindsay, Norene. 1986. *The Physically Disabled Traveler's Guide*. Toledo, OH: Resource Directories.

Fay, Frederick A., and Minch, Janet. 1976, October. *Access to Recreation: A Report on the National Hearing on Recreation for Handicapped Persons*. Architectural and Transportation Barriers Compliance Board, Department of Health, Education and Welfare, Office of Human Development, Rehabilitation Services Administration. Published by Tufts/New England Medical Center, Medical Rehabilitation Research and Training Center, No. 7.

Haight, Sherrel Lee, and Fachting, Daniel D. 1986, June/July. "Materials for Teaching Sexuality, Love and Maturity to High School Students with Learning Disabilities." *Journal of Learning Disabilities* 19 (6): 344–50.

Litvak, Simi, Zukas, Hale, and Heumann, Judity E. *Attending to America: Personal Assistance for Independent Living, A Survey of Attendant Service Programs in the United States for People of All Ages with Disabilities*. Berkeley, CA: World Institute on Disability.

Lunt, Suzanne. 1984. *A Handbook for the Disabled: Ideas & Inventions for Easier Living*. New York: Charles Scribner's Sons, 48, 106, 223.

May, Elizabeth Eckhardt, Waggoner, Neva R., and Boettke, Eleanor. 1974. *Independent Living for the Handicapped and Elderly*. Boston: Houghton Mifflin, Chapter 8.

National Association of Rehabilitation Research and Training Centers, 1986. *Directory of the Rehabilitation Research and Training Centers*, Washington, DC 20202.

Newstandt-Noy, Cory D. 1988, May. "A New Approach to Recreational Rehabilitation." *Journal of Visual Impairment and Blindness.* 195, 196.

Pflueger, Susan. 1977. *Independent Living, Emerging Issues in Rehabilitation.* Washington, DC: Institute for Research Utilization, 52.

Rehab Brief, 1987. "Telephone Services and Equipment for Disabled People," Department of Education, Washington, DC 20202. Vol. X, No. 3.

Rehab Brief, 1988. "Living Less Restrictively in the Community." Washington, DC: Vol. X1, No. 5.

Savitz, Harriet M. 1978. *Wheelchair Champions: A History of Wheelchair Sports.* John Day: New York, NY.

Simmons, Richard. "Exercise and Nutrition." In *A Positive Approach is at Municipal Airport.* Millville, NJ: Positive Approach, Inc., 36, 42.

Snider, Harold W. 1985. *The United States Welcomes Handicapped Visitors.* Brooklyn, NY: Society for the Advancement of Travel for the Handicapped.

"Ten Questions and Answers about Air Travel for Wheelchair Users." Eastern Paralyzed Veterans Association. (ND) Queens, NY 11370-1178.

The Voice of the Physically Challenged. 1988, December. Rockville Centre, NY, 14.

Weiss, Donna Valenti. 1988, July/September. "Accessible Vacations." *Journal of Rehabilitation,* 8-9.

Weiss, Louise. 1986. *Access to the World: A Travel Guide for the Handicapped.* Revised edition. New York: Henry Hold.

Wilkes, Penny. 1988, Spring. "Bed & Breakfast." *Accent on Living,* 32-36.

Witter, Dianne C. 1988, March/April. "She's Opening Arts' Doors for Us." *Arthritis Today.*

Chapter 5
New Technology

The decade of the 1980s has been characterized by exciting new developments in the field of technology to help people with all types of disabilities reach their maximum functioning levels. During the 1990s the most important mission for all persons working in the fields of rehabilitation and special education will be to find ways to bring the latest advances in technological development to the attention of children and adults with disabilities.

LEGISLATION

An increased emphasis on technology was apparent in the rehabilitation legislation of the 1980s. PL 99-506, the Rehabilitation Act of 1986, legitimized the use of technology to expand independence of persons with disabilities (see also Chapter 6). In Section 508 (a) (l) of Title VI of the act the principle of electronic "curb cuts" in computers is established. This means that equipment sold to the federal government must be "transparent," that is, it must have the ability to be adapted for accessibility built-in to all hardware to be there when needed. As principal procurer of equipment, the government has therefore ensured that all computers and other electronic equipment will be so equipped.

The National Institute on Disability and Rehabilitation Research, so renamed in this act, is charged with the development and efficient distribution of new technologies, foreshadowing a pressure on the states to make use of assistive devices and other technologies, such as computers, in rehabilitation, and to provide appropriate concrete channels for implementing these activities. One state which took the lead in this area was Minnesota, which created a Team on Technology for People with Disabilities as reported in the Spring 1987 issue of *Computer-Disability News* (National Easter Seal Society 1987). The report of the Minnesota Initiative, available free from the Office of the Governor, State of Minnesota, St. Paul, MN 55155, might assist other states in their activities.

In the summer of 1988, the Technology-Related Assistance for Individuals With Disabilities Act (PL 100-407) was passed by both houses of Congress, and signed by President Reagan. This act will help states begin linking people of all ages who are disabled with assistive technology. Essentially, under Title I, the act creates a competitive state grant program to serve as a catalyst for increasing the availability of and funding (both public and private) for assistive technology devices and services (*Mainstream* 1988). The Department of Education's Office of Special Education and Rehabilitative Services (OSERS) hoped to make the first state grants during fiscal 1989, but at this writing the regulations had not yet been developed, nor the complete funding allocated.

Three-year grants were to be awarded to as many as 10 states the first year, 20 more states in 1990, and the remaining states in 1991. These will be renewable for another two years. States will review the policies and practices of public and private organizations in providing and paying for assistive technology devices and services and will implement comprehensive strategies to expand opportunities for people with disabilities to obtain assistive devices and technology-related assistance. States' activities may include identifying and evaluating technology needs, providing devices and services, disseminating information, providing training and technical assistance, collecting data, sponsoring public awareness and outreach activities, and aiding community-based organizations and partnerships.

Title II of this Act includes a study on financing technology to be conducted by the National Council on Disability, the creation of a National Information and Program Referral Network, under the auspices of the Department of Education; training grants to be used to defray the cost of training individuals to train others in the use of assistive devices, and public awareness grants for national media campaigns, conferences, and public recognition programs (especially for employers); and grants to commercial developers of technology for individuals with disabilities and to insurers which facilitate the acquisition of or provide funding for devices. Also provided is funding for demonstration and innovation projects, including applied research and development for the design of customized devices and combinations of devices; funding to provide incentives for producing limited market devices; and a loan program for purchasing assistive technology devices for individuals with disabilities (Mainstream 1988).

The Center for Special Education Technology, at the Council for Exceptional Children, 1920 Association Drive, Reston, VA 22091, promotes appropriate use of computer, video, and audiotechnology in special education and provides information services to educators, parents, product developers, publishers, and others interested in technology for special needs children. The Center can be contacted in four ways: HOTLINE: answers specific information needs: 1-800-873-TALK, Monday thru Friday; TECH.LINE: a monthly bulletin board on SPECIALNET providing current and topical information; TECH-TAPES: 1-800-345 TECH: over 200 taped messages containing special education technology information, available 24 hours a day; SPECIALNET ID: TECH CENTER.

PERSONAL COMPUTERS AND SPECIAL NEEDS

The use of computer technology to reduce the barriers confronted by individuals with disabilities has been the principal exciting development of the 1980s. The challenge of the 1990s will be to disseminate information about this new technology to all people with disabilities and to provide the evaluation and training necessary to enable them to make use of it.

Most children with disabilities are now being introduced to computers in their schools; however, adults have not received this computer education. By making use of the rehabilitation and special education information and evaluation centers provided by the major computer producers, it is now possible for them to obtain the knowledge they need. However, at times persistence is needed in order to find the right place to secure the appropriate evaluation. Primarily, what it takes is the desire to try something new. Lest they doubt their ability to do this, let me say that this book is being written on a Macintosh using a word processing program that I found relatively simple to learn with a bit of coaching. Moreover, I never mastered the intricacies of the electric typewriter and therefore made the transition from an old manual typewriter to the word processor in one easy jump. Having mastered it, I never looked back.

My intention here is not to try to present the myriad programs now available to users with disabilities, or to explain the intricacies of how this remarkable machine works. It will suffice that we discuss in a very general way what the computer can do for persons with disabilities, and where and how rehabilitation professionals and consumers may inquire about obtaining the information, evaluation, and training required to enable purchasing the appropriate hardware (computer equipment), software (the programs that operate on this equipment), and firmware (programs that are less flexible than software because they stay in the machine) with the proper special adaptations that will allow usage.

What Personal Computers Can Do

In 1984 Frank G. Bowe wrote a small book entitled *Personal Computers and Special Needs* in which he foreshadowed the developments that would occur during the remainder of the decade of the 1980s (Bowe 1984). In his book Bowe outlined the many areas of life that would be touched by the personal computer, including education, employment, control of the environment (such as turning on and off light switches, radio dials and television channels), communication and recreation. The groups to be served would include deaf persons, blind persons, people with speech and language problems, and those with mobility impairments, mental retardation, and learning disabilities.

People with disabilities have been unable to work for several reasons, but the major cause has been employer bias. In the past many companies believed that persons with disabilities could not work as well as able-bodied persons. Today a number of companies, led originally by such organizations as IBM, DuPont, AT&T, and Control Data, are proving that given the correct work environment and tools, known as "reasonable accommodation" aids and devices, people with disabilities can do productive work (Bowe 1984).

Persons with physical impairments find doing the simplest chores around the house exhausting and commuting to and from work problematic. With the kinds of aids now available, many of these problems can be eliminated. Special switches exist for persons having control of only an eyelid or a toe, or an eye, Communication devices for the speech impaired and for the use of blind persons have reached highly sophisticated stages of development. There are speech synthesizers, voice recognition software, braille computer printers, and attachments that enlarge information on a computer screen up to 16 times normal size.

Education of children with disabilities is now aided by computer-assisted instruction, beneficial to youngsters with learning disabilities or mental retardation, as well as to those students needing special devices to do their school work. The educational environment has changed as a result of the microcomputer. The need for individualized learning materials for children with disabilities was recognized in the 1970s, and now the microcomputer is being used to create that educational environment suited exactly to the needs of each child (Hagen 1984).

Morever, teaching children with disabilities to use personal computers at home for homework, for recreational games, and for the operation of environmental controls, is a valuable addition to their curriculum. This knowledge will open up to many of them paths of future employment.

The early predictions have come to fruition in ways that most of us could never have dreamed possible. Computer advances that were intended for the general consumer electronics market have enabled persons with disabilities to become more independent and self-sufficient, increasing work and study skills, and the advanced technology is becoming less expensive (*Mainstream* 1988).

Unless otherwise referenced, much of the following overview has been adapted from "Technology for Persons with Disabilities—An Introduction" distributed by the IBM National Support Center for Persons with Disabilities. Permission for its use was granted by the center.

Computer Technology for People with Mobility Impairments

For people with mobility impairments that affect motor control, computer technology can provide much independence in daily living and work activities. However, the computer will require modifications so that it can become accessible. Each person has a different need, and so evaluation of ability and prescription of special devices is of utmost importance. Some people with physical disabilities can use a standard computer keyboard, but may be typing with one hand, with only one or two fingers, a head pointer, a mouthstick, a handstick, or with reduced fine motor control. Keyguards with holes positioned over each key prevent accidental key strokes. Single finger programs allow operations of keys so that two or more keys do not have to be pressed simultaneously, a most important adaptation. For the typist able to use only one hand, the keyboard layout can be redesigned to meet the user's needs. Expanded keyboards, with larger keys for those who can only manage large areas, and miniature keyboards for those with limited range of motion are also available.

Persons with a physical disability that also affects the muscles used in speaking may benefit from technology that can enhance oral communication. In such cases, portable devices that provide synthesized speech output or written output can aid communication. These devices can be used alone, or in some cases used in conjunction with the computer.

A computer program making use of a switch or voice recognition system, connected to an environmental control device, can enable an individual to operate lights, a radio, television, telephone, heating or air conditioning, motorized drapes, or almost any other electrical appliance. Banking from the home, computerizing telephone directories for use with adapted telephones, marketing from home, are all possibilities that can make use of computers.

The choice of a switch, which can be turned on or off by sipping and puffing, wrinkling the eyebrows, head or mouth sticks, using a toe, or scanning, such as eye scanning, or morse code, or voice recognition by which a computer can accept spoken commands, are all adaptations now available to the person with severe mobility impairment.

For children with physical disabilities playing is often difficult because of the inability to manipulate objects. In addition to specially adapted toys, the use of the computer for recreation, so prominent now in the games of able-bodied youngsters, can also give the disabled the experience of play. Special programs can produce music or other sounds, create visual displays on the computer monitor, generate speech, or activate toys. Computer games and graphics programs which enable a child who is disabled to draw are some of the possibilities.

Computer Technology for People with Speech and Language Disabilities

Speech and language disorders include defects of articulation, voice production, and rhythm; cleft-palate speech; delayed speech development; and disorders associated with hearing impairments or brain damage, such as cerebral palsy.

Special computer programs have been developed to assist the speech or language-impaired person to develop or re-develop adequate articulation or language skills. Cognitive rehabilitation software can identify and treat cognitive deficits in stroke and brain-injured persons, concentrating on the detection and retraining of language function, such as perceptual deficits, memory, categorization, sequencing, and association.

Computer Technology for People Who Are Visually Impaired

For those with low vision, the standard computer output on a screen display or printed page usually presents a major obstacle. Magnification adaptations, such as magnification lenses placed in front of standard displays, larger characters created on standard displays, alternative displays, and, for printed output, larger characters and more readable fonts can help. For persons who are blind, computerized audio output allows the user to read by hearing the information that is being displayed on the computer screen. Braille is also available as an output alternative for blind persons. Some braille devices currently in use include braille printers that produce embossed paper output and paperless tactile displays that use retractable pins to form braille characters. Software programs are required to perform the necessary translations to braille files used by the braille devices.

To enable persons who are blind to use the keyboard, some modifications, including key indicators such as dimples/dots or felt appliques, and key replacements (larger, or more unique) can be used for the often-used keys. However, voice recognition (the ability of a machine or computer to recognize human speech) can control and command the computer and create text without the use of the keyboard. The uses of voice technology were explained by Raymond Kurzweil in an interview published in *SAINT (Special and Individual Needs Technology)* in December 1987.

Speech synthesizers allow audio output during data entry, thus providing immediate feedback as information is entered by the user unable to visually verify as he or she goes along. Audio output aids, such as talking phone directories, talking calculators, and general file management products, spelling checkers, and online thesauri, as well as the use of telephone lines to perform such activities as exchanging machine-readable information, accessing remote data-banks of information, and sharing ideas via electronic bulletin boards, are some of the many ways in which persons with visual impairments are able to use computer technology.

Computer Technology for People Who Are Hearing Impaired

Hearing impairment presents difficulties in communication; however, interaction with a device such as a personal computer presents no essential difficulty. Moreover, computers can provide for two-way communication, in home or job, with anyone with a touch-tone telephone. It can also provide for other means of communication through telecommunications—for example, electronic bulletin boards, local area networks, and mainframe communication systems. As explained by Kurzweil, voice technology can be used to communicate with people who are deaf. The person communicating talks into the speech recognizer, while the deaf person reads the speech that appears on a video screen (SAINT 1987).

Bell Communications Research (Bellcore) is experimenting with a system called Deafnet, or Telecommunications for the Deaf. This system would facilitate the communication between hearing and hearing-impaired persons by further utilizing computers, eliminating the need for a relay operator when using a Teletypewriter for the Deaf (TDD). In some cases users would not have to purchase special equipment. For a demonstration of this system and more information, contact Bell Communications Research, 435 South Street, Morristown, NJ 07960 (NARIC 1988).

Persons in the United States who are deaf work in almost all occupational fields and use a variety of means to communicate. With the advent of computer databases and computer networks, much of government and industry communications are implemented today through the nonverbal direct communications between a terminal and a remote database. Thus the computer has greatly enhanced the job opportunities available, especially for those with hearing impairments. In the area of education, computers can serve as teaching tools to increase a person's skills or in basic education for replacing verbal classroom teaching of subjects such as reading, writing, and mathematics.

Computer Technology for People Who Are Mentally Retarded

Personal computers can be powerful tools to help persons who are retarded to attain greater use of their abilities. For the person requiring repetition or exposure to information to learn a skill, a personal computer allows an exercise to be repeated, without change, any number of times, thus permitting the user to progress at his or her own pace. A computer can also track the progress of the student, detect areas that require additional attention, and log this information for review by the teacher at the end of the session. The computer can then be programmed to begin a remedial exercise.

Touch boards allow a user to bring out sounds, musical tones, or change the color of the display. Materials can be presented in the same manner for a slow learner as it is for a faster paced student but there is no need for both to proceed at the same speed. It is possible to provide displays that will communicate with people who are severely retarded at their level. Pictures of basic needs can be furnished on touch pads and screens, coordinated so that the person can touch what he or she wants and have that need communicated verbally or electronically to another location, where the need can be recognized and action taken to meet the need (*Mainstream* 1989).

Computers can be used to drill students in learning basic living or occupational skills as well as educational activities. Job activities and behavioral techniques can be explained, drilled, and tested to improve skills and behavior to make the individual more employable.

Using Computers to Help Children with Down Syndrome, by Jeffrey Willner (1989, Down Syndrome Society, 666 Broadway, New York, NY 10012), examines ways in which a child with Down's Syndrome might benefit from using a computer at home and addresses the issues in choosing a computer and software for children and adults with this disability.

Computer Technology for People with Learning Disabilities

The learning-disabled (LD) person is usually of average or above average intelligence and may have one or more learning disorders. Cognitive impairments may also refer to attention deficit disorder (ADD), or other minimal brain dysfunction. In school the child with learning disabilities can benefit tremendously by using microcomputers. Education can be aided in the following ways:

For strengthening visual perception, color, graphics, motion and highlighting can aid the LD student by helping him or her to read line-by-line or by alleviating problems in distinguishing important details from background when studying designs or diagrams.

For reading and following instructions, reading material can be presented through voice output if necessary.

Writing problems can be helped with word processors that can not only check spelling but grammar and phrases as well.

Memory can be helped by repetition of information and there are computer programs to assist in instruction for sequencing and organizational skills. The computer provides a structured environment which will filter out extraneous stimuli, and provide necessary repetition.

For the working person with a learning disability it is critical to match the person's strengths with the work to be done. Use of a computer can make an important difference in an employee's performance.

SPECIAL SERVICES RELATED TO COMPUTERS

There are special resources now available to persons wishing to obtain information about where to go to be evaluated for the purpose of purchasing a personal computer and training in its use. There are also directories offering a tremendous number of software programs. Finding out about this rapidly changing field can be very confusing and information can become quickly obsolete. Therefore the following is an account of available sources to obtain the latest information.

While many personal computers on the market are compatible with the special switches and software available, the two major producers of personal computers, IBM and Apple, have set up special offices and programs for persons with disabilities where they can take the first steps toward becoming computer literate. The services listed here have been derived from the materials sent on request from these offices.

IBM

IBM has established the National Support Center for Persons with Disabilities at 4111 Northside Parkway, Atlanta, GA 30327 (1-800-426-2133 Voice/TDD). A call to this center produced for me the following information, all of it free upon request.

IBM has established a program with the National Easter Seals Society, which has now been extended to include the United Cerebral Palsy Association and Courage Center in Golden Valley, Minnesota, designating certain of their centers nationwide where persons with disabilities can go to find out how they can be evaluated for equipment. A listing of these centers, which now number over 30, located in over 20 states, can be obtained from the IBM National Support Center in Atlanta. The major purpose of the program is to offer financial discounts on the purchase of an IBM personal computer to qualified persons with disabilities. (In some cases, such as for use in a job situation, or to enable greater independent living, federal insurance programs may also be tapped for financial aid.)

Also in the information packet sent out on request is an introduction and overview of the technology available to persons with disabilities, as well as a listing of agencies and associations, with both national and regional office addresses, that deal with persons with disabilities. A listing of suppliers of software and hardware, primarily for audio and speech and braille products, cassette producers, closed circuit TV equipment, special keyboard and keyguard producers, magnification producers and non-vocal communication aids producers is available as well as listings of producers of printers and print programs, readers, switches, synthesizers, and word processors.

Upon requesting further information, IBM will supply extensive resource guides for persons with each of the above-listed impairments which include hardware and software programs and cover all of the needed adaptations for specific disabilities. Support groups and other contacts are listed at the back of each guide. Additional programs offered by IBM include a Special Needs Systems Group which oversees the development and manufacture of IBM products for persons with disabilities, and the Special Needs Initiatives and Programs Office which coordinates research projects and reviews product design. There is also a Special Needs Exchange, an innovative, online information resource for teachers, parents, students, university faculty, allied health professionals, school administrators, and others interested in educational computing for persons with special needs. This exchange is available nationwide through the CompuServe Information Service. In addition to information about IBM software and services, it also provides information on educational software for IBM systems from third-party publishers and public domain educational software. The Exchange is coordinated by LINC Resources, Inc. and is sponsored by the IBM Corporation as a public service.

An IBM Rehabilitation Training Program, under the sponsorship of state rehabilitation agencies, trains and places individuals with disabilities as computer programmers. Under joint funding by IBM and the Rehabilitation Services Administration in the Federal Department of Education, an additional 30 programs have been established which have been very successful (over 80 percent of the graduates finding jobs as computer programmers) (IBM 1988). A listing of where these programs are available may be obtained from the IBM Support Center in Atlanta.

IBM entertains requests from publicly supported organizations for equipment donations limited primarily to agency programs engaged in job training for the economically disadvantaged and the physically disabled, and to selected institutions of higher learning for use in educational activities.

Apple Computer, Inc.

Apple maintains an Office of Special Education at 19925 Stevens Creek Boulevard, Cupertino, CA 95014. Established in 1985, this office works with rehabilitation engineers and therapists, developers of software and hardware products that make Apple computers accessible, and with advocates, parents and children with disabilities. A request to this office produced the following information.

Apple maintains an online database of information called Special Education Solutions, describing hardware, software, organizations and publications which support computer users who are disabled. Sent upon request is a publication entitled *Connections*, drawn from this database. Addresses are given for obtaining general information as well as for a selection of the companies that manufacture and distribute a wide range of devices for persons with visual or mobility impairments, learning disabilities, or speech and hearing disabilities.

The complete contents of Special Education Solutions has been published by DLM, Inc. Entitled *Apple Computer Resources in Special Education and Rehabilitation*, this 400-page publication also includes a description of the roles computers can play in the lives of children and adults with disabilities, together with listings of organizations and publications that support these users. (DLM, Inc., One DLM Park, Allen, TX 75002, 800-527-4747). The entire Solutions database is also on AppleLink®.

Solutions has also been made a part of SPECIALNET, the nation's largest telecommunications service devoted to serving the needs of professionals in special education and rehabilitation. For information about a subscription to SPECIALNET write to Suite 315, 2021 K Street, NW, Washington, DC 20006.

An additional resource is The Apple Bulletin Board, an electronic drop-in center also available on SPECIALNET. It is a place to ask or answer questions, to meet colleagues, to learn about new products or innovative applications in special education and rehabilitation. Apple's SPECIALNET address is Apple.OSEP.

Apple, Inc., has also initiated a National Special Education Alliance, a partnership, among grassroots community organizations, third-party vendors, and professional associations for the purpose of increasing awareness, understanding, and implementation of microcomputer technology to aid individuals with disabilities. Each center conducts training seminars, and product fairs, and offers individual consultations, and is electronically linked to every other center, as well as to major national databases and bulletin boards. Unlike IBM, which has worked through Easter Seals and UCP, Apple has utilized special technology centers whose addresses are listed in *Connections*. The Alliance was conceived by Apple's Office of Special Education in cooperation with the Disabled Children's Computer Group (DCCG), 2095 Rose Street, Berkeley, CA 94709, a community-based resource center with a membership of 1,200 parents, teachers, and disabled individuals. Since new centers will be added by the time this book is published, it is best to contact Apple or DCCG fo an updated list.

Apple conducts ongoing research through new product development, and consults regularly with rehabilitation engineers. Apple is actively involved with the Government/Industry Task Force on Computer Accessibility by Individuals with Disability, and with the national task force working to develop Guidelines for the Design of Computers and Information Processing Systems to Increase Access by Persons with Disabilities.

Once the first hurdle of choosing a computer and apppropriate special devices has been overcome it becomes an ongoing challenge to choose software. Apple Connections asks what does the computer need to do? Learn basic academic skills? Play games? Write letters, articles, stories? Search online databases? Control aspects of the environment? In addition to Special Education Solutions, several other sources are suggested.

The International Software Database Corporation (accessible via AppleLink) lists The Apple II Guide (telephone 800-The Menu) containing more than 7,700 software programs, and the Mac Menu (telephone 800-Mac Menu) listing more than 2,000 titles for the Macintosh. All software is classified by subject, and each listing gives a brief description of the product, manufacturer, and price. Purchasing can be done directly from this catalog.

The Special Education Software Center, a federally supported clearinghouse for information on commercially available software for special needs, provides listings tailored to request (800-327-5892).

Public Domain refers to programs that are either free or available for a very small fee. Although they are of variable quality this is an inexpensive route that should be explored. Further information about Apple public domain software resources can be requested from:

Big Red Apple Club   Public Domain Exchange
1105 S. 13th Street   673 Hermitage Place
Norfolk, NE, VA 68701   San Jose, CA 95134

Apple Computer offers computer equipment at discounted prices to educational institutions, teachers and administrators, and also donates equipment to organizations serving humanitarian causes. For further information regarding Apple's donation policy, contact:

Department of Corporate Grants
Apple Computer, Inc.
20525 Mariani Avenue MS 5B
Cupertino, CA 95014

COMPUTERS IN HIGHER EDUCATION

An article entitled "Computer Accessibility for Students with Disabilities" (Kramer 1988) published in the journal *Academic Computing*, states that, as computer-based instruction is integrated into the curriculum, accessibility is taking on a new dimension. Interpreters for deaf students, readers and recordings for blind students, and ramps for mobility-impaired students are not enough to ensure full access to postsecondary opportunity.

There are now hundreds of thousands of students with disabilities in the higher education system. Computer access for these students is a necessity since all departments incorporate use of computers into their curricula and future disabled college freshmen undoubtedly will come in with computer literacy learned in elementary and secondary schools. Kramer enumerates many of the adaptations now available for students with disabilities and indicates that this equipment needs to be made available in computer labs on campus. One helpful idea in the area of notetaking is use of the small portable computers such as Zygo Notebook or the Zenith 181, eliminating problems with making copies and illegible handwriting. Notes can be printed out for as many students as necessary or copies can be made on disk (Kramer 1988). This article is of particular importance because it appeared in a journal which is read by all persons in the field of academic computing, rather than just by the community of the disabled.

An encouraging report from *HEATH* (1986) indicated that many post-secondary institutions were beginning to buy specialized computer products to attract students with disabilities. Most report an eagerness on the part of these students to acquire computer knowledge, which will help them to become employable.

Kramer makes the following recommendations for establishing campus accessibility:

- Survey what hardware, software, and adaptive equipment are currently available on campus
- Establish the spectrum of needs of students with disabilities based on requirements of their programs of study
- Establish a central consulting center
- Create a loan center for adaptive equipment and software to reduce the need for multiple purchases or purchases of equipment for a student who might need a specific item for only one term
- Provide training for staff
- Establish sharing agreements for labs without wheelchair access, and continue wheelchair access improvements
- Explore sources of funding for a high-tech center for students with disabilities, faculty and staff (Kramer 1988).

COMPUTERS IN VOCATIONAL REHABILITATION

Acknowledging the tremendous capacity of computers to process, store, retrieve and transmit information, the vocational rehabilitation system in America began, during the 1980s, to appreciate the variety of advantages available from computer use (Growick 1983). These advantages can be seen in the facilitating of the work of the rehabilitation counselor with the client in the rehabilitation process, in assisting management personnel with program maintenance, in improving the learning systems, and facilitating independent living options.

In a study written for NIDRR in 1983, and distributed by NARIC, Bruce Growick summerized the literature that pertained to these categories and discussed some future applications for computers in vocational rehabilitation. Documents analyzed by Growick described the use of computers in the interpretation of psychological and vocational tests and in aiding the counselor in administering tests to clients with a need for alternative means of response. Storing and retrieving detailed diagnostic information on clients were discussed in several articles. Recommendations suggested by Growick include the examination of computer-based occupational information systems to determine the relative advantages and disadvantages of each when combined with variables such as disability type, economic resources, etc; the encouragement of use of desktop computers by rehabilitation professionals and other agency personnel; consideration by rehabilitation counselors of the variety of jobs available from the computer industry, including the potential for homebound employment; computer and information management components to be built into the graduate education program for rehabilitation students; and encouragement of in-service training programs in the use of the computer for professionals already in the field.

Many of the suggestions made in this paper have been adopted in the United States. A recent article entitled "A Computerized Case Management System," by Glen MacDonald (1988), describes in detail the development of a system by the Canadian Paraplegic Association, Manitoba Division, to organize the service delivery component of that agency. This case management and data retrieval system, in place for two years, has made for better organization of work. Future directions include sharing online data and networking, extending the system to include documentation of the time required to deliver services, and eventually, enabling direct data entry into desktop terminals, so that each can enter data directly (MacDonald 1988). Both Growick and MacDonald mention computer use in the formulation of the Individualized Work Rehabilitation Plan (IWRP), as mandated by the Rehabilitation Act of 1973 (PL 93-112).

ROBOTICS IN REHABILITATION

The many devices now available to people with disabilities have not been enumerated in this chapter, since the information is too extensive, changes rapidly, and is readily available from the sources indicated. One exciting development that should be mentioned, however, is in the area of robotics, where research is ongoing and must be closely watched.

Richard A. Foulds of the Tufts Rehabilitation Engineering program in his monograph entitled *Interactive Robotic Aids—One Option for Independent Living: An International Perspective* (1986) includes papers written by rehabilitation robotics research and development experts from the United States and abroad. The information was summarized in a *Rehab Brief* (1987) entitled "Robotics and Rehabilitation."

Some of the solutions resulting from the development of technology for the exploration of space, deep-sea, and radioactive environments are now being used to enable people with severe disabilities to control their environments. The use of robotic manipulators to substitute for the lack of manual skills is being explored in several projects. Robotic devices can be task specific or can be used as general manipulation instruments. They can provide action at a distance, be used in unstructured environments, or carry out preprogrammed tasks within highly structured environments. They can be used to manipulate larger and heavier objects than an individual could handle with body-actuated manipulation aids (*Rehab Brief* 1987).

Examples of projects being conducted in five different countries were summarized in this *Rehab Brief*. The original report, available from the World Rehabilitation Fund, 400 East 34th Street, New York, NY 10016, offers more technical descriptions of the equipment and more complete discussions of the configuration, price, and accomplishments of specific devices.

In France, the Spartacus project, originally intended to stimulate the development of industrial robotics, conducted a feasibility study to develop and test a telemanipulator, controllable by people with high-level spinal cord lesions. These configurations of the equipment allowed participants to pour liquids, obtain objects from shelves, open cupboard doors, eat, light a lamp, draw or paint, or drink using a special mode that combines tilting and lifting a cup or glass, simultaneously while being controlled by a single signal. This last action was considered a "landmark" since it showed that a certain level of confidence and dexterity in controlling the system had been obtained.

In Canada, the Neil Squire Foundation created a manipulator that could perform tasks done by personal assistants and was approximately human size. This robot, called M.O.M. (a Machine for Obedient Manipulation), is designed as a work station manipulator. M.O.M. can pick up a manual from a bookshelf and place it in front of an individual, turn pages, pick up, serve, and replace a drink, serve up a mouthstick, load a diskette into a computer, pick up an electric shaver and shave a person, brush hair and brush teeth. It is hoped that a "second generation" M.O.M. will incorporate artificial intelligence, giving the user better control and allowing the arm to be mounted on a wheelchair.

From the Netherlands comes the report of a wheelchair-mounted robot (the Cobra Manipulator), which can perform many of the above-mentioned functions as well as operate environmental controls such as light switches, radios, TVs and door locks. Developed by a doctor and his son who has muscular dystrophy, this robot can be manipulated by light finger control or other switches if needed. Wheeling through the house requires simultaneous manipulation of the robotic control as well as wheelchair movement. Other activities possible with this manipulator are playing games such as chess, and woodworking.

From the United States come reports of three independent vocational work station studies. Boeing Computer Services has sponsored a project to experiment with a speech-controlled workstation for quadriplegic programmers and analysts. The workstation has a microcomputer system that supports and is driven by two voice-recognition products and a voice communication product. Here the hardware configuration allows single voice commands to produce the equivalent of multiple key strokes, permitting the user to handle filing in a file cabinet, handle floppy diskettes, adjust a printer according to command, and perform miscellaneous support activities. Special placement of the equipment is required and each station requires special programming; however, a quadriplegic computer operator is functioning independently in a business programming environment at Boeing Computer Services using this equipment.

The Rehabilitation Engineering Center in Wichita, Kansas, helped develop a work station robot that allows disabled people to work at assembly line tasks. Workers at Center Activities in Wichita are performing these tasks on a subcontract with the Boeing Company. An element of judgment is necessary in these operations, and the robot could not do the work alone.

The Johns Hopkins University Applied Physics Laboratory has developed a robot arm/work table system enabling high-level quadriplegics to execute manipulative tasks with little or no attendant assistance. This research program had reached a stage where a manufacturing prototype had been fabricated and it was in the final stages of evaluation when Foulds's monograph was written (Foulds 1986). This monograph concluded by asking how development in robotics could be brought to the average consumer with disabilities. A limited market of just several hundred thousand users has stood in the way, just as it did in the development of new wheelchair designs. (Until very recently, wheelchair models had not been changed very much since the 1940s.) Robotic development must include the fact that evaluation and training must be conducted in rehabilitation or hospital settings, each user must have a custom system specially designed, manufacturers would need to train sales and service personnel, some products would need to be prescribed by a physician, and clearly, cost on the one hand and market size on the other minimize the profit potential for private manufacturers (*Rehab Brief* 1987).

It would seem, however, that many of these same problems existed when it became a priority to evaluate individuals who were severely disabled for microcomputer use and then custom design systems for them. Perhaps if representatives from government, industry, and the rehabilitation field work together to accomplish the costly research, design, development, production, and dissemination of robotic devices, use by these consumers can come about.

ADDITIONAL SOURCES OF INFORMATION

"Computer Technology for Handicapped Persons—Some Questions and Answers," Facts Reference Sheet
National Library Service for the Blind and Physically Handicapped
The Library of Congress
Washington, DC 20542
Linda Redmond (September 1987).

American Foundation for the Blind
National Technology Center
15 West 16th Street
New York, NY 10011

Clearinghouse on Computer Accommodations
18th and F Streets NW
Washington, DC 20405

Center for Special Education Technology
Council for Exceptional Children
1920 Association Drive
Reston, VA 22091

SPECIALNET
National Association of State Directors of Special Education
2021 K Street NW, Suite 215
Washington, DC 20006

CompuHelp
National Association of Blind and Visually Impaired Computer Users, Inc.
PO Box 13652
Roseville, CA 95661-1352

Computer Users in Speech & Hearing
Department of Speech Pathology & Audiology
University of Southern Alabama
Mobile, AL 3668

DEAFNET
SRI International
333 Ravenswood Avenue
Menlo Park, CA 94025

Computer Periodicals

Closing the Gap (bimonthly)
PO Box 68
Henderson, MN 56044

Computer-Disability News (quarterly). Free
National Easter Seal Society
70 East Lake Street
Chicago, IL 60601

Catalyst (quarterly)
Western Center for Microcomputers in Special Education, Inc.
1259 El Camino Real, Suite 275
Menlo Park, CA 94025

Computer Science Update
National Federation of the Blind
3530 Dupont Avenue
Minneapolis, MN 55412

Online Bulletin Boards

Committee on Personal Computers
and the Handicapped (COPH-2)
(publishes Link and Go
[quarterly])
2030 Irving Park Road
Chicago, IL 60618

National Association of Blind and
Visually Impaired Computer Users
PO Box 1352
Roseville, CA 95661

4-Sights Network
c/o Greater Detroit Society for the
Blind
16625 Grand River
Detroit, MI 48227

Handicapped Educational Exchange
(HEX)
11523 Charlton Drive
Silver Spring, MD 20902

Handicapped Users Database
c/o Compuserve Information Service
5000 Arlington Center
Columbus, OH 43220

Deaf Communication International
PO Box 247
Fayville, MA 01745

Deafnet-West Coast
333 Ravenswood Avenue
Menlo Park, CA 94025

VA Rehabilitation Data Base (available via CompuServe)
Office of Technology Transfer
Veterans Administration
103 South Gay Street
Baltimore, MD 21201

REFERENCES

Apple Computer, Inc. 1988. *Apple Computer Resources in Special Education and Rehabilitation*. Allen, TX: DLM Teaching Resources, Inc.

Apple Computer, Inc. 1987. *Connections: A Guide to Computer Resources for Disabled Children and Adults*. Cupertino, CA: Office of Special Education, Apple Computer, Inc.

Bowe, Frank G. 1984. *Personal Computers and Special Needs*. Berkeley, CA: Sybex, 2 ff.

Computer-Disability News. 1987, Spring. Chicago: National Easter Seal Society 4 (1): 1.

"DEAFNET: A New System of Communication. 1988, Spring. *NARIC Quarterly* 1 (1): 14.

Foulds, Richard, 1986. *Interactive Robotic Aids—One Option for Independent Living: An International Perspective*. Monograph No. 37. New York: World Rehabilitation Fund.

Growick, Bruce, 1983. *Computers in Vocational Rehabilitation: Current Trends and Future Applications*. National Rehabilitation Information Center.

Hagen, Dolores. 1984. *Microcomputer Resource Book for Special Education*. Reston, VA: Reston Publishing Co.

Hall, Marion. 1989. *Abledata Information Sheet*. Newington, CT: Newington Children's Hospital.

IBM. 1988. *Technology for Persons with Disabilities—An Introduction*. Atlanta, GA: National Support Center for Persons with Disabilities.

In the Mainstream. 1988, September/October. Vol. 12 No. 5, MIN Report No. 8, "Legal Update, Technology-Related Assistance for Individuals with Disabilities Act of 1988," Mainstream, Inc.

In the Mainstream. 1989, January/February. Vol. 14, No. 1, MIN Report No. 2, "How Computers Can Assist Individuals with Specific Disabilities," 6.

Information from HEATH. 1986, May. Health Resource Center, American Council in Education, Washington, DC 20036, Vol. 5, No. 2, 1.

Kramer, Krista. 1988, September. "Computer Accessibility for Students with Disabilities." *Academic Computing*, 26–27, 38–39.

MacDonald, Glen. 1988. "A Computerized Case Management System." *Canadian Journal of Rehabilitation* 1 (4): 24–47.

National Easter Seal Society. 1987, Spring. "State Initiatives." Computer Disability News, Chicago, IL 60612. Vol. 4, Issue 1.

National Library Service for the Blind and Physically Handicapped. 1987, September. *Facts: Computer Technology for Handicapped Persons—Some Questions and Answers.* Washington, DC: Library of Congress.

"New Assistive Technology Program on Drawing Board at Ed Department." 1988, August. *Education of the Handicapped* 14 (8): 1, 11.

"New Law Provides Grant Money to States." 1988, September. *New York State Advocate: Newsletter of the State Advocate for the Disabled* 11 (9): 1.

Rehab Brief. 1987. *Robotics and Rehabilitation.* Department of Education, Washington, DC 20202, Vol. X No. 2.

Special and Individual Needs Technology (SAINT). 1987, December. "An Interview with Raymond Kurzweil," Reader's Digest, Inc., McLean, VA 22101, Vol. 1 No. 4.

PART III

Rehabilitation and Special Education: Information for Professionals

Chapter 6
Rehabilitation

Most people with disabilities need a variety of services from birth to adulthood, generally called rehabilitation and defined as a process through which a person reaches his or her highest level of self-sufficiency. For the congenitally disabled, this process might better be defined as habilitation. It is achieved through a combination of medicine and therapy, education, and vocational training. The goal of rehabilitation is the greatest degree of independence for each person, but the word independence means different things to different people. For some, independence may mean education, vocational training, and a job as a productive member of society. For the disabled it may mean a sheltered workshop with opportunities to socialize with others. For some, it may mean work at home and/or simply achieving an independent living situation.

MEDICAL REHABILITATION

Medical rehabilitation has come of age in the past few decades, giving people with disabilities the chance to minimize the destructive effects of disability, whether the result of disease or accident, congenital, or the consequence of deterioration because of age. Rehabilitation medicine seeks to restore normal functioning to the greatest possible degree.

Medical rehabilitation may take place in a comprehensive rehabilitation hospital or in a center that specializes in the treatment of a special disability, such as spinal cord injury, burns, stroke, or other conditions. The special departments involved include physical, occupational, and speech therapy; recreation; psychology; social work; rehabilitation counseling; and prosthetics (devices attached to the body) and orthotics (equipment used by disabled people) now included in the profession of rehabilitation technology (originally called rehabilitation engineering). An important department in many such facilities is "activities of daily living" (ADL), a simulated apartment living area in which a patient can learn to execute the daily tasks that will allow him or her to function independently. Rehabilitation units in general hospitals function in conjunction with the medical departments to provide consulting services.

VOCATIONAL REHABILITATION

Vocational rehabilitation can be defined as a series of actions moving toward a goal. The goal can be full or part-time competitive employment, supported employment, sheltered or voluntary work, self-employment, homebound employment, housekeeping and independent living, or any combination of these. Their purpose is to develop disabled persons' abilities to their highest functioning levels. In the vocational rehabilitation movement, many terms are used that should become familiar to anyone wishing to work in the field as part of the professional rehabilitation team. Prevocational evaluation, work evaluation, work adjustment and job placement, and on-the-job training (OJT) are all used to define the testing and training given to a client in any type of training facility (Cull and Hardy 1975).

The rehabilitation agency is a facility that provides or secures services for the rehabilitation of vocationally disadvantaged persons. The services of such an agency include coordinating and counseling in one or more of the following: evaluation, work adjustment, physical or occupational therapy, the fitting and use of prostheses, and job placement. Rehabilitation agencies include public, state-supported, voluntary local units in hospitals; the Veterans Administration; insurance companies; sheltered workshops; rehabilitation centers; or speech and hearing clinics. "Rehabilitation centers may be independent or part of a hospital that provides an integrated program of medical, psychological, social, and vocational services for rehabilitative purposes" (Garrett and Levine 1973).

A sheltered workshop may be loosely defined as "a nonprofit organization that provides employment to handicapped persons and that is certificated by the wage and hour division of the Department of Labor, as covered by special minimum-wage provisions for at least some of the handicapped persons employed at the organization" (Greenleigh Associates, Inc. 1976). The Vocational Rehabilitation Act Amendments of 1968 substitute "rehabilitation facility" for "workshop." To the layperson or librarian looking for information, these differences in definition can be confusing. Often a rehabilitation facility provides comprehensive services that include those provided by rehabilitation agencies, as well as long-term employment for severely disabled persons in sheltered workshop-type settings. In many cases remedial education is also provided. Sheltered workshops can also be of a transitional type in which the client is offered the opportunity to perform in a work adjustment setting in order to achieve good work habits and performance, attitudes, and knowledge of the world of work itself (Cull and Hardy 1975).

REHABILITATION COUNSELING

Rehabilitation counseling is still a fairly young profession. Like other, older professions, it is now beginning to question whether the rehabilitation generalist can handle the entire job or whether efforts need to be made to analyze the counselor's jobs with an eye toward restructuring and developing new career ladders in favor of support personnel. There was an attempt to fill this vacuum in 1974 with a pilot project first authorized by Congress under the Rehabilitation Act of 1973, which provided for an ombudsman, an advocate, within the state rehabilitation agency, who would, while respecting the client/counselor relationship, assist clients with personal problems. Success led to an expansion of the project and today most states have client assistance programs (CAPS). The rehabilitation counselor must try to coordinate and integrate all the other professional information, develop job opportunities or modified work opportunities, interpret tests to clients, help them with personal problems, understand the contributions of the related disciplines and the functions of the sheltered workshop, as well as other types of rehabilitation facilities.

REHABILITATION TECHNOLOGY

Rehabilitation engineering was a profession that developed during the 1970s and 1980s and was defined as the application of engineering and other sciences in combination with medicine to improve the quality of life of persons with disabilities (Reswick 1980). In the late 1980s it was felt that the designation rehabilitation "engineering" did not include the various types of therapists and specialists in the field of prosthetics and orthotics, and occupational, physical, and speech therapists who work in this field but who are not engineers in the strict sense of that word. These professionals are now updating their skills and broadening their practices to become knowledgeable in the application of new materials and electronic devices. Therefore an attempt is being made to change this term to rehabilitation technologist. No doubt both terms will continue to be used for some time.

Rehabilitation technologists must work with health professionals in health care settings or with rehabilitation counselors in vocational rehabilitation settings. They need to understand the special problems inherent in marketing medical devices and must be prepared to counsel industry before a manufacturing project is undertaken (Reswick). They may be employed by a research and development group or in private industry or other private rehabilitation delivery systems.

PROFESSIONAL ORGANIZATIONS

Since the 1960s the number of professional organizations dedicated to rehabilitation has increased. Additional organizations to those listed below may be found in the *Encyclopedia of Associations*, Katherine Gruber (ed.), *National Organizations of the US*, Vol. I, Gale Research Company, Book Tower, Detroit MI 48226.

The National Rehabilitation Association, 633 South Washington Street, Alexandria, VA 22314, established in 1925, continues to be the major organization in the field. It holds annual meetings and publishes the *Journal of Rehabilitation*.

The American Rehabilitation Counseling Association, 5999 Stevenson Avenue, Alexandria, VA 22304, is a division of the American Association of Counseling and Development (formerly the American Personnel and Guidance Association). It publishes the *Rehabilitation Counseling Bulletin*.

The Association of Rehabilitation Nurses, 2506 Gross Point Road, Evanston, Il 60201, established in 1978 was formed by those now in the profession of Rehabilitation Nursing which was developed by the insurance industry.

The National Council on Rehabilitation Education, c/o Jennifer Madox, 2921 Ermine Way, Farmers Branch, TX 75234, has established standards for credentials in the profession of rehabilitation counseling. It represents academic training programs and research projects related to the field of rehabilitation education.

The National Association of Rehabilitation Facilities (NARF), PO Box 17675, Washington, DC 20015, founded in 1969, combines the National Association of Sheltered Workshops and Homebound Programs (NASWHP) and the Association of Rehabilitation Centers. It is the only organization that represents rehabilitation facilities of all types in the United States today. It maintains records on all rehabilitation facilities and publishes *The Rehabilitation Facilities Sourcebook*, a comprehensive directory, that is kept updated.

The Commission on Accreditation of Rehabilitation Facilities (CARF), 101 North Wilmot, Suite 500, Tucson, AZ 85711, established in 1966, is sponsored by all principal rehabilitation facilities such as NARF, Goodwill Industries, the National Rehabilitation Association (NRA), Spinal Cord Injury Association, American Occupational Therapy Association, American Academy of Physical Medicine and Rehabilitation, the National Association of Jewish Vocational Services, and United Cerebral Palsy for the purpose of establishing standards for operation. It publishes *The Report* (a monthly newsletter) and a standards manual.

The Council of State Administrators for Vocational Rehabilitation (CSAVR), 1055 Thomas Jefferson Street NW, Washington, DC 20007, established in 1940, acts as an advisory body to federal agencies and develops policy affecting rehabilitation.

The National Association of Rehabilitation Professionals in the Private Sector, PO Box, 218, Blue Jay, CA 92317, established in 1977, represents the work of private industry and other private rehabilitation professionals.

The American Congress of Rehabilitation Medicine, 78 East Adams, Chicago, IL 60603, was established in 1921 and publishes the journal *Archives of Physical Medicine*.

The Association for the Advancement of Rehabilitation Technology (formerly Rehabilitation Engineering Society of North America, RESNA), 401 Connecticut Avenue NW, Suite 700, Washington, DC 20036, was established in 1980 in response to the development of rehabilitation engineering research as a new field employing science and technology to improve the quality of life for people with disabilities.

The President's Committee on Employment of People with Disabilities was established in 1945 by joint resolution of Congress to provide information about maximum employment opportunities for people who are physically disabled, mentally retarded, and mentally ill. It publishes the periodical *Worklife*.

LEGISLATION OF THE 1970s

The Rehabilitation Act of 1973

The year 1973 was significant in the history of rehabilitation in the United States. The ninety-third Congress passed a set of rehabilitation amendments that completely recodified the Vocational Rehabilitation Act as originally passed in 1920 and subsequently enlarged in 1943, 1954, 1965, and 1968. The two major thrusts of the act were to place emphasis on expanding services to the most severely handicapped individuals and to place the responsibility for the ultimate rehabilitation of people with disabilities squarely on the shoulders of society as a whole. The ultimate effect of this far-reaching legislation has yet to be felt, but in time it will and must result in improving the quality of life for all disabled people and bringing them into the mainstream of society (PL 93-112, 1973).

The bill was originally written with five titles. Title 5, in four sections, is the most well-known to the general public, and Section 504, in particular, is a revolutionary breakthrough, a benchmark for all the disabled people of this country. It states as follows: "No otherwise qualified handicapped individual in the United States, as defined in Section 7(6), shall, solely by reason of his handicap, be excluded from participation in, be denied the benefits of, or be subjected to discrimination under any program or activity receiving Federal financial assistance" (PL 93-112 1973).

In addition, Section 501: Provides for the hiring of disabled federal civil service employees under an affirmative action program, Section 502: Establishes an Architectural and Transportation Barriers Compliance Board, and Section 503: The "affirmative action" clause, provides that any company with federal contracts in excess of $2,500 must employ qualified handicapped individuals.

The following year in Section 111(a) of the Rehabilitation Act Amendments of 1974 (PL 93-516), Congress amended the definition of "handicapped individual" for purposes of Section 504 and the other provisions of Titles 4 and 5 of the Rehabilitation Act so that the definition is no longer limited to the dimensions of employability as it was. For the purposes of Section 504, a handicapped individual is defined as "any person who (a) has a physical or mental impairment which substantially limits one or more of such person's major life activities, (b) has a record of such an impairment, or (c) is regarded as having such an impairment." This makes it clear that Section 504 was intended to forbid discrimination against all individuals with handicaps, regardless of their need for or ability to benefit from vocational rehabilitation services.

On April 28, 1977, Joseph A. Califano, then secretary of HEW, issued the regulations for Section 504 which had been written into law in 1973 (*Federal Register* 1977). Although the law limited compliance to recipients of federal funds, the American way of life ensures that most schools, universities, libraries, businesses, and even museums are recipients of some federal funds in the form of grants of some kind. In brief, the Califano regulations provided, among other regulations, that all new facilities must be barrier-free; programs in existing facilities must be made accessible; employers must hire the handicapped if reasonable accommodations can be made; and handicapped children must receive free education appropriate to their needs (see also PL 94-142).

As interpreted in the regulations, Section 504 became the "equal access" law, and the word access the catchword for the 1970s to describe what people who are disabled want—access to education, employment, recreation and travel, and independent living opportunities. Books have been written using the word access in the title, and the 1970s will be known as the time when the United States began to grant equal access to a normal life, under the law, to people of this country who are disabled.

On August 14, 1978, four policy interpretations were issued by the Office of Civil Rights of the Department of HEW to interpret further the department's regulations issued under Section 504 of the Rehabilitation Act of 1973. These regulations have direct bearing on libraries, which are mentioned as an example. Here the policy interpretation of "program accessibility" is expanded to allow flexibility in selecting means of compliance. Extensive structural changes are therefore not necessary if other methods can be found to make services available to the mobility-impaired. Libraries, for example, may deliver books by bookmobile or special clerical aide to an "alternate site." The regulations go on to say that priority should be given to methods that offer handicapped and nonhandicapped people programs in equivalent settings.

A knowledge of the range of resources—professional reading guidance, periodical reading rooms, information and referral services, club meeting facilities and other programs offered by the typical library—should make plain the paradox implicit in these two statements. It is hoped, therefore, that librarians will not be satisfied with the option of alternative service mentioned in these regulations and will recognize that people with disabilities need access, to the greatest extent possible, to the library premises.

Developmental Disability: Definition

Since the late 1960s and early 1970s the concept of the least restrictive environment has been the principle used to design services for people with disabilities, including people with developmental disabilities. The Developmental Disabilities Assistance and Bill of Rights Act (PL 94-102) lent support to this principle by mandating that services be provided to people with developmental disabilities in the setting "least restrictive of the person's personal liberty" (Taylor, Biklen and Knoll 1987).

The Developmental Disabilities Services and Facilities Construction legislation of 1970 (PL 91-517) was a landmark in that it substituted the term "developmental disability" for "mental retardation." Eligibility was expanded to a broader class which was defined as persons with "a disability attributable to mental retardation, cerebral palsy, epilepsy, or another neurological condition of an individual found . . . to be closely related to mental retardation, or to require treatment similar to that required for mentally retarded individuals. . . ." (Burgdorf 1980).

PL 94-103 amended the 1970 legislation in several important ways. First, it required states to spend at least 30 percent of their formula grants on deinstitutionalization activities and to incorporate deinstitutionalization into the state plans required by the statute; second, it included a bill of rights for people who are developmentally disabled and third it added autism as a developmental disability (Castellani 1987).

The 1978 Rehabilitation Amendments (PL 95-602) do not enumerate a list of specific impairments, but change the definitions from categories to functional definitions. Developmental disability requires substantial functional limitations in three or more areas of major life activities. PL 95-602 also retains the requirement that the disability arise before the person reaches the age of 18 and continues past the age of 22.

LEGISLATION IN THE 1980s

Public Law 98-221

On February 22, 1984, President Reagan signed Public Law 98-221, the Rehabilitation Act Amendments of 1984, designed to revise and extend the Rehabilitation Act of 1973. This legislation provided an extension in state grant funding through fiscal year 1986, and extended all other programs for three more years. It established a separate authority for the Helen Keller National Center for Deaf-Blind Youth and Adults, established the National Council on the Handicapped as an independent agency within the federal government, and required the development of standards for evaluation of existing independent living centers and projects with industry.

Public Law 99-506

Public Law 99-506 was signed on October 21, 1986, to extend and improve the Rehabilitation Act of 1973. Two provisions to the act signal exciting new changes in the concept of service to people with disabilities. The first is an increased emphasis on rehabilitation engineering and technology. As defined in the Act, the term rehabilitation engineering means "the systematic application of technology, engineering methodologies, or scientific principles to meet the needs of and address the barriers confronted by individuals with handicaps (disabilities) in areas which include education, rehabilitation, employment, transportation, independent living, and recreation." In addition, the National Institute on Disability and Rehabilitation Research is charged with the development and efficient distribution of new technologies (*Computer-Disability* Spring 1987).

The second exciting feature is Section 508 (a)(1) of Title VI, entitled "Electronic Equipment Accessibility" which has been explained in Chapter 5.

LEGISLATION: 1988 AND 1989

In 1988 a new amendment to the Rehabilitation Act of 1973 was signed into law. PL 100-630 changes "National Employ the Handicapped Week" to "National Disability Employment Awareness Month" and gives the President's Committee on Employment of People with Disabilities the authority to accept money and other contributions. It also changes the name of the National Council on the Handicapped to the National Council on Disability.

Other bills passed in 1988 include the National Deafness and Other Communication Disorders Act. This law (PL 100-553) establishes a National Institute on Deafness and Other Communication Disorders within the National Institute of Health. Also, the Protection and Advocacy for Mentally Ill Individuals (PL 100-509) establishes separate legislation to provide protection and advocacy services for persons who are mentally ill (*New York State Advocate* 1988).

In September 1988 the Senate Subcommittee on the Handicapped and the House Subcommittee on Select Education held hearings on the proposed Americans with Disabilities Act of 1988, S.2345 and H.R. 4498. Over 200 supporters of the legislation packed a Senate chamber to listen to testimony of persons with disabilities who believed that the act would help mainstream them into American society. The bill would outlaw discrimination on the basis of handicap by state and local governments, certain employers and housing providers, the broadcasting and communications industry, and in public accommodations and transportation (*Handicapped Americans Report* 1988).

Although the bill had strong bipartisan backing in both houses in Congress and was endorsed by more than 50 national organizations representing people with a wide variety of disabilities, and was supported also by the Leadership Conference on Civil Rights, and both presidential candidates, it was not enacted during the 100th Session of Congress. (*Mainstream* 1988). [As of late 1989, it had only passed the Senate.]

CURRENT GOVERNMENT STRUCTURE

On October 17, 1979, the Department of Health, Education and Welfare was split into two departments, creating a separate Department of Education and a Department of Health and Human Services. At the present time the Department of Education consists of six major offices, covering elementary and secondary education, postsecondary education, vocational education, educational research and improvement, civil rights, and the Office of Special Education and Rehabilitative Services (OSERS). OSERS also includes the National Institute on Disability and Rehabilitation Research, formerly the National Institute of Handicapped Research. In addition, the Department of Education is responsible for the laws relating to Gallaudet University, the American Printing House for the Blind, the National Technical Institute for the Deaf in Rochester, New York, the model secondary school for the deaf (Kendall School), the Architectural and Transportation Barriers Compliance Board, and the National Council on Disability. The Office for Developmental Disabilities, the President's Committee on Mental Retardation, and the Assistant Secretary for Human Development have remained with the Department of Health and Human Services.

The Rehabilitation Services Administration (RSA) within OSERS has direct responsibility for supervising the state offices of vocational rehabilitation. These departments are funded by the federal government with monies earmarked for client service, used in a network of local offices staffed by rehabilitation counselors working directly with disabled clients. These clients may be physically, mentally, or emotionally disabled, or deaf or hearing impaired. Clients with visual impairments are served by a separate network in most states. Any person with a substantial employment disability who can become employable within a reasonable period of time may be eligible.

Employment may be defined as competitive or sheltered employment or homemaking, and these interpretations have been broadened to include the achievement of some form of independent living and also the attempt to employ new technologies that enable the person with severe physical and mental disabilities to become employable. Guidelines set up in the 1970s mandate an emphasis on individuals who are most severely disabled.

Expenses for some services are on a shared basis with the client. The Office of Vocational Rehabilitation works closely with departments of mental hygiene, social service, and labor, the Workmen's Compensation Board, health and correction facilities, and many public and private voluntary service agencies. Usually young adults who have come out of special schools or programs are referred immediately to their local Office of Vocational Rehabilitation (OVR) for further service. Persons who become disabled later in life should be informed that they may apply to the OVR office nearest their homes by letter, phone, or in person. Local offices are listed in the telephone directory; see Appendix C for state listings.

In addition to the departments of vocational rehabilitation administered by the individual states, there is a rehabilitation network of federal offices organized in 10 regions throughout the United States, Puerto Rico, and the Virgin Islands (see Appendix B). These offices are the local monitoring agencies of federal government monies. The states spend the dollars allocated to them, but must report on that money to the regional OSERS office. Certain specific projects are originated directly at the federal level and continue to be administered by the federal government, although the region is kept informed.

NATIONAL INSTITUTE ON DISABILITY AND REHABILITATION RESEARCH (NIDRR)

The National Institute of Handicapped Research was created in 1978 by Public Law 95-602. The Rehabilitation Act Amendments of 1986 (PL 99-506) changed the Institute's name to the National Institute on Disability and Rehabilitation Research. NIDRR is located within the Rehabilitation Services Administration and is responsible for allocation of funding for research in all areas of rehabilitation of the disabled, and of dissemination of the information generated by this research (NIDRR n.d.). Information is disseminated through newsletters, regional conferences and/or the development and distribution of technical assistance guidelines. Areas of research investigation might include: studies and analyses of industrial, vocational, social, physical, psychological, economic, and other factors affecting the rehabilitation of disabled individuals. Research activities include international research, joint projects with other federal agencies and with private industry, research related to children with disabilities and the elderly, and projects in rural areas. To carry out this research the Institute administers Rehabilitation Research and Training Centers (RRTC) located in many areas of the country and specializing in work with individuals with different types of disabilities. Most centers also offer vocational rehabilitation services to ensure that a continuity of rehabilitation care is maintained after clients are discharged.

NIDRR also supports Rehabilitation Engineering Centers (REC) in the United States and abroad to develop methods of applying advances in medical technology and scientific achievement to the problems of persons with disabilities. Each center is encouraged to establish official working relationships with institutions of higher learning in medicine, engineering and related sciences.

A significant part of the work of NIDRR is to disseminate its research findings to disabled persons and the rehabilitation community. In order to focus attention on outstanding examples of "grassroots" programs in particular core areas, NIDRR currently funds four Regional Diffusion Network projects (RDN) located in Regions I, II, VI and IX (Liberti 1987).

Also sponsored by NIDRR is the publication *Rehab Briefs*, extremely useful four-page distillations of topics of current interest in the rehabilitation field. They are available free from National Institute on Disability and Rehabilitation Research, US Department of Education, Mailstop 2305, 400 Maryland Avenue, Washington, DC 20202.

NATIONAL REHABILITATION INFORMATION CENTER (NARIC)

NIDRR also administers the work of the National Rehabilitation Information Center (NARIC) which has recently moved from its location at the Catholic University Library School to be administered by Macrosystems, Inc. Its address is NARIC, 8455 Colesville Road, Suite 935, Silver Spring, MD 20910-3319. Its toll-free telephone number is 800-34-NARIC.

NARIC collects a wide range of information about rehabilitation from many sources, and updates and maintains it. Much of this information can be identified through its bibliographic database REHABDATA. NARIC collects NIDRR research reports and other reports and papers, periodicals, audio-visuals, publications from the RRTCs and RECs, pamphlets, and *Rehab Briefs* (see below). NARIC accepts reference requests by mail, electronic mail, phone, or walk in. Patrons visiting the facility have access to all resources in the library. Customized responses to requests involve database searches, library research, and referrals to experts and supporting agencies. NARIC is open weekdays (except federal holidays) from 8 am to 8 pm. Some services are available free of charge while others are on a cost-recovery basis. NARIC publishes *NARIC Quarterly, a Newsletter of Disability and Rehabilitation Research and Resources.*

REGIONAL REHABILITATION CONTINUING EDUCATION PROGRAMS (RRCEPS)

In the early 1970s a network of service called RRCEPS was established directly under the Rehabilitation Services Administration (RSA). Its purpose was to meet the continuing education needs of rehabilitation professionals. Fourteen training offices were set up across the country in each of the RSA regions. Staff members of these agencies are professionals, trained to understand the needs of rehabilitation counselors. Periodic meetings with state agency directors and with members of professional organizations such as NRA, NCRE, and ARCA are held and committees formed to help with specific training needs. Workshops are generally organized throughout the region, training packages are developed, and annotated bibliographies are prepared.

Some of these continuing education programs maintain resource libraries, which are made up of training modules developed by the various RRCEPS. Oriented toward providing training in job counseling skills, they perform a valuable service for the rehabilitation counselor in counseling theory. To add to their service resources, libraries which consist of professional training materials could be expanded to include information on daily living needs of clients (as outlined in Chapter 4) as well as a realistic picture of the job availability market. A listing of all of the RRCEPS may be obtained from: The Rehabilitation Services Administration, Switzer Building, 330 C Street, SW, Washington, DC 20036.

THE HELEN KELLER CENTER

The Rehabilitation Act of 1973 (PL 93-112) made provision for the establishment of a national center for deaf-blind youth and adults, to be called the Helen Keller Center and to be administered under the auspices of the originally designated National Institute of Handicapped Research. The 1984 amendments (PL 98-221) established a separate authority for the Helen Keller Center, and the 1986 Rehabilitation Act (PL 99-506) renewed this mandate. Headquarters for this facility, which had operated on a smaller scale as a function of the Industrial Home for the Blind, was dedicated in October 1976 (PL 93-112). The main building, in Sands Point, Long Island, was named in memory of Mary E. Switzer.

The center provides facilities for housing and training for up to 50 deaf-blind individuals over the age of 18. Extensive evaluative and rehabilitative services include training in orientation and mobility, communication, and life skills, for periods ranging from several months to several years. A major effort is made to develop and assist in the appropriate placement of clients in work settings when training is completed.

A nationwide network of field services through nine regional offices provides consultation and technical assistance to deaf-blind persons and their families, locating, assisting, and refering deaf-blind individuals to the most appropriate program for comprehensive services. Field offices and headquarters offer training to new and prospective professionals who plan to work with the deaf-blind population.

A computerized national register of deaf-blind persons is maintained at Sands Point. The periodical *NAT-CENT NEWS* is published three times a year and is available from the Helen Keller National Center, 111 Middle Neck Road, Sands Point, New York 11050. Its editor, Robert J. Smithdas, who has been deaf and blind since before the age of five years, is assistant director of the center. He has written eloquently of the special isolation caused by the loss of both sight and hearing and of the neglect that deaf-blind people have, until very recently, experienced in society (Smithdas 1979). The center also produced two captioned films, "Raising the Curtain" and "The World at His Fingertips," and publishes the *Directory of Agencies Servicing the Deaf-Blind and Curriculum Models* (Russell 1986).

Now operating at the center is TAC, Technical Assistance Center/Helen Keller National Center, which provides technical assistance in support of comprehensive and coordinated services to facilitate the transition of youths who are deaf-blind, upon attaining age 22, from education to age-appropriate community-based activities, including work and living options, in the least restrictive environment (TAC/HKNC). Regional meetings, conferences, workshops, on-site and off-site consultations, in-service training for parents and paraprofessionals (short term), and information and referral services are provided.

THE NATIONAL COUNCIL ON DISABILITY

The National Council on Disability is an independent federal agency comprising 15 members appointed by the President of the United States and confirmed by the Senate. It is charged with reviewing all laws, programs, and policies of the federal government affecting individuals, and making such recommendations as it deems necessary to the President, the Congress, the Secretary of the Department of Education, the Commissioner of the Rehabilitation Services Administration, and the Director of the National Institute on Disability and Rehabilitation Research.

The council was directed to submit to the President and Congress, by February of 1986, a report to assess all federal laws and programs affecting persons with disabilities, with legislative recommendations. This report was entitled "Toward Independence," and a second report entitled "On the Threshold of Independence" was submitted in January 1988. The second report details progress on legislative recommendations from "Toward Independence." Both of these reports are available from the National Council on Disability, 800 Independence Avenue SW, Suite 814, Washington, DC 20591.

CLEARINGHOUSE ON THE HANDICAPPED

Within the Office of Special Education and Rehabilitative Services, Room 3132, Switzer Building, Washington, DC 20202-2319, the Clearinghouse, created by the Rehabilitation Act of 1973, responds to inquiries and researches and documents information operations serving the field of disability on the national, state, and local levels. It offers information, particularly in the areas of federal funding for programs serving people with disabilities and federal legislation affecting the handicapped community. The Clearinghouse offers *OSERS News in Print*, a newsletter, a *Summary of Existing Legislation Affecting Persons with Disabilities* (August 1988), and a *Pocket Guide to Federal Help for Individuals with Disabilities.*

REFERENCES

Burgdorf, Robert L., Jr., ed. 1980. *The Legal Rights of Handicapped Persons, Cases, Materials & Text.* Baltimore and London: Paul H. Brookes Publishing Co., 30, 31.

Castellani, Paul J. 1987. *The Political Economy of Developmental Disabilities.* Baltimore and London: Paul H. Brookes Publishing Co., 24, 25.

Closing the Gap. 1987, February/March, 5 (6).

Closing the Gap. 1987, December; 1988, January, 6 (5).

Computer-Disability. 1987, Spring. National Easter Seal Society, 4 (1).

Cull, John G., and Hardy, Richard E. 1972, 1975. *Vocational Rehabilitation: Profession and Process.* American Lecture Series in Social and Rehabilitation Psychology. Springfield, IL: Charles C. Thomas, 14, 18–19, 35, 49, 505.

Disability Programs (formerly *Handicapped Americans Report*) May 5, 1988, Business Publishers, Inc., Silver Spring, MD, 83.

Federal Register. May 4, 1977, 22676–702

Garrett, James F., and Levine, Edna S. 1973. *Rehabilitation Practices with the Physically Disabled.* New York: Columbia University Press, 6, 7, 14.

Greenleigh Associates, Inc. *The Role of the Sheltered Workshop in the Rehabilitation of the Severely Handicapped,* 1976, November, 8.

In the Mainstream. 1978, November/December. Vol. 3, No. 4. Mainstream, Inc.

In the Mainstream. 1988, November/December. MIN Report No. 7. "Americans with Disabilities Act Gets Hearing Endorsements," Mainstream Inc.

Liberti, Ellen J. 1986, Fall. *Keys to Creative Growth: Regional Diffusion Networks, in Question.*Washington, DC: NARIC.

New York State Advocate. 1988, Vol. 11, No. 12.

The 1986 Directory of National Information Sources on Handicapping Conditions and Related Services. 1986, June. Winchester, MA: Harold Russell Association, Inc.

Reswick, James B. 1980. "Rehabilitation Engineering." *Annual Review of Rehabilitation.* Vol. 1. New York: Springer Publishing Company, Inc., 55–79.

Smithdas, Robert, J. 1979, January. "Lest We Forget." In *NAT-CENT News* 19 (2), 1–4.

Taylor, Steven J., Klein, Douglas B., and Knoll, James (eds.). 1987. *Community Integration for People with Severe Disabilities.* New York: Teachers College Press.

Chapter 7
Concepts in Rehabilitation: Past, Present, Future

In the past 25 years tremendous changes have taken place in the lives of people with disabilities. The field of rehabilitation, an amalgam of public and private agencies, has grown into a vast network, continually attempting to push back the barriers, both medical and vocational, that prevent disabled people from reaching their fullest potential. Contact agencies existing in most states include vocational rehabilitation offices, client assistance programs (CAPS), governors' committees, protection and advocacy agencies, special education agencies, state parent representatives, and model Independent Living Centers (ILC). Some of these agencies will be discussed in other chapters.

This chapter will trace historically the ways in which concepts have developed over the years and changed during the 1980s. It will highlight the most important movements now in the forefront of the rehabilitation field and predict certain trends for the future. As a start, a look at just a few of the key organizations in the private sector that play a role in the field of rehabilitation is in order.

PRIVATE ORGANIZATIONS

Many private organizations contribute to the work of advocacy and information for and about people with disabilities; some were established early in the century and others were formed during the 1970s and 1980s. It is not possible to list all of them, although many are mentioned in other chapters of this book. The 1986 *Directory of National Information Sources on Handicapping Conditions and Related Services*, published by Harold Russell Associates, Inc., was developed under contract with NIDRR. This fourth edition contains up-to-date information (the third edition was published in 1982) on 398 organizations, listed in categories including advocacy organizations, federal government, professional and trade organizations, schools and clinics, and much more. It is an invaluable source of information. For some of the following descriptive material the author is indebted to this directory.

The National Easter Seal Society Incorporated, 70 East Lake Street, Chicago, IL 60601, founded in 1919, is the nation's oldest and largest voluntary health agency serving disabled people. Easter Seal societies administer their programs through some 2,000 separately incorporated affiliates. These local offices operate rehabilitation and treatment centers, sheltered workshops, resident and day camps, hospitals and other services and offer physical, occupational, vocational and speech therapy, vocational evaluation, testing and counseling, special education programs, and social clubs. The Easter Seal Research Foundation makes grants to finance investigation in fields that directly relate to the needs of their clients. Their professional journal *Rehabilitation Literature,* regrettably, has ceased publication. Monographs and other materials are published, however, and an annual publication catalog is available free of charge. Local Easter Seal offices are listed in telephone directories.

The National Clearing House of Rehabilitation Materials is part of the Rehabilitation Counselor Training Program at Oklahoma State University. Since 1962, it has disseminated such materials as abstracts, monographs, articles, final reports, booklets, audio and videotapes, and slide presentations in the areas of rehabilitation and special education to professionals in the field. These professionals are asked to notify the clearinghouse about newly developed materials. All items received are listed in *MEMO,* distributed quarterly. Current procedures for dissemination of materials are available on request. The clearinghouse also produces materials of its own.

The March of Dimes Birth Defects Foundation, 1275 Mamaroneck Avenue, White Plains, NY 10605, was originally founded in 1938 by Franklin Roosevelt as the National Foundation for Infantile Paralysis. Since that time, its scope has grown to include all birth defects, and its name has been changed to reflect that growth; 2,500 chapters nationwide are listed in local telephone directories. The goal of the foundation is to prevent birth defects, and numerous programs in medical research and education are funded toward this end. Information about birth defects is provided to the general public and professionals. Brochures, pamphlets, fact sheets, bibliographies and other materials are available on request. The latest scientific findings on birth defects are transmitted to schools of medicine and nursing and other medical centers, hospitals, and health professionals. The foundation publishes the *International Directory of Genetic Services,* a comprehensive listing of medical centers in the United States and other countries which provide genetic counseling; the *Birth Defects Atlas* and *Compendium,* the first book to standardize names and descriptions of nearly 800 congenital anomalies; and *Syndrome Identification,* an international journal on congenital disorders. Information may be obtained by calling or writing foundation headquarters in White Plains, New York.

The Academy of Dentistry for the Handicapped (ADH), 211 E. Chicago Avenue, 21st Floor, Chicago, IL 60611, is an organization of dentists, dental hygienists, and allied professionals. It provides educational services to professionals and information and referrals to persons with disabilities who are seeking dental treatment. Written and audiovisual materials are available. A bimonthly journal and a referral directory of dentists who treat disabled persons are available. One of the practical medical rehabilitation problems facing disabled people and the parents of disabled children is the care of teeth. Many dentists are not familiar with the manner in which various orthopedic disabilities react on their structure and condition.

Accreditation Council for Services for Mentally Retarded and Other Developmentally Disabled Persons (ACMRDD), 4435 Wisconsin Avenue NW, Suite 202, Washington, DC 20016, is a national, independent, voluntary accrediting body for agencies serving persons with developmental disabilities. Established in 1969 as a component of the Joint Commission on Accreditation of Hospitals, the Council was reorganized as an independent, not-for-profit corporation in 1979. Its 10 sponsoring organizations include the major developmental disability advocacy groups. The council responds to questions, offers workshops and consultation to help agencies implement accreditation standards, and provides information concerning requirements for quality services for developmentally disabled persons.

The national headquarters of the **Association for Retarded Citizens of the United States (ARC)**, located at 2501 Avenue J, Arlington, TX 76006, has as its goals to prevent mental retardation, find cures, assist those who are mentally retarded in their daily living, and provide support for their families. ARC sponsors research studies on prevention and cure, training volunteers who work with mentally retarded persons, developing demonstration models for educational, training, and residential facilities, developing advocacy systems, and furthering employment opportunities for persons who are mentally retarded. ARC has 1,300 state and local units, providing a variety of direct services, including day care, sheltered workshops, preschool programs, and transportation services. ARC answers inquiries, publishes pamphlets, monographs, audiovisual materials, and newsletters, and provides access to ARCNET, an electronic mail network. Some materials are available in Spanish.

American Deafness and Rehabilitation Association (ADARA), 814 Thayer Avenue, Silver Spring, MD 20910, is an organization of professionals and community persons active in the field of deafness in all areas of rehabilitation. It has two affiliate organizations, the National Association of State Agencies for the Deaf (NASAD) and the American Society of Deaf Social Workers (ASDSW). ADARA sponsors forums, conferences, and workshops, offers free information on all topics of deafness, careers, university programs, job opportunities, and publishes the quarterly *Journal of Rehabilitation of the Deaf* as well as a bimonthly *ADARA Newsletter* and occasional special publications and monographs. A listing of publications is available from the national office. (See Chapter 9 for additional organizations on deafness, as well as the *Encyclopedia of Associations* or the *Directory of National Information Sources on Handicapping Conditions and Related Services*) (Russell 1986).

American Foundation for the Blind (AFB), 15 West 16th Street, New York, NY 10011, was established in 1921 to help the blind and visually impaired acquire improved rehabilitation services and educational and employment opportunities, and to aid those persons in daily living activities. AFB provides legislative consultation to government agencies and advisory services to local agencies and schools. The foundation manufactures or adapts and sells more than 400 devices, on which they have done technological research, including braille watches and games for adults and children. AFB records and manufactures about 500 talking books per year for the Library of Congress, National Library Service for the Blind and Physically Handicapped (see Chapter 9). AFB publishes pamphlets and films about blindness, deaf-blindness and visual impairments, and eye disorders. Single copies of public education materials are free in print form. Films may be rented or purchased. AFB publishes the *Directory of Agencies Serving the Visually Handicapped in the United States* and the *International Guide to Aids and Appliances for Blind and Visually Impaired Persons*, as well as the *Journal of Visual Impairment and Blindness*.

National Federation of the Blind, 1800 Johnson Street, Baltimore, MD 21230 is a federation of 50 (plus DC) state and 400 local organizations of individuals who are blind. It monitors legislation; evaluates present programs; promotes needed services; conducts seminars; supports research, and publishes results. It publishes the *Braille Monitor*.

There are many other organizations serving visually impaired persons and they may be located in the *Encyclopedia of Associations* or the *Directory of National Information Sources on Handicapping Conditions and Related Services* (Russell).

The National Spinal Cord Injury Association, 600 West Cumming Park, Suite 2000, Woburn, MA 01801, is a voluntary health agency. It encourages research on all aspects of paraplegia; refers individual paraplegics to the best available sources of care; publishes the newsletter *Spinal Cord Injury Life*; distributes brochures, pamphlets, and fact sheets; organizes seminars and conferences; and permits on-site use of its holdings.

Paralyzed Veterans of America (PVA), 801 18th Street NW, Washington, DC 20006, is a national organization founded in 1947 and chartered by Congress in 1971. It is charged with the responsibility of representing veterans in their claims before the Veterans Administration. PVA is a federation of autonomous local chapters, which join with the national organization in an attempt to improve veterans' benefits and achieve such goals as barrier-free design. PVA's services to veterans include overseeing hospital and rehabilitation treatment; locating suitable housing; encouraging driver education programs and adapted mass transportation; adjudicating claims before federal, state, and local agencies; and supporting legislation to assist all disabled individuals. PVA also has a research foundation to review requests for funding and award grants, particularly in the area of spinal cord research. Publications issued by PVA include *Paraplegia News*, a monthly magazine; the magazine *Sports 'N Spokes*, and monographs on selected topics. PVA also has available a variety of access information bulletins on such topics as adaptable housing, doors and entrances, elevators and lifts, kitchens, ramps, stairs and floor treatments, and many more. Originally published by the National Center for a Barrier Free Environment, which no longer exists, these are very valuable, offering concise information. Write to national headquarters or contact a local chapter. These are listed in telephone directories under slightly different names, such as Eastern PVA, in New York City.

To service persons with severe speech impairments, **TRACE Research and Development Center for the Severely Communicatively Handicapped**, is located at the University of Wisconsin at Madison. Its goal is to provide individuals who are severely physically disabled and speech-impaired with some form of communication. A number of centers in the United States and abroad are working to develop devices in this area, and exciting breakthroughs are taking place. *Communication Outlook*, a quarterly newsletter about new developments in communication aids and techniques, is published by TRACE in conjunction with the Artificial Language Laboratory of Michigan State University. It is available through the International Society for Augmentative and Alternative Communication (ISAAC), which also publishes the *Journal of Augmentative and Alternative Communication*.

The American Association for the Advancement of Science, Project on Disability is an interesting prototype for possible similar projects in other professional fields. Think of the opportunities that could be opened to qualified people who are disabled if all professional organizations began to develop activities in this area. Established by a group within the American Association for the Advancement of Science, the project is designed to explore the barriers that deter people with disabilities from participation in education and employment opportunities in science. It develops programs to improve the opportunities in science education to youth, to train science educators, and to inventory science resources for students who are disabled. Accessibility to professional meetings is a special objective. Information on careers in science is made available to interested students who also can be referred to an individual in the association who both has expertise related to his or her career choice and is a person with a similar disability who can give the student advice and support. Their directory of disabled scientists has been republished (1987 edition) and is available from the association at 1333 H Street NW, Washington, DC 20005.

Just One Break (JOB), 373 Park Avenue, New York NY 10016, was founded in 1949 by Eleanor Roosevelt, Orin Lehman, and Bernard Baruch, and was incorporated in New York City in 1952. Its original purpose was to assist disabled veterans returning from World War II in rejoining the work force. Its services were later expanded to aid all handicapped adults in achieving employment in business and industry. No fees are charged, and JOB has an impressive placement rate. Although JOB's activities are in the greater New York area, it distributes information about its operations nationwide to rehabilitation facilities and educational institutions. It conducts research and demonstration projects in the area of placement of disabled people, answers telephone and mail inquiries, refers inquiries to other information centers, and provides brochures, pamphlets, and fact sheets.

Mainstream, Inc., 1030 15th Street NW, Suite 1010, Washington, DC 20005, is a national nonprofit organization founded in 1975 for the purpose of increasing employment opportunities for people with disabilities by working with employers and the disabled community to develop cost-effective solutions to problems inherent in the process of mainstreaming into the workplace. Information services and technical assistance are offered on a consulting basis. Mainstream conducts conferences on job analysis, reasonable accommodations, physical accessibility, legal concerns, and interviewing and recruiting techniques. Since 1983, Mainstream has operated Project LINK, a national job development and placement model that matches qualified applicants with available jobs in Washington, DC, and Dallas, Texas. A bimonthly newsletter, *In the Mainstream*, reports on programs, relevant legislation and administrative and judicial activities. The Mainstream Information Network responds to inquiries on all handicap employment issues. Mainstream has produced a manual for company trainers, *Successful Mainstreaming of Disabled People into the Workplace*, as well as pamphlets on specific disabilities, medical standards in employment, insurance, and section 503. Most pamphlet information is available on cassette. Publications and services can be purchased individually or on an annual subscription basis.

The National Organization on Disability (NOD), 910 16th Street NW, Suite 600, Washington, DC 20006, is a privately funded successor organization to the US Council for the International Year of Disabled Persons. Established in 1982, it works to support grassroots community-based efforts to improve the lives of disabled people. To date there are 50 state chapters and approximately 1,700 local chapters of NOD. An annual program is sponsored for community partners at which cash prizes are awarded for progress made toward integrating citizens with disabilities into community life. NOD encourages organizations, corporations, and others to support local efforts, emphasizing partnership between able-bodied and individuals with disabilities in developing cooperative programs.

The Association for Persons with Severe Handicaps (TASH), 7010 Roosevelt Way NE, Seattle, WA 98115, (206) 523-8446, is an organization serving people with severe physical handicaps and profound mental retardation. Formerly the American Association for the Education of the Severely/Profoundly Handicapped, the organization was founded in 1974 to respond to changes in legislation affecting persons with disabilities and address their needs for services. TASH chapters are being chartered at local levels to facilitate increased involvement in local concerns and to date has chartered or is developing chapters in 33 states and several Canadian provinces. TASH publishes a monthly newsletter, and a quarterly journal. Additional publications include four volumes of *Teaching the Severely Handicapped*, and *Methods of Instruction with Severely Handicapped Students*. A publications list is available on request. TASH holds an annual conference, maintains lists of parents, and has a parent-to-parent network.

Founded in 1952 by Dr. Henry Viscardi, the **Human Resources Center** in Albertson, NY 11507, has been a pioneer in the rehabilitation and special education fields. The author has been associated with the center for 25 years. The Center is composed of five coordinated units: (l) Abilities Inc., which runs a work demonstration center that employs disabled adults in industrial operations; (2) Human Resources School, which offers tuition-free education to over 230 severely disabled children; (3) the Research and Training Institute, which conducts research relating to persons with severe disabilities and employment; (4) Rehabilitation Services, which conducts programs of work evaluation, training, job development, and career placement for persons with disabilities; and (5) The Industry-Labor Council (see below). The information dissemination arm of the Human Resources Center is the Rehabilitation Research Library. Functions of the library are described in detail in Chapter 11. Publications available from the center include titles on employment, placement, attitudes, and driver education. Recent publications include a handbook for professionals on vocational rehabilitation for learning-disabled adults and a reference manual for managers responsible for implementing corporate affirmative action and equal employment opportunity programs. Any lay or professional person may request information from the center, and requests are received from consumers, professionals in education and vocational rehabilitation, and members of business and industry.

REHABILITATION IN THE 1980s

During the decade of the 1980s several major concepts have emerged to add to the many rehabilitation services offered and to the groups of disabled persons who are served. These concepts which have characterized the current rehabilitation movement are supported employment; participation of the private sector in the field of rehabilitation; rehabilitation of clients with traumatic brain injury (TBI); rehabilitation of clients with severe learning disabilities (SLD); and rehabilitation of the elderly and the homebound.

Supported Employment

Sheltered Workshop

The Forerunner: Traditionally the sheltered workshop played an important role in the vocational rehabilitation of people with severe disabilities. In 1974, Greenleigh Associates was contracted by the Department of Health, Education and Welfare to conduct a congressionally mandated evaluation of sheltered workshops in the United States [Entitled "The Role of the Sheltered Workshop in the Rehabilitation of the Severely Handicapped" (Greenleigh 1976)]. The Greenleigh study was a benchmark in the sheltered workshop program in that it summarized and evaluated the state of this movement as it has developed in the United States.

The successful workshop needed to be concerned with the interests of its clients and to create a viable business enterprise if a work atmosphere was to be maintained. Although the first sheltered workshop in the United States opened in 1838, the greatest growth in this movement occurred from the 1960s on. The Greenleigh study concentrated its statistical data on workshops starting operation in 1964. Reportedly, by the second quarter of 1975, there were 2,766 certificated workshops, both for the blind and those with physical and mental disabilities (Greenleigh 1976). Four out of five workshops are operated by voluntary nonprofit organizations and associations. Most have working relationships with state offices of vocational rehabilitation, which usually involve the provision of services to clients on a fee basis. There is therefore an interdependent relationship between the government and the agencies that operate workshops. The following material will outline the development of the sheltered workshop idea, which has changed dramatically.

Sheltered Industrial Employment

The Prophecy: In the first *Annual Review of Rehabilitation* (1980), Carolyn Vash's chapter, "Sheltered Industrial Employment," is based on her monograph of the same title (1977). She is concerned with work opportunities for people with severe disabilities who cannot fit easily into traditional positions. Vash views the entire spectrum of opportunity in the marketplace with an eye toward breaking down the artificial barriers, sometimes primarily attitudinal, that stand between the person who is severely disabled and the potential work opportunity afforded him or her.

Vash makes a distinction between the term "shelter" and the term "accommodation," which is some adjustment that must be made for the worker who is not necessarily disabled in order for his or her other life obligations to be met. Vash explains that ". . . accommodation is something an employer provides to enable a worker to perform up to standards. Shelter is something the employer provides for selected employees who are unable to meet the standards" (Vash 1988).

We are living at a time in which, sometimes, jobs are modified to meet the needs of workers, rather than asking workers to make all adjustments. In addition, modern technology is expanding and architectural modifications are taking place that are accelerating the process of accommodation. Although Vash deals with all types and degrees of disabilities, she deals only with one handicap—vocational. Mainstreaming in the workplace, according to Vash, can take place at many levels from homebound, or totally sheltered employment; to semi-integrated units in mainstream industry with significant accommodation or shelter; through full integration in industry with some accommodation; to competitive employment with no accommodation or shelter (Vash 1980).

Vash's prophetical reflections on the future of sheltered employment include financial issues such as the cost factor, unionization, marketing, and federal subsidies. Mainstreaming in employment requires more work in the area of job development and an expanded role for the rehabilitation technologist in helping with worksite and machine modifications. Other accommodations mentioned are flex-time and job sharing.

Vash deplores irrelevant training for jobs that do not exist and reiterates the need for accurate information on job and labor markets. She concludes with an examination of the philosophical implications of the question "which is the better way . . . welfare or wages?" Her answer is if people with disabilities are working, regardless of the costs of accommodation or shelter to the employer, or the need for government subsidy, at least they are no longer being supported on the welfare roles. Vash's ideas have taken root during the 1980s in concrete ways, resulting in the development of the idea of supported employment.

The Concept of Supported Employment

The Fullfillment: The concept of supported employment was first authorized under the 1984 Rehabilitation Act Amendments which extended the Developmental Disabilities Assistance and Bill of Rights Act (PL 94-103) of 1975. States became eligible for funds for advocacy, planning, and demonstration projects for people with severe intellectual and other developmental impairments. Forty states were awarded grants for employment-related activities and half of these developed supported employment programs (*Rehab Brief* 1987). By 1986, 27 states were involved in supported employment projects. The 1986 amendments to the Rehabilitation Act (PL 99-506) defined supported employment as:

> "competitive work in integrated settings—a) for individuals with severe handicaps for whom competitive employment has not traditionally occurred, or b) for individuals for whom competitive employment has been interrupted or intermittent as a result of a severe disability, and who, because of their handicap, need ongoing support services to perform such work." The key words here are "ongoing support services."

In the past, in order to become eligible for OVR services, an individual with disabilities had to demonstrate a high probability that, if services were provided, independent employment without further use of public monies for job support would result. Supported employment makes no such claims; in fact, it is addressed solely to the people who will always need public support in order to remain employed (*Rehab Brief* 1987). It focuses on employment and training in actual jobs rather than on preparation for employment. It uses the place/train as opposed to the train/place approach; i.e., the person is trained on the job in job skills and work-related behaviors. Employment is real work performed for industry-based wages and produces valued goods or services. Supported employment is one option for individuals with mental retardation, severe physical disabilities, sensory impairments, long-term mental illness, traumatic brain injury, and multiple disabilities. Persons with any of these disabilities who are able to work independently would not be candidates for supported employment (President's Committee on Employment of People with Disabilities, Fact Sheet).

Several types of programs currently exist. The four prevalent models are:

1. **The individual placement model**: One individual is placed in a job in a community business or industry. Training is provided on the job site by a job coach. When performance reaches the employer's standards, training and on site support is gradually reduced to a stable minimum.
2. **Enclave**: An enclave consists of a small group (generally five to eight) of individuals with disabilities working within a local business. Support is

provided on site by a job trainer who may work for the supported employment organization or for the host company. The trainer generally remains on site with individuals throughout their employment.

3. **Mobile Crew**: A mobile crew consists of a number of workers (again generally five to eight) who work for a company that secures service contracts around the community. The crew moves from contract site to contract site. Above training conditions apply.

4. **Benchwork model**: Some individuals need more supervisory attention and exhibit behavioral problems. This last model shares many features of the traditional sheltered workshop. Integration is achieved here by locating the workplace near stores, restaurants, etc., offering integration opportunities during breaks, lunch hours, and before and after work.

In conjunction with the first 10 supported employment demonstration projects funded by RSA, the University of Oregon (with funding provided by NIDRR) is testing the development of a Supported Employment Information System (SEIS). This system will provide specific data on individuals in supported employment in the demonstration states (*Rehab Brief* 1987). Berkeley Planning Associates is both developing methods for client performance, and developing a private sector business model which may be used to expand supported employment opportunities (Berkeley Planning Associates 1986).

A climate of opportunity has been developed during the 1980s to envision new employment options for people with severe disabilities. The future lies in the hands of employers, service providers, parents, and people with disabilities to realize these opportunities.

Private Sector Participation

Projects with Industry

Earlier attempts to broaden the concept of cooperation between industry and business and the rehabilitation field need to be outlined here. Projects with Industry (PWI), funded in 1968 by the 1968 amendments to the Vocational Rehabilitation Act, had as its objectives to establish projects designed to prepare individuals with disabilities, especially severe disabilities, for competitive employment, using the concept of on-the-job training in the world of real work. Experiments in the early 1970s originated in California, where Ranchos Los Amigos Hospital created job slots for people with disabilities within the staff itself. Another example was the Jacksonville, Florida, Restaurant Association's PWI to fill a serious personnel shortage in restaurant jobs. Both IBM and Goodwill Industries sponsored PWIs.

Projects with Industry is a partnership between business/industry and rehabilitation, which is guided by a formal "Business Advisory Council" (BAC). BACs set policy and dictate the scope and quality of training. They are composed primarily of business managers who have technical expertise in the area of training emphasized in the project (*Rehab Brief* August 1985).

The State Vocational Rehabilitation Agency (or the state agency for the blind) serves as the link between the person with a disability and the employer, providing assistance and support by selecting candidates on the basis of their abilities and potential. The agency provides any special services needed to prepare them for jobs. The difference between this idea and the current supported employment concept lies in the word "competitive." Only those disabled individuals who can ultimately function in a competitive setting are chosen.

The program has proved eminently successful, growing during a 20-year period from three original projects with funding of $450,000 to approximately one hundred projects with a budget of $13 million (*Rehab Brief* 1985). A link among all of the Projects with Industry, both in the United States and in other countries, is the umbrella group Inter-National Association of Business, Industry and Rehabilitation (I-NABIR).

In recent years, possibly as a result of the PWI concept, and with the blessings of I-NABIR, rehabilitation, industry, and labor have opened vital lines of communication regarding employment of individuals with disabilities, however, the rehabilitation practitioner is oriented toward serving and concerned with quality of life issues, while business people are trained to achieve tangible measurable goals in sales and marketing and are concerned with efficiency and cost-effectiveness (*Rehab Brief* 1985). PWI tries to help business, labor, industry, and rehabilitation meet one another's expectations while achieving their individual goals.

IRA (Intracorp)

One of the first dozen PWIs funded was an outgrowth of the new concept in medical and vocational rehabilitation pioneered by the Insurance Company of North America (INA) during the 1960s. A series of regional offices was set up throughout the country, staffed by rehabilitation coordinators and rehabilitation nurses, a profession that was new at that time. The teams worked together with medical personnel to obtain an early evaluation of a patient who was a victim of accident or injury. The determination of cost of rehabilitation, wherever possible, was made to include vocational retraining with the objective of productive reemployment. The cost of rehabilitation, borne by the insurance company, was in all instances more economically sound for the company than a large payment to a client for a lifetime of inactivity. For the client, the value was self-evident.

The rehabilitation activities in INA were taken over by a separate subsidiary called International Rehabilitation Associates, Inc. (IRA) which was able to contract services to other insurance companies as well as to INA clients. IRA has now become a subsidiary of a network of companies called Intracorp, with a vastly enlarged ability to handle the medical and vocational needs of clients. Intracorp offers comprehensive services performed by registered nurses, case managers and vocational counselors. These include medical review, medical case management, auditing services for hospital bills, and other financial matters, Mental Health Services (ACORN), and short-term and long-term disability. Intracorp is nationwide, including Alaska and Hawaii, and has offices in Canada and Australia. For further information contact: International Rehabilitation Associates, Inc. (an Intracorp Company), Chesterbrook Corporate Center, 701 Lee Road, Wayne, PA 19087, (800) 345-1075.

Corporate/Industry Participation

In the early 1980s economic conditions and the philosophy of the Reagan administration made necessary a search for alternative funding in place of government support services as RSA support for individual projects decreased.

With continued emphasis on the "marketing" approach to vocational rehabilitation, business and industry members have been encouraged to contribute directly to social programs. Many large and medium-sized companies are also federal contractors,and are therefore bound by Section 503 of the Rehabilitation Act of 1973 as amended, the affirmative action law for disabled people. One way for them to demonstrate their commitment to affirmative action is to develop linkages with potential recruitment sources such as rehabilitation agencies. Many of them have become involved in various areas of assistance, one being direct contributions of money to rehabilitation facilities, and another being contribution of personnel. Employees may be given release time to volunteer, while executives on loan work full-time, typically for one or two years, in a nonprofit agency that needs their management expertise. Equipment, materials, and office space may be donated (McCarthy 1986).

In many cases employers have taken advantage of a labor pool supplied by the education system and have even become involved in career education programs, bringing business representatives into the schools and sending students to industrial sites. For example, the IBM work experience program for hearing-impaired students gives college students the opportunity for summer jobs at IBM in professional fields like accounting, computer programming, and engineering, sometimes leading to permanent employment at IBM (McCarthy 1986).

Corporate efforts also have assisted in the functional independence of persons requiring assistive devices, one outstanding example being the volunteer work of the more than half a million current and retired employees of the Bell System who belong to the Telephone Pioneers of America. They have custom designed and constructed devices such as the beeping audio softball for players who are blind and an instrument to teach children who are deaf how to modulate their speech by color-graphic feedback.

CIVITEX is a database for obtaining program profiles on model projects involving corporate collaboration. This service of the Citizens Forum on Self-Government, 1601 Grant Street, Suite 250, Denver, CO 80203, offers searches which can be ordered and received by calling 800-223-6004 and talking to a CIVITEX staff person (McCarthy 1986). The fee is $25 for 10 searches, discounted for members.

The Job Accommodation Network (JAN), P.O. Box 468, Morgantown, WV 26505 (800-JAN-PCEH Voice and TDD), is a database which brings together information about practical steps taken by employers to make accommodations for functional limitations of employees and applicants with disabilities. It was created by the President's Committee on Employment of Persons with Disabilities and is housed at the West Virginia Rehabilitation Research and Training Center. It contains specific information about how individual tasks can be performed by persons with limitations. JAN consultants may provide referrals to placement services, government agencies, private facilities, or rehabilitation technologists. There is no charge for the service, but users are asked to provide information about accommodations made so they can be shared with others.

Private-for-Profit Rehabilitation

It is obvious that the decades of the 1970s and 1980s have been periods of great change for the rehabilitation movement, and continuing legislation of the 1980s has led to an increase in the participation of the private sector. Another aspect of this development has been the private-for-profit concept of rehabilitation service, where rehabilitation counseling is provided on a fee-for-service basis. As a result, career opportunities in the profession of rehabilitation counseling have expanded and changed somewhat in their orientation. Some of this growth can be attributed to federal action. The Occupational Safety and Health Act of 1970 (PL 91-596) called for the creation of a National Commission on State Worker's Compensation Laws. This commission issued a report in 1972 which contained 84 recommendations for improvement of worker's compensation programs, several relating to vocational rehabilitation (Lynch 1987). As a result, and in response to other factors, since the early 1970s, private-sector rehabilitation has experienced a great increase in revenues and numbers of clients served. Industrially injured workers comprised the bulk of the clients at first, but expansion soon occurred in many other types of insurance cases, in a sense following the lead of INA, which was a pioneer in the field. In order to function effectively in this setting, traditional counselor roles and counseling strategies must be modified emphasizing accountability for their procedures and opinions under the scrutiny of the legal system (Lynch 1987).

Industry Labor Council (ILC)

The Industry Labor Council was established in 1977 as an outgrowth of the White House Conference of Handicapped Individuals as an arm of the Human Resources Center, in Albertson, Long Island. It is a fee-for-membership resource, responding to corporate and labor needs in the employment and retention of disabled individuals by providing information and technical assistance. It has over 110 corporate and union members, representing such diverse industries as pharmaceuticals, communication, petroleum, electronics, and high technology.

The council assists professionals in these industries in their day-to-day responsibilities for planning and implementing the affirmative action efforts of their organizations. ILC can help companies recruit workers with disabilities, can conduct site accessibility surveys, and provide guidelines to help overcome barriers and modify worksites. ILC develops and conducts training programs for all staff levels. Its annual national conference affords an opportunity to meet colleagues from diverse industries and areas (Fact sheet n.d.).

Rehabilitation of Persons with Traumatic Brain Injury (TBI)

A major rehabilitation challenge faced during the past few years has been in the area of traumatic brain injury. Advances in emergency medical service and operating room procedures are saving the lives of people with head trauma who would have died 5 or 10 years ago. Referrals to rehabilitation agencies, therefore, have increased rapidly, necessitating an immediate increase in the knowledge and skill of the rehabilitation counselors working with these individuals (McAlees 1987).

Typically, the person with head injury is male, between the ages of 15 and 24 years, usually injured in an automobile accident. To illustrate the scope of the problem, while spinal cord injury occurs at the rate of 5 per 100,000 persons a year, TBI is occurring at the rate of 200 per 100,000 persons a year (Rehab Brief 1987).

While persons with TBI incur much cognitive and psychosocial dysfunction, they do not want to be considered to be mentally retarded, or mentally ill, or even learning disabled. Improvement can continue to take place over long periods of time. It is necessary, therefore, that very special techniques be developed to assist in their rehabilitation. The following organizations are working in the field and can supply information:

The National Head Injury Foundation, Inc., 333 Turnpike Road, Southboro, MA 01772, is an advocacy organization providing information and resources. Many states have local support groups. A free catalog of publications is available.

The following are NIDRR-supported Rehabilitation Research and Training Centers in brain injury/stroke:

Research and Training Center for Head Trauma and Stroke, New York University Medical Center, 400 East 34th Street, New York, NY 10016. The center has published an annotated bibliography of research on vocational outcome following head trauma (2nd ed.), February 1986, by Kay Thomas, Ora Ezrachi, and Marie Cavallo. An annotated list of publications by Margaret Brown was published in March 1986.

Rehabilitation Research and Training Center, Emory University, 1441 Clifton Road NE, Atlanta, GA 30322.

The Rehabilitation Institute of Chicago, Northwestern University, Department of Rehabilitation Medicine, 345 East Superior, Chicago, IL 60611.

Rehabilitation Research and Training Center for Brain Injury and Stroke, University of Washington, Department of Rehabilitation Medicine, RJ-30, Seattle, WA 98195.

The Journal of Head Trauma Rehabilitation, Gaithersburg, MD: Aspen Publishers. Began publication in 1986 and provides information on clinical management and rehabilitation.

A NARIC Resource Guide on Head Injury provides additional resources (NARIC 1987).

Rehabilitation of Persons with Specific Learning Disabilities

Another important area of rehabilitation that has developed during the 1980s is counseling, training, and placement of adults with learning disabilities. Major interest in the field of learning disabilities did not begin until the early 1960s and 1970s. Before that time persons with learning disabilities were not recognized as having a handicapping condition.

According to the most widely used definition of learning disabilities (as stated in PL 94-142; see Chapter 8), a learning disability is a disorder in one or more of the basic processes involved in using spoken or written language in the presence of normal or above-average intelligence. The disorder may manifest itself in problems related to listening, thinking, speaking, reading, writing, spelling, or doing mathematical calculations. Each person is affected differently and to a different degree. It is thought that about three percent of the population has learning disabilities.

In 1981 the word "adults" was added to the title of the Association for Children with Learning Disabilities. It was not until the late 1970s that professional attention began to concentrate on the diagnosis and treatment of adults with Specific Learning Disabilities (SLD) as separate from the services offered to children. Recognizing the fact that children with learning disabilities were not, as often thought, "outgrowing" their learning and behavior problems, parents and advocates pressured the field of vocational rehabilitation for services. Until the 1980s, SLD was not recognized as a disability by the medical community, and thus the vocational rehabilitation (VR) program could not provide services. But in 1980 the *Diagnostic and Statistical Manual of Mental Disorders*, 3rd ed. published by the American Psychiatric Association, and the 1980 edition of the *International Classification of Diseases*, published by the World Health Organization, both included specific learning disabilities in one category of development delay disorders. Based upon this recognition, RSA recognized LD for vocational rehabilitation services. Naturally, there must be a demonstrated presence of serious functional limitations and a real need for VR services over a period of time. Some persons with learning disabilities can compensate for their problems so well that they are barely noticeable and have found vocations in which they can use their areas of strength, but many people with LD do need counseling. The specific laws and codes have continued to refine precise definitions while efforts to serve this population have continued.

Based upon the history of the identification of learning disabled students in the schools, assumptions may be made that it will take some years to locate eligible SLD adults, compile data, more sharply define the group of disabilities in this category, and refine diagnoses. This work is continuing and may well prove adult SLD to be one of if not the most prevalent handicapping conditions in rehabilitation (Newill, Goyette, and Fogarty 1984; see also Chapter 5).

A President's Committee publication entitled "Supervising Adults with Learning Disabilities" (SuDoc 461-566-814/25964, 1985), points out that any job will be appropriate commensurate with the person's level of intelligence and ability. In fact, positions requiring creativity may take advantage of an SLD person's slightly different way of looking at the world so that what they produce can be exciting, amusing, and innovative (Brown 1985). We might remember here that such well-known persons as Albert Einstein, Thomas Edison, and Nelson Rockefeller were learning disabled.

Job accommodation needs of the learning-disabled employee may include arranging for someone to help with math and statistics if necessary (dyscalculia), providing a typewriter or dictating machine to draft materials (dysgraphia), if possible, providing good clerical support, accommodating hyperactivity with a private office area to avoid excess stimulation, providing clear and concise instructions, and arranging for someone to review important documents before they are put into final form (Robinson 1984; see also Chapter 5).

Research initiatives were stimulated when the Ninth Institute of Rehabilitation Issues Prime Study Group addressed the Rehabilitation of Clients with Specific Learning Disabilities (1982). In March 1983, NIDRR sponsored a conference on this topic, and in 1984 awarded a four-year Research and Demonstration Project grant to the Woodrow Wilson Rehabilitation Center, Fishersville, VA, which focused on improved delivery of vocational rehabilitation services to adolescents and adults with learning disabilities. At this writing, Woodrow Wilson has now received a new grant that will work to help smaller centers replicate what they have done at their very large (600 bed) center. The Ohio State University College of Education and the Human Resources Center in Albertson, New York, have several grants in the field of SLD, focusing on transition from high school to work, or college, and from college to work. A full account of these programs will be found in Chapter 8 on special education.

An RSA workgroup, formed in 1983, included many state vocational rehabilitation administrators, and contributed extensive statements of short-term and long-term policy guidelines. Continuing efforts to refine definitions focus on distinguishing between work-related limitations and academic limitations in the classroom (Sanchez 1984).

Self-help groups of learning-disabled adults began to exist as early as the late 1970s. In 1980, the President's Committee on Employment of People with Disabilities held a national meeting of learning-disabled adults. The people there decided to form the National Network of Learning Disabled Adults (Brown 1984). Articulate learning-disabled adults help rehabilitation professionals to understand more about their needs, and many have spoken at training sessions. For more information about these activities contact the Association of Children and Adults with Learning Disabilities (ACLD), 4156 Library Road, Pittsburgh, PA 15234, or the National Network of Learning Disabled Adults, 808 North 82nd Street, F-2, Scottsdale, AZ 85257.

Rehabilitation of Older People

Medical technology has succeeded in extending life expectancy during the last few decades. At the same time, changes in mandatory retirement laws have extended working life, and many older people continue working even after retirement age. Gerontologists now tend to refer to the young-old (persons 65-74) and the old-old (75 and above). The rehabilitation profession is increasingly having to deal with rehabilitation in the group who have become disabled through physical changes due to the aging process. Often this involves a diminishing of or change in work, the preservation of an independent life style assisted by available support services for physical care, the preservation of mental health, and to aid social adjustment.

In the article "Rehabilitation of Older People" in the *Annual Review of Rehabilitation*, Jane E. Myers presents an excellent review of the literature on the history of changes in statistics of our increasingly older population and the legislation now in effect that relates to rehabilitation of older people. Dr. Myers states that older people have been viewed in negative ways by society in general and by members of the rehabilitation professions. However, attitude changes are indicative that rehabilitation of older persons will become one of the important aspects of the rehabilitation counseling field into the 1990s and counselors will find themselves working with a new array of agencies and programs (such as departments for the aged) that can be used as resources.

Aging with a Major Physical Disability

In *Rehab Brief* (Vol. X No. 11 received January 1988), aging with a major physical disability is discussed. This *Rehab Brief* was based on the book *Aging with a Disability*, by Roberta Trieschmann (1987). This group is a fairly new population because, prior to World War II, individuals with physical disabilities were not visible in society; a majority did not survive acute injury or illness. The development of sulfanilamides and antibiotics in the 1930s and 1940s changed survival statistics of people with spinal cord injury. The polio epidemics of the 1940s and 1950s enlarged this population. Now both groups are aging.

A whole range of physical problems may occur among people with spinal cord injury as outlined in the above-mentioned *Rehab Brief.* Physical problems of muscle weakness, breathing difficulties, etc., are being experienced by people who have had polio (*Rehab Brief* 1986).

Five environmental factors that influence the quality of life for this group are identified by Trieschmann:

1. **Money:** living with a disability is expensive.
2. **Interpersonal support:** a network of family and friends is very important.
3. **Knowledgeable health professionals:** few local doctors know enough about long-term disability to treat their patients adequately.
4. **Community support services:** personal assistants become important, and home health and meal services should be integral parts of our health and rehabilitation systems.
5. **Role models:** peer counseling and support groups can play important roles. To this end, over 120 support groups have been formed to assist polio survivors. The International Polio network (IPN) was established by Gazette International Networking Institute (GINI). GINI which has maintained this network through its journal *Rehabilitation Gazette* publishes *Polio Network News* for IPN members who also receive national and international directories of polio support groups, clinics and physicians. Annual membership dues are $5 for polio survivors and $15 for health professionals. Write GINI, 4502 Maryland Avenue, St. Louis, MO 63108.

The Disability Task Force of the National Gray Panthers, a cross-generational advocacy organization, is implementing a plan to establish three resource centers across the country, located at 2632 Belmont Road NW, #226, Washington, DC 20009; 1027 East Concordia Drive, Tempe, AZ 85282; and PO Box 771, Fort Bragg, CA 95437 (*First Dibs* 1988). The Newsletter *First Dibs* has published a bibliography in the area of the disabled elderly (July–August 1988).

Two research and training centers are concerned with the problems of aging. These are:

Rancho Los Amigos Medical Center
    Rehabilitation Research and Training Center on Aging
    7600 Consuelo Street
    Downey, CA 90242

Rehabilitation Research and Training Center for Rehabilitation of
    Elderly Disabled Individuals
    Box 590
    3400 Spruce Street
    Hospital of the University of Pennsylvania
    Philadelphia, PA 19104-4283

Disabled Homebound People

Severely disabled homebound people were identified in the Rehabilitation Act of 1973 as a priority population for service. This seemed to have important implications for state rehabilitation agencies. While homebound clients who were severely disabled had not received appropriate rehabilitation services over the years, advances in medical science, rehabilitation technology, and new philosophies in job modification, as well as new modes of transportation, and the demands of this homebound group themselves combined to change this picture somewhat. Rusalem (1974) estimated that there were more than two million disabled Americans who were homebound. A significant document, developed to aid in promoting service to this group was *The Rehabilitation of the Severely Handicapped Homebound* (June 1977), an outgrowth of the work of the Fourth Institute on Rehabilitation Issues, held in Dallas, Texas. It developed training guides to assist counselors in instituting programs for the disabled homebound, detailed programs already developed in many areas of the country, and suggested models for homebound employment, as well as possibilities for bringing clients out of the home whenever possible by using the most recent advances in all areas of rehabilitation.

During the 1980s, the growing use of computer systems has created a demand for skilled workers in fields like computer programming and word processing. At the same time, increasing costs of urban office space have provided an economic incentive for the use of home-based workers. Also, high-speed telecommunication systems permit the retrieval of work assignments to and from homebound workers (Kuhlman 1988). There have been, therefore, an increasing number of successful efforts. Such programs as the IBM computer programmer training program, and Lift, Inc., have placed hundreds of homebound individuals with disabilities in programming jobs nationwide (Kuhlman 1988).

Lift, Incorporated, is one example of a private, not-for-profit, corporation that trains people who are intellectually qualified but physically disabled for computer programming. The company was founded in Chicago, in 1975 and operates there and in New York, Los Angeles, and other major cities throughout the United States. Lift has served over 50 major corporations in the fields of insurance, banking and finance, manufacturing, consumer goods, and others (Lift, Inc. 1985). Qualified candidates are selected through state vocational rehabilitation organizations, rehabilitation hospitals, VA centers, organizations for the disabled, and by word of mouth referrals.

Each candidate is matched with a corporation which agrees to employ him/her after training. Lift then trains the candidate by audiovisual programs self-administered plus home tutors. The successful candidate is then employed by Lift under contract with an employer for one year, after which the company agrees to employ the candidate directly for at least one more year. The training period lasts for six months. Candidates who are severely physically disabled, but intellectually qualified, are given preference, and typical disabilities are quadriplegia as a result of spinal cord injury, cerebral palsy, muscular dystrophy, and polio.

Hourly wages are competitive with those of the average able-bodied entry-level programmer. While the employee works at home on a remote computer terminal, he or she must come to the office at least once a week to receive assignments, attend staff meetings, etc. Lift's headquarters are at 350 Pfingsten Street, Suite 103, Northbrook, IL 60062.

REFERENCES

Berkeley Planning Associates. 1986, July. *Development of Performance Measures for Supported Employment Programs, Final Report.* Contract No. 300-85-0138. Available from NARIC.

Brown, Dale. 1984, April–June. "Self-Help Groups for Learning Disabled People and the Rehabilitation Process." *Journal of Rehabilitation* 50 (3).

Brown, Dale. 1985. *Supervising Adults with Learning Disabilities.* President's Committee on Employment of the Handicapped. Washington, DC: U.S. Government Printing Office.

The Directory of National Information Sources on Handicapping Conditions and Related Services. 1986, June. Winchester, MA: Harold Russell Associates, Inc.

First Dibs. Disability Information Brokerage System, Tucson, AZ, 4–5.

Greenleigh Associates, Inc. 1976, November. "The Role of the Sheltered Workshop in the Rehabilitation of the Severely Handicapped." New York, NY: 8.

ILC Fact Sheet. Industry-Labor Council on Employment of Handicapped Individuals, National Center on Employment of the Disabled, Human Resources Center, Albertson, New York.

Kuhlman, Gregory A. 1988, April–June. "Follow-up of a Word Processing Training and Employment Program for Homebound Persons with Disabilities." *Journal of Rehabilitation,* 55–59.

Lift Inc. 1985. "A Description of the Operations of Lift, Inc., Computer Programming for the Severely Disabled." Northbrook, IL 60062.

Lynch, Ross K., and Beck, Richard J. 1987. "Rehabilitation Counseling." In Parker, Randall M., ed. *Private Sector in Rehabilitation Counseling: Basics & Beyond.* Austin, TX: Pro Ed, 225–46.

McAlees, Daniel. 1987, November. "Traumatic Brain Injury." In McCray, Paul, ed. *RTC Connection.* University of Wisconsin-Stout, Vol. 8, No. 3, Menomonie, WI 54751, 1–5.

McCarthy, Henry. 1986, May. "Corporate Social Responsibility and Services to People with Disabilities." *Journal of Rehabilitation Administration.* Vol. 10, No. 2, 60–70.

Myers, Jane E. 1985. "Rehabilitation of Older People." In *Annual Review of Rehabilitation.* Vol. 4. New York: Springer Publishing Company, 1–54.

NARIC, Resource Guide: Head Injury. 1987, March. National Rehabilitation Information Center, Washington, DC.

Newell, Barry H., Goyette, Charles H., and Fogarty, Thomas W. 1984, April–June. "Diagnosis and Assessment of the Adult with Specific Learning Disabilities." *Journal of Rehabilitation* 50 (3): 34–38.

President's Committee on Employment of People with Disabilities. 1988. *Fact Sheet on Supported Employment.* Washington, DC.

Rehab Brief. 1985, August. "Projects With Industry-Training for Partnership." Department of Education, Washington, DC. Vol. VIII, No. 8.

Rehab Brief. 1986. "The Late Effects of Poliomyelitis." Vol. IX, No. 9.

Rehab Brief. 1986. "The Silent Epidemic: Rehabilitation of People with Traumatic Brain Injury." Vol. IX, No. 4.

Rehab Brief. 1987. "Aging with a Major Physical Disability." Vol. X, No. 11.

Rehab Brief. 1987. "Supported Employment." Vol. X, No. 1.

The Rehabilitation of the Severely Handicapped Homebound. 1977, June. Youth Institute on Rehabilitation Issues (report from the study group), Dallas, TX.

Regional Rehabilitation Continuing Education Programs. *Newsletter.* Region 2. Buffalo, NY: State University of New York at Buffalo.

Robinson, Elizabeth. 1984, April–June. "Techniques for Job Hunting." *Journal of Rehabilitation* 50 (3): 93.

Rusalem, H. 1974. *The Characteristics and Rehabilitation Experience of Homebound Applicants for State Vocational Rehabilitation Agency Service.* Monograph of the Programmatic Research Project on the Rehabilitation of Homebound Persons. New York: Federation of the Handicapped.

Sanchez, Susan. 1984, April–June. "Where Do We Go from Here: A Look to the Future in the Rehabilitation of Learning Disabled Persons." *Journal of Rehabilitation*, 82–89.

Trieschmann, Roberta B. 1987. *Aging with a Disability*. New York: Demos Publications.

Vash, Carolyn L. 1980. "Sheltered Industrial Employment." In *Annual Review of Rehabilitation*. Vol. 1. New York: Springer Publishing Company, 80–120.

Chapter 8
Special Education

HISTORY

Before rehabilitation can take place, children born with disabilities, as well as young people who become disabled during their school years, must be educated to the highest level of their ability. It has only been in the twentieth century in the United States that educational opportunity has been extended in some measure to children and youth with disabilities, and only in the 1970s that the principle of a full and equal education for exceptional children began to be implemented nationwide. Now, at the end of the 1980s, we have seen a giant leap forward, with major emphasis being placed at the present time on early childhood intervention, and at the other end of the spectrum, on career preparation at the secondary or postsecondary level, known as transition from school to work.

By 1911 many large city school systems had established special schools and special classes for children with disabilities, and a number of states began to subsidize special programs by paying the excess costs of maintaining special classes. In 1919 the National Easter Seal Society was founded, focusing attention initially on the orthopedically disabled and gradually including children with all types of disabilities.

The major thrust of the volunteer movement came in the 1940s and 1950s with the organization of such groups as the National Association for Retarded Children (now the National Association for Retarded Children and Adults) and the United Cerebral Palsy Association. Local groups developed informally as gatherings of people sharing a common problem. They came together to help their children and to help themselves by providing each other with psychological support. Public education was not accepting its responsibility toward many groups of these children.

Parent groups began to sponsor and encourage a wide diversity of activities, including education (originally through private schools and finally through the public school systems) and the establishment of teacher training programs. Other types of projects included sheltered workshops, vocational training centers, diagnostic facilities, parent education, preschool and postschool facilities, research, therapy, and medical services (Cain 1976).

In the 1920s the United States established a division of special education in the Federal Bureau of Education, with Elise Martens as its first director (Velleman 1964). Martens encouraged the states to enact legislation to aid children with disabilities. The Social Security laws of 1935 included $3 million to aid the states in developing programs for physically disabled children. A special division was established in the Children's Bureau in the Department of

Labor and later transferred to the Department of Health, Education and Welfare. Today the Bureau of Education of the Handicapped is located in the Office of Special Education and Rehabilitation Services (OSERS) in the Education Department. Special Educational services are administered by the states through the divisions of their education departments. Local school districts receive approval for placement of exceptional children from the Commissioner of Education.

In 1958, although gains had been made in the education of children with disabilities, fewer gains were made for the orthopedically disabled and those with special health problems than for any other group. Only one-fourth of the disabled in the country between the ages of 5 and 17 were receiving an appropriate education. Moreover, the overwhelming number of these children enrolled in special programs—83 percent—were being served on the elementary level. Very few opportunities existed for high school students who were disabled to receive an appropriate education (Velleman 1964).

With the growth of special education in this century have come alternative facilities. The first answer to the challenge came with the residential school, which still offers the solution to complete 24-hour care for children with disabilities. Educational programs in these facilities are minimal; however, residential schools for deaf and blind children often offer effective educational programs. Current trends in residential care are toward smaller facilities, with the children located closer to home to encourage week-end and vacation visits with the family, and even eventual placement in the public school (National School Public Relations Association 1974).

Day school instruction has become popular since the 1950s, including private schools run with state support, schools run by parent groups or organizations such as Easter Seals and United Cerebral Palsy, schools run by the states, and some administered by public school systems (National School Public Relations Association 1974). Day school institutions take many forms, as listed below:

1. **Special education classes** housed in regular schools.
2. **Special schools** for children with disabilities or for special categories of disabilities.
3. **Cooperative services** available on a regional basis where children are transported to the school for all or part of the day.
4. **Resource rooms** in schools where children go for special instruction geared to their disabilities.
5. **Itinerant teacher** services where teachers travel from school to school to teach and tutor children, and serve as consultants to classroom teachers, often bringing special materials. Itinerant services often include teachers of the blind and the deaf and such special personnel as speech therapists.
6. **Mobile facilities** whereby vans with special equipment and special education teachers visit schools to provide diagnosis, consultation, in-service training, new materials and equipment, and actual teaching of some children.
7. **Homebound instruction.** Until the legislation of the 1970s children with orthopedic disabilities were on home instructional programs. These "hidden youngsters" were served by a teacher for the homebound who visited the home a few hours per week but who never saw the youngsters in a classroom or socializing with other children.

The legislation of the 1970s and 1980s has improved the picture dramatically. During the 1986-87 school year the majority of children and youth with disabilities received special education and related services in settings with able-bodied students. Over 26 percent were in regular classes, 41 percent in resource rooms, and another 24 percent in separate classes within a regular education building, accounting for over 92 percent of disabled placements (US Department of Education 1988). According to the department's tenth annual report in 1988, over 4.4 million students were served during the 1986-87 school year, representing 6.47 percent of the population between 3 and 21 years of age. Federal officials are confident that because of the child-find programs instituted by the states in response to legislation, almost all children in need of special educational services are receiving them. While statistics are easily manipulated and difficult to analyze accurately, there is certainly no doubt that Public Law 94-142 and subsequent legislation of the 1980s have made dramatic changes in the education of children and young adults with disabilities in this country.

LEGISLATION

Beginning in the 1950s, and accelerating since the late 1960s, a consumer movement, led by organizations of parents of children with disabilities, has forced action with regard to the education of exceptional children. Many state legislatures responded with laws making educational opportunity for these children mandatory, breaking away from the custodial care philosophy that had characterized their schools and providing substantive learning experiences. By the mid-1970s almost all states had adopted mandatory education statutes for children with disabilities. An appropriate education for every child who is disabled began to be regarded as an inalienable right, just as it is for every other citizen. These laws, in many instances, included additional provisions such as the training of special education personnel and the acquisition of needed facilities and materials. In addition, many states bagan to pass laws mandating education for the disabled children of preschool age (National Advisory Committee on the Handicapped 1976).

Since the mid-1960s, the federal government has significantly increased its support of education for children with disabilities. In 1965 the Elementary and Secondary Education Act (ESEA) was passed (PL 89-10). Title I of this act included coverage of children with disabilities. Major amendments gave greater emphasis to special education. The first of these, PL 89-313 (1965), provided support for the education of these children in state-operated schools and hospitals and, in a special provision in some states, in private, state-supported schools. The second, PL 89-750 (1966), added Title VI to ESEA, which established the Bureau of Education of the Handicapped and the National Advisory Committee on the Handicapped.

In 1972 the Fleischmann Committee of New York, after a two-year study, published a prophetic report pinpointing special education needs and proposing means for identifying and diagnosing problems (Fleischmann 1972). Many of its recommendations were incorporated into the "child find" requirement of PL 94-142 (1975).

The Education of the Handicapped Act, PL 91-230, passed in 1973 and amended by PL 93-380 in 1974, provided a comprehensive federally funded program of service to children with disabilities. Public Law 91-230, Sections A through G, provided for the strengthening of educational services to exceptional children (Part B), early education for children with disabilities and centers for deaf/blind children and their parents (Part C), the recruitment of educational personnel and the dissemination of information on educational opportunities for the disabled, and the preparation of teachers and support personnel such as physical education and recreation teachers (Part D), the promotion of research in curriculum areas (Part E), the provision of media services and captioned film loans (Part F), and provision for research in the establishment of model centers for children with specific learning disabilities (Part G). Part A of this law deals with general provisions and definitions (National School Public Relations Association 1974).

Public Law 93-380, the Educational Amendments of 1974, authorized greater aid to the states and supported the principle of placing children with disabilities in the least restrictive educational environment, commensurate with their needs. It also specified due process requirements, protecting the rights of this group of children and requiring the states to develop plans setting forth how and when each expects to achieve the desired goals.

In November 1975, PL 93-380 was broadened by the enactment of an even more significant measure, the Education for All Handicapped Children Act, known as PL 94-142 (1975). The new bill called for a massive expansion of the authorized levels of the basic state grants program. PL 94-142 is unique in that it makes a very specific commitment to the broadening of educational opportunity to exceptional children. Unlike other federal education laws, it has no expiration date. It sets forth as a national policy the proposition that education must be extended to persons with disabilities as their fundamental right. It has four major purposes:

1. To guarantee the availability of special education programming to children and youth who require it.
2. To ensure fairness and appropriateness in decision making concerning special education to children and youth with disabilities.
3. To establish clear management and auditing requirements and procedures regarding special education at all levels of government.
4. To assist state and local governments through the use of federal funds (Ballard 1977).

PL 94-142 revised only Part B of the Education of the Handicapped Act. The other components, Parts A and C–G, remained unchanged and continued in operation. Many of the requirements of PL 94-142 were stated in the Education Amendments of 1974. All programs under these acts were administered through the Bureau of Education of the Handicapped, which is now located in the Office of Special Education and Rehabilitation Services (OSERS), in the Department of Education.

Handicapped children are defined by the act as "mentally retarded, hard of hearing, deaf, orthopedically impaired, other health impaired, speech impaired, visually handicapped, seriously emotionally disturbed, or children with specific learning disabilities who, by reason thereof, require special education and related services" (Ballard 1977). The two requirements for child eligibility are that the child has one or more of these disabilities, and that the child requires special education and related services. Not all children with disabilities require such services. Many of them are able to attend regular school programs without program modification.

Under PL 94-142, an Individualized Educational Program (IEP) must be prepared for each child with disabilities by the agency currently providing educational services for the child. A district committee called Committee on Special

Education (CSE), made up of a teacher or administrator of special education, a psychologist, a physician and a parent advocate, must approve the plan. IEPs must include:

1. A statement of the child's present level of educational performance.
2. A statement of annual goals, including short-term instructional objectives.
3. A statement of the specific educational services to be provided to such a child and the extent to which the child will be able to participate in the regular educational program.
4. The projected date for initiation and anticipated duration of such services.
5. Appropriate objective criteria and evaluation procedures and schedules for determining on at least an annual basis whether instructional objectives are being achieved.

The IEP is a management device only, and the teacher cannot be held accountable should the child fail to achieve the anticipated academic growth. Methods are set up that give the child's parents the right of approval of the plan and the right to judicial review if they do not find it satisfactory, thus strengthening the rights of the parents. If federal funds were to continue, availability of an education for every child in the district between the ages of 3 and 21 had to be guaranteed by September 1980.

The provisions of PL 94-142 were to be seen in conjunction with Section 504 of the Rehabilitation Act of 1973. Since Section 504 set forth the civil rights of all disabled Americans, it also applied to all children with respect to public education. PL 94-142 was called, mistakenly, the "mainstreaming" law. Although it did result in making it easier for some children to be placed in regular classrooms, the concept of appropriate placement in "the least restrictive environment" (LRE) was the intent of the law, and special classes have not disappeared altogether. Mainstreaming has served especially in those areas where children have not been receiving an appropriate education, or any education at all.

Using monies provided for the purpose of locating children with disabilities most states instituted "child find" programs, and as a result of these activities located two age groups where the largest numbers of unserved children seemed to exist, birth to 5 years old and 16 to 21 years old. Ultimately these findings resulted in legislation in the 1980s directed at programs for preschoolers and in extensive transition from school to work programs for adolescents "aging out" of the educational system.

In 1983, Public Law 98-199, the amendments to the Education for Handicapped Children Act, set aside funds to support secondary education programs and transitional services as well as personnel and parent training. The Carl D. Perkins Vocational Education Act (PL 98-524), signed by President Reagan in October 1984, made funds for vocational programs accessible to all persons, including the handicapped. Moreover the act intended to improve the quality of vocational education programs to give the nation's workforce the marketable skills needed to improve productivity and promote economic growth.

In 1986 Congress passed the Education of the Handicapped Act Amendments of 1986 (PL 99-457). Signed in October 1986, its purpose was "to amend the Education of the Handicapped Act, to reauthorize the discretionary programs under that Act, to authorize an early intervention program under that

Act for handicapped infants and toddlers and their families, and for other purposes" (OSERS 1987).

It therefore becomes the policy of the US to provide financial assistance to states to develop and implement a statewide interagency program of early intervention services for disabled infants, toddlers, and their families, and to facilitate coordination of payment from federal, state, local and private sources. Disabled infants and toddlers are individuals from birth through age two who need early intervention services because they are experiencing developmental delays, as determined by the states and as measured by appropriate diagnostic instruments and procedures, in one or more of the following areas: cognitive development, physical development, language and speech development, psychochosocial development, or self-help skills; or have a diagnosed physical or mental condition which has a high probability of resulting in developmental delay. An Individualized Family Service Plan (IFSP) must be developed by a multidisciplinary team, including the parent, and each IFSP must be reviewed at six-month intervals and evaluated annually. With parental consent, early intervention services may commence prior to the completion of the assessment (Exceptional Parent 1988).

The National Information Center for Handicapped Children and Youth (NICHCY) published a special edition of their *News Digest* entitled "Early Intervention for Children Birth through Two Years" (Number 10 1988). Also available from NICHCY is "A Parents' Guide to Accessing Programs for Infants, Toddlers and Preschoolers with Handicaps." For free copies of both publications write to NICHCY, PO Box 1492, Washington, DC 20013.

The Education of the Deaf Act of 1986, Public Law 99-371, was signed on August 4, 1986, "to authorize quality educational programs for deaf individuals throughout the United States, to reenact and codify certain provisions of law relating to the education of the deaf, and for other purposes."

NATIONAL NETWORK OF PARENT CENTERS

During the 1970s parents had used their organizations to play a major role in bringing about revolutionary changes in the education of children with disabilities and defining a new role for themselves in the educational process. But when their rights were established, as provided for under PL 94-142, few parents were prepared to assume their new responsibilities on behalf of their children. They began to form coalitions of parents in their own regions and states, cutting across disabilities and run by and for parents of children with disabilities. The term "parent center" was used to describe the organized training and information efforts of these coalitions. Since 1975 the federal government, through grants and contracts, has supported these organizations, initially through pilot projects which grew, by 1980, to 30 coalitions of parents of children with disabilities.

In 1983, in recognition of the role of parents in the educational process, the Education of the Handicapped Act Amendments, PL 98-199 included a section mandating establishment of a national program of parent-run projects now known as Parent Training and Information (PTI) programs. As of this writing (1989) there are 49 Parent Training and Information programs in 37 states and territories (*Coalition Quarterly* 1987–88).

Public Law 98-199 also mandated that a program of technical assistance be established for the new parent projects. Out of this mandate grew the Technical

Assistance for Parent Programs (TAPP) project, funded by the Office of Special Education and Rehabilitative Services (OSERS) through a cooperative agreement with the Federation for Children with Special Needs, 312 Stuart Street, Boston, MA 02116 (which had been the first pilot project funded in 1975). A five-year goal of the network is to foster leadership among the members of PTI through workshops, conferences, on-site and telephone consultations, and other collaborative and networking activities. Five regional centers cover the country. TAPP publishes the *Coalition Quarterly*. Addresses for the PTI Network and TAPP programs may be obtained from the Federation for Children with Special Needs in Boston.

THE COUNCIL FOR EXCEPTIONAL CHILDREN

The Council for Exceptional Children (CEC), 1920 Association Drive, Reston, VA 22091, is the professional oraganization to which most educators in the field of exceptional children belong. It was founded in 1922 and has 54 state federations and over 950 local chapters. Its principal purpose is the advancement of the education of exceptional children and youth. It cooperates with all organizations interested in the education of exceptional children and promotes standards for professional personnel. Its official journal, *Exceptional Children,* includes articles on the latest educational research in this area. *Teaching Exceptional Children*, another journal published by CEC, offers practical ideas to the classroom teacher.

The CEC Department of Governmental Relations monitors and analyzes policies concerning exceptional children, conducts policy research in this area, and works to encourage policies favorable to the development of exceptional children. The Department of Professional Development sponsors an annual convention, numerous topical conferences, and other training activities.

The council has 13 divisions which focus on particular aspects of special education (Periodicals available to nonmembers by subscription are listed in parentheses.): Association for the Gifted (*Journal for the Education of the Gifted*—available to libraries only), Council for Administrators of Special Education, Council for Children with Behavioral Disorders (*Behavioral Disorders*), Council for Educational Diagnostic Services (*Diagnostique*), Council for Learning Disabilities (*Learning Disabilities Quarterly*), Division of Mental Retardation (*Education and Training of the Mentally Retarded*), Division of Early Childhood Education, Division of Children with Communication Disorders, Division on the Physically Handicapped, Division for the Visually Handicapped, Teacher Education Division, Division on Career Development, and Technology and Media division.

Although CEC's user group is the 0–21-year-old population, much of their information is also applicable to the adult disabled (Russell 1986). CEC has an in-house database, Exceptional Child Education Resources (ECER), which contains documents entered into ERIC by the Clearinghouse on Handicapped and Gifted Children (operated by CEC as one of the 16 ERIC clearinghouses), as well as other special education materials not appropriate to the ERIC system, such as textbooks and doctoral dissertations in special education. ECER has been searchable online since 1971. *Exceptional Child Education Resources* is the print index and abstract for the ECER database. Custom computer searches of the ECER, ERIC, and other databases are available from CEC for a charge, and reprints of previous searches on selected popular topics may also be ordered.

FOUNDATION FOR EXCEPTIONAL CHILDREN

The Foundation for Exceptional Children is also located at 1920 Association Drive, Reston, VA 22091, but is separate from CEC. It was established in 1972 to serve the needs of exceptional children and youth by addressing the educational, vocational, social and personal needs of children with disabilities as well as the neglected educational needs of gifted children. The foundation is a public organization and is supported from public memberships, foundations, corporations, bequests, and special gifts. In 1987, a group called The Friends of the Foundation was established to enable highly visible Americans, to support the foundation as well as outstanding persons in the arts, athletics, academia, and the business community, including Senator Robert Dole. It supports numerous awards and programs for exceptional children, and publishes *Focus*, a quarterly newsletter.

TEACHER PREPARATION

Federal funding during the 1960s established training grants for teachers. Research and development centers were established in major universities, focusing on early childhood education, learning characteristics of disabled children, curriculum and materials development, and innovations in teacher education (Connor 1976). Recent concerns about staff have centered upon questions of qualifications, the quality of teachers in the field, the uniqueness of each child, and the need to educate teachers to meet the educational needs of all children with disabilities. With the advent of the concept of least restrictive environment (LRE), all teachers will need to learn about techniques for educating exceptional children. A general broadening of their base of knowledge, a cross-culturalization, is coming about whereby teachers are being prepared to teach in many new and innovative settings, and to meet the needs of all kinds of children with physical, mental, and learning disabilities.

The 1987 edition of the *National Directory of Special Education Personnel Preparation Programs* (CEC 1987) expands and updates the 1983 edition and contains information about 1,165 programs, including those that prepare special education personnel in all areas: teachers, special education administrators, speech-language pathologists, audiologists, physical therapists, occupational therapists, and professionals who provide adaptive physical education services. To this list must be added secondary school teachers in the field of vocational education, whose contribution to the education of young adults with disabilities is becoming more and more important as the problem of "aging out" (leaving school, and the special education network of services) and transition from school to work becomes a major focus.

The federal government, through the Special Education Personnel Development program, funded and administered by the Office for Special Education and OSERS office of educational programs (OSEP), funded 98 new and 254 continuation grants for fiscal year 1987. These funded programs focus primarily on training of teachers of preschool children; instructional personnel for students with severe and profound handicaps, emotional disturbance, autism, visual handicaps and deafness; speech pathologists; and others. Additional grants supported the preparation of leadership personnel and support personnel such as school psychologists, paraprofessionals, and career transition teachers.

Parent training and information projects are also funded under this program (US Department of Education 1988).

RESEARCH

Medical research has had a positive influence on the population of children with disabilities. It has reduced the number of children in danger of blindness from retrolental fibroplasia. It has discovered methods for treating some disorders such as the birth defect phenylketonuria (PKU) and has provided a means for early identification of some congenital disorders such as hemophilia and muscular dystrophy by means of amniocentesis. The Alpha-Fetoprotein Blood Test can determine early in pregnancy if there is a neural tube defect which can cause the birth defects of anencephaly, or spina bifida (Stony Brook 1982). Polio was virtually eliminated by the invention of the Salk vaccine. Ongoing neurological research continues through the National Institute of Health and the National Institute of Mental Health, and in the Department of Health and Human Services, and in the fields of epilepsy, autism, cerebral palsy, learning disabilities, emotional disturbance, and other areas.

The number of federally funded programs in the field of special education research has exploded in the past 10 years to the point where it would be impossible to enumerate them all. Research in special education is funded by the Division of Innovation and Development in OSEP (the Office of Special Education Programs) in OSERS. An ERIC/OSEP special project on interagency information dissemination was established by the ERIC Clearinghouse on Handicapped and Gifted Children to facilitate the dissemination of information about research in special education. The activities of the special project include the annual publication of a series of directories of research projects as well as a master directory listing all projects. Also published is a series of research summaries and research briefs for teachers. Information is available from the Clearinghouse on Handicapped and Gifted Children, CEC, 1920 Association Drive, Reston, VA 22091.

In 1987, research included field-initiated research (29 new and 60 continuation grants), student-initiated research (13 new grants, providing support for student researchers), and a number of grants in department-directed research (US Department of Education 1988).

REGIONAL RESOURCE CENTERS

There are six regional resource centers (RRC) that help state education departments develop programs and services for children with disabilities. These centers are located throughout the country (see Appendix D for addresses) and each RRC serves an average of nine states. They provide information and training for agencies, institutions, and organizations regarding techniques for submitting applications for grants, contracts and cooperative agreements; assistance with respect to early intervention services for handicapped infants and toddlers and their families; and many other technical resources.

Another network of services is that of Resource Access Projects (RAPS). These were funded in 1976 by the Agency for Children, Youth and Families, in the Department of Health and Human Services. Their mandate is to provide training programs and technical assistance to Headstart programs which must provide 10 percent of their services to children with disabilities. The emphasis here is on facilitating mainstreaming of children with disabilities by showing how special therapeutic services can be provided in the mainstream. The RAPS work directly with private nursery school programs and with the early childhood direction centers which were established to diagnose and properly refer and place disabled preschoolers. A listing of the RAPS is in Appendix D. Early childhood direction centers may be located through each state's department of special education.

Another network, the National Early Childhood Technical Assistance System (NEC*TAS), is funded through the Office of Special Education Programs, US Department of Education, as part of Public Law 99-457, the Education of the Handicapped Act Amendments of 1986. NEC*TAS brings together individuals and organizations with expertise in technical assistance, research, and support services. Six collaborative organizations comprise the system (see Appendix D). The goals of NEC*TAS during its four-year contract are to assist states in developing policies and practices to improve comprehensive services for young children with special needs and their families, to help community agencies develop their capacity to provide comprehensive services, and to facilitate the national exchange of timely information.

MAINSTREAMING

Ever since the passage of Public Law 94-142, with its provision that children with disabilities should be educated in the least restricted environment for each child, the educational controversy has continued as to just how restricted that environment should be. A paper released to the public in June 1988 by the Office of Special Education Programs (OSEP) indicated that statistics from one state to another are very different concerning the removal of students with disabilities from the regular school. The variation among states suggests that "something is affecting placements other than the needs of children, and whatever those things are, they are more powerful than the IEP process" (Bellamy 1988). It is this author's opinion that in many areas of the country these influences include the fact that more special education services are available, and parents choose to take advantage of them. Reinforcing this opinion is the fact that the report shows industrialized states more likely than rural states to use separate placements.

At this writing it is too early to assess the reaction to the aforementioned data. There is no question, however, that attitudinal changes have occurred, allowing for tremendous change to take place in integrating students with severe physical and mental disabilities into the mainstream of education. The need has arisen for auxiliary personnel, such as nursing staff, to become knowledgeable about the health needs of special students. Two recently published books dealing with this subject are *Program Models for Mainstreaming: Integrating Students with Moderate to Severe Disabilities* by Michael S. Berres and Peter Knoblock (eds.), Aspen Publications, Rockville, MD 1987, and *Mainstreaming Handicapped Children: Outcomes, Controversies, and New Directions* by C. Julius Meisel, ed., Erlbaum Associates, New Jersey and London. The first book offers models of successful programs in the mainstreaming of students with visual, hearing, orthopedic, and mental disabilities, including an account of integrating autistic children. The models seem not unlike earlier ones, with the difference that IEPs, with parent participation, offer greater assurance than before, that all disabled children identified by the local districts must be provided for in the most advantageous settings for their particular needs.

At the Human Resources School for Physically Disabled Students in Albertson, New York, more students are being mainstreamed outside the school than previously, and the school is beginning to see more multiply disabled students. Most mainstreamed students, especially those with moderate to mild disabilities, have been successful in fully integrated classrooms.

Mainstreaming of Deaf Students—NTID

An interesting report "Toward Equality: Education of the Deaf" was published by the Commission on the Education of the Deaf at the beginning of 1988. It requested the slowing up and reversal of mainstreaming for many deaf students. The commission was established by the Education of the Deaf Act of 1986. Its chair, Frank Bowe, stated that "The state of the art in deaf education today, at all levels, is unsatisfactory, and Congress must share the blame" (Education of the Handicapped 1988). The report recommended that educators put less emphasis on placing students in the least restrictive environment and instead emphasize the appropriateness of the services offered each child, based on severity of hearing loss, academic level and learning style, communicative needs, and many others. Consideration should be given to placing deaf students in special schools and, when necessary, upgrading these facilities.

Further, the commission recommended the establishment of a comprehensive service center to serve the approximately 100,000 deaf Americans who do not qualify for postsecondary education. Television captioning should be increased, and training program standards should be developed for teachers, educational interpreters and rehabilitation specialists in the field of deafness ("Report: Many Deaf People Undereducated," New York State Advocate 1988).

In the field of higher education, the commission recommended establishing 10 regional service centers to help deaf people. At the present time, 48 percent of the full-time deaf students are enrolled in the two national programs established by federal law, at Gallaudet University in Washington, DC, and the National Technical Institute for the Deaf (NTID) at the Rochester Institute of Technology.

The commission also recommended that research funding now allotted to Gallaudet University be available to all institutions (Education of the Handicapped 1988). Deaf persons selecting non-specialized colleges often encounter an irregular pattern of opportunities and support services, due to insufficient training of staff, lack of support personnel, inadequate funding, and undefined admission policies (HEATH 1987). Of the 3,000-plus institutions of higher education in the US 1,300 are reported in the Oryx Press *Directory of College Facilities and Services for the Disabled*, as offering support services to hearing-impaired students in some way.

Gallaudet University is well known as the only liberal arts college for the deaf in the United States. Perhaps less well known is The National Technical Institute for the Deaf, the world's only technological college designed exclusively for hearing-impaired students, as one of the nine colleges of the Rochester Institute of Technology. More than 1,250 deaf students enroll at NTID from all 50 states, DC, and the US territories, about half from special schools for hearing-impaired students and half from mainstreamed situations. NTID provides technological and professional education for hearing-impaired students;

prepares professionals to work with the hearing impaired; and conducts research into the social, educational, and economic needs of hearing-impaired people. Research has also included the development of a system to encode and hide captions on motion picture film, and the development of a looseleaf notebook with carbonless, pressure-sensitive paper for use by notetakers.

Since NTID is part of the Rochester Institute of Technology students may enroll into any of the other eight colleges and about one out of every six students do so. Hearing and hearing-impaired students live together, and dormitories are equipped with special signal lights, 24-hour information desks, and telephones with built-in amplifiers. Other college facilities such as the library, bookstore, athletic fields, swimming pool, gymnasium, and ice rink are shared by NTID students.

NTID is partially funded by the US Department of Education. It was created by Congress in 1965 and admitted its first students in 1968. Students use a variety of communication methods, including American Sign Language, signed English, speech and speech-reading, depending on individual preference, and severity and age at onset of the hearing impairment. Notetakers and tutors are available to crossover students (Facts You Can Use 1987).

NTID publishes a catalog of educational resources that lists several publications related to hearing impairment. To order materials or for further information contact:

Rochester Institute of Technology
NTID
Division of Public Affairs
One Lomb Memorial Drive
PO Box 9887
Rochester, NY 14623-0887

SECONDARY SCHOOL PROGRAMS

An educationally significant trend during the 1980s has been the development of innovative secondary school programs for young adults with disabilities. Before the deinstitutionalization movement of the 1970s and 1980s, and the legislation in PL 94-142, secondary education programs for disabled students were rare, outstanding examples being the Spaulding High School for students who are orthopedically disabled in Chicago, Illinois, and the Human Resources School in Albertson, Long Island. By 1972, 75 percent of special education services were still at the elementary level, with students being retained until their "aging out" in most states at the legal age of 21, or dropping out in their teens. Institutionalization kept many young adults in segregated programs (Wilcox and Bellamy 1982).

During the 1980s we began to see the first generation of students to enjoy the benefits of the "right to education" legislation. With some seven years of elementary education behind them, these students were different from earlier generations who had no access to educational programs or were institutionalized (Bellamy et al. 1985). Many of these young adults were returning to the mainstream, although data in the early 1980s indicated that many special education students were still simply dropping out of school.

In their book *Design of High School Programs for Severely Handicapped Students*, Barbara Wilcox and G. Thomas Bellamy outlined curriculum needs for young adults with disabilities. It is, of course, important that students with academic ability have access to a full academic curriculum in preparation for postsecondary education. For those students not academically oriented, new materials must be developed that are age appropriate. And all young adults with disabilities need to begin to place an emphasis on practical applications of what they are learning with goals that are very different from those on the elementary level, i.e., success after graduation, vocational career preparation, independent living possibilities, recreation and use of leisure time, modes of communication, etc. (Wilcox and Bellamy 1982). Parents and students must have available to them sufficient information about postsecondary opportunities of all kinds, including college programs, of which guidance counselors must be made aware. School librarians must assume a knowledgeable and positive role in obtaining information and making it available to teachers, counselors, psychologists, parents, and others involved in the planning process (see Chapter 10).

In an article entitled "Education and Career Preparation for Youth with Disabilities" by Bellamy et al., the authors develop the concept of career preparation on the secondary level. They mention technological advances as offering rising expectations for employment, and state that "the great majority of persons with disabilities should be able to enter full-time, self-supporting employment upon completion of their education" (Bellamy et al. 1985). The article goes on to delineate in detail the elements of career preparation curricula, including the acquisition of job skills, work-support skills (defined as social behavior on the job), and a breadth of training to ensure skills for advancement, and points out that entry could be made into employment after high school or after a period of postsecondary education.

The Council for Exceptional Children (CEC) has published "Secondary Special Education: A Guide to Promising Public School Programs," which presents 60 secondary-level special education programs (available from the Council for Exceptional Children, 1920 Association Drive, Reston, VA 22091).

TRANSITION FROM SCHOOL TO WORK

In 1984, Madeleine Will, then Assistant Secretary for Special Education and Rehabilitative Services (OSERS), issued a policy statement that has influenced the field of Special Education and Rehabilitation in the second half of the 1980s. In it she introduced the concept of transition from school to work. The paper was called "Bridges from School to Working Life" (Will 1984). Transition is a period that includes high school, the point of graduation, additional postsecondary education or adult services, and the initial years in employment. Will states that transition services can be grouped into three classes that reflect the nature of public services used to provide support as the passage is completed. The first involves movement from school either without services or with only those that are available to the population at large; the second involves use of time-limited services that are designed to lead to independent employment at the termination of service; and the third involves use of ongoing services for those disabled individuals who do not move to unsupported work roles. Here the supported work models outlined in Chapter 7 would come into play. The paper goes on to outline research and demonstration needs to be funded by OSERS.

The need for these services was demonstrated in the early 1980s with unemployment figures for special education graduates approaching 50 to 60 percent (Hasazi, Gordon, and Roe 1985). The federal government reacted to this need with the Education of the Handicapped Amendments PL 98-199 in 1983, and with PL 99-437 in 1986, authorizing funds for research, training, and demonstration projects in the area of transition (Everson and Moon 1987).

Transition services should begin two to four years before leaving school and continue for several years afterward, involving the school system, state developmental disability/mental retardation agencies, vocational rehabilitation agencies, and other organizations, and services should be coordinated with private sector programs, involving business and industry as well as the voluntary agencies which provide employment-related services (Elder 1988). The secondary special education teacher and administrators must take the responsibility for coordinating with rehabilitation services. An individualized transition plan (ITP) and the inclusion of a vocational rehabilitation representative in the final years of school is essential. The role of the vocational educator, trained to teach specific occupational skills, emphasized in the Carl D. Perkins Act of 1984, is also essential. For many secondary students and young adults with moderate and severe disabilities, occupational therapists, physical therapists, speech therapists, psychologists, nurses and social workers must also play an active service role during the transition years (Everson and Moon 1987). The individual student must, of course, be an active member of the planning team.

As evidence that this new approach is being increasingly accepted by lawmakers and administrators of public programs, the Supplemental Security Income (SSI) program has recently been modified to encourage employment of persons who because of disability were previously considered unable to engage in gainful employment. The 99th Congress changed the law to make it possible for persons with disabilities to engage in paid work without risking their Medicaid coverage and other benefits (see Chapter 3). At this writing the Department of Health and Human Services has established a working group on policies affecting mentally retarded and other developmentally disabled persons which is considering changes in the Medicaid programs to assist states by providing more funds for group homes, home care, and vocational services (Elder 1988). Elder, Special Assistant to Secretary of Health and Human Services, concludes her article by pointing out that it costs less to provide appropriate transitional and supported employment services than to continue to maintain people in community programs which do not have an employment outcome.

EDUCATION OF PEOPLE WITH LEARNING DISABILITIES

During the 1980s the number of students identified with learning disabilities has more than doubled, making it the largest of the disability groups being served by the schools. Understanding of what the disability is has grown tremendously, with the need to establish special programs and teaching practices for these children. The most commonly used definition is taken from the Education for All Handicapped Children Act of 1975:

> The term "children with specific learning disabilities" means those children who have a disorder in one or more of the basic psychological processes involved in understanding or in using language, spoken or written, which disorder may manifest itself in imperfect ability to listen, think, speak, read,

write, spell or do mathematical calculations. Such disorders include such conditions as perceptual handicaps, brain injury, minimal brain dysfunction, dyslexia, and developmental aphasia. Such term does not include children who have learning problems which are primarily the result of visual, hearing, or motor handicaps; of mental retardation; of emotional disturbance; or of environmental, cultural, or economic disadvantage (PL 94-142 1975).

A fact sheet prepared by Dale Brown of the President's Committee on Employment of People with Disabilities for the ERIC Clearinghouse on Handicapped and Gifted Children lists and describes all of the visual and auditory problems in sequencing, perception, and discrimination that are associated with learning disabilities (Brown 1980). By definition, learning disabilities have nothing to do with overall intelligence and indeed, many LD students are of average or above average intelligence. LD cannot be cured, but rather students are taught to compensate for their deficiencies and learn in accordance with strengths.

Learning disabilities have been variously attributed to neurological, environmental or emotional factors, but in recent years the emerging consensus is that they constitute neurological problems, some of which seem to have genetic bases. Medical research has centered upon trying to find abnormalities in brain structure. Boys diagnosed as learning disabled outnumber girls by a ratio of five to one, but the reason is not apparent.

Learning-disabled students are mainstreamed to the greatest extent possible, augmented with additional tutorial assistance. Only a small percentage are in special schools. More and more school districts are identifying LD students very early and placing them in special classes until such time as greater maturity might enable them to feed into regular classes. Learning-disabled high school graduates have been going to college in much greater numbers than ever before. Consequently, colleges have had to establish programs that will assist them with tutorial and other needs. These programs have been growing rapidly. A newsletter called *College "Helps"* (*College-Handicapped and Exceptional Learners Programs and Services*) is published by Partners in Publishing, 1419 West First Street, Tulsa, OK 74117. It reports on the many support programs that colleges and universities have developed to assist intelligent learning-disabled young adults who wish to go to college. Partners in Publishing also publishes a national directory of four-year colleges, two-year colleges, and postsecondary training programs for young people with learning disabilities (P.M. Fielding, ed.), a video tape on preparation of LD students for postsecondary education, and other materials, all listed on the last page of the newsletter.

In Chapter 7 the discussion on adult learning disabilities includes services now available through offices of vocational rehabilitation. At the present time, educators are looking at secondary-level programs with an eye toward transition to either higher education or work. As with other groups of young people with disabilities, it is very important that LD high school students be referred by education teachers to rehabilitation counselors at least one year before leaving school. Even if the student plans to attend college, it is important to develop an individual written rehabilitation plan (IWRP) to be used as a guide to facilitate the eventual transition from school to work. Work-related skills should be taught before students leave school (Drake and Whitten 1986).

At the Human Resources Center in Albertson, New York, several transition grants from OSERS are being used to operate various research and training programs for learning-disabled young adults, aimed at helping them make this transition. A three-year transition grant from OSERS which ended in 1987 examined the process for LD students moving from high school to college. Two workbooks were produced through this grant:

> *From High School to College: Keys to Success for Students with Learning Disabilities* (Michaels 1988) presents the strategies and techniques developed in this model project, and offers guidelines for replicating similar types of transitional support services at other sites. Information is given for high school, college and rehabilitation professionals.

> *How to Succeed in College: A Handbook for Students with Learning Disabilities* (Michaels 1988) is a workbook for learning-disabled high school students to assist them in their transition to college. It includes, among others, sections on self-awareness, "how to" tests to establish learning styles, strengths and weaknesses, and worksheets to help plan work schedules, techniques to aid recall, typical college tests, how to make use of information resources and enlist the assistance of college personnel, choosing the right major, and setting goals. Information about these books can be obtained from the Learning Disabilities Project, the National Center on Employment and Disability, Human Resources Center, Albertson, NY 11507.

A second grant from OSERS in operation at this writing, enables the center to help LD students make the transition from college to employment through vocational testing and counseling and support during the college experience. Students who may prove to be unable to negotiate college, or community college programs successfully would then become eligible for testing and training through a third grant project, Transition from High School to Employment. This program works with LD young adults not going to college, offering evaluation, training, job placement, and support counseling after placement. A manual entitled *Transitional Services for High School Students with Disabilities* (Michaels and Swirsky 1987) describes the services offered by Human Resources Center under this grant. Since the grant under which this program operated is now concluded, these services are being offered school districts on a "fee-for-service" basis.

A research-oriented grant at Human Resources Center is allowing a curriculum specialist to write curricula for use in both regular and special educational settings for the purpose of improving secondary services for learning-disabled students. Support personnel such as guidance counselors and administrators will be included in the program. A second year of the project includes training, and during the third year the information will be disseminated nationally.

The Rehabilitation Services Program at Ohio University College of Education has developed a model program to assist selected learning-disabled students with the transition from high school to work and/or postsecondary education. The program operated with a federal grant with the assistance of several central Ohio schools.

In 1987 a fact sheet from the Clearinghouse on Handicapped and Gifted Children described Attention Deficit Disorder (ADD), a diagnosis for children with distinct behavioral characteristics that do not fit the criteria in PL 94-142 for learning disabilities or emotional/behavior disorders. These children display inappropriate inattention, impulsivity, and sometimes hyperactivity. ADD is often diagnosed as secondary to other learning difficulties which may range from learning disabilities to emotional disturbance. The earlier the diagnosis can be made and remediation begun the better the chances of avoiding other complicating difficulties (Scott 1987). Information about learning disabilities and ADD can be obtained from:

The Association of Children and Adults with Learning Disabilities (ACLD)
4156 Library Road
Pittsburgh, PA 15234

The Orton Dyslexia Society
8415 Bellona Lane
Towson, MD 21204

The 1987-88 Directory of Facilities and Services for the Learning Disabled, Twelfth Edition
Academic Therapy Publications
20 Commercial Boulevard
Novato, CA 94947

The Coalition to ADD Attention Deficit Disorder to 94-142
PO Box 242
Osseo, MN 55369

Challenge (a newsletter available on subscription)
Challenge, Inc.
PO Box 96
Byfield, MA 01922

A minibibliography of Readings for Parents and Teachers of Learning Disabled Children, 1986, is available from the ERIC Clearinghouse on Handicapped and Gifted Children., 1920 Association Drive, Reston, VA 22091.

HIGHER EDUCATION

Almost all colleges and universities receive funds from the Department of Education, and are, therefore, affected by Section 504 of the Rehabilitation Act of 1973. This was a much needed development as many university campuses were inaccessible to disabled students.

In 1965, several existing federal laws were recodified and expanded into the Higher Education Act (PL 89-329), which established, as one of its provisions, a national policy of increasing accessibility of disadvantaged students to postsecondary education. Subsequent amendments added a variety of new grant and loan authorities and revised others. The latest amendment (PL 99-498, 1986) in Title VII authorizes construction/renovation grants and loans to institutions of higher education. Among the purposes for which funds may be used are bringing academic facilities into compliance with the Architectural Barriers Act of 1968 and Section 504 (Summary of Existing Legislation 1988).

Some universities—for example, the University of Illinois, University of Missouri, St. Andrew's Presbyterian College in North Carolina, the University of California, and Emporia State College in Kansas—led the way some years ago in making architectural and program changes for students with disabilities. Wright State University in Ohio pioneered during the 1970s the establishment of attendant services for severely disabled students. The number of students with disabilities prepared to enter college has grown in recent years because of improved high school curricula.

The 1986 edition of the *Directory of College Facilities and Services for the Disabled*, Oryx Press, Phoenix, AZ, Carol and James Thomas, eds., is the most up-to-date major directory available but a new edition is forthcoming. Students will have to investigate locally for any other programs suitable for their particular needs. The *Guide to Colleges for Learning Disabled Students*, Mary Ann

Liscio (ed.), was published by Academic Press, Inc., in 1984. A more up-to-date directory for students with learning disabilities may be obtained from the newsletter called *College "Helps."* For all students with disabilities, information is available from HEATH and from AHSSPPE. A pamphlet entitled "How to Choose a College: Guide for the Student with a Disability" was published as a joint project of HEATH and AHSSPPE in 1986.

CLEARINGHOUSES FOR THE HANDICAPPED AND OTHER INFORMATION RESOURCES

National Information Center for Handicapped Children and Youth (NICHCY), Box 1492, Wrshington, DC 20013, is a free information service that helps parents, educators, caregivers, and advocates to improve the lives of children and youth with disabilities. NICHCY is funded through a cooperative agreement between the US Department of Education under OSEP and Interstate Research Associates, Inc., 7923 Jones Branch Drive, Suite 1100, McLean, VA 22102, and operates the national clearinghouse on the education of the handicapped. It produces fact sheets, directories, and newsletters, and maintains resource files for each of the states and territories by organization and by subject. Two newsletters published by NICHCY are *News Digest*, circulated quarterly and focusing on special education concerns, and *Transition Summary*, a compilation of articles on transition issues that is distributed semiannually.

LINC Resources Inc., 4820 Indianola Avenue, Columbus, OH 43214, funded by the US Department of Education, Office of Special Education Programs, is available to access free information services (toll-free 800 772-7372). LINC maintains a database of special education media and materials which is highly selective and kept up to date, offers information on marketing for anyone who has developed special education media, helps in locating nonprofit special education publishers, and publishes reports synthesizing current literature and research results about selected instructional methodologies.

Workshops, planned and conducted by LINC, are held in conjunction with the annual meetings of the American Speech-Language-Hearing Association (ASHA), The Association for Persons with Severe Handicaps (TASH), and the Council for Exceptional Children (CEC). Publishers' workshops are held annually, to encourage publishers to enter, continue, or expand their efforts in the special education market. SpecialNet and Compuserve users can contact the center by sending messages to LINC (LINC Information Sheet 1988).

LINC publishes *LINC Notes*, a highly informative series of monthly newsbriefs to the publishing industry. Also available is its SpecialWare Database, containing 775 descriptions of software programs for special education including materials for early childhood to adult education and mildly handicapped to severely handicapped. LINC is also assisting IBM on their Special Needs Exchange project, an online information resource sponsored by the IBM Corporation as a public service for teachers, researchers, administrators, and others. To request information send a message, via SpecialNet electronic mail, to IBM.LINC, or contact the IBM Corporation.

HEATH (Higher Education and Adult Training for People with Handicaps) Resource Center, One Dupont Circle, Suite 670, Washington, DC 20036-1193, is a clearinghouse and information exchange center for resources on postsecondary education programs for persons with disabilities. A program of the American Council on Education, it operates the National Clearinghouse on

Postsecondary Education for Handicapped Individuals, which is funded by OSEP. Topics covered include educational support services, opportunities on American campuses, vocational-technical schools, adult education programs, independent living centers, and other training opportunities after high school.

Fact sheets and research papers are available from HEATH on a variety of topics including access, audio-visual materials, hearing impairments, financial aid, learning disabilities, and much more. HEATH publishes a newsletter entitled *Information from HEATH* tri-annually which includes information about laws, regulations, and other items of interest. An annual resource directory contains an annotated listing of over 100 national organizations which can provide additional information on postsecondary education and handicapped individuals. There is no charge for HEATH publications and they are all available on cassette from the National Library Service for the Blind and Physically Handicapped (see Chapter 9).

The National Clearinghouse on Careers and Employment in Special Education is a new clearinghouse which was first funded by OSEP in 1987 and is operated by the National Association of State Directors of Special Education (NASDSE). It assumes some of the functions previously performed by the National Clearinghouse on the Education of the Handicapped, and concentrates on disseminating information concerning career opportunities in special education, and identifying training programs around the country. It is located at CEC.

Association on Handicapped Student Service Programs in Postsecondary Education (AHSSPPE) is a national, nonprofit organization of persons from all 50 states, Canada, and other countries, which is interested in promoting full participation of individuals with disabilities in college life. Established in 1978, the association disseminates information on postsecondary education for students with disabilities, and serves as a resource to individuals currently engaged in providing support services to these students as well as to individuals and organizations interested in expanding/improving access for such students to higher education. It sponsors numerous workshops and conferences focused on solutions in upgrading the quality of available services. The association holds an annual conference. AHSSPPE may be reached at PO Box 21192, Columbus, OH 43221.

National Information Center on Deafness (NICD) located at Gallaudet University, 800 Florida Avenue NE, Washington, DC 20002, was established in 1980 to meet the need for accurate, current information on topics dealing with deafness. It provides experts in the field of deafness at Gallaudet as well as names of national, state, and local programs and services from its in-house resource collection. NICD provides either direct information, printed materials, and/or, when appropriate, referrals to other helpful resources. Fact sheets and resource listings include such areas as teletypewriters for the deaf, alerting and communication devices, hearing ear dogs, financial aid for hearing-impaired students, travel resources for hearing-impaired people, and reading lists on topics in education of deaf children. Single copies of publications are provided free, as are all information services.

The National Center for Research in Vocational Education at the University of California (2150 Shadhuck Avenue, Sutie 600, Berkeley, CA 94704-130) carries out applied research in vocational education, disseminates findings, and offers planning and evaluation assistance to help agencies and organizations solve educational problems related to career planning and conducts leadership training programs. Its databases RIVE (Resources in Vocational Education and

VECM (Vocational Education Curriculum Materials) include some materials for special needs students. The National Center subcontracts work to five other research institutions. One of them, the Center at the University of Illinois, College of Education (345 Education Building, 1310 South Sixth Street, Champaign, IL 61820) operates the Technical Assistance for Special Populations Program (TASPP) and is publishing a series of briefs dealing with aspects of populations with special needs.

ERIC Clearinghouse on Adult, Career, and Vocational Education is located at 1900 Kenny Road, Columbus, OH 43210.

For all persons wishing to stay abreast of legislation, programs, and funding for special education, an extremely valuable newsletter is *Education of the Handicapped*, a biweekly publication from Capitol Publications, Inc., 1101 King Street, PO Box 1453, Alexandria VA 22313-2053.

Exceptional Parent magazine (Psy-Ed Corp. 1170 Commonwealth Avenue, Boston, MA 02134) is now publishing an annual *Directory of Organizations* (latest edition is in the September 1989 issue of the *Journal*). It lists information and advocacy service agencies, parent-governed groups, government agencies, and professional organizations.

REFERENCES

Aiello, Barbara. 1976, February. "Especially for Special Educators: A Sense of Our Own History." *Exceptional Children* 42, 246.

"Amendment to Education of the Handicapped Act." 1988, January/February. *Exceptional Parent*, 17.

Ballard, Joseph. 1977. "Public Law 94-142 and Section 504—Understanding What They Are and Are Not." Reston, VA: Council for Exceptional Children, 1.

Bellamy, G. Thomas. 1988. "State Variation in Placement of Children with Handicaps in Segregated Environments." Washington, DC: Education Department.

Bellamy, G. Thomas, Wilcox, Barbara, Rose, Heidi, and McDonnell, John. 1985, October. "Education and Career Preparation for Youth with Disabilities." *Journal of Adolescent Health Care* 6 (2): 125-35.

Brown, Dale. 1980. "Learning Disabilities." Fact Sheet, ERIC Clearinghouse on Handicapped and Gifted Children.

Cain, Leo F. 1976, May. "Parent Groups: Their Role in a Better Life for the Handicapped." *Exceptional Children* 52: 432-37.

Connor, Frances P. 1976, April. "The Past Is Prologue: Teacher Preparation in Special Education." *Exceptional Children* 42: 369.

Drake, Gregory A., and Witten, Barbara J. 1986, Spring. "Facilitating Learning Disabled Adolescents' Successful Transition from School to Work." *Journal of Applied Rehabilitation Counseling* 17 (1): 34-37.

Education of the Handicapped. 1988, March. "Commission Faults Deaf Education in Report to Congressional Panel." Capitol Publications, Inc. Alexandria, VA 22313-2053.

Elder, Jean K. 1988, January/February. "Transition from School to Work." *Exceptional Parent*, 27-29.

Everson, Jane M., and Moon, M. Sherril. 1987. "Transition Services for Young Adults with Severe Disabilities: Defining Professional and Parental Roles and Responsibilities." *Journal of the Association for Persons with Severe Handicaps (JASH)* 12 (2): 87-95.

Hasazi, S. B., Gordon, L. R., and Roe, C.A. 1985. "Factors Associated with the Employment Status of Handicapped Youth Exiting High School from 1979-1983." *Exceptional Children* 5 (6): 455-69.

HEATH Resource Center. 1987, May. "ADD Sometimes Overlaps." Washington, DC: Information from HEATH, 5–6.

HEATH Resource Center. 1987, May. "Post Secondary Education Opportunities for Students Who Are Hearing Impaired." Washington, DC: Information from HEATH, 1–2.

LINC Information Sheet, June 1988.

Meisel, C. Julius, ed. 1986. *Mainstreaming Handicapped Children: Outcomes, Controversies, and New Directions*. London: Lawrence Erlbaum Associates, Publishers.

Michaels, Craig A. 1988. *From High School to College; Keys to Success for Students with Learning Disabilities; Strategies to Facilitate Transition for College, High School and Rehabilitation Professionals*. Albertson, NY: Vocational Rehabilitation Services Division, National Center on Employment and Disability, Human Resources Center.

Michaels, Craig A. 1988. *How to Succeed in College: A Handbook for Students with Learning Disabilities*. Albertson, NY: Vocational Rehabilitation Services Division, National Center on Employment and Disability, Human Resources Center.

Michaels, Craig, and Swirsky, Jessica. 1987. *Transitional Services for High School Students with Disabilities*. Albertson, NY: Vocational Rehabilitation Services Division, National Center on Employment and Disability, Human Resources Center.

Montgomery, Judy K. 1986. "Mainstreaming Orthopedically Handicapped Students in a Regular Public School." In Berres, Michael S., and Knoblock, Peter. *Program Models for Mainstreaming: Integrating Students with Moderate to Severe Disabilities*. Rockville, MD: Aspen Publishers, 169–91.

National Advisory Committee on the Handicapped. 1976. *The Unfinished Revolution: Education for the Handicapped, 1976 Annual Report*. Washington, DC: Department of Health, Education and Welfare, Office of Education, 3, 4.

National Directory of Special Education Personnel Preparation Programs, 1987 Edition. 1987. Washington, DC: Teacher Education Division of the Council for Exceptional Children, National Information Center for Children and Youth with Handicaps.

National School Public Relations Association. 1974. *Educating Children with Special Needs: Current Trends in School Policies and Programs*. Arlington, VA, 23.

National Technical Institute for the Deaf. 1987. "Facts You Can Use." Pamphlet, Rochester, NY.

Neural Tube Defect Laboratory. 1982. *Screening for Neural Tube Defects: A New Blood Test for Pregnant Women*. Stoney Brook, NY: State University of New York at Stony Brook.

New York State Commission on the Quality Cost, and Financing of Elementary and Secondary Education. *The Fleischmann Report: A Report on the Quality, Cost, and Financing of Elementary and Secondary Education in New York State*. 1972. "Children with Special Needs."

Newsletter. "Summary of Selected Legislation Relating to Handicapped Individuals." 1987, Spring. *OSERS News in Print*. Department of Education, Washington, DC 20202, 8.

The 1986 Directory of National Information Sources on Handicapping Conditions and Related Services. 1986, June. With update supplement, 1987. Winchester, MA: Harold Russell Associates, Inc.

Program-Funded Activities Fiscal Year 1987. 1988. Washington, DC: Department of Education.

"Report: Many Deaf People Undereducated." 1988, May. *Newsletter of the State Advocate for the Disabled*. 11 (5): 1, 8.

Schmitt, Patricia, Cartledge, Gwendolyn, and Growick, Bruce. 1988, Spring. "Addressing the Transition and Social Skill Needs of Learning Disabled Adolescents and Adults." *NARIC Quarterly* 1 (1): 1, 6–13, 17.

Scott, Mary E. 1987. "Attention Deficit Disorder (ADD)." *Digest 445*. Reston, VA: ERIC Clearinghouse on Handicapped and Gifted Children.

Summary of Existing Legislation Affecting Persons with Disabilities. 1988, August. Clearinghouse on the Handicapped. US Department of Education, Pub. E-88-22014. Washington, DC 20202-2524, 21.

"To Assure the Free Appropriate Public Education of All Handicapped Children" (Education of the Handicapped Act, Section 618, as amended by PL 98-199). 1988. Tenth Annual Report to Congress on the Implementation of the Education of the Handicapped Act, Washington, DC, Department of Education.

Velleman, Ruth A. 1964. "School Library Service for Physically Handicapped Children; An Account of the Library Program at the Human Resources School, Albertson, NY." Master's Thesis, Palmer Graduate Library School, C.W. Post College of Long Island University, Brookville, NY, unpublished, 3–8.

"What Is the TAPP Network?" 1987–88, Winter. *Coalition Quarterly*. National Network of Parent Centers, Inc. Technical Assistance for Parent Programs Network. Vol. 5, No. 4, 1.

Wilcox, Barbara, and Bellamy, G. Thomas. 1982. *Design of High School Programs for Severely Handicapped Students*. Baltimore: Paul H. Brookes Publishing Co.

Will, Madeleine. 1984, March/April. *Bridges from School to Working Life, Programs for the Handicapped*. Clearinghouse on the Handicapped.

PART IV

Library Applications

Chapter 9
The Public Library

Public libraries are the backbone of library and information services in the United States, and they have always led the way in providing special patrons, such as blind, homebound, and institutionalized individuals with basic reader services. During the decades of the 1970s and 1980s, people with disabilities emerged in far greater numbers than ever before from homes and institutions, making great strides toward becoming active participants in society. "Access" became the word that characterized this phenomenon—access to education, employment, housing, and recreation, access to the right to live in dignity with some measure of independence, whether or not employment is feasible. For all people, the quality of life is the most important goal, not its length or its economic productivity. Information services to this special population must continue to reflect their changing life requirements. Most public libraries operate active outreach programs, serving the disabled with recreational reading materials in book or alternative format under the mandate of the National Library Service for the Blind and Physically Handicapped of the Library of Congress.

LEGISLATION

The Library Services and Construction Act as amended in 1984 (PL 98-480) is composed of six titles. Title I includes providing basic grants-in-aid to the states to provide library services for patients and inmates in state-supported institutions and persons with physical handicaps. To receive specialized library services, an individual with a physical handicap (including a person who is blind or otherwise visually handicapped) must be . . . "certified by a competent authority as unable to read or to use conventional printed materials as a result of physical limitations." (Summary of Existing Legislation 1988).

A draft bill entitled "Library Improvement Act of 1989" has now been circulated for comments. This bill proposes to establish a library improvement program for economically disadvantaged or handicapped individuals and to repeal both the Library Services and Construction Act and Title II of the Higher Education Act (see Chapter 10). Libraries should be alerted to watch for its passage.

LIBRARY SERVICE TO PEOPLE WITH DISABILITIES

People who are physically disabled have the same recreational reading tastes as their able-bodied peers. Although a book may sometimes prove inspirational, in most cases people with disabilities are interested in well-written books that depict the human condition in all its aspects, through good fiction, nonfiction, or biography. Offering these people a book about someone with a disability, unless it is in response to a request, is presumptuous and to be avoided. In addition to recreational reading, many people with disabilities need the library for professional reading materials.

As school and university programs are shaped to accommodate students with disabilities, more and more of them will be entering the professions. All of these needs can be handled easily by the professional librarian when these people are able to use print materials. Sources for alternate formats will be discussed below.

Access to the physical library premises is, of course, a basic necessity. Chapter 12 outlines the architectural adaptations which can make a library accessible. Adaptations can also make it possible for librarians with disabilities to work in the public library environment.

A question often asked by public librarians is how they can reach people with disabilities who live in their communities but who are not using the library. As with any other library user, those with physical disabilities sometimes must be lured to the library with a little extra effort. Some librarians have found that, after building what they consider to be an accessible library, patrons who are physically disabled still do not appear. In one such library, it was found that no reserved parking had been provided. The following suggestions may encourage such greater library use:

1. Wherever possible, when planning architectural adaptations, include people with disabilities on the planning team to ensure that alterations are feasible.
2. Publicize. After physical adaptations have been made to the library building, a news story in the local press may spark interest.
3. Set aside two or three reserved parking spots (see Chapter 12) appropriately marked with the symbol of access or a sign stating "reserved for persons with disabilities." This in itself is an advertisement to the community that the library staff is aware of this population and is anxious to serve them.
4. A newsletter is an excellent way to publicize what the library has to offer and can be sent legitimately to all homes in the area. One of the most difficult things to find are actual names of people with disabilities living within a district. It may even be a violation of privacy to do this. Moreover, it is impossible to judge to what extent an individual perceives him or herself to be disabled. Elderly or infirm people may also benefit from some of the materials acquired or the architectural modifications made. The newsletter might mention the acquisition of special reference materials. In addition, an item in the local press indicating that a special collection is being developed in this area may bring patrons in or to the telephone.
5. Club activities sometimes bring surprising results. In one public library, the reference librarian in Port Washington, New York, had an interest in CB radios and started a hobby club. Four teenagers in wheelchairs arrived to attend the first meeting.

6. Children's librarians will find much of the reference information collected in the library to be helpful in answering questions raised by the parents of youngsters with disabilities. In addition, efforts can be made by children's librarians to determine which special schools in their areas do not have librarians, and they can offer to develop story hours or help teachers acquire special materials.
7. Clubs, church groups, or schools for persons who are deaf may be contacted to offer service. Persons who are deaf or hearing impaired often hesitate to come to the library for fear they will not be understood.
8. The increase in nonbook materials in all public libraries, such as musical recordings on disc or record and videotapes, should be publicized and methods of borrowing explained. For persons who spend much time at home, the advent of the VCR has helped broaden horizons.
9. Above all, librarians must be aware of what can and cannot be answered by supplying a book. It is important to make sure that the patron has had appropriate medical information. For example, in the case of low-back pain symptoms, books containing exercises will not help, and may even prove harmful, unless the specific problem has been diagnosed and the exercises prescribed or approved by a physician. Persons seeking information that is rehabilitative in nature should be referred first of all to a rehabilitation facility. If the person is disabled, the local vocational rehabilitation office should be suggested, where a rehabilitation counselor can make the proper referral. Local offices are listed in the telephone directory.
10. The State Governor's Committee may be consulted for additional suggestions on the information needs of people with disabilities (a listing of all governor's committee addresses is available from the State Relations Department, President's Committee on Employment of Persons with Disabilities, Washington, DC 20036.

REFERENCE MATERIALS

At one time it was thought that services to people with disabilities was only the responsibility of the National Library Service (NLS) for the Blind and Physically Handicapped. But public libraries now realize that there are many more facets to service. Public librarians can exercise their own professional creativity in shaping special services. A Harris Poll conducted in March of 1988, in conjunction with the International Center for the Disabled, revealed that many people with disabilities are still not familiar with services available to them and a majority find it difficult to find out about these services. It is an ongoing challenge, therefore, for public libraries to do more to reach this population. Basic information can be found in Chapters 3 and 4 of this work. Information should be made available about legal and financial rights, as well as transportation and travel, recreation, sports, sexual information, adaptive devices, special clothing, home adaptations, and sources for information about independent living. Chapter 5 outlines the uses of the computer as it has benefited people with disabilities, and includes sources for information in this important area.

While the information provided here is on a national level, public librarians will wish to develop local community resource files in order to provide useful references. In many cases, national organizations have local chapters. Social service agencies can be of help in providing community resource material. It will be useful to include in reference files addresses of organizations offering information about specific disabilities, as listed in Chapter 2. It is important for parents of babies born with disabilities to find information when they look for it in the public library. Much of it is in pamphlet form and can be obtained for vertical files at little or no cost. Periodicals which should be available to the public are *Accent on Living, Paraplegia News, Exceptional Parent, The Journal of Visual Impairment and Blindness, The Deaf American,* and *A Positive Approach.*

To the extent that particular public libraries serve professional populations in either the rehabilitation or special education fields, information, books, and periodicals in these fields should be acquired. Periodicals might include, in addition to those mentioned above, the *Journal of Rehabilitation, Exceptional Children, Journal of Learning Disabilities,* and the *Journal of Rehabilitation of the Deaf.*

Basic newsletters for libraries wishing to remain current on legislation are *Report on Disability Programs* and *Education of the Handicapped. Report on Disability Programs* is available on recorded cassette for blind and visually impaired people, thanks to the Washington Volunteer Readers for the Blind, Inc., of Washington, DC. These copies may be obtained through local NLS regional libraries.

Reference materials for all libraries should include the following basic directories:

Directory of Information Sources on Handicapping Conditions and Related Services, prepared by Harold Russell Associates, for the Office of Special Education and Rehabilitative Services, U.S. Department of Education, Washington, DC, 1986 plus supplement (or latest edition)

National Resources Directory: An Information Guide for Persons with Spinal Cord Injury
600 West Comming Park, Suite 2000
Woburn, MA 01801 (August 1985 or latest edition)

A Handbook for the Disabled: Ideas and Inventions for Easier Living by Suzanne Lunt
New York: Charles Scribner's Sons, 1984.

A Directory of Agencies Serving the Deaf-Blind
Helen Keller National Center
111 Middle Neck Road
Sands Point, NY 11050

Directory of Services for Blind and Visually Impaired Persons
American Foundation for the Blind
15 West 16th Street
New York, NY 10011 (23rd ed. 1988)

Directory for Exceptional Children
Porter-Sargent Publishers Inc.
11 Beacon Street
Boston, MA 02108 (latest edition)

American Annals of the Deaf: Reference Issue
814 Thayer Avenue
Silver Spring, MD 20910
> This reference issue, published annually in April, supplies information on programs and services for deaf persons in the United States including educational, rehabilitational, social, and recreational resources. Most information is listed by state.

Resource Guide to Organizations Concerned with Developmental Handicaps
American Association of University Affiliated Programs for Persons with Developmental Disabilities (annually)
8605 Cameron Street, Suite 406
Silver Spring, MD 20910
> A much more extensive listing may be found in the *Directory of National Information Sources on Handicapping Conditions and Related Services* (1986).

Reference services offered by the reference section of the National Library Service for the Blind and Physically Handicapped of the Library of Congress include the publication of informative bibliographies that are updated continually. In addition, use can be made of the reference resources at NARIC, and the ABLEDATA computerized bank of devices. The bibliography of this work is organized by topic and may be consulted for additional books, periodicals, and newsletters.

Libraries with access to ABLEDATA will not need extensive files of commercial catalogs. However, for quick reference it is useful to have a few basic ones on file.

Accent on Living Buyer's Guide, Annual.
Supplied with a subscription to Accent on Living Magazine, or purchased from the publisher, this handy little guide indexes advertisers, addresses of manufacturers, service organizations, periodicals and local dealers. Topics covered include automobile controls, vans, clothing, reading aids, recreation, sports, travel, furniture, gardening, sexuality, mobility aids, films and publications.

Ways and Means
Capability Collection Resource Catalogues
Wagner Associates
28001 Citrin Drive
Romulus, MI 48174 (1-800-221-4413 in Michigan; 1-800-654-2345 outside Michigan)
> This is a mail-order catalog listing over 1,000 products from several hundred manufacturers for activities of daily living.

Clio, Inc.
3957 Mayfield Road
Cleveland, OH 44121 (800-321-0595)
> Catalog of products for activities of daily living and medical equipment.

Equipment for Rehabilitation and Special Education
J. A. Preston Corporation
60 Page Road
Clifton, NJ 07012 (800-631-7277)
> Catalog of materials for activities of daily living, medical equipment, special furniture, as well as special equipment for children in a complete line of perceptual training materials. These include physical therapy equipment, tricycles, bicycles, and other mobility aids, specially adapted games and puzzles, and much more.

Prentke Romich
1022 Heyl Road
Wooster, OH 44691
Catalog of communication aids.

Products for People with Vision Problems
American Foundation for the Blind
15 West 16th Street
New York, NY 10011 (1988-89 new ed. forthcoming)
A catalog of products including household items, games, education materials, communication aids, clocks and timers, health care, kitchen equipment, mobility aids, recreation, tools, watches, and writing aids.

L S & S Group
Products for the Visually Impaired
PO Box 673
Northbrook, IL 60065 (1-800-468-4789)
A mail order catalog listing a full range of products and including computer adaptations, sports equipment, and educational materials for children.

Independent Living Aids, Inc.
27 East Mall
Plainview, NY 11803
Lists devices for easier use of all kinds of aides for independent living for persons with limited hand use, or limited vision.

The Assistive Devices Center
Products for Deaf and Hard of Hearing People
Clarke School for the Deaf
Center for Oral Education
McAlister Building
Round Hill Road
Northampton, MA
Lists all types of signaling devices for environmental awareness.

NATIONAL LIBRARY SERVICE FOR THE BLIND AND PHYSICALLY HANDICAPPED

The Library of Congress began its service to people who are blind and handicapped on March 3, 1931, when President Herbert Hoover signed into law the Pratt-Smoot Act, mandating that embossed books be provided to adult blind residents of the United States, and that these books be circulated through a number of libraries designated as regional centers. An amendment to the bill providing recorded books as well was added in 1932. After being funded, the talking books program was inaugurated in 1934. In 1962 the Pratt-Smoot Act was amended to authorize "a library of musical scores, instructional texts, and other specialized materials. . . ." (Majeska 1988). And in 1966, President Lyndon Johnson signed a bill amending the Pratt-Smoot Act to extend service to persons who are physically handicapped and who cannot use conventional printed material. This now includes those who are learning disabled and who must be certified by a physician as being unable to use print materials.

In the more than 50 years that this program has been in operation it has gone through many changes involving equipment development as well as the expansion of public library capabilities through which services to the reader are delivered. Interested persons can read about the history of this remarkable development in two works developed and published by the National Library Service for the Blind and Physically Handicapped, and available from the US Government Printing Office: *That All May Read: Library Service for Blind and Physically Handicapped People*, National Library Service 1984, and *Talking Books: Pioneering and Beyond*, Majeska 1988, which details the hardware development that has taken place through the decades, including the evolving of recording machines from disc to cassette, and the refinement of methods of braille processing. The development of the cassette player, with voice indexing, may be followed in detail in *Talking Books: Pioneering and Beyond*. Services to children have been outlined in *R Is for Reading, Library Service to Blind and Physically Handicapped Children* (Eldridge 1985).

Publicizing the ways in which the collection can be accessed by its reading public is an ongoing project of NLS. The publications *Braille Book Review* and *Talking Book Topics*, bimonthly magazines listing books produced since the previous issues, are supplemented by many catalogs and bibliographies which are available at regional and sub-regional libraries.

The NLS Network

The nationwide network of agencies cooperating with NLS in Washington, DC, includes hundreds of state and local agencies: regional libraries, subregional libraries, deposit and demonstration collections, multistate centers, and machine-lending agencies. NLS provides the materials and equipment while network agencies provide space, staff, and all aspects of library service to persons with print handicaps. The network of cooperating libraries is divided into four regions: the west, the north, the south and the midlands. The libraries belong to their own regional conferences, headed by an elected chairperson. Regional conferences generally make it possible to exchange information geared toward more efficient delivery of service and expansion of outreach services.

NLS materials are made available to eligible users through regional libraries, which serve patrons directly or establish subregional libraries to do so. There are 56 regional libraries, administered in whole or in part by a state library agency, and 97 subregional libraries. In some states programs are administered jointly by the state library agency and another state agency such as the department of education. Regional libraries receive both state and federal funds.

Subregional libraries are local, usually public libraries, or library systems, designated by a regional library, with the approval of NLS, to provide service to individuals in a specified area of the regional library's total jurisdiction. Twenty-two states have established subregional or branch service patterns. Funding may be provided entirely from local sources or from a combination of state, local, and federal sources. One of the great strengths of the NLS program is that the librarians in the entire network have a great deal of flexibility in carrying out the basic mandate of the program. Over the years, in my travels around the country, I have found great differences in the ways in which the program is administered and in the level of service provided.

By 1980 findings about the use of the NLS program, numbers of nonusers, and of potential users were submitted to NLS based on a survey conducted in 1977 by the American Foundation for the Blind. Among significant findings, the nonuser study showed that 43 percent of the eligible population had never heard of the NLS program. The study noted that, although health care professionals were in an ideal position to refer people, they had a poor track record.

It would seem that until health care agencies have libraries, an ideal I have long espoused, the onus is on the public library, specifically the subregional library, to continually reach out to the community, to make persons aware of this very important service. Two years later another survey was conducted with no sharp changes in readership reported. NLS has been making a great effort, during the last two decades, to reach potential users via brochures, posters, a slide show, regional workshops and conferences, and broadcast television public service announcements. Statistics of numbers of users have been difficult to update, as the population changes constantly, with older users dropping out and new users coming in. However, the report *Library Resources for the Blind and Physically Handicapped*, issued by the department in 1988 and available from NLS, is not only a directory of all regional and subregional libraries, but contains a chart with detailed statistics by state, on readership and circulation numbers, budget, staffing, and size of collections. While this is an excellent reference, it does not contain an overall analysis of readership patterns.

Automation

In 1982 NLS investigated proposals for a complete data processing and telecommunications system (NLSNET) to link NLS regional libraries, multistate centers, and machine-lending agencies. This system has enabled greater production control. During the 1970s complete computerization of bibliographic records made it possible for a computer output microfiche (COM) catalog called *Reading Material for the Blind and Physically Handicapped* to appear in 1977 with subsequent cumulative quarterly editions. Moving toward the goal of developing the microfiche catalog into a union catalog of materials for blind and physically disabled people, NLS began a cooperative cataloging project with network libraries, and to this end adapted the MARC (machine readable cataloging) system of the Library of Congress. Network libraries that produce books and are willing to lend them outside their own areas submit cataloging forms to NLS for input into the MARC records. Other agencies, such as Recording for the Blind, Inc. (see below), and the National Library of Australia, joined the cooperative cataloging project. Since 1980 Bibliographic Retrieval Services, Inc. (BRS), a national information retrieval network, has processed a tape copy of the NLS computer file, by an indexing method that makes access to the records highly simplified. The system is searched regularly by more than a dozen network libraries, by Recording for the Blind, and by the National Library of Australia via satellite.

Children's Services

When Leslie Eldridge compiled *R Is for Reading*, in 1985 it was her finding that children were not using NLS to the same extent as were adults. Differences between this service and public library service to children seemed to work against recorded materials. The browsing aspect of other libraries is missing. Children can choose from catalogs and consult *Talking Book Topics*, but that is not the same as being able to hold a book in one's hand and decide whether to read it. Selection is left up to the librarian in many cases (Eldridge 1985). Talking Books should be able to motivate reading by supplying books on tape appropriate to the age level of students who are blind, physically disabled, or the learning-disabled student who would not otherwise be able to read appropriate age-level books. Many children use the service through itinerant teachers either in regular schools serving students with disabilities or in special school settings. It is certainly the task of the school and the public librarian to make parents aware of the service and how to apply for it. Eldridge found that many teachers were unaware of up-to-date children's literature and recreational reading possibilities of all kinds. Here again the school or public librarian must take the lead. NLS is continuing to explore ways to publicize service to children and young adults and make the service more appealing to them.

Volunteers

Volunteers have always played a significant role in NLS services. Even before NLS was established, volunteers were providing reading materials for blind individuals. A 1980 study showed that volunteers were contributing services in all areas, including narration of tapes, proofreading, binding, labeling and packaging braille, and transcribing large type. Telephone Pioneers repair cassettes and in some areas do repair work in patrons' homes, making the service more personal. Some volunteers read to individuals, transport patrons to and from the library, deliver machines and books, and provide reading guidance. Others work in outreach and administration, including speaking to community groups, recruiting volunteers, and scheduling labor. The 1980 study estimated that the net value of the volunteer contribution was at least $3 million. National Library Service provides technical training to volunteers, certifying them in braille transcription through Library of Congress courses taken by correspondence or through local groups.

Reference Services

The reference service division publishes a *Directory of Library Resources for the Blind and Physically Handicapped*, giving the addresses, phone numbers and names of the librarians or directors of regional libraries. This directory is produced annually. Librarians throughout the network receive many requests for information of all kinds from their patrons. In order to assist in answering these requests, the reference services department supplies many bibliographies which are periodically updated. A partial listing includes:

Bibles and Other Scriptures in Special Media, 1988
Braille Instruction and Writing Equipment, 1986
From School to Working Life: Resources and Services, 1985
Information for Handicapped Travelers, 1987
Reading Materials in Large Type, 1987
Reading, Writing, and Other Communication Aids for Visually and
    Physically Handicapped Persons, 1986
Library and Information Services to Persons with Disabilities (ref.
    bibliography no. 89–1), 1989.

RADIO READING SERVICES

Radio reading services bring news, features, sports, business, opinions, advertisements and other materials over a closed circuit signal tied in with local FM radio stations. A special receiver pretuned to the service is needed to listen.

The receivers look like ordinary table-model radios, some with earphone jacks for private listening, some with automatic timers and tape recorders attached so that programs can be recorded for later listening. Most radio reading services are on the air around the clock or most of the day and night. The Association of Radio Reading Services (ARRS) was formed in 1977 to promote the growth of radio reading services throughout the country and to provide for the development and sharing of new technology, and mount a unified effort in the pursuit of conducive legislation and public awareness of this valuable service. More than 100 radio reading services now provide reading to approximately 125,000 persons (ARRS 1988).

Persons are eligible if they are print-handicapped because of blindness, visual impairment, or severe physical disability. Receivers are on loan and remain the property of the service. Programs are read by volunteers who are specially trained. Some 7,000 of them serve each week, a phenomenal example of volunteering in the United States. Services do their own fund-raising, with funds coming from local or state governments; foundations or service clubs; businesses or corporations; labor unions; or listeners and friends of the service. Some services are affiliated with state or voluntary agencies serving blind persons, some have been set up as nonprofit corporations, some are supported by local FM stations, some by public radio stations, and some are supported by colleges, universities, and libraries.

The Intouch Network Inc., the radio reading service based at 322 West 48th Street, New York, NY 10036, was established in 1977. Intouch is a member of ARRS, with a very large readership. It provides programs to other radio reading services around the country and operates 24 hours a day. One hour a day is devoted to Spanish-language periodicals. Local radio reading services can be contacted for an application to obtain the service. It is important that local libraries have on file the telephone numbers of these services. To obtain a national directory supplying addresses and telephone numbers of radio reading services contact: The Association of Radio Reading Services, Inc., 1745 University Avenue, St. Paul, MN 55104.

CHOICE MAGAZINE LISTENING

Choice Magazine Listening (CML) selects and records writings from print magazines. Every other month, this free service offers its subscribers 8 hours of articles, fiction, and poetry, chosen from over 100 contemporary periodicals and read by professional voices onto 8 rpm phonograph records (record players with this speed are provided through National Library Service for the Blind and Physically Handicapped). CML is a project of the nonprofit Lucerna Fund. It welcomes new subscribers on a first-come first-served basis. To subscribe write to: Choice Magazine Listening, PO Box 10, Port Washington, NY 11050. Talking books users may also obtain subscriptions through their talking books librarian.

RECORDING FOR THE BLIND, INC. (RFB)

Recording for the Blind (RFB) is a private, nonprofit service organization with administrative headquarters and Master Tape Library in Princeton, New Jersey. Thirty-one recording studios around the nation use the talents of 4,000 volunteers to fulfill RFB's mission, which began originally for blinded war veterans 40 years ago, but has been expanded to provide recorded educational books free on a loan basis to persons who cannot read standard printed material and whose print handicap results from a visual, physical, or specific learning disability. Once registered, RFB borrowers have free access to all aspects of the service, including the over 80,000-title master tape library, the recording program and the subject reference service. The recording program provides that in the event that a title is not available, a borrower may request that a recording be made by sending two copies of the material with the request. College students should make their requests in the spring, for a fall semester course, thus allowing time to locate a reader knowledgeable in the subject area to prepare the material.

Since 1975, Media Services and Captioned Films, in the Office of Special Education and Rehabilitative Services (OSERS), has, through contract with RFB, assisted in providing students with materials. Borrowers must be registered with RFB at the Princeton office. Schools, agencies, or their representatives are not eligible as borrowers. Borrowers must list exact title and author of work needed, as well as copyright date and edition.

LOW-VISION PATRONS

Persons with low vision should be directed to a low-vision clinic where ophthalmologists or optometrists have had specialized training in dealing with this disability. Librarians should be aware of the aids that are available for persons with low vision. Nonoptical aids include large-print materials, reading stands, reading and writing guides, and high-intensity lamps. Some sources of nonprint nonoptical materials can be found in the *American Foundation for the Blind's Products for People with Visual Problems*, published annually in large type. The reference circular "Reading, Writing and Other Communication Aids for the Visually and Physically Handicapped" (1986) is available from the NLS. Optical aids include lens systems such as spectacles, contact lenses, telescopic lenses, microscopic lenses, clip on lenses, loops and hand-held telescopes, and electro-optical systems such as illuminated magnifiers, projection magnifiers, and closed circuit television. By acquiring some of these aids librarians can expose the partially-sighted person to their diversity (Klauber and Covino 1981).

LIBRARY SERVICE TO PEOPLE WHO ARE DEAF AND HEARING IMPAIRED

Many public libraries have developed services for deaf and hearing-impaired people during the 1980s, stimulated by the leadership of the Forum on Library Service to the Deaf Population of ASCLA, as well as by published works by Alice Hagemeyer, librarian for the deaf at the Martin Luther King Public Library in Washington, DC, (Hagemeyer 1979, 1988) who also prepared a chapter in the first edition of this book, and *Library Service to the Deaf and Hearing Impaired* (Dalton 1985).

The development of a collection and services for the population of deaf and hearing-impaired persons in the community will be successful if efforts are made to involve them in suggestions for such service and in the subsequent use of the library. Dalton states that resource development on deafness and hearing impairment should not be considered special or outreach, but should be fundamental to and an integral part of the library program on the basis that the library should serve everyone in the community (Dalton 1985).

Equipment and Staffing

Public libraries should have a teletypewriter for the deaf (TDD) so that patrons who do not have such equipment at home will be able to use it to contact public agencies for essential information. For information on purchasing a suitable machine write to: Teletypewriters for the Deaf, Inc., 814 Thayer Avenue, Silver Spring, MD 20910. Information for purchasing home equipment should be kept on file for deaf patrons. Libraries should also consider installing a sound system for use at meetings held in the library.

The staff of the library might benefit by asking a person who is hearing impaired to teach the staff rudimentary sign language and other ways of communicating with patrons. Other duties could include initial contact with the deaf community, developing of a reference collection, conducting a deaf awareness week at the library, and arranging for captioned film programs (Hagemeyer 1979).

Developing the Collection

Because severe hearing loss at birth or in early childhood causes difficulties in communication and impedes the development of language, reading levels of many people who are deaf may be below that of their intellectual abilities. Consequently, high-interest low-vocabulary materials will be appropriate. Recreational reading should also include books relating to deafness such as Joanne Greenberg's *In This Sign* and Paul West's *Words for a Deaf Daughter* (Hagemeyer 1979) and Joanne Greenberg's newest book *Of Such Small Differences* (1988) about a man who is blind and deaf. Book selection for young adults might be aided by *Notes from a Different Drummer*, 2nd ed., by Barbara Baskin and Karen Harris (Bowker 1984).

Because many people with hearing loss learn primarily through sign, most ideas, concepts, stories, and information must be presented visually to be understood. For this reason, well-illustrated books are needed in the library collection. Signed stories and other books are available, as well as collections of songs for signing, which include music, the lyrics, and accompanying sign language (Dalton 1985). Dalton also recommends developing a kit for parents of children who are deaf to include annotated bibliographies, descriptions of possible home problems, the laws relating to the deaf and hearing impaired, travel, and recreation.

Communicating with Hearing People, better known as *The Red Notebook*, is a looseleaf service providing information about deafness and services for and by the deaf comunity. Developed by Alice Hagemeyer, it is available for sale by The National Association of the Deaf (NAD) and free annual supplements are supplied by Friends of Libraries for Deaf Action (FOLDA), an advocacy organization established in January of 1986. *The Red Notebook* includes 15 sections including definitions of deafness, library services, history, culture, laws, older adults, community services, programs, and resources, etc. FOLDA was organized by Hagemeyer as a nonprofit service and volunteer organization to improve library and information services to the deaf community, to encourage the entrance of people into the profession of library science and other related careers, and to improve the deaf community's awareness of their rights and potential, as well as to alert the public to the strengths and needs of their fellow citizens who are deaf (Hagemeyer 1988). In addition to supplements to *The Red Notebook*, FOLDA publishes *CROSSROADS*, a newsletter put out twice a year. Alice Hagemeyer is the founder and president of FOLDA.

Captioned Films for the Deaf

The Media Services and Captioned Films Division of the Office of Special Education and Rehabilitative Services (OSERS) began in 1959, after the enactment of Public Law 85-905 in 1958 which authorized the establishment of a free loan service of captioned theatrical films for persons with hearing impairments. The law was amended in 1962 (PL 87-715), in 1965 (PL 89-258), and in 1968 (PL 90-247), and later became known as Part F of the Education of the Handicapped Act. The amendments broadened the scope of the program to include research and training in the use of media, production, acquisition, and distribution of educational media. Activities included closed captioned television. While the amendments did not change the original intent of alleviating the wide gap—educational, cultural, and social—between persons with hearing impairments and persons with normal hearing, they did provide for the promotion of educational media to improve the educational environment of other persons with handicaps in addition to those with hearing impairments.

The Education of the Handicapped Act of 1986 (PL 99-457) repealed section 653 of Part F, Centers on Educational Media and Materials for Persons with Handicaps, and created a new Part G to carry out these activities. Part F, as amended, is now responsible only for: (1) Captioned films for the deaf program; (2) Closed Captioned Television; (3) Recording for the Blind; (4) National Theatre of the Deaf; and (5) Educational Media and Materials for Persons with Hearing Impairments. Captioning covers educational films, theatrical films, and closed captioned television.

Educational Films

Educational films are distributed through 58 depositories free of charge to any school or program that is registered for service and has at least one child with a hearing impairment in the classroom. The only cost to the user is return postage. Teachers from public school systems, day schools, and residential schools for the deaf review titles and make recommendations for captioning, which is done during the summer months. Theatrical films are distributed free of charge to groups of six or more persons with hearing impairments who have registered for service. Schools or groups of persons with hearing impairments may apply for an account number by writing to: Captioned Films for the Deaf, Modern Talking Picture Service, 5000 Park Street North, St. Petersburg, FL 33709.

Closed Caption Television

Captions for television programs are encoded onto line 21 of the broadcast signal and are made visible on any television set equipped with a special decoder. To coordinate the work of the networks that pioneered this system and carry it further, the National Captioning Institute (NCI), 5203 Leesburg Pike, Suite 1500, Falls Church, VA 22041, was created. The institute is a nonprofit entity with federal funding covering approximately 40 percent of the current programming available; the networks provide approximately 30 percent and corporate advertisers, foundations, and contributions account for the remaining 30 percent. NCI is now producing captioning for videocassettes. A full account of the work of the National Captioning Instititute will be found in Chapter 3.

Sources of Information

The **Alexander Graham Bell Association for the Deaf**, 3417 Volta Place, Washington, DC 20007, maintains a library in the field of deafness, disseminates printed materials, and answers inquiries from people who are hearing impaired, their families, professionals, and the general public. It publishes the journal *Volta Review*, an annual monograph and a newsletter, as well as a variety of books and audiovisual materials concerning the psychological, social, and educational implications of hearing loss.

Gallaudet University, 800 Florida Avenue NE, Washington, DC 20002, maintains a library in all subject areas relating to deafness (available on interlibrary loan) and offers assistance and bibliographies to libraries wishing to develop a collection. Gallaudet Media Distribution Service distributes videocassettes, videotapes, and 16-mm films on sign language instruction, signed educational films, and materials on deafness. The Gallaudet University Press publishes two catalogs, the *Gallaudet University Press Catalog* and the *Public Services Materials Catalog*. Gallaudet also operates a national information center on deafness and a national information center on deaf-blindness.

Organizations

National Association of the Deaf (NAD), 814 Thayer Avenue, Silver Spring, MD 20910, is a consumer-oriented organization for professionals and lay persons which recommends and promotes legislation on behalf of people who are deaf in areas of education and rehabilitation. It sponsors a communication skills training program to upgrade instructional skills of teachers of sign language. Information services include addresses of schools, camps, interpreters, homes for aged deaf, sources of devices, hearing-ear dogs, and professional providers including medical specialists and speech therapists. It also offers information regarding legislation and legal rights. Books and audiovisual materials are available for sale, as well as three periodicals: *The Deaf American*; the *Broadcaster*, a monthly newspaper; and the *Interstate*, a newsletter focusing on state issues and news. NAD also has an extensive library and markets *The Red Notebook*.

Telecommunications for the Deaf, Inc. (TDI), 814 Thayer Avenue, Silver Spring, MD 20910, serves people with deafness and hearing impairments and the general public with information about telecommunications, ensures access to telecommunications technologies and services, supports legislation for installing TDDs in all public places, publishes an *International Telephone Directory* of TDD users annually, which includes TDD numbers of federal, state, and local agencies and businesses and organizations that serve persons who are deaf and hearing impaired.

Registry of Interpreters for the Deaf, Inc. (RID), 814 Thayer Avenue, Silver Spring, MD 20910, is a membership organization of professional interpreters whose main purpose is to certify interpreters and transliterators. RID and its state affiliates actively advocate for the use of interpreters for people who are hearing impaired and deaf and RID maintains a current list of certified interpreters in the US (by state) which is made available to over 160 interpreter referral-service agencies. *Interpreter View* contains professional articles, job openings, and training program announcements.

Deafpride, Inc., 1350 Potomac Avenue SW, Washington, DC 20013, is a nonprofit organization which works for the human rights of people who are deaf and their families by providing opportunities for them to develop their potential as advocates. It offers activities and programs in leadership and advocacy, family life, deaf culture, technical assistance, and sign language programs. It provides interpreting services and can provide speakers and panelists from the deaf community. *The Advocate* is Deafpride's quarterly newsletter.

Other organizations within the deaf community are: American Society for Deaf Children (ASDC); Association of Late Deafened Adults (ALDA); Children of Deaf Adults (CODA); and Self Help for Hard of Hearing People, Inc. (SHHH) (Hagemeyer 1988). Many other groups can be found under either "deaf" or "hearing" in the *Encyclopedia of Associations*, Gale Research Co., latest edition.

ASSISTING PEOPLE WITH PHYSICAL DISABILITIES

Some librarians have not had a great deal of experience in dealing with persons with disabilities. A feeling of apprehension or timidity is normal under such circumstances. At the end of Chapter 1 of this book some helpful hints have been offered. In addition to those mentioned the following ideas may also provide some guidance:

1. Many people in wheelchairs can move to other seats, usually with little or no help. If they do this in the reading room do not move the wheelchair out of their reach.
2. A visually impaired person needs to know you are there. Address him or her directly, and signal if you must move away or need to end the conversation.
3. Do not pet guide dogs. They are working and must not be distracted.
4. When offering to help the visually impaired person around the library allow him or her to put a hand on your arm and walk slightly behind you. When offering a seat, place the person's hand on the back or arm of the chair.
5. When working with hearing-impaired persons do not hesitate to use paper and pencil to communicate when necessary.
6. Remember that there are many kinds of hearing and visual impairments, and some persons are not entirely deaf or blind.
7. Do not be afraid to ask speech-impaired persons to repeat themselves, even three or four times. They will be happy to do this. Do not finish sentences for them. Do not simplify your own speech or raise your voice to be understood. Remember that physical impairments do not indicate lack of intelligence (Kalusza 1987) .
8. Do not assume that very small persons with disabilities are children. Many people with osteogenesis imperfecta, cerebral palsy, dwarfism, or other disabilities look very young or are undersized. Speaking with simplified speech, assuming lack of intelligence, or assuming that a person is a younger child when that person is a teenager or an adult is very painful to

them and will cause them to avoid the library. When in doubt it is better to ask than to risk offending.

THE LIBRARY AND THE LEARNING DISABLED

In the Summer 1987 edition of *Interface*, the newsletter of ASCLA, Dale Brown, a staff member of the President's Committee on Employment of People with Disabilities, tells about her experiences in the public library as a learning-disabled student. As she explains it, the library is sometimes the only place where young people are able to receive individualized instruction from an adult. Libraries are quiet and undistracting, which is helpful to those who are hyperactive and need silence to concentrate. The wealth of different types of resources allows for locating something that can be adapted to their unique learning styles (Brown 1987).

All of the materials provided for patrons who are blind and physically disabled, such as the Kurzweil reading machine, Visualtek, large-print collections, computer programs, as well as new reader materials for people with low literacy levels, will be helpful to persons with learning disabilities. Also helpful are videos, films, and records; many learn best through using two senses. Quiet areas are helpful and study carrels are preferred (Brown 1987).

For people with learning disabilities it is the librarian who provides the crucial link. For example, the patron may not be able to find a book on the shelf because of a problem seeing the call numbers in order. A little extra instruction in using the card catalog, patience with those persons who lose their library cards because they might have difficulty seeing them when they are surrounded by other objects and cards or are not well-organized, and a willingness to repeat directions several times will be rewarded (Brown 1987).

LEKOTEK CENTERS

Many public libraries are now maintaining toy libraries for lending purposes. One idea that might be a useful one for public libraries is the establishment of a Lekotek Center. Lek is the Swedish word for play, and tek connotes library. The word Lekotek means play library. It is a worldwide system of play materials for children with special needs which offers counseling for parents on using play to help their children. Lekotek has an extensive library of toys, therapeutic play materials, and books and operates a preschool mainstreaming project and a computer project for Lekotek children and their families. Lekoteks are staffed by certified Lekotek leaders with backgrounds in special education or child development. Family visits are made by appointment and toys and materials are loaned to the family for a period of time. Lekotek announced plans in 1988 for a new technology division called Innotek, which will provide technology-related resources to families with children with special needs ("New Technology Division Opens at Lekotek," *Computer-Disability News* 1988).

One public library that established a Lekotek Center was the East Rockaway Public Library on Long Island. Funding was obtained through the Outreach Program of the Nassau Library System, through a grant from New York State, and there is no fee charged to the families who participate in this program. In Illinois, the Galesburg Public Library has also established a

Lekotek Center. Public libraries wishing to find out more about establishing such a program may contact the East Rockaway Public Library or the Outreach Program at the Nassau Library System, 900 Jerusalem Avenue, Uniondale, NY 11553 or the Galesburg, IL Public Library.

SERVICE TO SENIORS

It is often a problem for people to obtain information about special community services; however, for the older person, who is often disabled, it can be especially overwhelming. It was in recognition of this situation that Senior Connections was established as a joint project between the Adelphi University School of Social Work and the Palmer School of Library and Information Science of Long Island University. It was initiated in 1984 when the School of Social Work received a federal grant from the Administration on Aging to conduct an interdisciplinary Information and Referral (I & R) training project for librarians and social workers in public libraries (Levinson 1988).

The project takes place in Nassau County where many of the public libraries participate. A corps of library and social work students work together with senior volunteers in the operation of the service. Grants from the New York State Legislature in 1985 and 1986 have enabled this library-based I & R program to continue to operate with a growing number of older volunteers and student interns under the supervision of faculty from both professional schools. The older volunteers find working with Senior Connections very appealing since the public libraries are accessible to them and they are helping their peers. Students and senior volunteers receive training in providing I & R services.

Senior Connections includes support services, counseling, and consumer advocacy to individuals, families, agencies, self-help groups, and other organizations primarily concerned with older persons, many of whom are disabled. The originator and director of the program is Professor Risha W. Levinson of the Adelphi University School of Social Work, in Garden City, NY. Information about initiating a Senior Connections program may be obtained from her.

JOB ACCOMMODATIONS FOR LIBRARIANS WHO ARE DISABLED

Many people with disabilities work in public libraries. Library directors who hire them find that they are able to do the jobs they are trained to do and require minimum adaptations of the environment. However, in many cases, negative attitudes prevent persons trained as librarians, or clerical workers, from obtaining positions. Many people with disabilities who are qualified to work cannot find jobs and the library profession can do a great deal to alleviate this situation. I have always felt that it should even be possible for library schools to encourage qualified disabled persons to take the library degree, and to work together with local libraries to place them upon graduation. The many professional duties in a library, including acquisitions, reference, and working with children, can all be performed by librarians who are physically disabled if they are provided with accessible parking and entrances to the library. In addition, many clerical jobs can be performed by disabled persons. Some will need reasonable accommodations. In some cases a disabled person can be paired with another person to divide duties. Working at the front desk can be carried out by a person in a wheelchair although shelving books would have to be done by someone else. Computers have a myriad of uses and can be adapted for persons with all disabilities (see Chapter 5). Contact local rehabilitation agencies such as the Office of Vocational Rehabilitation or the Commission for the Blind for names of persons who might have qualifications that could enable them to work in the library. Gallaudet University offers undergraduate introductory work in library science and capable students are encouraged to go on to graduate work.

The computerized database JAN (Job Accommodation Network) is a national information source and consulting service for employers wishing to hire qualified workers with disabilities. Employers can call (JAN 1-800-JAN-PCEH) and can find out how other employers have dealt with similar situations.

The President's Committee on Employment of Persons with Disabilities, Washington, DC 20036, has the following publications available free: "Employers Are Asking about Accommodating Workers with Disabilities"; "Employers Are Asking about Making the Workplace Accessible to Workers with Disabilities"; "Disabled Americans at Work"; "The Law and Disabled People—Selected Federal and State Laws Affecting Employment and Certain Rights of People with Disabilities." Another source of information on occupational opportunities is Mainstream, Inc., 1200 15th Street NW, Washington, DC 20005. A bi-monthly newsletter, *In the Mainstream*, is available and a list of other publications include items on interviewing, accommodating, and supervising individuals with specific disabilities (Brown 1987).

In 1981 the American Library Association passed a policy on "Employment of Disabled Persons in Libraries," stating that the association (1) supports equal employment opportunities and affirmative action for persons with disabilities and (2) believes hiring individuals with disabilities for library positions is consistent with good personnel and management practices. A full copy of the policy with interpretations and guidelines is available from ALA/OLPR (The Office for Library Personnel Resources), 50 East Huron, Chicago, IL 60611. There is also a new group within ALA for disabled librarians.

ASSOCIATION OF SPECIALIZED AND COOPERATIVE LIBRARY AGENCIES (ASCLA)

The American Library Association, the national professional organization for librarians, deals with library service to persons with disabilities through ASCLA (Association of Specialized and Cooperative Library Agencies), which is divided into three sections. Two of the sections are concerned with state library agencies and multi-library organizations. The third section is the Libraries Serving Special Populations Section (LSSPS) and is organized into six forums serving the impaired elderly, prison populations, health care, bibliotherapy, the blind and physically handicapped, and the deaf.

ASCLA publishes the newsletter *Interface*. The Summer 1987 issue, edited by Eunice Lovejoy, featured articles by librarians who are involved in outreach services to persons with disabling conditions. The issue was part of the effort of a joint committee which included ASCLA and representatives of other units within ALA to mark the United Nations Decade of Disabled Persons, consisting of the years 1983-1992. The articles in this issue included, among others, tips for making libraries accessible, ways in which librarians can work with people with learning disabilities, library service to persons with disabilities in rural areas, and a program for training and employing people with disabilities. In an article on computers in the public library, Mary A. Roatch, Special Needs Center Supervisor of the Phoenix Public Library, describes the array of special computers that make it possible for persons who are blind and visually impaired to gain electronic access to print (Roatch 1987). A room that is equipped with computers, as well as other aids such as Kurzweil reading machines, optacons, and visualteks, can make it possible for visually disabled persons to become active users of the public library.

INTERNATIONAL RELATIONS

In 1974 NLS approached the International Federation of Library Associations (IFLA) about sponsoring an organization devoted to the needs of libraries for patrons who are blind or physically handicapped. In 1977 the Working Group of Libraries for the Blind, renamed in 1979 the Round Table of Libraries for the Blind, was established under the Hospital Libraries Section of IFLA. Meetings of the group are, or were at the time this author attended a meeting, heavily weighted toward standardization of equipment and toward service to patients in hospitals. Since then the Round Table on Libraries for the Blind has become a separate section and has continued to remain strong, holding three days of preconferences before the annual August conference of IFLA. The section on hospital libraries has become the section on service to the disadvantaged, which, I am told, includes service to the physically disabled. I am doubtful that this is satisfactory and I feel that IFLA continues to need strengthening in this area. A working group on service to the deaf was established in 1983 in the section on service to the disadvantaged, under the able guidance of Phyllis Dalton, who has worked to bring it into existence. In March 1984 the first issue of the *Deaf Newsletter* was published, providing an international exchange on activities in the area of library service to the deaf and hearing impaired (Dalton 1985).

REFERENCES

Association of Radio Reading Services, *Hello World*, pamphlet, 1988.

Baskin, Barbara H., and Harris, Karen H. 1984. *Notes from a Different Drummer: A Guide to Juvenile Fiction Portraying the Handicapped*. New York and London: R. R. Bowker.

Brown, Dale. 1987, Summer. "The Library: Individualized Learning for Learning Disabled People." *Interface* 9 (4): 4, 6.

Brown, Dale. 1987, Summer. "Workers with Disabilities—A Hidden Human Resource." *Library Personnel News* 1 (3).

Dalton, Phyllis. 1985. *Library Services for the Deaf and Hearing Impaired*. Phoenix, AZ: Oryx Press, 152, 159, 162, 314.

Directory of National Information Sources on Handicapping Conditions and Related Services. 1986. Harold Russell Associates, US Department of Education. Washington, DC.

Eldridge, Leslie, ed. 1985. *R Is for Reading*. Library Service to Blind and Physically Handicapped Children, National Library Service for the Blind and Physically Handicapped. Washington, DC: The Library of Congress.

Greenberg, Joanne. 1988. *Of Such Small Differences*. New York: Henry Holt and Co.

Hagemeyer, Alice. 1988, August. *Cross Roads*. District of Columbia Public Library, Washington, DC, Vol. 5, No. 8.

Hagemeyer, Alice. 1988, November. "A Quick Guide to Resources for the Deaf Community." News Release. District of Columbia Public Library, Washington, DC.

Hagemeyer, Alice. 1979. "Special Needs of the Deaf Patron." In *Serving Physically Disabled People: An Information Handbook for All Libraries.* New York: R. R. Bowker Co., 156.

Kaluzsa, Karen. 1987, Summer. "Tips for Helping a Person with a Physical Disability in the Library." *Interface* 9 (4): 2.

Klauber, Julie, and Covino, Joseph. 1981, Fall. "The Partially Sighted: Low Vision and the Library." *The Bookmark* 40 (1): 41, 42.

Levinson, Risha W. 1988. "The Social Services Perspective: Networking, New I & R Teams in Library-Based Services: Librarians, Social Workers, and Older Volunteers." In *The Reference Librarian*, No. 21. The Haworth Press, 121–32.

Massis, Bruce. 1988, October. Library Director, Jewish Guild for the Blind, telephone conversation.

Massis, Bruce. 1988. "A History of the IFLA Section of Libraries for the Blind." *Soviet Library Journal*, forthcoming issue.

Majeska, Marilyn Lundell. 1988. *Talking Books: Pioneering and Beyond.* National Library Service for the Blind and Physically Handicapped. Washington, DC: The Library of Congress.

National Library Service for the Blind and Physically Handicapped. 1984. *That All May Read.* Second Printing. Washington, DC: The Library of Congress.

"New Technology Division Opens at Lekotek." 1988, Summer. *Computer-Disability News* 5 (1): 1.

Roatch, Mary A. 1987, Summer. "Computers in the Public Library Assist Blind Persons to Read and Write." *Interface* 9 (4).

Summary of Existing Legislation Affecting Persons with Disabilities. 1988, August. US Department of Education, Office of Special Education and Rehabilitative Services, Clearinghouse on Handicapped. Washington, DC, 20.

Chapter 10
School and University
Libraries

The special nature of the problems of exceptional children makes it imperative to have an increasing degree of communication among the educational disciplines that deal with their development. The traditional practice of educating school librarians separately from teachers, preschool teachers separately from elementary school teachers, and secondary school personnel separately from everyone else should be changed, because the exceptional teenager and adult are products of their childhood experiences, and their learning problems stem from the infancy period. Teachers and librarians must understand the total child—average or exceptional—and how he or she learns before they can educate the child successfully.

At first the ramifications of PL 94-142 were far-reaching in the encouragement of this type of interdisciplinary activity. Journals in such diverse professional fields as home economics, art education, and school guidance carried articles about how the implementation of this law would affect school programs in each subject area. However, I do not believe that this has carried over significantly into course work at the university level.

Since many children who are physically disabled have appeared in the regular school population, and those still in special school situations are required to have a richer education—similar to their able-bodied peers—it is inevitable that changes will have to occur in the field of school library service. School library/media specialists are finding themselves without the backgrounds to acquire the materials and develop programs for these children.

Chapter 8 of this work discusses some of the history of the development of special education, updates information on the laws that have been enacted since PL 94-142, and presents a picture of the field as it exists at this time. Needs of the child with disabilities from birth to 5 years of age, and of the young adult aging out of the educational system, from ages 16 to 21 (transition), have been addressed in legislation, and a new emphasis is being placed on the needs of children with learning disabilities. Secondary programs, almost nonexistent 10 years ago in most areas of the country, are now receiving more attention, and new curricula address the specific needs of young adults.

THE HUMAN RESOURCES SCHOOL LIBRARY PROGRAM

The Library Media Center at the Human Resources School (where the author served as head librarian for 25 years) is discussed here as a demonstration model for library service to children who are orthopedically disabled as well as children with neurological impairments and special health problems. The school is one of the components of the Human Resources Center, a private, nonprofit organization in Albertson, New York, that serves people with physical disabilities [see also chapters 7 and 11].

Human Resources School offers a tuition-free education to more than 200 children. Chartered by the Board of Regents of the State of New York, it provides a full academic and extracurricular program to previously homebound children from infancy through high school. Founded in 1962, the program began with 20 children of average or above average intelligence, and disabilities stemming from brain damage (such as cerebral palsy); special health problems like hemophilia; orthopedic disabilities like osteogenesis imperfecta and arthrogryposis; neuromuscular disorders such as muscular dystrophy, dysautonomia and dystonia; and spina bifida, a neurological and orthopedic impairment. There were also children with congenital anomalies and those who had experienced crippling diseases and accidents that produced paraplegia and quadriplegia.

All of the children had been receiving home instruction in their own school districts. Because of meager instruction and a great deal of time spent in hospitals, most of them were reading below grade level and had read very little before coming to Human Resources School. The story of the designing of the new school building, which was erected in 1964, is told by its founder, Henry Viscardi, in his book *The School* (Viscardi 1964). A new building to house high school classes opened in the Spring of 1989 and was dedicated in September 1989 as The Henry Viscardi High School.

The design of the school library and its program were described by the author in "A Library for the Handicapped," an article appearing in *School Library Journal* (Velleman 1966).

The original library was a warm, carpeted interior room at the heart of the school. Special features included a wood-burning fireplace, a picture window overlooking a greenhouse, a lowered card catalog, and accessible shelves and tables. Ten years later, the original library was more than doubled in size and transformed into a library media center. Architectural features of this facility were described in *Library Adaptations for the Handicapped* (Velleman 1974).

The Collection

It is basically accepted that the reading and leisure-time interests of our students are very similar to those of their able-bodied peers. Accordingly, our book collection has been developed to include the very best standard and new materials in the areas of fiction, nonfiction, biography, and reference. There are, however, elements of exceptionality in our population that lead to certain adaptations. Books about the disabled are purchased only when they have literary merit, since our students are quick to sense inaccuracies and insincerity in this sensitive area. A ratio of fiction to nonfiction which is slightly greater than the average school collection has made it possible to supply much of the students' leisure reading material and to compensate for a somewhat lower usage of public libraries.

Rapid growth of the paperback book business has also been of great assistance. A collection of approximately 1,000 paperbacks, inexpensive, lightweight, and easily handled by students with upper extremity weakness, has proved very popular. Nonfiction and elementary level fiction books are cataloged and shelved with the hardcover books. On the secondary level, a paperback book rack for fiction draws an appreciative public. Paperback books on the elementary level are used to send home with those youngsters who are not yet ready for the responsibility of checking out the hardcover books, and in general to supplement the regular book collection.

For the small segment of the student body with limited or no vision, whose primary disability is orthopedic, large-print books are a part of the collection. Tapes for textbook materials are obtained upon request of the teaching staff from Recording for the Blind. The Industrial Home for the Blind, a local depository for materials from the American Printing House for the Blind, loans the school large print text materials, and the public library supplies cassettes and tapes from the National Library Service for the Blind and Physically Handicapped of the Library of Congress.

Some of the students require a longer than average period of time to develop their learning skills. Widespread reading retardation was at first attributed only to the fact that many of the original students had been receiving homebound instruction. In addition, a considerable amount of school time was (and still is) lost because of prolonged hospital stays. Although these factors are important, it also becomes obvious that sensory deprivation plays an important role in reading development.

The original library collection included perceptual training materials such as those from Teaching Resources and Developmental Laboratories, which were housed centrally in the library media center. As Human Resources School grew in size, these items were placed in K–3 and developmental classrooms so that they were readily available to classroom teachers on a daily basis. Similarly, those classrooms contain adapted toys and other realia. However, it is possible for an imaginative librarian working with children who are disabled to provide such equipment in the library (see Chapter 9, Lekotek). A very good description of the types of toys, games, puzzles, and other realia appropriate for developing large and small muscles, mastering perceptual skills, developing cognitive skills, and exploring the environment at various age levels can be found in the book *The Disabled Child in the Library: Moving into the Mainstream* by Linda Lucas and Marilyn H. Karrenbrock (1983).

Because of the broad range of abilities on any given grade level, the student book collection—except for a picture and easy-reading book corner—has not been divided between the elementary and secondary schools. The combined book collection enables all students to progress at their own rates, avoiding a feeling of inadequacy in those who work below their chronological age levels. Small color stickers on the spines of the books serve to alert the library staff to those books that have large print or are high-interest, low-vocabulary books.

The media collection includes a full complement of 8-mm films, film loops, sound and silent filmstrips, recordings, audio cassettes, video cassettes, and study prints in all curriculum areas. These materials are cataloged and color-coded and cards are filed in the card catalog with the book collection cards.

An important part of the library is a full professional special education collection for the use of the school staff, which includes books, journals, newsletters, and vertical file materials in the areas of physical disabilities and special curricula for disabled children. Included in the professional library are materials for the use of the children's parents, who are always welcome and are encouraged to ask for information in all areas of living and management of their children at home. Knowledge of community and national resources and services available to people with disabilities enables us to answer reference questions from both staff and parents. A file of field trips to adapted facilities, as well as information about adapted college campuses, and much of the information contained in resources discussed in chapters 3 and 4 round out our files.

The Library Program

The library program at Human Resources School was developed in the belief that a school library is indispensable to the total academic progress of its students and that one of the serious disadvantages of a home instructional program is the absence of professional reading guidance and the lack of diversified library materials in both print and nonprint formats. The aims of the school library media program are the encouragement of reading, the provision of a variety of learning materials in all subject areas, the use of many forms of media to develop creative ability, and the teaching of library skills.

To this end, we have developed a rounded library program at Human Resources school, specially tailored to the population. One rather widespread problem we have discovered is that parents find it difficult to take children to the public library. We try to encourage visits and offer information as to the accessibility of the various branch libraries in our area. There are other factors besides architectural barriers, however, that cause parents difficulty in transporting the children to various activities: loss of sleep, not uncommon with children such as those with muscular dystrophy, who must be turned over several times a night; difficulty in transporting wheelchairs; and giving equal attention to other siblings. For these reasons we have tried to create a school library program on the elementary level that is a combination school and public library program. Although the library is always open for research on a flexible scheduling basis in such curriculum areas as social studies and science, to offer a complete service we schedule one library period per week, from nursery school through the sixth grade. During this period, the children report to the library for 20 to 30 minutes of activity, usually a story hour. This is followed by a book selection session during which the librarian is joined by the classroom teacher and teacher assistant to offer a high degree of individual reading guidance. Such individualization is necessary becuase some youngsters work on or above grade level, while others work below their levels and require special help in selecting reading materials.

Children who are disabled are not anxious to read about people with disabilities. However, when a disabled character in a book is presented in a positive way, they are quick to notice and respond. One good example is *Moon Man* by Tomi Ungerer (1967). In this story about the Moon Man who comes to earth, his return to the moon, after a series of adventures, is engineered by a group of learned scientists. A board meeting is attended by a distinguished-looking gentleman in a wheelchair. The obvious message is that although he is physically disabled, he is obviously mentally able and occupationally active. Kindergarten students at Human Resources School who were read this story for the first time noticed the man in the wheelchair before the librarian picked up on it. This type of positive portrayal is most welcome at all levels by people who work with children with disabilities. In addition to the use of good literature during story hours, an attempt is made to reach each child in a special way. The librarian often structures story hours to build upon concepts introduced in the classroom and by speech and learning resources teachers.

Slow-learning older children, too old for picture books, but with very short attention spans and immaturities, are often reached with books about emotions such as *I Was So Mad* by Norma Simon (1974) and *Alexander and the Terrible, Horrible, No Good, Very Bad Day* by Judith Viorst (1973). When kindergarten and first-grade classes show problems in interpersonal relationships, our school psychologist and teachers like to use books about friendship. *Curious George Goes to the Hospital* by H. A. Rey, and other books about hospital, clinic, and doctor visits are in constant use with children who are disabled and must spend so much of their time in these environments.

Since children with disabilities often live in a very restricted physical world, story hours are organized around books about other countries or cities, supplemented by films, sound filmstrips, and music pertaining to these cultures. Middle elementary children reading below grade level do well with these kinds of programs. Our large media collection includes book and film strip sets of picture books produced by Weston Woods.

Storytelling techniques for children with physical disabilities do not differ appreciably from those used for their able-bodied peers. One helpful hint, however, is that children with minimal brain damage respond in an overwhelmingly positive way when a character in the story is given his or her name. This identification is very great and often serves to keep the child from wandering off, or brings him or her back to the group and encourages active participation. Creative activities in the library include having the children produce their own books.

On the secondary level the use of the library is extremely flexible. Group instruction in advanced reference is offered from the seventh to the tenth grades, depending on the scholastic ability of the groups involved. The librarian works with the business and guidance teachers to acquaint high school students with sources of career information. Recent trends in education have reflected an increase in awareness of the need for an early start in career education. How much more important is this concept for youngsters with disabilities who have difficulty in preparing themselves for the world of work, and for females who are disabled and who must cope with physical disability and also face possible sex discrimination.

An important function of the library is to support special grant activities with the acquisition of appropriate materials. The librarian continually peruses the professional literature for information to this end. Teachers are provided with materials in all curriculum areas, and the library staff solicits their requests and suggestions for purchase and apprises them of new research findings in areas of special education, suited to their field of expertise. Reports are obtained, often on microfiche, and with the cooperation of the Rehabilitation Research Library at Human Resources Center a listing of professional periodicals is circulated and the teachers are asked to indicate which periodicals would interest them. The tables of contents of all professional journals are photocopied and circulated as requested, and staff are encouraged to request specific articles, which are supplied to them. Periodical titles in both rehabilitation and special education fields are listed in the bibliography of this book.

Working with Parents

A very important aspect of the Human Resources School Library program is direct contact with the parents of the students. Most of these parents need a tremendous amount of support, which is offered through individual and group discussions with the school psychologists, social workers, and other professional personnel. Each year, the librarian sets up a display of special materials at the traditional parent open house, and more important, whenever there is a meeting of parents who are new to the school, supplemented with a talk by the librarian to point out specific materials and to state that she is always available to answer reference questions. Often, a parent who has heard this talk for a number of years will really "hear" it for the first time when the information becomes pertinent to the particular situation in that home. Materials discussed range from supportive literature to specialized books and materials in the areas of prosthetics and orthotics, wheelchairs, bathroom and kitchen design, travel information, recreation, dentistry for children who are disabled and much more. The librarian is currently working with the social-work staff to make this information file more accessible.

The Concept of Death

Many of the children at Human Resources School have terminal disabilities, such as muscular dystrophy of the Duchenne type. Very few school years go by without the death of one or more of our students. Some of these deaths are expected; others are quite sudden and unexpected. The librarian has learned to purchase supportive literature in this area. Such books, however, are never put out on general display at parent nights. It is felt that some of the parents are not yet ready to cope with this concept as it relates to their own children. A certain amount of sensitivity is required to know when such books may be offered. Generally, we wait until they are requested, or we suggest to the psychologist or social worker that this literature is available. Teachers have also requested that we obtain such literature to help them to deal with their own feelings and those of the students in the classroom.

Dealing with the concept of death is most difficult for those students with terminal disabilities, most of whom, by the time they reach adolescence, are aware of their own diagnosis. Pamphlets about these disabilities are given to these students upon request utilizing the advice of the psychologist. Sometimes younger children are afraid that "the same thing will happen to them," although they may not have a terminal disability. They need to be reassured. For younger children books like *The Tenth Good Thing about Barney* (Viorst 1972), *The Dead Bird* (Brown 1958), and *The Saddest Time* (Simon 1986) are sometimes useful to stimulate discussion about feelings in this area. Books for staff and parents include *The Dying Child* (Easson 1981), *How Do We Tell the Children?* (Schaefer and Lyons 1986), *Helping Children Cope with Separation and Loss* (Jewitt 1982), and, for siblings, *Losing Someone You Love* (Richter 1986). Other titles are listed in the bibliography at the end of this book.

Sex Education

Special information about sex and the disabled (see Chapter 13) is kept on hand in the library for the use of the professional staff. Students seldom approach the librarian directly for this information. However, when requested it is freely given. Of course, the general nonfiction section of the library contains many books on puberty, reproduction, childbirth, and so on, and children are encouraged to take these books home at an early age. It is recognized, however, and the fact dealt with, that children with disabilities have different physical growth rates than their able-bodied peers, and often their sexual needs must be handled differently from the norm. Reference materials in this area may be found in Chapter 4 and in the bibliography at the end of this book.

SCHOOL LIBRARIANS: WHAT CAN THEY DO?

Exceptional children are being placed in regular school programs in greater numbers than ever before. Librarians in these schools are frequently without the background to deal with the needs of these children. The librarian is confronted with a new challenge and an opportunity to extend service to groups that have in the past been excluded from the library. Librarians must expand their own knowledge of the nature of exceptionality and its implications for the learning process.

Access to the Library

Architectural barriers should be eliminated wherever possible. Although the school librarian must work within the framework of the school and is dependent on the administration for cooperation, the law is on the side of making facilities accessible. It is the obligation of the professional person involved to attempt to make facilities and programs available if there is a student who can benefit from the service (see Chapter 12).

Additional light for low-visioned children can be provided by high-intensity lamps, and the level of illumination increased by means of walls of pastel colors, white ceilings, bulletin boards with light backgrounds, gray-green or blue-green chalk boards, and dull finish furniture. Carpeting should be light in color. Easily accessible storage space and shelves can be used for supplies for the student with visual disabilities such as large type and braille dictionaries and encyclopedias, braillewriters, special paper, desk easels, and magnifiers. Other adaptations might include large print signs, bulletin boards with large pictures and little detail outlined in dark colors (Kirk 1976). Children with little or no residual vision rely on the tactile and aural modes. Recorded books are desirable and tactile and other sensory materials can be used for teaching purposes and during story hours (Lucas and Karrenbrock 1983).

For the child who is hearing impaired or deaf, sight is his or her prime mode of obtaining information and therefore no obstruction between student and speaker should prevail. During story hours the child who is hearing impaired must be sitting directly in front of the librarian, the light shining on the librarian's face and backlighting eliminated. Drapes should be used to keep out bright sunlight and minimize glare. Carpeted rooms absorb sounds, reduce noise levels, and enhance the deaf child's ability to pick up speech sounds when possible (Batt 1976). Tests have indicated that there are more vision problems among youngsters than in the general hearing population so it is imperative to minimize eye strain (Sangster 1981). Fire alarms and school bells can be signaled with a flashing light (Lucas and Karrenbrock 1983).

Children with hand impairments may require tapes or recordings since automatic page turners, though available, are expensive and seldom operate efficiently. In some cases, special reading stands may be required. The Reference Circular "Reading, Writing and Other Communication Aids for Visually and Physically Handicapped Persons" (1986), can be obtained from the National Library Service for the Blind and Physically Handicapped Reference Section in Washington, DC. Traditional audiovisual equipment must be evaluated by the librarian; bulk, weight, portability, amplification, magnification, and ease of operation become important variables when considered for use with exceptional children.

In addition to the problems in communication encountered by blind and deaf children, many students who are severely physically disabled such as those with cerebral palsy may have a severe speech impairment. The work being done at TRACE in Madison, Wisconsin is documented in the quarterly newsletter, *Communication Outlook*, a publication of the International Society for Augmentative and Alternative Communication (ISAAC) which also publishes a journal and newsletter.

Dealing with Students' Physical Disabilities

Possible physical problems encountered by the librarian will cover a broad range; in general, however, the librarian must deal with excessive fatigue, the frequent need to report to the nurse for medication, or simply the problem of mobility or accessibility. More specifically, the nature of the disability will dictate the type of problems that can be expected. Chapter 2 defines many of the disabilities that will be seen in the schools in greater numbers than ever before. Those definitions should be read in conjunction with the following pages, which describe some limitations that will directly affect library use and the librarian.

Children with osteogenesis imperfecta are generally small in stature. Usually the disability does not directly affect their intelligence, which sets them apart from disabled children with learning problems. A distinctive facial characteristic makes them easily identifiable to professional staff and to each other. As these children grow older, their condition is apt to stabilize and the fear of breaking bones diminishes. The wheelchair basketball team at Human Resources School often has many members with osteogenesis imperfecta, and they are anything but cautious in their movements. Low tables are useful for these students into their teen years. However, they are very resourceful and are able to get out of their wheelchairs and use the floor to look at books or take notes. With a positive attitude, children with this disability can easily become part of the library program.

Arthrogryposis, a congenital disability of the joints, can affect just the upper or the lower extremities with varying degrees of severity. Limitations in the library would involve inability to reach shelves or to carry books, and the student with hand limitations might not be able to handle media or write independently without some sort of adjustment. Often all that is needed is to tape a paper to a table and adjust a pencil. This disability is purely physical. It does not affect intelligence and children perform entirely within normal ranges.

The muscular disabilities include many subgroups, all of which affect the muscles to varying degrees. The most common that affects children (predominantly male) is the Duchenne type, which is progressive and terminal. With the emphasis on mainstreaming, efforts have been made to retain MD students in school. Academically they will be able to achieve in a normal manner until such time as extreme weakness makes it impossible for them to continue in class on a regular basis. Physically they will begin to require electric wheelchairs when they are no longer able to push themselves, and then the help of an aide in taking out books, writing assignments, and so on. Their hands will have to be positioned so that a book can be held open. A great deal of physical attention must be given to students with advanced muscular dystrophy to keep up with their work. Sometimes a student's position must be changed very often, or his or her head must be propped up. Books may have to be placed on reading stands. With sufficient physical help, however, students are able to function with some success.

Children with postpoliomyelitis symptoms, paraplegia, or quadriplegia will be able to function with whatever muscle power they have. What is lost cannot be regained, but the conditions are not terminal. Some of the accommodations made for children with muscular disabilities may have to be made for them as well.

Children with spina bifida may manifest the same physical characteristics as paraplegics, quadriplegics, and children with postpolio symptoms, with the additional problem of loss of sensory input. Children with spina bifida exhibit a wide range of intellectual ability. Some children have average to above-average intelligence. However, the presence of hydrocephalus at birth, which causes brain damage, can result in learning problems. Children with spina bifida often show a pattern of what is called "cocktail chatter." Since they spend much time with adults, their verbal ability appears to be high, but it is characterized by stereotypical phrases and a superficial understanding of language concepts. Therefore, care must be taken not to misinterpret their intellectual ability. Because of incontinence in early childhood, these children have not been mainstreamed to any great extent. However, new methods of emptying bowel and bladder mean that children with spina bifida require less nursing care during the day and are able to be placed in regular school programs. Their library performance will be similar to that of their able-bodied peers. Hand usage will be good, and if architectural adaptations are made, they will have no trouble integrating into the regular library program.

The physical manifestations of cerebral palsy vary widely, as does intellectual ability. In the past, children with mild to moderate forms of this neurological disorder have been mainstreamed. But cerebral palsy may be the most severe of the physical disabilities seen in the schools as a consequence of mainstreaming. People who are severely palsied require a great deal of physical care. Often they are taken to be younger than they are because of communication problems, as many cerebral palsied people have unclear speech. Because they are unable to express their feelings fully, intelligence and other capabilities often remain locked inside. Accommodating the child with cerebral palsy in the library may require a great deal of physical adjustment, with the help of an aide to handle books, other students to take duplicate notes during reference lessons, and above all, a positive attitude in terms of attempting to understand the speech patterns of the child. This can be done once the librarian realizes that these children do not mind repeating over and over again, and it is acceptable behavior to let them know that you do not understand. In the case of students with exceptionally poor speech or none at all, further adaptations may have to be made in the form of communication boards or computerized equipment (see Chapter 5).

One of the less common neurological disorders is familial dysautonomia. It results in a childlike appearance, and those affected seem younger than their years. Sometimes they look mildly retarded. Students can be ambulatory, may be short in stature, or may have a severe enough form of the disease to be in a wheelchair. With appropriate architectural modifications, these students should be able to function in a regular school setting with proper medical supervision. Librarians working with them should be made aware of problems that may occur at any time, such as dizziness, inability to breathe properly, and unawareness of injury to a limb. The librarian should be able to summon medical help when it seems indicated. Educationally, these children show a delayed development, but they are capable of working within the normal academic range with some individualized help.

Children with dwarfism have a problem of body image, not so much during their elementary years, but more so as they get older and enter high school. Everything in the world is too high. Sometimes they have trouble walking distances and must use walkers or wheelchairs.

In general, children with disabilities usually lack social experience and, therefore, are more immature and unworldly than their able-bodied peers. Many children who are disabled have high verbal ability and low performance, which may be characterized by perceptual problems or simply the inability to perform fine motor tasks as quickly as able-bodied children. Library media specialists can play a role in assisting other staff members to understand these disabilities by acquiring pamphlet materials listed in Chapter 2. Teachers, nurses, and other professional personnel will benefit from this information. In addition, *Physically Handicapped Children: A Medical Atlas for Teachers*, edited by Eugene E. Bleck and Donald Nagel, would be a most useful acquisition. It describes many of the physical disabilities with which children will enter the schools. The medical terminology is simple and educational, and classroom procedures are detailed.

Serving Students Who Are Blind or Visually Impaired

Students who are visually disabled should participate in all library activities. Blind children can enjoy films when someone describes what is taking place on the screen and most students will be able to see much of the action if they sit close enough. Rear projection screens are ideal as they allow children to get as close as necessary without blocking the image (Henne 1978). Storytelling is enjoyed by blind children when the stories chosen have good descriptive narrative and do not depend on illustrations. The storyteller must rely solely upon the voice to convey the action of the story. Voice changes to convey different characters or animals is also enjoyed. Realia can be passed around to be touched or sniffed. It is helpful to consult a teacher or tutor to ascertain a child's experience level. Children who are blind often have no concept of sizes, shapes, or texture (Brown 1976).

Special curriculum materials in braille, large print, and recorded format, as well as reading aids, equipment, and supplies such as note paper and Braillon for students who are blind and visually impaired, are available through the American Printing House for the Blind (APH), PO Box 6085, Louisville, KY 40206-0085. APH is the oldest national agency serving the blind in the United States. It is legally mandated to supply materials for children in educational settings who are legally blind, meaning those who have a measured visual acuity of 20/200 or less in the better eye, after correction, or who have a visual field no greater than 20 degrees. However, many of these children are visual learners, some even functioning well with regular print. Children with field defects may have an inability to see peripherally or may have "blind spots" in their visual fields (Corn and Martinez 1986).

A central catalog maintained by the American Printing House is a compilation of their own materials produced in recorded form, braille, or large print, as well as materials listed in the catalog of Recording for the Blind in Princeton, New Jersey. All American Printing House materials are obtained in each state through local educational outlets, and copies of the central catalog are available locally through state agencies that serve children who are blind.

Many local agencies, such as the Industrial Home for the Blind in New York, will produce books in large print, much of the time utilizing volunteer help, where such books are not available. These books will usually be produced in 14-point print or larger for those visually impaired students needing these materials. Schools should provide large print copiers which will enable teachers, or librarians to reproduce pages of text in large print for students with vision problems. Local school districts will probably be obligated to sustain the cost of this and other needed equipment for a specific child because of PL 94-142. In special schools for children who are blind and visually impaired, the card catalog is often brailled on one side and in large print on the other. Unless schools are prepared to make this modification, and unless there is a good deal of material available in alternate format in the library, visually impaired students will need individualized assistance in doing work that involves library research. Auxiliary personnel are obtainable under 94-142, although for many years before that, students in mainstreamed situations were already provided with tutors.

Parents should be told about the National Library Service for the Blind and Physically Handicapped of the Library of Congress (which provides recorded recreational reading materials for the print handicapped, usually called talking books) and the availability of this service through the local public libraries should be made known. Children who are blind or visually impaired, those who cannot use their hands or, because of neurological impairments, cannot read traditional print materials are eligible. Certification by a school official such as the librarian, the teacher, or an administrator will be sufficient to obtain the service. In the case of children with learning disabilities, the certification of a medical doctor is necessary. Where appropriate, duplicate equipment is often placed in a school setting such as the library.

A very useful pamphlet, available free of charge in quantity from the American Foundation for the Blind (AFB), 15 West 16th Street, New York, NY 10011 is "When You Have a Visually Handicapped Child in Your Classroom: Suggestions for Teachers," by Anne Lesley Corn and Iris Martinez. School librarians might wish to make these available to teachers. Also published by AFB is a complete and very useful text, *Foundations in Education for the Blind and Visually Impaired Child* by Geraldine Scholl (1986).

Serving Students Who Are Deaf or Hearing Impaired

Students who are deaf or hearing impaired who enter regular school programs will represent a very great challenge to the librarian. They encompass a broad range of disability levels, and the child who is prelingually deaf is already at a disadvantage when entering school. The average hearing child brings 5,000 words to kindergarten; the deaf child usually has no language when entering school. Education has been divided, and is still divided today, over methods of instruction. The aural/oral method, advocated by the Alexander Graham Bell Association, is still followed today by many schools although the total communication method has gained acceptance with many educators of the deaf who have found that only 30 to 40 percent of words can be perceived by lip reading and the rest must be guessed. Total communication advocates use a combination of methods, depending on what is best for each child: amplification of hearing, lip reading, signing and finger spelling, as well as gestures and body movements. Ameslan, the sign language used by adults who are deaf, has also been used with some success with children who are autistic and brain injured.

Children who are hearing impaired can benefit from high-interest, low-vocabulary materials which promote their skills and provide stimulating reading. Since these children learn primarily by sight, concepts must be presented in visual format, as abstract concepts and words with multiple meanings are difficult for them to comprehend. Library books should contain controlled vocabulary, simple syntax, and clear and illustrative pictures. It is possible to obtain books written in signed English, brightly illustrated, that have the text and signs printed together. Some stories are written especially for the young child. Some popular children's books have sign translations printed on dry stick paper applied directly to the book (Sangster 1981). Storytelling is most effective when many visual materials are used, and library skills must be presented in visual format, one concept at a time (Metcalf 1979). When librarians do not have signing skills it is sometimes possible to use the services of a volunteer from the community, or a parent, to present a story hour. Special instructional techniques in storytelling for children who are deaf are detailed by Patrick Huston in *The Special Child in the Library* (1976). The Gallaudet University Press produces picture books and other materials; captioned films and film strips are important media for children who are deaf and hearing impaired.

Serving Students with Mental or Emotional Disabilities

Children with mental disabilities often have short attention spans and are easily distracted. HI/LO materials are needed and often large print is helpful. Subject matter should be short and simple, with only the necessary information included. Materials leading from the concrete and the known to the more abstract and unfamiliar will be most successful (Lucas and Karrenbrock 1983). Storytelling technique should include short simple plots and very concrete concepts. Tales about animals, family life, and children their own age will have appeal, as well as stories about fears or concerns about which the children cannot verbalize. Stories with exotic locales or a great deal of fantasy are to be avoided. Illustrations should be representational rather than impressionistic, large, uncomplicated, and executed in primary colors. Folk tales and others with sequential plots that employ a great deal of repetition and rhyming will be successful with all children, but particularly with this group (Baskin and Harris 1976). Because of the many types of materials in the library media center, older students who are mentally disabled can often find that the opportunity to work in an individualized manner can be helpful. Magazines about sports, driving, or even such magazines as *National Geographic* can be used for their illustrations. Film strips can convey ideas in simpler language than books.

Emotionally disabled children can be difficult and often do not come to the library. However, sometimes when the classroom environment is too overwhelming a child who is emotionally disabled can be handled successfully by a sensitive librarian by being given a secluded and quiet spot to work, appropriate materials, or a job to do in the library which will convey a sense of responsibility.

Children with learning disabilities are receiving much more understanding than ever before in the schools and universities. School librarians can refer to chapters 7 and 8 for references in this field. It is important to know that when a learning disability involves a reading problem these children may need to learn by listening to tapes and using sound filmstrips. Those who are categorized as print handicapped are entitled to talking books and parents should be so informed. The opportunity to work independently, in a quiet space in the library, without distraction, can be beneficial to children who are hyperactive learning disabled. They are often of average or above average intelligence and so need to be reached with materials on their own grade level and will enjoy story hours along with able-bodied children.

Involving Parents

One of the basic provisions of PL 94-142 is the Individualized Education Program (IEP) which was described in Chapter 8. Regulations for the preparation of this individualized plan include recognition of the parent as an official member of the educational team and as an advocate for the child. To a greater extent than ever before, school professionals must work with parents and allow them an influential voice in determining what is best for their children. The library media specialist will be in a position to render an information service in trying to find information that will help parents and staff to work together and understand one another.

School librarians must recognize that parents are not a homogeneous group. They have different educational, cultural, and ethnic backgrounds and will need different types and levels of information (Kroth and Brown 1978). In addition, parents require different kinds of information at different stages in their children's lives. Most parents share fear, frustration, disappointment, and other difficulties in child rearing beyond that experienced by parents of able-bodied children. Often they have encountered ignorance among doctors and educational personnel. Stages of denial, guilt, and a search for help sometimes turn into militance. School personnel are, therefore, in need of professional information to assist in handling conferences with parents responding with a wide range of emotional responses to extremely difficult situations.

In recent years several books have been written for parents to help them understand the ways in which they can provide trusts for their children with disabilities without endangering their federal assistance programs. In addition, guardianship programs for children who are mentally disabled can also be arranged. See Chapter 8 for titles of books that would be helpful to obtain for the parent information section of the school media center.

Attitudes toward Students

In Chapter 8 many sources of information for special classroom materials are mentioned. School library media specialists will need to familiarize themselves with these sources and where they can be accessed locally. The catalogs of the Council for Exceptional Children, the Association for Children with Learning Disabilities, and other professional organizations should be obtained for the library.

The most important aspect involved in placing exceptional children in regular school programs will, of course, be attitudes. Youngsters need to be seen in terms of their abilities rather than their disabilities and death must be seen as part of the life process. There is an abundance of good literature that offers positive portrayals of children with disabilities. It is important that the able-bodied students read some of this literature which can be ordered by using *Notes from a Different Drummer* (Baskin and Harris 1984) or *The Bookfinder* (Dreyer 1977).

For the child who is functioning on a lower level than his or her able-bodied peers, the librarian can play a nonthreatening role by drawing on materials especially developed for lower achieving children. The library is one place where the child may perform at his or her own academic level in an accepting and uncritical environment. Intellectual and cultural deprivation may have narrowed the educational background of the child with disabilities. The library has the potential to compensate partially for this disparity. In the library the special child can experience success on his or her own level and can share experiences with the able-bodied child.

COLLEGE AND UNIVERSITY LIBRARIES

The *Directory of College Facilities and Services for the Disabled* by James and Carol Thomas (1986) is the most up-to-date source of information about adapted college and university facilities (new edition forthcoming in 1990). It includes information about the majority of postsecondary institutions within the United States and Canada. For each school information is given on the physical terrain, special support services, auxiliary aids such as note takers, personal and campus assistants, movement of classes when necessary, names of resource persons, and numbers of disabled students enrolled, divided by categories. Facilities are listed such as dormitories, classrooms, gymnasium, cafeteria, library, etc., and percentages of accessibility given. Reader services include equipment for brailling or taping, optacons, Kurzweil readers, and large print screens. Speech adaptors for computers, and TDDs for students who are hearing impaired are also available at many schools. Copies of this directory should be made available in high school libraries, and brought to the attention of guidance counselors.

While this source can be used as a starting point, librarians should assist guidance counselors in attempting to find out about schools in their particular areas. Most schools have made some adaptations for almost all students with disabilities. Surely a campus that is built on a hillside, or has many buildings with flights of steps, will be difficult for a person in a wheelchair, even with special scheduling of classes. Common sense must be exercised in choosing an appropriate school. Obviously new buildings must conform to architectural standards for the accommodation of students with disabilities.

SPECIAL MATERIALS AND EQUIPMENT

In addition to the usual library materials that must be made available in special formats, it is helpful to the student with disabilities if the library staff acquires an understanding of their informational needs in the areas of activities of daily living, legal rights as disabled citizens, the independent living movement, local community services, and, in particular, the services of the Office of Vocational Rehabilitation and the Commission for the Blind. In most cases students will already be aware of these departments as their schooling is often funded by them.

Especially useful is a file of travel guides offering information about adapted facilities, as well as Amtrak, airlines, and bus regulations. These are of help to students wishing to return home or travel independently on vacation. Recreational information about camping, skiing, or other sports for the blind or physically disabled are welcome. Many schools now have wheelchair basketball teams and send students to participate in the national wheelchair sports events and the paralympics.

The college or university library can play a leading role in assisting students with disabilities. If staffing resources permit, it is often useful to designate a librarian as coordinator of resources, who can work closely with the department for special-needs students and with the students themselves to determine how the library can upgrade services. Use of the many reference sources outlined in this text will help make it possible to locate information more easily. A file of maps of the campus, indicating accessible entrances to buildings, is of great use, as is a tactile map for blind students. Of course, access to the library itself is of utmost importance to students in wheelchairs. Chapter 12 outlines the major provisions for such accessibility. Further provision might include modified carrels to accommodate wheelchairs, special keys for elevators, and access to special floors or collections during extended hours. Telephone information centers, where students can call in to determine if a specific book is available and have it held or picked up by a designated helper, can be a boon for students who are mobility impaired. Building adaptations can be helpful if made with imagination.

Provisions for blind and visually impaired students might include reference works in large print. The World Book has been recorded by the American Printing House for the Blind. Listings of essential library telephone numbers can also be made available in large print and braille. Other provisions can include specialized equipment in listening/taping/reading rooms such as TV magnifiers, talking book machines, page turners, braille typewriters, Edna Lite magnifiers, optacons and Kurzweil reading machines, as well as the new personal Kurzweil reading machine. This personalized Kurzweil reader represents an exciting new breakthrough in technology with interfacing capabilities to computer devices. Although the introductory price will be high for blind persons wishing to purchase personal machines, the American Foundation for the Blind is planning a low-interest loan program. Information can be obtained from AFB or Personal Reader Department, Kurzweil Computer Products, 185 Albany Street, Cambridge, MA 02139.

Library materials that are helpful to the hearing-impaired college student include those that simplify and clarify reading materials. Such books as *The Dictionary of Idioms for the Deaf,* by Maxine T. Boatner and John E. Gates (1975), explain words and short phrases in simple, exemplary sentences (Ritter

1981). Of course lists of captioned videotapes and films and the way in which they can be borrowed or rented should be made available to students who are hearing impaired. Librarians wishing to develop a collection of materials on deafness, provide information on interpreters, or assist the college that is providing programs to train workers in the field of deafness should call upon other colleges with in-depth materials, for instance, Gallaudet University, the Rochester Institute of Technology, the California State University at Northridge, the Registry of Interpreters, or the National Association of the Deaf (Ritter 1981).

EDUCATING LIBRARIANS TO SERVE PEOPLE WITH DISABILITIES

During the 1970s, in many workshops around the country, attempts were made to interest schools of library and information science in offering courses in library service to people with disabilities. While some gains have been made, many schools do not offer such special coursework, although many incorporate relevant material into other courses. It makes sense to have concepts dealing with information needs of the disabled population permeate the whole curriculum, since all librarians will be seeing members of this population (Whelan 1981).

Special and medical library coursework should include rehabilitation information, public library coursework should make mention of the information and referral possibilities for patrons with disabilities, and training for school library media specialists should certainly include work with exceptional children. However, this author believes that the wealth of material available and the differing needs of persons with different disabilities makes it desirable to continue to advocate the introduction of at least one special course into the curricula of schools of library and information science dealing with service in all types of libraries to people with disabilities.

REFERENCES

Baskin, Barbara H., and Harris, Karen H. 1976. "Storytelling for the Young Mentally Retarded Child." In Baskin, Barbara H., and Harris, Karen H., ed. *The Special Child in the Library.* UMI, 114.

Baskin, Barbara H., and Harris, Karen H. 1984. *More Notes from a Different Drummer.* New York: R.R. Bowker Co.

Batt, Doris, Sr. 1976. "The Hearing-Impaired Child in the Library." In Baskin, Barbara H., and Harris, Karen H., eds. *The Special Child in the Library.* UMI, 14.

Bleck, Eugene E., and Nagel, Donald A. 1982. *Physically Handicapped Children: A Medical Atlas for Teachers.* Orlando, FL: Grune and Stratton.

Boatner, Maxine T., and Gates, John E. 1975. *Dictionary of Idioms for the Deaf.* National Association for the Deaf.

Brown, Jean D. 1976. "Storytelling and the Blind Child." In Baskin, Barbara H., and Harris, Karen H., eds. *The Special Child in the Library.* UMI, 109.

Buscaglia, Leo, ed. 1975. *The Disabled and Their Parents: A Counseling Challenge.* Thorofare, NJ: Charles B. Slack, Inc.

Corn, Anne Lesley, and Martinez, Iris. 1986. *When You Have a Visually Handicapped Child in Your Classroom: Suggestions for Teachers.* New York: American Foundation for the Blind, 4.

Dreyer, Sharon Spredemann. 1977. *The Bookfinder: A Guide for Children's Literature about the Needs and Problems of Youth Aged Two to Fifteen.* Circle Pines, MN: American Guidance Service.

Easson, William M. 1981. *The Dying Child: The Management of the Child or Adolescent Who Is Dying*. Second Edition. Springfield, IL: Charles Thomas.

Henne, John F. 1978, December. "Serving Visually Handicapped Children." *School Library Journal* 25 (4): 36–37.

Huston, Patrick. 1976. "Storytelling." In Baskin, Barbara H., and Harris, Karen H., eds. *The Special Child in the Library*. UMI, 112.

Jewitt, Claudia. 1982. *Helping Children Cope with Separation and Loss*. Cambridge, MA: Harvard Common Press.

Kirk, Edith C. 1976. "Designing Desirable Physical Conditions in Libraries for Visually Handicapped Children." In Baskin, Barbara H., and Harris, Karen H., eds. *The Special Child in the Library*. UMI, 11.

Kroth, Roger, and Brown, Gweneth Blacklock. 1978, Summer. "Welcome in the Parents." *School Media Quarterly* 6 (4): 248.

Lucas, Linda, and Karrenbrock, Marilyn H. 1983. *The Disabled Child in the Library: Moving into the Mainstream*. Littleton, CO: Libraries Unlimited, 128, 156–68.

Mass, Carrel J., and Williams, Charles F. 1962. *The Assessment of College Experience of Severely Handicapped*. Gainesville, FL: University of Florida.

Metcalf, Mary Jane. 1979, January. "Helping Hearing-Impaired Students." *School Library Journal* 25 (5): 27–29.

Richter, Elizabeth. *Losing Someone You Love: When a Brother or Sister Dies*. New York: Putnam, 1986.

Ritter, Audrey. 1981, Fall. "The College Library Serving Hearing-Impaired Students." *The Bookmark: Library Service to the Disabled* 22, 24.

Sangster, Collette. 1981, Fall. "Library Service for the Hearing Impaired." *The Bookmark: Library Service to the Disabled*, 26.

Schaefer, Dan, and Lyons, Christine. 1986. *How Do We Tell the Children? A Parents' Guide to Helping Children Understand and Cope When Someone Dies*. New York: Newmarket Press.

Scholl, Geraldine, ed. 1986. *Foundations in Education for the Blind and Visually-Impaired Child*. New York: American Foundation for the Blind.

Thomas, James and Thomas, Carol. 1986. *Directory of College Facilities and Services for the Disabled*. Phoenix, AZ: Oryx Press.

Velleman, Ruth A. 1966, September. "A Library for the Handicapped." *School Library Journal* 13 (1): 48–52.

Velleman, Ruth A. 1971, Summer. "Serving Exceptional Children." *School Libraries* 20 (4): 27.

Velleman, Ruth A. 1974, October. "Library Adaptations for the Handicapped." *School Library Journal* 21 (2): 85–88.

Viscardi, Henry. 1964. *The School*. New York: Erickson.

Whelan, Lucille. 1981. "Educating Librarians to Serve the Disabled." *The Bookmark*, 51.

Chapter 11
The Rehabilitation Library

The decades of the 1970s and 1980s have seen great growth in the rehabilitation field, which now encompasses public and private agencies, private rehabilitation hospitals, general hospitals with rehabilitation units, public veterans administration hospitals, private rehabilitation centers, and sheltered workshops still operated by the earliest private organizations such as Goodwill Industries and the National Easter Seal Society. The federal government presides over a large network of vocational rehabilitation offices, administered through the individual state governments operating a network of local offices.

It would seem that access to information for activities of daily living, including devices and adaptations, education, employment, housing, travel and transportation, recreation, and a myriad of other needs, would be simple. A recent Harris poll tells us that this is not the case. According to this poll, taken under the auspices of the International Center for the Disabled (ICD), in 1986, a majority (53 percent) of people with disabilities said they found it difficult to obtain information about available services.

The chief purveyors of information, public librarians, have tried, in many cases, to supply some of this information. The federal government has mentioned in several laws the need for information banks for people who are disabled. The Client Assistance Project (CAP) was established within the rehabilitation agency system to act as an information ombudsman for the client, supplementing the work of the rehabilitation counselor. Why then is the system not working as well as it could? In this author's opinion there still remains a need for a subspecialty within the library profession to be called rehabilitation librarianship. There are many library students who major in special librarianship or medical librarianship, and their coursework could include this specialty.

Admittedly, the funding for establishing a library collection, no matter how small, administered by a professional librarian is often not available within the rehabilitation field. It is to be hoped, however, that with encouragement from the library profession and the training of people with an interest and competence in this field, opportunities such as the following will ultimately begin to be available and will be found:

1. At the state level, where some states have already pioneered in the establishment of libraries to service the state departments of vocational rehabilitation.
2. At the local level, where all vocational rehabilitation offices could benefit by having a trained librarian on the staff.
3. In all rehabilitation facilities.
4. In general and rehabilitation hospitals.
5. In Veterans' Administration hospitals.

6. In the offices of the rehabilitation research network.
7. In all private organizations, dealing with specific disabilities, including advocacy parent organizations that deliver services to children with disabilities.

ESTABLISHING A COLLECTION

Chapters 6 and 7 of this work outline the rehabilitation field, its history and development, the laws governing it, the principal projects in the forefront of the field today, and some of the organizations of importance. A perusal of these chapters will furnish a start in gathering materials. Libraries in organizations operating on government and private grants should include the *Federal Register, Commerce Business Daily,* and other sources on how to write and acquire grant monies, as well as the *U.S. Government Manual,* the *Congressional Yellow Book,* and the *Federal Yellow Book.* The *Encyclopedia of Associations,* the *Ulrich Index to Periodicals,* and other general reference sources should be included as well. State government directories for the local area as well as state medical directories which list physicians and their accreditation and training, are also valuable. The bibliography of this book should be a source for collection building and should be consulted under all appropriate headings.

Until recently, hospital and institutional librarians concerned themselves with two types of service: recreational reading for patients and scientific informational services to the medical and other professional staff. By adding information to their files in the fields of activities of daily living, rehabilitation technology, and other areas of need for professionals working with disabled patients who are returning home, hospital and institutional librarians could expand their usefulness one-hundredfold. Some hospitals have done this. Others, including very large and important teaching hospitals, have not done so yet.

Libraries in rehabilitation centers should include a full professional collection of books, journals, and research monographs and newsletters in the general field of rehabilitation which should be supplemented by specialized materials needed at the specific work site. At vocational rehabilitation offices, and rehabilitation centers active in the area of placement the collection should include information in the field of careers and employment opportunities for people with disabilities. The latest research in rehabilitation technology and, of course, the use of the computer, are important for the collection so that counselors will be aware of all new technological modifications that assist job productivity. While direct service to clients may be less likely than in a school or public library, the librarian should be prepared to offer information as requested pertaining to all of the daily living needs and legal and financial rights discussed in chapters 3 and 4.

Libraries serving facilities that include education will wish to obtain some special education materials to serve the professional teaching and administrative staff. Chapters 8 and 10 will be of help here. Parents of children who are disabled will need the information referred to in chapters 3 and 4 while hospital and medical libraries will emphasize materials in rehabilitation medicine, to serve physiatrists, social workers, physical and occupational therapists.

All rehabilitation librarians should include in their collections basic periodicals and newsletters in the field of rehabilitation and scan them constantly for new materials to keep the collection up to date. Special education journals and newsletters will be of use in facilities that include education. Of very great importance is a subscription to *Rehab Briefs*. Free from the National Institute on Disability and Rehabilitation Research, in the Office of Special Education and Rehabilitative Services, Washington, DC, these short, concise newsletters each deal with one important current topic in the field of rehabilitation, offering the major information as well as references for more in-depth perusal.

Principal directories that should be in the collection should include all of those listed in Chapter 9, such as the *Directory of National Information Sources on Handicapping Conditions and Related Services*, The *National Resource Directory from the National Spinal Cord Injury Association*, and *The Resource Guide to Organizations Concerned With Developmental Handicaps*, 1987–1988 edition, (a very valuable directory listing developmental and mental retardation centers around the country, as well as selected government agencies and programs, state mental retardation program directors, and other resources), and directories on facilities for blind and deaf individuals if the library serves these groups. In addition, the following directories are basic:

The Program Directory issued by the National Institute on Disability and Rehabilitation Research (NIDRR) (October 1988) or next annual edition.
Lists field-initiated research, model spinal cord injury systems, rehabilitation engineering centers, research and development projects, research and training (R & T) centers, small-business innovative research, utilization projects, and research training grants. It is indexed by program with a reference listing by state.

The Directory of Organizations Interested in People with Disabilities, produced by the President's Committee on Employment of Persons with Disabilities, the People to People Committee for the Handicapped and Disabled American Veterans. Published by Disabled American Veterans, 807 Maine Avenue SW, Washington, DC 20024 (June 1986, plus supplements).
This directory lists 100 organizations, many of them not listed elsewhere, as well as government agencies in employment security (regional office addresses), state offices of vocational rehabilitation, and commissions for the blind.

The CARF Directory of Facilities Serving People with Disabilities, Commission on Accreditation of Rehabilitation Facilities, 2500 North Pantano Road, Tucson, AZ 85715 (1986 or latest edition).
Lists facilities accredited by the commission, by state. It covers facilities with comprehensive in-patient rehabilitation programs, as well as programs in infant and early childhood, vocational evaluation, training and placement, spinal cord injury, brain injury, chronic pain centers, outpatient medical centers, independent living, residential and respite care, alcohol and drug abuse, psychosocial programs and programs in industry.

The Rehabilitation Facilities Sourcebook, National Association of Rehabilitation Facilities, PO Box 17675, Washington, DC 20041 (annually).
Lists all rehabilitation facilities in the US organized by listings of metropolitan areas served, followed by an alphabetical cross-reference by state. Also lists the chapter offices of NARF around the country.

A Guide to Periodicals on Disability & Rehabilitation, published by NIDRR, will be forthcoming in 1989 replacing a previous directory published by NARIC under its old contract which is no longer available.

A Readers'/Writers' Guide to Periodicals in the Disability Field by The Committee to Promote Writing in Disability Studies, 2nd ed. English-Language International, Joseph L. Baird, Kent State University, Kent, OH 44242 (1987).
This directory also lists periodicals, with information about how to submit articles for publication, length, format, etc.

National Directory of Rehabilitation Facilities Offering Vocational Evaluation and Adjustment Training to Hearing-Impaired Persons by Paula Marut, Douglas Watson, and Diane Buford (August 1984).
Arkansas Rehabilitation Research and Training Center on Deafness and Hearing Impairments, 4601 West Markham Street, Little Rock, AR 72205.
Programs are listed by regions.

Directory of Agencies & Organizations Serving Deaf/Blind Individuals, (October 1988), Helen Keller National Center for Deaf/Blind Youths and Adults, 111 Middle Neck Road, Sands Point, NY 11050.
Public and private organizations are listed by state and range of services, such as day programs, residential, group homes, vocational evaluation, training and placement, parent education and training, advocacy, and research.

Commercial catalogs that would be helpful to have for quick reference are listed in Chapter 9. The key periodicals in the field, which should be in all rehabilitation libraries are as follows:

Accent on Living (quarterly)
Box 700
Bloomington, IL 61702

American Journal of Physical Medicine and Rehabilitation (bimonthly)
Williams & Wilkins for the Association of Academic Physiatrists
428 E. Preston Street
Baltimore, MD 21202

American Rehabilitation (quarterly)
Rehabilitation Services Administration (RSA)
330 C Street SW
Washington, DC 20202

Deaf American (quarterly)
National Association of the Deaf
814 Thayer Avenue
Silver Spring, MD 20910

Journal of the American Deafness and Rehabilitation Association (ADARA) (monthly)
PO Box 55369
Little Rock, AR 72225

Journal of the Association for Persons with Severe Handicaps (quarterly)
The Association for Persons with Severe Handicaps (TASH)
7010 Roosevelt Way NE
Seattle, WA 98115

Journal of Rehabilitation (quarterly)
National Rehabilitation Association
633 S. Washington Street
Alexandria, VA 22314

Journal of the Multi-Handicapped Person (quarterly)
Plenum Publishing Corporation
233 Spring Street
New York, NY 10013
This is a new journal which will publish original research and clinical reports covering all multi-handicapped populations including deaf/blind, blind/mentally retarded, and emotional disturbed/mentally retarded persons.

Journal of Visual Impairment & Blindness (monthly except July and August)
American Foundation for the Blind
15 W. 16th Street
New York, NY 10011

Mental and Physical Disability Law Reporter (bimonthly)
American Bar Association
1800 M Street NW
Washington, DC 20036

Rehabilitation Gazette (annually)
4502 Maryland Avenue
St. Louis, MO 63108

RESNA: Rehabilitation Technical Review (quarterly)
Suite 700
1101 Connecticut Avenue NW
Washington, DC 20036

Worklife (replacing *Disabled USA*)
(quarterly)
President's Committee on
Employment of People
with Disabilities
Washington, DC 20036

Other journals would include professional journals in the fields of rehabilitation counseling, rehabilitation administration, speech and hearing, physical and occupational therapy, prosthetics and orthotics, careers for persons with disabilities, and client-oriented journals such as *A Positive Approach, Mainstream (California), Breakout, Sports N' Spokes,* and *Paraplegia News.* For those libraries with special education requirements, the *Journal of Special Education, Exceptional Children, Exceptional Parent,* and the *Journal of Learning Disabilities* are appropriate.

Newsletters to be included in rehabilitation libraries are the following:

Report on Disability Programs
(formerly Handicapped Americans
Report) (biweekly)
Business Publishers Inc.
951 Pershing Drive
Silver Spring, MD 20910-4464

In the Mainstream (bimonthly)
Mainstream Inc.
1030 15th Street NW
Suite 1010
Washington, DC 20005

First Dibs (semiannually)
A Disability Information Brokerage
System
PO Box 1285
Tucson, AZ 85702

ICTA Inform
Newsletter of the ICTA Information
Centre
Swedish Institute for the
Handicapped and Rehabilitation
International
Box 303, S-161 BROMMA
Sweden

Computer-Disability News
The Computer Resource Quarterly
for People with Disabilities
National Easter Seal Society
70 E. Lake Street
Chicago, IL 60601

Closing the Gap
PO Box 68
Henderson, MN 56044

Additional important references for rehabilitation libraries include *The Handicapped Requirements Handbook* issued by the Federal Programs Advisory Service, Thompson Publishing Group, 1725 K Street NW, Suite 200, Washington, DC 20006, and updated by monthly supplements which are invaluable for tracking current legislation.

The resources and services of NARIC, the National Rehabilitation Information Center, have been described in Chapter 6. Now located at 8455 Colesville Road, Suite 935, Silver Spring, MD 20910-3319 (toll-free number 800-346-2742, voice or TDD), NARIC should be a major resource for the rehabilitation library.

NARIC maintains REHABDATA, a bibliographic database of the disability and rehabilitation literature, and an updated thesaurus should be obtained from the center. The 20,000 entries are each represented by a record containing a short abstract and 10 information fields describing the holding. Each entry is assigned up to 5 descriptors using terms from the thesaurus. The contents of REHABDATA are categorized into research reports, journal articles, and reference resources. NARIC's in-house collection contains copies of most items listed in REHABDATA. Photocopies for uncopyrighted documents are available at a nominal rate. REHABDATA can be accessed through NARIC or through BRS. The REHABDATA file name is "NRIC." NARIC accepts requests through TDD, electronic bulletin boards, telephone, mail, and personal visitation. Directly contacting a staff person is usually the best method for obtaining information. Recently, NARIC issued a subject index for the *Rehab Brief* collection. Since the *Rehab Briefs* are such an important resource, this index is a most valuable tool for accessing back issues on special topics (NARIC 1988).

The three major commercial vendors, BRS, DIALOG, and SDC Information Services (ORBIT retrieval system), all offer databases on handicapping conditions. Many of the databases listed below are accessible through one or another of these systems.

ABLEDATA: This database of assistive devices was administered through NARIC, which lost this contract. After a gap of over a year in data collection, ABLDATA was awarded to its original developer, Marion Hall, at the Adaptive Equipment Center at Newington Children's Hospital, in Newington, Connecticut. ABLEDATA can be accessed through the Adaptive Equipment Center (for information or a search call 1-800-344-5405). It is also available to search through subscription to BRS. In cooperation with the Adaptive Equipment Center, the Trace Center at the University of Wisconsin–Madison will be distributing copies of the entire database to individuals or programs that wish to install ABLEDATA on personal computers. Initially, the distributed version of ABLEDATA will be for the MacIntosh computers only, but other Apple and IBM versions will be developed in the future (ABLEDATA 1989).

Accent on Information (Box 700, Bloomington, IL 61701) is operated by Cheever Publications, Inc., which also publishes the journal *Accent on Living* and an annual buyers' guide, as well as related publications. This system operates in response to specific questions posed by users and maintains an extensive library of information on aids for persons with physical disabilities. Less numerous citations are available for devices intended for persons with other kinds of impairments.

CIVITEX, a business information resource, not on-line at present, can be accessed by calling 800-223-6004 (see also Chapter 4).

CRISP is a large computer-based information system operated by the Statistics and Analysis Branch, Division of Research Grants, National Institutes of Health, US Department of Health and Human Services, Bethesda, MD 20892. The Computer Retrieval of Information on Scientific Projects (CRISP) was developed to facilitate the rapid dissemination of current scientific information on research projects supported through the various research grants and contracts programs of the Public Health Service or conducted intramurally by NIH and the National Institute of Mental Health. The file contains approximately 500,000 items, many of which report on research on disabling diseases and conditions, including cerebral palsy, mental retardation, spina bifida, and other congenital abnormalities, blindness, deafness, metabolic disorders, multiple sclerosis and other diseases of the nervous system, spinal cord injuries, amputation, mental illness, and all other major handicapping conditions.

CRISP will perform searches of the database on single specific topics (e.g., one particular disability) or generic data (e.g., all research support on cancer). Although there is no charge for routine searches to government agencies, public interest groups, other nonprofit organizations, and individuals, profit-making organizations must pay for searches (Russell 1986).

CTG (Closing the Gap Solutions) is a new information retrieval system focusing on products, use of computer services, and a large miscellany of information related specifically to disability and to special education. Contact: Closing the Gap, PO Box 68, Henderson, MN 56044.

Current Index to Journals in Education (CIJE) is a guide to periodical literature in education and is part of the ERIC family. It is sponsored by the Department of Education and is published by Oryx Press, Phoenix, AZ 85004.

ERIC (The Educational Resources Information Clearinghouse) is available on BRS, DIALOG, and SDC. Libraries that subscribe to the index *Resources in Education (RIE)* may deal directly with ERIC, or a local depository, usually at a major university, for current references retrieved through manual searching. For material that needs to be retrieved over a span of several years, a computer search would be advisable.

ECER (Exceptional Child Education Resources) is maintained by the Council for Exceptional Children. A subscription to the *ECER Index* allows for manual searches. For more in-depth searching, ECER is available on BRS or DIALOG.

EMBASE (formerly Excerpta Medica) is available on BRS and DIALOG.

Family Resources (National Council on Family Relations), a fairly new database, is available on BRS and DIALOG.

JAN is the job accommodation network, accessed by calling 800-JAN-PCEH (see also Chapter 7). Job match and discussions of job-site modifications to accommodate people with disabilities are included. Operated by the President's Committee on Employment of People with Disabilities. Contact: Job Accommodation Network, Box 468, Morgantown, WV 26505 (800-526-7234).

MEDLINE (National Library of Medicine) is available on BRS and DIALOG. Included are citations in the entire arena of health care and medicine, including rehabilitation and therapy. Operated by the National Library of Medicine. Contact: National Library of Medicine, MEDLARS Management Section, 8600 Rockville Pike, Bethesda, MD 29209.

NAHL, Nursing and allied health care, is available on BRS and DIALOG.

NTIS (National Technical Information Service) is available on BRS, DIALOG, and SDC.

PSYC, information on mental disorders, developed by the American Psychological Association, is available on BRS and DIALOG.

REHABDATA (National Rehabilitation Information Center) is available on BRS.

TECHNET is a model program of statewide assistance to people with disabilities, originally developed in Washington. For information on Technet and planned "subsidiaries" contact: The Resource Center for the Handicapped, 20150 45th Avenue NW, Seattle, WA 98155.

Vocational Education Curriculum Materials, The National Center for Research in Vocational Education, is available on BRS.

MODEL REHABILITATION LIBRARIES

There are several outstanding rehabilitation libraries in the United States today, albeit not nearly as many as there should be. The following accounts will provide examples of three different types of libraries: a small library in a nonprofit organization devoted to the needs of children and adults with disabilities; a large state vocational rehabilitation library; and a hospital library in a rehabilitation hospital.

The Human Resources Rehabilitation Research Library, Albertson, New York, 11507. The Human Resources Center (HRC), founded in 1962 by Dr. Henry Viscardi, is a private, nonprofit organization dedicated to providing educational, vocational, social, and recreational opportunities for people who are severely disabled. The center's programs encompass work demonstration; vocational evaluation; job training and placement; academic, career and adult education; and research. Its four units are (1) Abilities Incorporated, a work demonstration center that employs disabled adults (2) the Human Resources School, which offers tuition-free education to over 230 children with severe disabilities; (3) the Research and Training Institute, which conducts research relating to persons with disabilities; and (4) Rehabilitation Services, which conducts programs of work evaluation, training, job development and career placement for the disabled.

The Rehabilitation Research Library was established in 1962 to serve as an information arm for the entire organization, and to disseminate its publications. Monies to operate the library come from the various grant projects awarded to the center, as well as from a small foundation grant which provides a yearly stipend. A full-time certified librarian, operates the library with the assistance of a part-time assistant who is responsible for fulfillment of publication requests, as well as many other duties. The library loans or rents a few center-produced films. Some clerical and duplicating functions are provided by trainees in the rehabilitation programs of the center.

The library is physically accessible to persons with disabilities, but space is at a premium. For this reason, vertical-file material is housed in a Lectriever, a revolving shelf system built by the Sperry Corporation which holds approximately 50 shelves of material in a relatively small area. The book and periodical collection consists of approximately 2,000 books and 200 periodical and newsletter subscriptions, which reflect the needs of the professional people in the organization. General works in the area of rehabilitation, psychology, and attitudes toward the disabled are supplemented by works in the fields of rehabilitation counseling and special education and, to a much lesser extent, rehabilitation medicine.

The library reflects the major purpose of the center, which is employment of people with disabilities. Principal fields now in the forefront, as described in Chapter 7, are well-represented with current works, many in monograph form, in the areas of supported employment, transition from school to work, and new technology. Films and video training materials, some produced by the center, are also available.

Because very little material in rehabilitation medicine is acquired for the collection, the library relies on contact with the Medical Society of Nassau County, whose librarian networks with the center informally when medical information is needed. The library is also a member of the Long Island Library Resource Council (LILRC), a reference network that links public, university, and special libraries and provides special materials on interlibrary loan. Books for HRC staff members are borrowed for specific periods of time, while periodical articles are supplied on a fee basis, a system in which the library receives credit for articles supplied to LILRC against those borrowed from it. The library's holdings are listed in the Union Catalog so that books may also be loaned out through the LILRC system.

Periodical holdings are listed online using the library's IBM PC computer, and listings include the names of staff members requesting the table of contents of the particular journal. The library has access to databases on BRS.

The Human Resources Center also maintains a school library in the Human Resources School. While this library, a collection of approximately 10,000 books, is geared primarily to the children, there is a professional collection for the teachers and parents of the children in the area of special education. Audiovisual equipment, including JTV and VCR equipment, housed in the school library is at the disposal of the center staff when needed.

Each year the librarians circulate a joint memorandum to all staff members in the center and school, listing current periodical holdings in both libraries. Staff members check off those journals in which they have a professional interest. The names of staff members requesting each periodical are entered into the computerized periodical records at the research library. The tables of contents of all journals are then duplicated and circulated to those indicating interest. Staff members are then asked to circle titles of articles they wish to see, and copies of the articles are supplied to them. When, occasionally, a staff member requests the entire journal, it is signed out for a limited amount of time. This service, while expensive in terms of duplicating and staff time, is not as expensive as subscriptions to various current contents which are commercially available but do not include the journals specifically needed by the library's clientele. Supplying only the table of contents rather than circulating journals cuts down on loss, and time spent on various desks in the center. The system was initiated by the author, after many years of experience as administrator of the research library.

The research librarian also peruses the major periodicals and newsletters that come in to the library for the purpose of acquisition of new materials, and with an eye to supplying information to particular staff members. This requires an intimate knowledge of the fields in which each professional person in the center is operating. Often the librarian is called upon to assist a rehabilitation counselor who is seeking information for a particular client. The Industry Labor Council (see Chapter 7), a component of the center, receives many requests from industry and obtains information from the library. Literature searches are done on request to support grants being written at the center for government or private funding.

The Human Resources Center often hosts conferences and the librarian supports these conferences with displays of pertinent materials. Many persons tour the Center from all over the world but since the library is small and has a limited staff, visits by the public must be by appointment only. Requests for information are either handled by the research library or by an appropriate staff member. Students at neighboring colleges and universities in nursing, social work, rehabilitation counseling, and special education may also use the library by appointment. However, except for loans through LILRC, materials are circulated only in-house since the collection is too limited to allow borrowing outside the organization. The library is open from 8:30 am to 4:30 pm, Monday through Friday.

The Massachusetts Rehabilitation Commission Library, Fort Point Place, 27-43 Wormwood Street, Boston, MA 02210. From an account of a very small agency rehabilitation library that has always been run on a very minimal budget, we now turn to a description of the Massachusetts Rehabilitation Commission Library, one of the largest if not the largest, state rehabilitation libraries in the country, and a truly outstanding facility. The Massachusetts Rehabilitation Commission (MRC) is the name of the state office of vocational rehabilitation.

The library was established in 1963, is funded as a line item in the agency budget, and provides a collection in the field of vocational rehabilitation. It serves agency administrators, local Office of Vocational Rehabilitation (OVR) individuals who are disabled, employers of the disabled, health care providers, hospital staff, rehabilitation instructors, students, vocational rehabilitation counselors, and other government agencies. It can be reached by telephone or by TDD number. This library employs three professionals, two with library degrees. Its collection is estimated at 35,000 with subscriptions to 100 journals and other serials, monographs, texts, technical reports, a card catalog of journal articles, films, audios, and videos. Special reference collections include such materials as the *Encyclopedia of Deaf People and Deafness*, legal rights of handicapped persons, and making accessibility affordable. The entire collection is cataloged according to the Portal Rehabilitation Filing System, an adaptation of the Dewey Decimal System which was developed 30 years ago by Doreen Portal.

The library publishes a bimonthly newsletter and acquisitions list called *Bits and Pieces*, in which special new journal articles and other pertinent news are highlighted, followed by a new acquisitions listing, and the tables of contents of current journals. Frequent requests are received by mail from agency staff for copies of articles appearing in journals, and these are found, copied and mailed out at no cost. This service parallels a similar service at the Human Resources Center Rehabilitation Library. A "Users Guide to the Massachusetts Rehabilitation Commission Library, Boston, Massachusetts," is now under revision.

The library provides a centralized reference source to materials about persons with disabilities and, through *Bits and Pieces*, keeps the staff alert to new materials and subject areas in the field. Computer literature searches and bibliographies are provided, as well as computer product searches. Computer facilities include access to BRS and Medline. Agency subscriptions are ordered centrally through the library as well as subscriptions for supplemental reference needs of the staff who are involved in special programs. Educational materials are provided to assist counselors in completing graduate studies in vocational rehabilitation and to prepare staff for new assignments within as well as outside the agency.

The library is open from 8:00 am to 4:00 pm, Monday through Friday. The public may use the library when seeking information concerning the field of disability and may borrow materials. Information is available in all areas including devices and equipment. Many items can circulate with the exception of certain reference materials. All circulating materials may be charged out for three weeks by MRC staff, and for two weeks by the public, and in some cases materials can be mailed. Films are loaned to agency personnel and members of the rehabilitation community without charge and may be previewed in the audio department of MRC.

The library participates in interlibrary loan procedures. It has contact with all human service agencies and teachers and students of rehabilitation courses in universities and shares information nationally and internationally. The library director is on the advisory committee of the access center for the disabled of the Boston Public Library and is a member of the library board of the Perkins School for the Blind. Network memberships include the Boston Group of Government Libraries, the Boston Biomedical Library Consortium, and the Massachusetts Health Sciences Library Network (Holt 1988).

The Resource and Information Center for Disabled Individuals, Moss Rehabilitation Hospital, 12th Street and Tabor Road, Philadelphia, PA 19141. This is an excellent example of a library in a rehabilitation hospital. The resource center is a source of information on aspects of physical disability and rehabilitation and was created to meet the needs of individuals with disabilities, their families, and professionals working in the rehabilitation field. Examples of topics covered reflect their information needs, such as travel accessibility, attendant care, transportation, vocational rehabilitation, recreation, and adaptive equipment design and products. The center also has advocacy information available through its newsletter file and maintains information and referral listings of support groups and other programs and services.

In addition to the general rehabilitation topics mentioned, the resource center collection also maintains management materials for the hospital administration, as well as scientific professional information for the hospital staff, including physiatrists, therapists, social workers, and others. A patient library of light reading materials is also maintained.

A series of fact sheets have been developed on specific disabilities such as spinal cord injury, arthritis, head injury, and stroke. A definition of the disability is followed by bibliographies of professional literature, patient and family literature, and magazines (Fact Sheet 1988).

The resource center maintains a collection of printed materials of interest to professionals, people with disabilities, and their families, and is open to the public for on-site use. However, telephone or mail requests cannot be handled in great quantity because funding is not available for this service. The travel service is widely known and does respond to requests for information from the public. The Travel Information Service supplies information about accessibility and other pertinent data on a destination for a traveler with disabilities. An information package is supplied on up to three places, per request. A one month turnaround time is required for the service to process a request which is answered on a first come/first served basis. The service does not function as a travel agent and cannot make travel arrangements; therefore, the information package should be taken to a travel agent to plan the details of the trip. A $5.00 postage and handling fee (current schedule) is charged for each travel accessibility information package mailed. Checks must be made payable to the Moss Rehabilitation Hospital, and sent along with the request to: Travel Information

Service, Moss Rehabilitation Hospital, 12th Street and Tabor Road, Philadelphia, PA 19141.

It is recommended that the American Automobile Association (for members) be contacted, or another appropriate resource such as the Chamber of Commerce, for road maps since Moss cannot supply them. An information fact sheet on the Travel Information Service supplies the above details, as well as information about automobile hand controls, train travel, bus and air travel, and hotel chains which supply information on accessible accommodations and offer directories (Travel and Information Service Fact Sheet 1988). The resource center is funded by the hospital and also receives some monies from special grants.

CATALOGING

All special libraries must decide how to catalog their materials. Usually the collection is germaine to the parent facility, and a combination of systems sometimes is the only method that fits the specific needs. Putting a library completely online where only the library staff must use the materials can be the answer with subject heading designations. However, whenever other staff or the public needs access to the shelves, materials need to be organized to be "user friendly" and allow for browsing among subject areas. Some rehabilitation libraries, largely in medical facilities (such as the Moss Resource and Information Center) use the Medical Library classification system, in combination with Library of Congress classifications; others use Library of Congress classifications, with expansion in the vocational rehabilitation area. Some years ago a rehabilitation system, modeled after the Dewey Decimal system was devised by Doreen Portal, and subsequently abridged by Laura Edwards (now on the faculty of the College of Optometry in Philadelphia, PA). Edwards has recently made a further modification of this system. The Human Resources Center Library uses the Edwards abridgment for its vertical files, and Library of Congress classification for books. The Massachusetts Rehabilitation Commission Library uses the Portal system for its entire collection. However, no major steps have been taken in the United States to codify a rehabilitation filing system.

The Canadian Rehabilitation Council for the Disabled (CRCD) designed such a scheme in 1979 when it produced a filing system called "Keywords." The system was designed to accommodate the organization of literature relating to disability and rehabilitation and incorporated the classification schemes of CRCD and the Kinsmen Rehabilitation Foundation of British Columbia. An expansion was undertaken in 1982. The third edition, published in 1987, includes detailed introductions containing a general orientation to the system, which could help a nonprofessional librarian operating a small information center. This publication is in a loose-leaf format to allow for easy updating (CRCD News 1987). The system relies on the authority of the ABLEDATA and REHADATA Thesauri and subject descriptors of NARIC. Other bibliographic resources consulted include the Library of Congress Subject Headings and Sub-Divisions, Dewey Classification Scheme, Medical Subject Headings (MESH), and the Nordic Information System on Technical Aids for Disabled Persons (Jaeggin 1985). Keywords is in use in Canada, as well as in other countries, including Australia. For further information on this system contact: Maureen Vasey, CRCD Director of Information Resources and Communications, or Robert Jaeggin, CRCD librarian, One Yonge Street, Suite 2110,

Toronto, ON Canada, M5E. To order a copy of the CRCD Rehabilitation Classification Scheme send a check for $10.00 plus $2.00 for postage and handling, made out to the Canadian Rehabilitation Council for the Disabled.

CONCLUSION

In order to help rehabilitation librarians function effectively there is still a need for a complete rehabilitation database that coordinates all of the existing databases which provide pieces of the information puzzle. There is also a need for a complete indexing of the journals in the field of rehabilitation, some of which are indexed in *Index Medicus*, some in *Psych Abstracts*, and some in *Current Index to Journals in Education (CIJE)*. Some are not completely indexed anywhere, but provide their own indexing at the end of each year.

REFERENCES

ABLEDATA Information Sheet. 1989, January. Newington, CT.

Fact Sheet. National Rehabilitation Information Center, Silver Spring, MD.

Fact Sheet. Resource Center, Resource and Information Center for Disabled Individuals, Moss Rehabilitation Hospital, Philadelphia.

Fact Sheet. Travel Information Service, Resource and Information Center for Disabled Individuals. Moss Rehabilitation Hospital, Philadelphia.

Holt. June, *Bits & Pieces.* 1988, September/October. Massachusetts Rehabilitation Commission Library.

Jaeggin, Robert B. 1985. "C.R.C.D. Rehabilitation Classification Scheme." *Bibliotheca Medica Canadiana* 7 (3): 1–171.

"New CRCD Rehabilitation Classification Scheme." 1987, September. *CRCD News.*

REHABDATA, A Bibliographic Database of the Disability and Rehabilitation Literature, National Rehabilitation Information Center, Silver Spring, MD 20910-2319.

Chapter 12
Barrier-Free Design for Libraries

Three basic guides are available for librarians wishing to modify their premises to make them accessible to people with disabilities. With the help of these references it should be possible to make at least some adaptations to old buildings and to ensure that new buildings are accessible in accordance with federal regulations. Those libraries receiving federal funds must offer accessibility, however, most librarians now realize that it is important to modify their facilities under any circumstances in order to serve this segment of their user population.

Schools of architecture are offering information about barrier-free design in their course work, and librarians serving such schools should have references in their files to assist professors and students. For this purpose, refer to the bibliography which contains several additional entries.

The American National Standards Institute (ANSI) published its original general specifications for the elimination of architectural barriers in 1961. Known as the ANSI standards, the latest edition, issued in 1986, is entitled "Providing Accessibility and Usability for Physically Handicapped People" and can be obtained from ANSI at 1430 Broadway, New York, NY. It offers general standards and measurements in all areas of accessibility.

In 1984 a study entitled "Uniform Federal Accessibility Standards" was published jointly by the four regulatory agencies: General Services Administration, Department of Defense, Department of Housing and Urban Development, and the US Postal Service. It can be obtained from the Architectural and Transportation Barriers Compliance Board, Washington, DC 20202. It offers officially accepted government standards in all areas, and contains a one-page suggestion about libraries.

Planning Barrier Free Libraries (Library of Congress 1981) has not been updated but remains available from the National Library Service. Essentially, it is a complete guide for library directors and librarians wishing to build or remodel a library to be a part of the National Library Service Network of libraries for the blind and physically handicapped.

Some basic guidelines are listed here to help librarians who wish to begin giving some thought to modifying their facilities. This information has been culled from the above guides. Information is required in two areas: (1) general information which is necessary for all public buildings, such as wheelchair measurements, curb cuts, parking areas, ramps, door widths and thresholds, restrooms, telephones, elevators, corridor widths, and floor space; and (2) specific requirements for libraries, including stack widths, reference table and carrel heights, and optimum heights for circulation desks and card catalogs.

The population for which adjustments must be made includes

1. Nonambulatory disabled: those with permanent or temporary injury with some degree of paralysis to lower and/or upper limbs.
2. Semi-ambulatory disabled: persons who walk with difficulty, including people using crutches, braces, walkers, amputees, people with pulmonary or cardiac ailments, and persons with arthritis.
3. People with neuromuscular impairments, which may cause lack of control and/or faulty coordination.
4. Blind or visually impaired people.
5. Deaf or hearing-impaired people.
6. People disabled due to aging.

STANDARDS FOR BARRIER-FREE DESIGN

The standard model collapsible wheelchair of tubular metal construction most commonly in use is 42 inches long (see Figure 1), 25 inches wide when open, and has a fixed turning radius of 18 inches, wheel to wheel, and 31.5 inches from front to rear structure. Average turning space is 60 x 60 inches. A minimum width of 60 inches is required for two individuals in wheelchairs to pass each other.

FIGURE 1. Average Measurements for Standard Collapsible Wheelchair

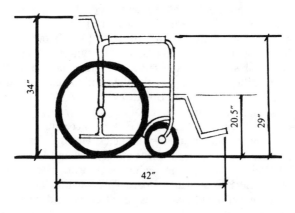

In parking areas, spaces that are accessible and close to the building should be set aside and identified for people with disabilities. An area at least 12 feet wide is adequate and provides room for a person with disabilities to get out of the car and into a wheelchair. This is about the width of a regular parking space plus an area of approximately 4 feet next to it, preferably crosshatched so that it is obviously designated as a "no parking" space for another car, with appropriate signage (Figure 2).

FIGURE 2. Parking for a Disabled Person

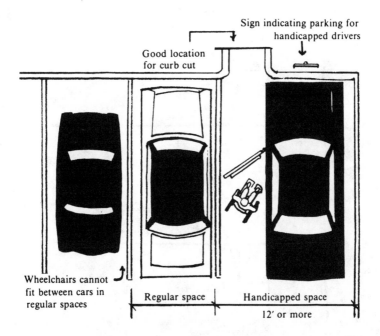

Parking for a disabled person may be perpendicular, as above, diagonal, or parallel to the curb. For parallel parking the curb and sidewalk on the right side of the car is preferred. Two percent of the total number of parking spaces, or a minimum of one space, should be set aside for patrons with physical disabilities.

There should be a passageway so that the person need not wheel or walk behind other parked cars, as well as curb cuts and ramps into the building (Figure 3).

FIGURE 3. Walkway and Ramp Specifications

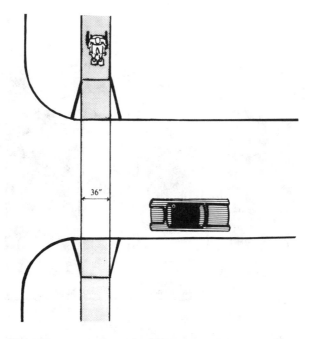

Walkways and ramps should align across the roadway. Ramps and walkway should be at least 36 inches wide; curb height should not exceed 6 inches.

Ramps may not have a slope greater than a 1 foot rise in 12 feet and must have a handrail on at least one side where the rise is greater than 10 feet, as well as a level area at the top at least 4 feet square (large enough for entry by a wheelchair) (Figures 4 and 5).

FIGURE 4. Illustration of Ramp Length

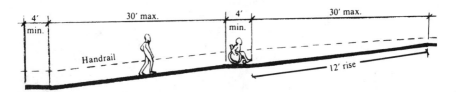

The maximum length of the ramp between platforms is 30 feet.

FIGURE 5. An Illustration of a Ramp Platform

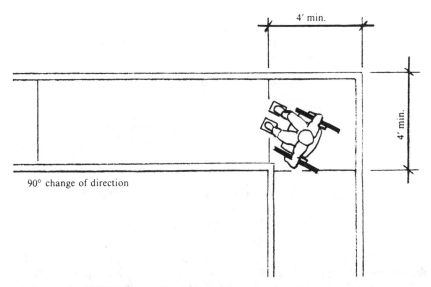

90° change of direction

A 4-foot square platform is needed wherever there is a change of direction on a ramp since it is very difficult to turn a wheelchair on a ramp slope.

At least one primary entrance to the building shall be usable by persons in wheelchairs, with a door no less than 32 inches wide, easy to operate (no heavier than 10 pounds of pressure), with a see-through panel if possible, as well as a kickplate from the bottom of the door to at least 16 inches from the floor, made of a material to withstand wear and tear from bumps by wheelchair foot pedals, wheels, or crutches. Thresholds should be flush with the floor, and abrupt changes in level should be avoided at the entrance. Figure 6 shows maneuverability of wheelchairs on the push side of the door, side approach.

FIGURE 6. Doorway Dimensions

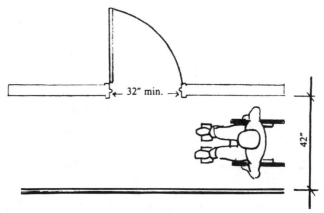

Maneuvering space on the push side of the door, side approach; minimum of 42 inches for corridor or walk width.

Switches and controls for lights, heat, ventilation, windows, draperies, fire alarms, and all similar controls of frequent or essential use should be placed within reach of individuals in wheelchairs (at a maximum height of 48 inches) (see Figure 7).

FIGURE 7. Area of Reach from a Wheelchair

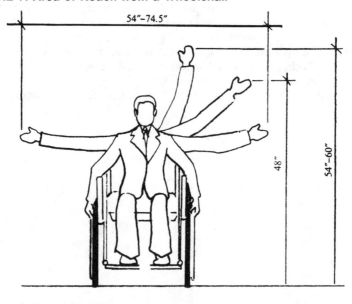

Raised letters and numbers to identify offices, reading rooms, or stacks should be placed conveniently at about 5-foot height for the use of people who are blind. Doors that might lead to areas not intended for use, or that are dangerous, should be identified by knurled door knobs or handles. Audible and visual warning signals should be installed for people who are blind and deaf.

Low-hanging signs, ceiling lights, and other objects that protrude in corridors or traffic ways should be avoided (a minimum height of 7 feet from the floor is recommended). Maps with raised features or letters showing locations of materials are useful.

The two most formidable barriers for those who are partially sighted are stairs and locating public restrooms, and then determining whether the restrooms are for men or women. The leading edges of stairs, on both the runner and the riser, should be marked with a 2-inch-wide strip of paint or nonskid material that has a color and gray value in high contrast to the color and gray value of the rest of the stairs.

Restrooms should be marked with protruding panels on the exterior face of the doors, about 2 feet square and 1/4 inch thick. The men's restroom panel should be one simple, geometric shape (for example, rectangle) and the one on the women's restroom door should be a distinctly different shape (perhaps a circle or a triangle). These panels should also be of distinctly different colors and gray values from one another and from the doors on which they are mounted. Existing restroom stalls can, in some instances, be modified at little cost. If the stall is wide enough to accommodate a wheelchair, the door and door jams may be removed and a full curtain substituted for privacy.

Restrooms (Figure 8), telephones, and elevators (Figure 9) should be made accessible by providing appropriate space and fixtures, and in the case of elevators audible signals, whenever possible, should be installed for patrons who are blind. Telephones and water fountains should be low enough (48 inches from the ground) to be accessible to persons in wheelchairs.

FIGURE 8. Dimensions for Restroom Stall

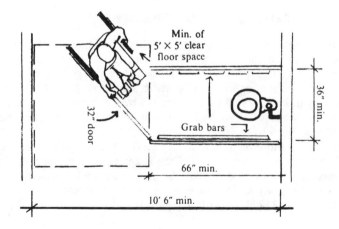

Restroom stall should have grab bars on both sides.

FIGURE 9. Control Panel Layout

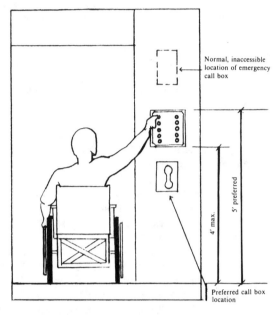

Bottom of elevator control panel should be no higher than 4 feet, with the panel top no higher than 5 feet (average highest reach from a wheelchair is 5 feet as shown in Figure 7). Elevator controls should be push-buttons with raised letters.

LIBRARY ADAPTATIONS AND ACCESSIBILITY

In some cases, providing access to the library building and personal service thereafter may be all that a very old and inaccessible library can accomplish until adequate funding or a new building allows for greater improvements. Access to the building, or even an alternate service such as a bookmobile or home delivery of books, is all that is required by law, according to policy three, issued by the Office of Civil Rights as one of six interpretations relating to Section 504 of PL 93-112 (Federal Register 1978.) However, when librarians realize how much more there is to library service than home delivery of books, they will certainly wish to make all of the adaptations they can possibly afford to allow people who are disabled to take part in all library activities. In many cases it will be possible for libraries to improve access to reading areas, circulation desk, and book stacks (see Figure 10).

FIGURE 10. Illustration of Passage Specifications

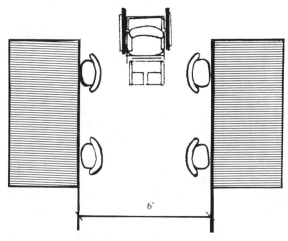

Area between library tables and book stacks should be at least 6 feet wide for easy passage.

The card catalog should be 18 to 48 inches from the floor with a 36-inch maximum height preferred. An adjacent work surface should be 29 inches from the floor. Should remodeling be a problem, the card catalog, an essential tool, may be made accessible by lowering the base to 16 inches; however, removing a drawer and placing it on a low table may serve as a viable alternative. An able-bodied patron might be happy to perform this function should a librarian not be readily available.

Checkout counters and information desks should be no higher than 36 inches from the floor. Tables should be 29 inches from the floor and apronless, or with recessed aprons. Carrels should be 29 inches from the floor, a minimum of 30 inches wide, with a preferred width of 34 inches and a 20-inch depth.

NETWORK LIBRARIES

Planning Barrier Free Libraries: A Guide for Renovation and Construction of Libraries Serving Blind and Physically Handicapped Readers (1981) is an essential reference tool for library directors and librarians planning new or renovated quarters for a network library. While the guide suggests how to establish an "ideal" library, the size of the building will obviously be determined by the population to be served, the size of the staff, and the funds available. The guide recommends that the planning team include the library director, librarian, architect, and a member of the community who is blind or physically disabled. Various steps in the planning stage are suggested, including budget, as well as a determination of the number of "walk-in" patrons expected, since much of the work of the network library is done by mailing talking books to patrons' homes. The following recommendations are made:

- The lobby or waiting area should be large enough for wheelchairs to move freely from the lobby to all other areas. Eliminate sharp corners and protruding furniture legs by rounding the walls and selecting furnishings carefully. A desk for a receptionist should be placed as near the entry as possible. A predialed phone or a tactile map of the building would contribute to the independence of patrons.

- A reading and study area should include samples of new and unusual aids. Study carrels should be "wet," that is, wired for electrical outlets to accommodate playback equipment, Optacons, personal Kurzweil readers, Visualteks, etc. A card or microfiche catalog suspended from the wall is a good idea.

- A conference meeting room with adjustable counters, accessible tables, and carrels can be used for meetings of organizations of individuals who are blind and physically disabled, as well as for volunteers and other groups who work with the patrons. Games, toys, braille writers and typewriters, talking calculators, and other types of equipment can be closeted or recessed in this room.

- Detailed information is also offered for the bookstack area. These stacks will contain all the talking books, braille volumes, and a work area. Various types of shelves are suggested, including compact shelving (if storage space is at a premium) which moves on guides or tracks and is operated either manually or electronically.

- Depending on whether the library being planned is a regional or subregional facility, and the extent of its need for production and machine repair facilities, appropriate space will need to be allotted. This monograph offers complete information as to how to plan for these areas, as well as for shipping and receiving, mail sorting, etc. Site selection is also a very important consideration when planning access to the building for persons with disabilities, including ease of parking and walking or wheeling to the library, and for reaching the library (if in an urban area) by means of public transportation.

The rest of this monograph deals in detail with planning the architectural program, building schedules, and other important details. Repairing and renovating an existing building is certainly an alternative to constructing a new building. Many older buildings have a certain charm, but each building must be analyzed and evaluated for structure, utility systems, and adaptability to the functional and architectural program.

The monograph concludes with an accessibility checklist which is extremely useful to any library wishing to improve accessibility, a flowchart diagramming a suggested facility, and time charts for the renovation of an old library or the building of a new one.

REFERENCES

American National Standards Institute, New York. 1986. *Providing Accessibility and Usability for Physically Handicapped People.* ANSI A117.1.

Federal Register. 1978, August. Part 3, Office of Civil Rights, Department of Health Education and Welfare. Washington, DC: 4 (3): 36034–36036.

National Library Service for the Blind and Physically Handicapped. 1981. *Planning Barrier Free Libraries.* Washington, DC: Library of Congress.

Chapter 13
Book and Periodical
Resources for Core
Collections

Much of the information in this bibliography would be useful in all library and information settings. It is presented topically so that collections may be assembled according to individual needs. The works listed under "General" would be useful in all collections and public libraries could use this section as a basic core collection.

GENERAL

Directories

American Annals of the Deaf, Vol. 134, No. 2, April, 1989. (Reference Issue)
This yearly reference issue supplies information on programs and services for deaf persons in the US.

American Association of University Affiliated Programs for Persons with Developmental Disabilities. *Resource Guide to Organizations Concerned with Developmental Handicaps*, Silver Spring, MD: American Association of University Affiliated Programs for Persons with Developmental Disabilities (annually).

American Foundation for the Blind. *Directory of Services for Blind and Visually Impaired Persons in the United States*. 23rd ed. 1988. New York: American Foundation for the Blind.

Arkansas Rehabilitation Research and Training Center on Deafness and Hearing Impairment. *The National Directory of Rehabilitation Facilities Offering Vocational Evaluation and Adjustment Training to Hearing-Impaired Persons*. Edited by Paula Marut, Douglas Watson, Diane Buford. Little Rock, AR: Arkansas Rehabilitation and Training Center on Deafness and Hearing Impairment, 1984.

Directory for Exceptional Children. Boston: Porter-Sargent, 12th ed., 1990–91.

Eckstein, Richard M. *Handicapped Funding Directory: A Guide to Sources of Funding in the United States for Programs and Services for the Disabled*. 6th ed. Margate, FL: Research Grant Guides, 1988.

Federal Programs Advisory Service. Handicapped Requirements Handbook. Washington, DC: Thompson Publishing Group.
Covers federal laws pertaining to people with disabilities. Monthly supplements update and supply information on proposed changes in legislation. Available only from Thompson Publishing Group, 1725 K Street NW, Suite 200.

HEATH Resource Center. National Clearinghouse on Postsecondary Education for Handicapped Individuals, Resource Directory. Washington, DC: HEATH Resource Center, 1987.

Helen Keller National Center. *A Directory of Agencies Serving the Deaf-Blind.* Sands Point, NY: Helen Keller National Center 1988.

LINC Associates. *The Specialware Directory: A Guide to Software for Special Education.* 2nd ed. Columbus, OH: LINC Associates, 1986.

National Association of Rehabilitation Facilities. *1988 Rehabilitation Facilities Sourcebook.* Washington, DC: National Association of Rehabilitation Facilities, 1987.

National Association of Rehabilitation Professionals in the Private Sector. *NARPPS National Directory of Rehabilitation Professionals, Vocational/Medical Facilities, Products and Services.* Twin Peaks, CA: National Association of Rehabilitation Professionals in the Private Sector, 1988–89 ed.

National Spinal Cord Injury Association. *National Resources Directory: An Information Guide for Persons with Spinal Cord Injury.* Woburn, MA: National Spinal Cord Injury Association, 1985.

Nosek, Margaret A. et al. *Registry of Independent Living Programs.* Houston, TX: The Institute for Rehabilitation Research (TIRR), 1987.

Self, Phyllis, ed. *Physical Disability: An Annotated Literature Guide.* New York: Marcel Dekker, 1984.

The Source: Products and Services for Persons with Disabilities. Verndale, MN: RPM Press, 1987–88.

Thomas, Carol H., ed. *Directory of College Facilities and Services for the Disabled.* 2nd ed. Phoenix, AZ: Oryx Press, 1986.

U.S. Department of Education. Office of Special Education and Rehabilitation Services. National Institute of Handicapped Research. *Directory of National Information Sources on Handicapping Conditions and Related Services.* 4th ed. Washington, DC: Harold Russell Associates, 1986.

Independent Living

Hayle, Glorya. *The Source Book for the Disabled: An Illustrated Guide to Easier More Independent Living for Physically Disabled People, Their Families and Friends.* New York and London: Paddington Press, 1979.
Covers home adaptations, personal needs, sexuality, parenting the disabled child, leisure and recreation.

Hotte, Eleanor Boettke. *Self-Help Clothing for Children Who Have Physical Disabilities.* Rev. ed. Chicago: National Easter Seal Society, 1979.
A revised edition of a 1962 booklet.

Kreisler, Nancy, and Jack Kreisler. *Catalog of Aids for the Disabled.* New York: McGraw-Hill, 1982.
Details devices for personal care, communication, travel, and recreation. Includes names and addresses of useful organizations.

Lunt, Suzanne. *A Handbook for the Disabled: Ideas and Inventions for Easier Living. New York: Charles Scribner's Sons, 1984.*
Reference book detailing hundreds of devices for physically disabled people, to make life easier and more active. Also offers directions for home-made aids.

Pancsofar, Ernest, and Robert Blackwell. *A User's Guide to Community Entry for the Severely Handicapped.* Albany, NY: State Univ. of New York at Albany, 1986.
A guide for individuals with severe mental handicaps entering independent living arrangements. Covers transitions from home, how to work with attendant care providers, domestic skills, and leisure time activities. Lists funding sources.

New Technology

Association for the Advancement of Rehabilitation Technology. *Rehabilitation Technology Service Delivery: A Practical Guide.* Washington, DC: 1987.

Bender, Michael, Nancy M. Pinson-Millburn, and Lee Joyce Richmond. *Careers, Computers, and the Handicapped.* Austin, TX: Pro-Ed, 1985.
Discusses using the computer as a tool for implementing job skills.

Bowe, Frank. *Personal Computers and Special Needs.* Berkley, CA: Sybex, 1984.
Introduction to the uses of the computer for persons with all types of disabilities. Discusses what the personal computer can do to help people with disabilities achieve independence in the home or employment setting.

McWilliams, Peter. *Personal Computers and the Disabled.* New York: Quantum, 1984.
Covers what computers can do for physically disabled, hearing-impaired, visually-impaired, learning-disabled, or speech-impaired people. Includes a buying guide on purchasing a computer.

Webster, John G., Albert M. Cook, Willis J. Tompkins, and Gregg C. Vanderheiden, eds. *Electronic Devices for Rehabilitation.* New York: J. Wiley, 1985.

Barrier-Free Design

American National Standards Institute. *Providing Accessibility and Usability for Physically Handicapped People.* New York: American National Standards Institute A117.1, 1986.

Cary, Jane Randolph. *How to Create Interiors for the Disabled.* Illus. by Philip F. Farrell, Jr. New York: Pantheon Books, 1978.
Discusses how spaces and objects can be modified to suit motor limitations. Includes shelter, basic remodeling techniques, and "how to" diagrams.

Dunning, Glenna. *Architecture of Accessibility: Planning for the Disabled,* a partially annotated bibliography. Vance Bibliographies, Box 229 Monticello, IL 61856, 1989.

Eastern Paralyzed Veterans Association. *Wheelchair House Designs.* Jackson Heights, NY: 1989.
New booklet incorporating latest architectural standards.

General Services Administration, Department of Defense, Department of Housing and Urban Development, United States Postal Service. *Uniform Federal Accessibility Standards.* Architectural and Transportation Barriers Compliance Board, Washington, DC: Government Printing Office, 1984.

Library of Congress. National Library Service for the Blind and Physically Handicapped. *Planning Barrier Free Libraries.* Washington, DC: Government Printing Office, 1981.

Moakley, Terence J., and John D. Del Colle, eds. *Barrier Free Design: The Law.* 2 vols. New York: EPVA, 1986 and supplements.

Travel

Hecker, Helen. *Travel for the Disabled: A Handbook of Travel Resources and 500 Worldwide Access Guides.* Portland, OR: Twin Peaks Press, 1985.
Printed in large type for easy reading; includes addresses for both domestic and foreign access guides. Includes information on special camps, travel tips for air, sea, rail, and bus travel.

Lindsay, Rod W. and Norene Lindsay. *The Physically Disabled Traveler's Guide.* Toledo, OH: Resource Directories, 1986.

The Physically Disabled Traveler's Guide. Toledo, OH: Resource Directories, 1987.
Printed in easy-to-read large type. Includes a listing of accessible resorts.

Sygall, Susan. *A World of Options: A Guide to International Educational Exchange, Community Services and Travel for Persons with Disabilities.* Eugene, OR: Mobility International USA, 1985-86.

Walzer, Mary Meister. *A Travel Guide for the Disabled: Western Europe.* New York: Van Nostrand, Reinhold, 1982.

Weiss, Louise. *Access to the World: A Travel Guide for the Handicapped.* Rev. ed. New York: Henry Holt and Co., 1986.
Includes hotels and motels, access guides, airline policies, bus, train and ship accessibility, and practical travel hints.

Recreation

Cratty, Bryant J., *Adapted Physical Education for Handicapped Children and Youth.* Denver, CO: Love Publishers, 1980.

Nesbitt, John A., ed. *International Directory of Recreation Oriented Assistive Devices Sources.* Marina del Rey, CA: Lifeboat Press, 1986.

Saari, Joan. *Fitness Courses with Adaptations for Persons with Disabilities.* Loretto, MN: Vinland National Center, 1981.

Simmons, Richard. *Reach for Fitness: A Special Book of Exercises for the Physically Challenged.* New York: Warner Books, 1986.
Provides health and exercise guidelines for over 40 different physical and mental challenges. Includes nutrition information.

Winston, Lynn. *Recreation and Sports.* Bloomington, IL: Accent on Living Press, 1985.

Sex Information

Ayrault, Evelyn West. *Sex, Love and the Physically Handicapped.* New York: Continuum, 1981.
Competent and sensitive account of the importance of recognizing and developing normal feelings of sexuality in people with disabilities.

Baxter, Robert T., *Salvaging Our Sexuality: For Spinal Cord Injury and Related Disabilities in Distress.* East Orange, NJ: Medical Media Visuals, 1979.
Primarily for spinal cord injured people.

Chipouras, Sophia, Debra Cornelius, Susan M. Daniels, and Elaine Makas. *Who Cares? A Handbook on Sex Education and Counseling Services for Disabled People.* Washington, DC: George Washington Univ., 1979.
For consumers, professionals, and trainers. Contains literature summaries, books and journals, consultants and organizations.

Enby, Gunnel. *Let There Be Love: Sex and the Handicapped.* New York: Taplinger, 1975.

Gregory, Martha F. *Sexual Adjustment: A Guide for the Spinal Cord Injured.* Bloomington, IL: Accent on Living Press, 1974.
Written by a woman who is a counselor as well as the marriage partner of a spinal cord injured person.

Johnson, Warren R., with Winifred Kempton. *Sex Education and Counseling of Special Groups: The Mentally and Physically Disabled, Ill and Elderly.* Springfield, IL: Charles C. Thomas, 1975.
Deals with specific sex-related behaviors.

Mooney, T. O., T. M. Cole, and R. A. Chilgren. *Sexual Options for Paraplegics and Quadriplegics.* Boston: Little, Brown, 1975.
Written by a spinal cord injured person and two physicians as a guide to techniques.

Task Force on Concerns of Physically Disabled Women. *Within Reach: Providing Family Planning Services to Physically Disabled Women.* New York: Human Science Press, 1978.
Complements *Toward Intimacy.* Provides guidelines to providers of health care services.

Task Force on Concerns of Physically Disabled Women. *Toward Intimacy: Family Planning and Sexuality Concerns of Physically Disabled Women.* New York: Human Sciences Press, 1978.

REHABILITATION

The following books would provide a good basis for a core rehabilitation collection, especially in conjunction with the above. It is impossible to list the many monographs being issued by the research and training centers around the country. These monographs, as well as reports of seminars and conferences, can be obtained from them, as well as from reading the periodicals and newsletters in the field.

General

Berkowitz, Edward D. *Disabled Policy: America's Programs for the Handicapped. A Twentieth Century Fund Report.* New York: Cambridge Univ. Press, 1987.
Exposes contradictions in America's disability policies and suggests means for remedying them.

Bowe, Frank. *Handicapping America.* New York: Harper & Row, 1978.
Deals with attitudes toward disabled people.

Bowe, Frank. *Rehabilitating America: Toward Independence for Disabled and Elderly People.* New York: Harper & Row, 1980.
Suggests a five-point plan for rehabilitating disabled and elderly people.

Burgdorf, Robert L., Jr., ed. *The Legal Rights of Handicapped Persons, Cases, Materials and Text.* Baltimore: Paul H. Brookes, 1980.
With 1983 supplement. Provides very detailed account of legislation, with case studies.

Deegan, Mary Jo, and Nancy A. Brooks, eds. *Women and Disability: The Double Handicap.* New Brunswick, NJ, and Oxford: Transactions, Inc., 1985.
Recounts experiences of disabled women and provides advice for confronting daily problems.

Fine, Michelle, and Adrienne Asch. *Women with Disabilities: Essays in Psychology, Culture, and Politics.* Philadelphia: Temple Univ. Press, 1988.
Written from a feminist and disability rights perspective, discusses discrimination in the workplace and the failure of mainstream women to address their concerns.

Goldenson, Robert M., Jerome R. Dunham, and Charlis S. Dunham, eds. *Disability and Rehabilitation Handbook.* New York: McGraw-Hill, 1978.
A tremendous compendium of information with many contributors. Includes medical definitions of disabilities, definitions of health science professions concerned with rehabilitation. Covers civil rights and consumerism, independent living, educational programs, vocational rehabilitation, psychosocial aspects of disability, environmental barriers, recreation, statistics, and organizations interested in the disabled.

Hardy, Richard, et al., *International Rehabilitation: Approaches and Programs.* New York: Irvington, 1988.

Pan, Elizabeth, Thomas E. Backer, and Carolyn L. Vash, eds. *Annual Review of Rehabilitation.* 5 vols. New York: Springer, 1980–86.
Collections of articles that chronicle the progress of the rehabilitation movement throughout the 1980s. Of historical value.

Taylor, Lewis J., Margarie Colter, Gary Colter, and Thomas E. Backer, eds. *Handbook of Private Sector Rehabilitation.* Springer Series in Rehabilitation. New York: Springer, 1985.
Discusses the state of private-sector rehabilitation, relationship to the insurance industry, uses of the computer, marketing rehabilitation services.

Taylor, Steven J., Douglas Biklen, and James Knoll, eds. *Community Integration for People with Severe Disabilities.* New York: Teachers College Press, 1987.

Van Hasselt, Vincent B., Philip S. Strain, and Michael Hersen. *Handbook of Developmental and Physical Disabilities.* 1st ed. New York: Pergamon Press, 1988.

Wright, George Nelson. *Total Rehabilitation.* Boston: Little, Brown, 1980.

Rehabilitation: Medical

Dorland's Illustrated Medical Dictionary. 27th ed. Philadelphia: W. B. Saunders, 1988.

Handbook of Severe Disabilities. Edited by Walter C. Stolov and Michael R. Clower. U.S. Department of Education. Washington, DC: Government Printing Office, 1981.
Provides medical definitions of mental disabilities, many physical disabilities and neurological impairments, blindness, chronic pain, alcoholism, drug abuse, cardiovascular and pulmonary dysfunction, cancer, burns, spinal cord injury, with emphasis on training the rehabilitation counselor.

Kamenetz, Herman L. *Dictionary of Rehabilitation Medicine.* New York: Springer, 1983.

Nichols, P. J. *Rehabilitation Medicine.* 2nd ed. Woburn, MA: Butterworth, 1980.
Discusses physical and occupational therapy in arthritis, fractures, stroke, amputees, and heart attacks.

Rosenstein, Solomon N. *Dentistry in Cerebral Palsy and Related Handicapping Conditions.* Springfield, IL: Charles C. Thomas, 1978.

Stryker, Stephanie. *Speech After Stroke: A Manual for the Speech Pathologist and the Family Member.* 2nd ed. Springfield, IL: Charles C. Thomas, 1981.

World Health Organization. *International Classification of Impairments, Disabilities and Handicaps: A Manual of Classification Relating to the Consequences of Disease.* Geneva: World Health Organization, 1980.

Rehabilitation: Nursing

Sine, Robert D., ed. *Basic Rehabilitation Techniques: A Self-Instructional Guide.* 2nd ed. Rockville, MD: Aspen, 1981.

Rehabilitation: Psychology and Neuropsychiatry

Caplan, Bruce, ed. *Rehabilitation Psychology Desk Reference.* Rockville, MD: Aspen, 1987.
Covers psychological adjustment to spinal cord injury, traumatic head injury, stroke, chronic pain as well as family adaptations; includes section on sexuality.

Ciardiello, Jean A., and Morris D. Bell. *Vocational Rehabilitation of Persons with Prolonged Psychiatric Disorders.* Baltimore: Johns Hopkins Univ. Press, 1988.

Grief, Elaine, and Ruth G. Matarazzo. *Behavioral Approaches to Rehabilitation: Coping with Change.* Springer Series on Rehabilitation, edited by Thomas E. Backer, vol. 3. New York: Springer Publishing Co., 1982.
Discusses patterns of behavior, social and, psychological phenomena, coping with disability.

Krueger, David W., ed. *Rehabilitation Psychology: A Comprehensive Textbook.* Rockville, MD: Aspen, 1984.
A comprehensive textbook dealing with the emotional aspects of rehabilitation.

Lezack, Muriel Deutch. *Neuropsychological Assessment.* 2nd ed. New York: Oxford Univ. Press, 1983.

Lohr, James B., and Alexander A. Wisniewski. *Movement Disorders: A Neuro-psychiatric Approach.* New York: Guilford Press, 1987.

Manelli, Robert P., and Arthur E. Dell Orto, eds. *The Psychological and Social Impact of Physical Disability.* New York: Springer, 1984.

Meier, Manfred J., Arthur L. Benton, and Leonard Diller. *Neuropsychological Rehabilitation.* New York: Guilford Press, 1987.

Olshan, Neal H. *Depression: Causes and Treatment.* New York: Watts, 1982.

Wright, Beatrice. *Physical Disability: A Psychosocial Approach.* 2nd ed. New York: Harper & Row, 1983.
A classic text covering all aspects of the psychological aspects of disability.

Rehabilitation: Evaluation and Management

Berkowitz, Monroe, ed. *Measuring the Efficiency of Public Programs: Costs and Benefits in Vocational Rehabilitation.* Philadelphia: Temple Univ. Press, 1988.

Bolton, Brian. *Handbook of Measurement and Evaluation in Rehabilitation.* 2nd ed. Baltimore: Paul H. Brookes, 1987.

Brown, Roy I., ed. *Management and Administration of Rehabilitation Programs.* San Diego: College-Hill Press, 1986.
Covers a wide range of topics relating to employment of disabled people.

Castellani, Paul J. *The Political Economy of Developmental Disabilities.* Baltimore: Paul H. Brookes, 1987.
Discusses the effect of financial cost on the provision of community services to developmentally disabled people.

Erekson, Thomas L., and Anthony F. Rotatori. *Accessibility to Employment Training for the Physically Handicapped.* Springfield, IL: Charles C. Thomas, 1986.
Guide for teachers, administrators, and program designers.

Fuhrer, Marcus J., ed. *Rehabilitation Outcomes: Analysis and Measurement.* Baltimore: Paul H. Brookes, 1987.

Kiernan, William E., and Robert L. Schalock. *Economics, Industry and Disability: A Look Ahead.* Baltimore: Paul H. Brookes, 1989.

Rehabilitation: Counseling and Vocational Rehabilitation

Deneen, Lawrence J., and Thorvald A. Hesselund. *Counseling the Able-Disabled: Rehabilitation Counseling in Disability Compensation Systems.* San Francisco: Rehabilitation Publications, 1986.
Covers industrial rehabilitation fundamentals, workers compensation, vocational exploration, job placement, legislation, private/public rehabilitation, nurses' perspective.

Gandy, Gerald L., E. Davis Maratin, Jr., Richard E. Hardy, and John G. Cull, ed. *Rehabilitation Counseling and Services: Profession and Process.* Springfield, IL: Charles C. Thomas, 1987.
A complete revision of *Vocational Rehabilitation: Profession and Process,* 1972. An introductory text in rehabilitation counseling and a reference for the practicing counselor.

Haveman, Robert H. *Public Policy toward Disabled Workers: Cross-national Analyses of Economic Impact.* New York: Cornell Univ. Press, 1984.

Matkin, Ralph E. *Insurance Rehabilitation: Service Applications, Disability Compensation Systems.* Austin, TX: Pro-Ed, 1985.

McCray, Paul M. *The Job Accommodation Handbook.* Verndale, MN: RPM Press, 1987.

McLaughlin, Caven S., J. Bradley Garner, and Michael J. Callahan, eds. *Getting Employed, Staying Employed: Job Development and Training for Persons with Severe Handicaps.* Baltimore: Paul H. Brookes, 1987.

Parker, Randall M., ed. *Rehabilitation Counseling: Basics and Beyond.* Austin, TX: Pro-Ed, 1987.

Revision of earlier text. Provides updates in legislation, independent living, private sector rehabilitation, computer applications, and school-to-work transition.

Rasch, John D. *Rehabilitation of Workers' Compensation and Other Insurance Claimants: Case Management, Forensics, and Business Aspects.* Springfield, IL: Charles C. Thomas, 1985.

A textbook on private sector rehabilitation. Reviews early history, details the relationship to state and federal programs and policies within the insurance industry.

Rosen, Christine Duncan, and Joan P. Gerring. *Head Trauma: Educational Reintegration.* Boston and San Diego: College-Hill Press, 1986.

Covers anatomy of the brain, recovery, school planning, and learning theories.

Rubin, Jeffry. *Alternatives in Rehabilitating the Handicapped: A Policy Analysis.* New York: Human Sciences Press, 1982.

A collection of papers documenting the change in vocational rehabilitation in the 1980s.

Rudrud, Eric H., Jon P. Ziarnik, Gail S. Bernstein, and Joseph M. Ferrara. *Proactive Vocational Habilitation.* Baltimore: Paul H. Brookes, 1984.

For persons responsible for designing and/or providing vocational habilitation services to adults with mental retardation and developmental disabilities. Can also be applied to people with physical disabilities. Makes assumption that competitive employment is a realistic goal.

Rusch, Frank R., ed. *Competitive Employment Issues and Strategies.* Baltimore: Paul H. Brookes, 1986.

Covers employment models in several states, methods, work behavior training, support networks for individuals who do not achieve competitive employment.

Szmanski, Edna Mora. *Rehabilitation Counseling in Supported Employment: A Conceptual Model for Service Delivery and Personnel Preparation.* Baltimore: Paul H. Brookes, 1986.

Weisgerber, Robert A., Peter Dahl, and Judith A. Appleby. *Training the Handicapped for Productive Employment.* Rockville, MD: Aspen, 1980.

Mental Disability

Brown, Roy R. *Integrated Programs for Handicapped Adolescents and Adults.* New York: Nichols, 1984.

Discusses training models and concepts in academic areas as well as social education skills, including home management, budgeting, meal preparation, and family relationships, for developmentally disabled persons.

Gallagher, James J., and Peter M. Vietz. *Families of Handicapped Persons: Research Programs and Policy Issues.* Baltimore: Paul H. Brookes, 1986.

Provides accounts of the effect on families of a mentally retarded member.

Halpern, Andrew S., Daniel W. Close, and Debra J. Nelson. *On My Own: The Impact of Semi-independent Living Programs for Adults with Mental Retardation.* Baltimore: Paul H. Brookes, 1986.

Heal, Laird W., Janell I. Haney, and Angela R. Novak Amado. *Integration of the Developmentally Disabled.* Baltimore: Paul H. Brookes, 1988.

Ludlow, Barbara L., Ann P. Turnbull, and Ruth Luckasson, eds. *Transition to Adult Life for People with Mental Retardation: Principles and Practice.* Baltimore: Paul H. Brookes, 1988.

Pueschel, Siegfried M., ed. *The Young Person with Down's Syndrome: Transition from Adolescence to Adulthood.* Baltimore: Paul H. Brookes, 1988.
Covers biology of the maturing Down's Syndrome person, social integration, leisure, vocational training, psychological adaptation from school to employment, sexuality, marriage, and parenting.

Rotatori, Anthony F., John O. Schwenn, and Robert A. Fox. *Assessing Severely and Profoundly Handicapped Individuals.* Springfield, IL: Charles C. Thomas, 1985.

Employment, Transition, and Supported Employment

Bellamy, G. Thomas, Larry E. Rhodes, David H. Mank, and Joyce M. Albin, eds. *Supported Employment: A Community Implementation Guide.* Baltimore: Paul H. Brookes, 1988.
Provides program models, strategies for state leadership, parents, advocates and friends, and business participation.

Berkell, Dianne E., and James M. Brown. *Transition from School to Work for Persons with Disabilities.* White Plains, NY: Longman, 1989.
Textbook in special education, vocational education and rehabilitation. A reference for professionals on current issues relating to transition.

Gardner, James F. *Toward Supported Employment: A Process Guide for Planned Change.* Baltimore: Paul H. Brookes, 1988.

Hippolitus, Paul. *College Freshmen with Disabilities Preparing for Employment: Statistical Profile.* President's Committee on Employment of People with Disabilities and the American Council on Education. Washington, DC: 1987.

Wehman, Paul. *Transition from School to Work: New Challenges for Youth with Severe Disabilities.* Baltimore: Paul H. Brookes, 1988.

Wehman, Paul, and M. Sherril Moon. *Vocational Rehabilitation and Supported Employment.* Baltimore: Paul H. Brookes, 1988.

SPECIAL EDUCATION

The following books would provide a good basis for a core special education collection, especially in conjunction with the general works in the first section of the bibliography.

General

Anastasiow, Nicholas J. *Development and Disability.* Baltimore: Paul H. Brookes, 1986.
A psychobiological analysis for special educators.

Ballard, Joseph, Bruce A. Ramirez, and Frederick J. Weintraub, eds. *Special Education in America: Its Legal and Governmental Foundations.* Reston, VA: Council on Exceptional Children, 1982.
Interprets PL 94-142 and its consequences.

Bigge, June L. *Curriculum Based Instruction for Children with Special Needs.* Mountain View, CA: Mayfield, 1988.

Bigge, June L., and Patrick A. O'Donnell. *Teaching Individuals with Physical and Multiple Disabilities.* 2nd ed. Columbus, OH: Charles E. Merrill, 1982.
Provides overview of handicaps plus task analyses.

Bleck, Eugene E., and Donald A. Nagel. *Physically Handicapped Children: A Medical Atlas for Teachers.* 2nd ed. Orlando, FL: Grune and Stratton, 1981.
An excellent text for classroom teachers. Defines many physical disabilities in non-clinical terms.

Braddock, David L. *Federal Policy toward Mental Retardation and Developmental Disabilities.* Baltimore: Paul H. Brookes, 1987.

Brucker, Diane D. *Early Education of At Risk and Handicapped Infants and Toddlers and Pre-school Children.* Glenwood, IL, and London: Scott, Foresman & Co., 1986.

Calhoun, Mary L., and Margaret Hawisher. *Teaching and Learning Strategies for Physically Handicapped Students.* Baltimore: University Park Press, 1979.
Provides definitions of handicapping conditions, covers psychological aspects and appropriate educational programming.

Cratty, Bryan J. *Perceptual and Motor Development in Infants and Children.* 3rd ed. Englewood Cliffs, NJ: Prentice-Hall, 1986.

Cruickshank, William M. *Psychology of Exceptional Children and Youth.* 4th ed. Englewood Cliffs, NJ: Prentice-hall, 1980.
Update of a classic text.

Esterson, Morton M. *Related Services for Handicapped Children.* Boston and San Diego: College-Hill Press, 1987.

Freeman, Stephen W. *The Epileptic in Home, School and Society: Coping with the Invisible Handicap.* Springfield, IL: Charles C. Thomas, 1979.

Garwood, S. Gray, and Rebecca R. Fewell. *Educating Handicapped Infants: Issues in Development and Intervention.* Rockville, MD: Aspen, 1983.

Gliedman, John, and William Roth. *The Unexpected Minority: Handicapped Children in America.* New York: Harcourt Brace Jovanovich, 1980.
An innovative study by a psychologist and a political scientist, making the point that discrimination against disabled children begins early when their needs are perceived in terms of deviations from the norms of their able-bodied peers.

Hallahan, Daniel P., and James M. Kauffman. *Exceptional Children: Introduction to Special Education.* 3rd ed. Englewood Cliffs, NJ: Prentice-Hall, 1986.
Update of classic text.

Harel, Shaul, and Nicholas J. Anastasiow, eds. *The At Risk Infant: Psycho/social/medical Aspects.* Baltimore: Paul H. Brookes, 1985.

Haring, Norris G., and Linda McCormick. *Exceptional Children and Youth.* 4th ed. Columbus, OH: Charles E. Merrill, 1986.
Update of classic text.

Kirk, Samuel A. *Teaching Reading to Slow and Disabled Learners.* Prospect Heights, IL: Waveland Press, 1988.

Kirk, Samuel A., and James C. Chalfont. *Academic and Developmental Learning Disabilities*. Denver, CO: Love Publishing, 1984.

Kirk, Samuel A., and James J. Gallagher. *Educating Exceptional Children*. 6th ed. New York: Houghton Mifflin, 1989.
Update of classic text.

Linder, Toni W. *Early Childhood and Special Education*. Baltimore: Paul H. Brookes, 1983.

Losan, Stuart M., and Joyce Garskof Losen. *The Special Education Team*. Boston: Allyn and Bacon, 1985.
Discusses how to improve team problem solving and effectively involve parents.

Love, Harold D. *Teaching Mentally Handicapped Children: Methods and Materials—A Generic Approach*. Springfield, IL: Charles C. Thomas, 1984.

Mullins, June. *A Teacher's Guide to Management of Physically Handicapped Students*. Springfield, IL: Charles C. Thomas, 1979.
Discusses physical and health care needs in an educational setting.

Nelson, C. Michael, Roger B. Rutherford, Jr., and Bruce I. Wolford, eds. *Special Education in the Criminal Justice System*. Columbus, OH: Charles E. Merrill, 1988.
The first book to deal with this problem.

Sabatino, David A., and Ted L. Miller, eds. *Describing Learner Characteristics of Handicapped Children and Youth*. Orlando: Grune and Stratton, 1978.
An introductory text in assessment for preservice special education teachers and for inservice training. A diagnostic resource book.

Wallace, Helen M., Robert F. Biehl, Lawrence Taft, and Allan C. Oglesby. *Handicapped Children and Youth: A Comprehensive Community and Clinical Approach*. New York: Human Sciences Press, 1987.
Covers impact on the family, early intervention, respite care, and special education; includes definitions of some disabilities.

Wilcox, Barbara, and Thomas G. Bellamy. *Design of High School Programs for Severely Handicapped Students*. Baltimore: Paul H. Brookes, 1982.
Provides innovative approaches to creating realistic high school programs for students with disabilities.

Williamson, G. Gordon, ed. *Children with Spina Bifida: Early Intervention and Pre-school Programming*. Baltimore: Paul H. Brookes, 1987.
Provides information on family services, health issues, wheelchairs and other mobility aids, perceptual-motor performance, speech and language development, activities of daily living and classroom considerations.

Mainstreaming

Berres, Michael S., and Peter Knoblock. *Program Models for Mainstreaming: Integrating Students with Moderate to Severe Disabilities*. Rockville, MD: Aspen, 1987.

Meisel, C. Julius, ed. *Mainstreaming Handicapped Children: Outcomes, Controversies, and New Directions*. Hillside, NJ: Lawrence Erlbaum Associates, 1986.

Turnbull, Ann P., and Jane B. Schulz. *Mainstreaming Handicapped Students: A Guide for the Classroom Teacher*. Boston: Allyn and Bacon, 1979.

Career Planning

Feingold, S. Norma, and Norma R. Miller. *Your Future: A Guide for the Handicapped Teenager.* New York: Richard Rosen Press, 1981.

Mitchell, Joyce Slayton. *See Me More Clearly: Career and Life Planning for Teens with Physical Disabilities.* New York and London: Harcourt Brace Jovanovich, 1980.
Addressed to disabled young adults. Deals with attitudes, coping with disability, sexuality, legal rights, and strategies for making career decisions.

FAMILIES

Apolloni, Tony, and Thomas P. Cooke, eds. *A New Look at Guardianship: Protective Services that Support Personalized Living.* Baltimore: Paul H. Brookes, 1984.
For parents wishing to plan for long-range care and financial well-being of their disabled children.

Association for Retarded Citizens. *How to Provide for Their Future.* Arlington, TX: Association for Retarded Citizens, 1984.

Buscaglia, Leo. *The Disabled and Their Parents: A Counseling Challenge.* 3rd rev. ed. New York: Henry Holt and Co., 1983.
Third edition of a classic in the field of working with parents who have become advocates for their children.

Crump, Iris M., ed. *Nutrition and Feeding of the Handicapped Child.* Boston and San Diego: College-Hill Press, 1987.
Discusses effects of congenital disorders and those conditions requiring special dietary management, including gastrointestinal disorders.

Dickman, Irving, and Sol Gordon. *One Miracle at a Time: How to Get Help for Your Disabled Child—From the Experiences of Other Parents.* New York: Simon & Schuster, 1988.
Written by the father of a disabled child who compiled the results of a questionnaire he sent nationwide to the parents of disabled children. An account of frustrations, including difficulties in obtaining an accurate diagnosis, strains on the family, value of parent groups and networks, and where to look for help. Includes a chapter on sexuality.

Easson, William M. *The Dying Child: The Management of the Child or Adolescent Who Is Dying.* Springfield, IL: Charles C. Thomas, 1981.
The task of helping a child who is dying, whether of preschool, grade school, or adolescent age. Help for families and professional caretakers.

Featherstone, Helen. *A Difference in the Family: Life with a Disabled Child.* New York: Basic Books, 1980.
Written by a professional educator and mother of a severely physically and mentally disabled child. A sensitive and readable book about the difference that such a child makes in a family. Highlights stages of fear, anger, loneliness and guilt, and marital and sibling problems.

Fewell, Rebecca R., and Patricia F. Vadasy. *Families of Handicapped Children: Needs and Supports Across the Life Span.* Austin, TX: Pro-Ed, 1986.
Discusses roles of parents and siblings in families with disabled members, as well as roles of grandparents and extended family, including interaction with professionals.

Finnie, Nancie R. *Handling the Young Cerebral Palsied Child at Home.* New York: Dutton, 1975.
Contains practical hints covering all aspects of home care.

Fraser, Beverly, and Robert N. Hensinger. *Managing Physical Handicaps: A Practical Guide for Parents, Care Providers, and Educators.* Baltimore: Paul H. Brookes, 1983.

Goldfarb, Lori, Mary Jane Brotherson, Jean Ann Summers, and Ann P. Turnbull. *Meeting the Challenge of Disability or Chronic Illness: A Family Guide.* Baltimore: Paul H. Brookes, 1986.

Hofmann, Ruth B. *How to Build Special Furniture and Equipment for Handicapped Children.* Springfield, IL: Charles C. Thomas, 1974.
Covers functional furniture and includes simple blueprints of projects parents can build.

Jeter, Katherine. *These Special Children: The Ostomy Book for Parents of Children with Colostomies, Ileostomies and Urostomies.* Palto Alto, CA: Bull Publishing, 1982.
Comprehensive resource covering definitions, emotional reactions of family members, teachers, and classmates, and information about legal, financial, and psychological support. A valuable book in large paperback format that would be excellent for a parent's reference shelf.

Jones, Monica Loose. *Home Care for the Chronically Ill or Disabled Child.* New York: Harper & Row, 1985.
To assist parents caring for disabled children at home, this book covers meeting physical, medical, social, recreational, and travel needs as well as adolescent care and care for the dying child at home.

Kuklin, Susan. *Thinking Big: The Story of a Young Dwarf.* New York: Lothrop, Lee and Shepard, 1986.
Story of an eight-year-old dwarf who lives with his family and attends regular school.

Levy, Joel M., Philip H. Levy, and Ben Nivin. *Strengthening Families: New Directions in Providing Services to People with Developmental Disabilities and Their Families.* New York: Young Adult Institute, 1989.

Love, Harold D. *Behavior Disorders in Children: A Book for Parents.* Springfield, IL: Charles C. Thomas, 1987.

McConkey, Roy, and Dorothy Jeffree. *Making Toys for Handicapped Children: A Guide for Parents and Teachers.* Englewood Cliffs, NJ: Prentice-Hall, 1981.
A valuable resource for those frustrated by the lack of toys available for the child with special needs. Shows how to make simple, sturdy toys with a variety of uses.

Myers, Gary J., Sharon Bidwell Cerone, and L. Olson Ardis. *A Guide for Helping the Child with Spina Bifida.* Springfield, IL: Charles C. Thomas, 1981.
Account of problems confronting parents and children with spina bifida for health professionals, educators, and parents.

Powell, Thomas H., and Peggy Ahrenhold Ogle. *Brothers and Sisters: A Special Part of Exceptional Families.* Baltimore: Paul H. Brookes, 1985.
Authors are founders of the Sibling Information Network, which publishes a newsletter. Siblings of brothers and sisters with disabilities are in need of a special kind of understanding.

Power, Paul W., and Arthur Del Orto. *Role of the Family in the Rehabilitation of the Physically Disabled.* Baltimore: University Park Press, 1980.
How the family of children with physical disabilities can help in their rehabilitation and health care.

Prensky, Arthur L., and Helen Stein Palkes. *Care of the Neurologically Handicapped Child: A Book for Parents and Professionals.* New York: Oxford Univ. Press, 1982.
A practical and informative book for the parents of a neurologically disabled child. Covers roles of the specialists, includes special chapters on individual disabilities.

Roy, Ron. *Move Over, Wheelchairs Coming Through.* New York: Tichnor & Fields, 1985.
Recounts stories about active lives of youngsters in wheelchairs.

Russell, L. Mark. *Alternatives: A Family Guide to Legal and Financial Planning for the Disabled.* Evanston, IL: First Publication, 1983.
Primarily for parents of mentally retarded children, but applicable also to children with severe physical disabilities. Looks at estate planning, wills, trusts, guardianship, government benefits, taxes, insurance, and financial planning.

Russell, Philippa. *The Wheelchair Child.* Englewood Cliffs, NJ: Prentice-Hall, 1985.
How disabled children can enjoy life to the fullest: a practical guide to care, special furniture, education, work, and leisure time.

Schleichkorn, Jay. *Coping with Cerebral Palsy: Answers to Questions Parents Often Ask.* Baltimore: University Park Press, 1983.
A physical therapist provides practical answers to many questions.

Segal, Ellen, and Mark Hardin. *Adoption of Children with Special Needs.* Washington, DC: American Bar Association National Legal Resource Center for Child Advocacy and Protection, 1985.

Segal, Marilyn. *In Time and with Love: Caring for the Special Needs Baby.* New York: Newmarket Press, 1988.
For families and caregivers of handicapped children in the first three years and preteens.

Seligman, Milton ed. *The Family with a Handicapped Child: Understanding and Treatment.* Orlando, FL: Grune and Stratton, 1983.
Includes chapters on siblings, uses of bibliotherapy, counseling strategies, family and group therapy.

Thompson, Charlotte E. *Raising a Handicapped Child: A Helpful Guide for Parents of the Physically Disabled.* New York: Morrow, 1986.
Covers coping with the diagnosis, finding professional help, telling friends, relations, and siblings, handling financial costs, education, leisure, adolescence, and death.

Turnbull, H. Rutherford, Ann P. Turnbull, G. J. Bronick, Jean Ann Summers, and Constance Roeder-Gordon. *Disability and the Family: A Guide to Decisions for Adulthood.* Baltimore: Paul H. Brookes, 1989.
Answers to questions about planning for the future for families with children with physical or mental disabilities.

Webster, Elizabeth J. *Counseling with Parents of Handicapped Children: Guidelines for Improving Communication.* Orlando, FL: Grune and Stratton, 1977.

Weiner, Florence. *A Guide to Living with a Disability.* New York: St. Martin's Press, 1986.
Written by people with disabilities, their families, and friends.

Zang, Barbara. *How to Get Help for Kids: A Reference Guide to Services for Handicapped Children.* Syracuse, NY: Neal-Schuman-Gaylord Professional Publishers, 1980.
Services include diagnostic, medical, educational, vocational, respite care, financial and legal information. Includes a section on parent groups.

LEARNING DISABILITIES

Cordoni, Barbara. *Living with a Learning Disability.* Carbondale, IL: Southern Illinois Univ. Press, 1987.
Covers life after school, and communicating with and parenting the young adult with learning disabilities.

Goodman, Libby, and Lester Mann. *Learning Disabilities in the Secondary School: Issues and Practices.* Orlando, FL: Grune and Stratton, 1976.

Hammill, Donald D., and Nettie R. Bartal. *Teaching Students with Learning and Behavior Problems.* 4th ed. Austin, TX: Pro-Ed, 1986.

Johnson, Doris J., and June Blalock, eds. *Adults with Learning Disabilities: Clinical Studies.* Orlando, FL: Grune and Stratton, 1987.

Mangrum, Chaerles T. II, and Stephen S. Strichart. *College and the Learning-Disabled Student: A Guide to Program Selection, Development and Implementation.* Orlando, FL: Grune and Stratton, 1984.
Emergence of college programs for learning disabled students has necessitated guidance for these students. Covers legal rights, application to college, testing, basic skills remediation.

Myklebust, Helmer R. *The Pupil Rating Scale Revised: Screening for Learning Disabilities.* Rev. ed. Orlando, FL: Grune and Stratton, 1980.

Myklebust, Helmer R., ed. *Progress in Learning Disabilities.* Vol. 5. Orlando, FL: Grune and Stratton, 1983.
Provides technical definitions in the areas of language and math disorders.

Noyes, Joan, and Norma McNeill. *Your Child Can Win.* New York: William Morrow & Co., 1983.
A practical book for helping learning-disabled children at home. Includes explanations of testing procedures, questions parents can ask of professionals, and how to evaluate classroom activities, as well as recreational activities and games to improve language development, body image, and motor skills, and a listing of commercial games.

Osman, Betty, and Henriette Binder. *No One to Play With: The Social Side of Learning Disabilities.* New York: Random House, 1982.
Discusses social problems of the learning-disabled child, including problems within average families and those in crisis, as well as social problems of learning-disabled teenagers and adults.

Siegal, Ernest, and Ruth Gold. *Educating the Learning Disabled.* New York: Macmillan, 1982.
Contains introductory text, definitions, educational approaches, and interdisciplinary intervention.

Smith, Sally L. *No Easy Answers: The Learning Disabled Child at Home and at School.* New York: Bantam Books, 1981.
Very informative book by the founder of a school for intelligent children with severe learning disabilities, written for both teachers and parents. Covers how to work with learning-disabled children at school and at home, adolescent development, and legal rights.

Stevens, Suzanne H. *The Learning Disabled Child: Ways That Parents Can Help.* Winston-Salem, NC: John F. Blair, 1980.
Does not give activities to do in the home, but does offer a great deal of information that parents will find useful, including definitions, symptoms, how to communicate with the school, and offering understanding and positive support.

Wodrich, David L., and James E. Joy. *Multidisciplinary Assessment of Children with Learning Disabilities and Mental Retardation.* New York: Bowker, 1986.

BLINDNESS AND VISUAL IMPAIRMENTS

American Foundation for the Blind. *The Future of Work for Disabled People: Employment and the New Technology.* New York: American Foundation for the Blind, 1986.

Anderson, Mary Ellen, ed. *Competing in Terms of Equality: An Examination of Attitudinal Barriers Confronting the Blind in Competitive Employment and Related Areas and an Evaluation of Progress Achieved in Overcoming These Barriers.* Baltimore: National Federation of the Blind, 1982.

Bishop, Virginia E. *Teaching the Visually Limited Child.* Springfield, IL: Charles C. Thomas, 1978.
Of use to teachers with visually impaired students in a mainstreamed situation.

Harley, Randall R., and Laurence G. Allen. *Visual Impairment in the Schools.* 2nd ed. Springfield, IL: Charles C. Thomas, 1984.
A guide to a better understanding of the structure and function of the eye, its diseases, and the relationship of visual impairment and visual learning.

Harley, Randall R., Milo B. Truan, and La Rea Sanford. *Communication Skills for Visually Impaired Learners.* Springfield, IL: Charles C. Thomas, 1988.

Koestler, Francis A. *The Unseen Minority: A Social History of Blindness in the United States.* New York: McKay, David, 1976.
History of blindness in the U.S., including how services began and laws were enacted, as well as information about personalities who spurred these advances.

Lowenfield, Berthold. *Our Blind Children: Growing and Learning with Them.* 3rd ed. Springfield, IL: Charles C. Thomas, 1977.

Spiegel, Allen D., Simon Podair, nd Eunice Fiorito. *Rehabilitating People with Disabilities into the Mainstream of Society.* Park Ridge, NJ: Noyes Medical Publishers, 1981.

Vander Kolk, Charles J. *Assessment and Planning with the Visually Impaired.* Baltimore: University Park Press, 1981.

DEAFNESS AND HEARING IMPAIRMENT

Charlip, Remy, Mary Beth, and George Ancona. *Handtalk: An ABC of Finger Spelling and Sign Language.* New York: Parents Magazine Press, 1980.
Handtalk teaches two ways of communicating through sign language: by using a sign for a word or concept and by finger spelling. This book is a pleasure to look at, with striking photographs.

Fant, Lou. *The American Sign Language Phrase Book.* Chicago: Contemporary Books, 1983.

Fant, Louis J., Jr. *Ameslan: An Introduction to American Sign Language.* Acton, CA: Joyce Media, 1972.

Fant, Louis J., Jr. *Intermediate Sign Language.* Acton, CA: Joyce Media, 1980.

Fritz, Georgene. *The Hearing-Impaired Employee: An Untapped Resource.* Boston and San Diego: College-Hill Press, 1985.

Giangreco, C. Joseph, and Marianne R. Giangreco. *The Education of the Hearing-Impaired.* 2nd ed. Springfield, IL: Charles C. Thomas, 1976.
Written for parents, nurses, teachers, and other professionals working with the hearing impaired.

Grant, Brian, ed. *The Quiet Ear: Deafness In Literature.* Boston: Faber and Faber, 1988.

Greenberg, Joanne. *Of Such Small Differences.* New York: Henry Holt and Co., 1988.

Harris, Grace M. *Language for the Preschool Deaf Child.* 3rd ed. Orlando, FL: Grune and Stratton, 1971.
Discusses early intervention techniques for the development of language in the young hearing-impaired child.

Hart, Beatrice Ostern. *Teaching Reading to Deaf Children.* Washington, DC: Alexander Graham Bell Association, 1978.
A practical handbook for guiding reading growth pre-kindergarten through high school.

Jacobs, Leo M. *A Deaf Adult Speaks Out.* 2nd ed. Washington, DC: Gallaudet University Press, 1981.

Jamison, Steven L. *Signs for Computer Terminology: A Sign Reference Book for People in the Computing Field.* Silver Spring, MD: National Association of the Deaf, 1983.

Kaplan, Harriet, Scott J. Bally, and Carol Garretson. *Speechreading: A Way to Improve Understanding.* Washington, DC: Gallaudet University Press, 1984.
All deaf and hearing-impaired people use speechreading to some extent. Discusses the nature and process of speechreading, its benefits and limitations. Provides a source of information for hearing-impaired adults and parents of hearing-impaired children, and aids professionals in providing habilitation/rehabilitation services in classrooms and clinics.

Kretchmer, Richard, and Laura Kretschmer. *Language Development and Intervention with the Hearing Impaired.* Austin, TX: Pro-Ed, 1978.
Provides overview of thinking in the area of psycholinguistics and its application to the hearing impaired.

Levine, Edna S. *Lisa and Her Soundless World.* New York: Human Sciences Press, 1984.
Explains treatment techniques and lip reading, and introduces language of finger spelling.

Ling, Daniel. *Early Intervention for Hearing-Impaired Children: Oral Options.* Boston and San Diego: College-Hill Press, 1984.

Ling, Daniel. *Early Intervention for Hearing-Impaired Children: Total Communication Options.* Boston and San Diego: College-Hill Press, 1984.

Luterman, David M. *Deafness in Perspective.* Boston and San Diego: College-Hill Press, 1986.
Contains presentations from a national symposium on deafness, documenting changes during the 1980s in service delivery to deaf individuals.

Mykelbust, Helmer R. *Your Deaf Child: A Guide for Parents.* Springfield, IL: Charles C. Thomas, 1979.

Nix, Gary W. *Mainstream Education for Hearing-Impaired Children and Youth.* Orlando, FL: Grune and Stratton, 1976.
Discusses aspects of mainstreaming: psychological, pathological, audiological, and educational.

Northcott, Winifred H. *Curriculum Guide: Hearing-Impaired Children—Birth to Three Years—and Their Parents.* Washington, DC: Alexander Graham Bell Association for the Deaf, 1977.
Curriculum guide covering integration of a hearing-impaired preschool child into a nursery program, stages of receptive and expressive language.

Northern, J., and M. Downs. *Hearing in Children.* 3rd ed. Baltimore, MD: Williams and Wilkins, 1984.
A comprehensive description of the current state of knowledge of the audiological problems of children.

Oyer, Herbert J., Barbara Crowe, and William Haas. *Speech Language and Hearing Disorders: A Guide for the Teacher.* Boston: College-Hill Press, 1987.

Spradley, Thomas S., and James P. Spradley. *Deaf Like Me.* Rev. ed. Washington, DC: Gallaudet University Press, 1985.
One family's account of communication with a deaf daughter for the first time after perceiving futile hopes of oral education.

Sternberg, Martin L. *American Sign Language: A Comprehensive Dictionary.* New York: Harper & Row, 1981.

Deaf-Blind

Arkansas Rehabilitation Research and Training Center. *Strategies for Serving Deaf-Blind Clients.* 11th Institute on Rehabilitation Issues, University of Arkansas. Hot Springs, AR. San Antonio, TX: 1984.

Cadigan, Ellen and Roslye Roberts Geuss. *Sex Education: A Curriculum for the Deaf-Blind.* Watertown, MA: Perkins School for the Blind, 1981.

Goetz, Lori. *Innovating Program Design for Individuals with Dual Sensory Impairments.* Baltimore: Paul H. Brookes, 1987.

Perkins School for the Blind. *Sex Education: A Curriculum for the Deaf-Blind.* Watertown, MA: 1981.

Thompson, Joyce. *Assistive Devices for Deaf-Blind Persons.* Toronto: Canadian National Institute for the Blind, 1987.

Walsh, Sarah R., and Robert Holzberg. *Understanding and Educating the Deaf-Blind/Severely and Profoundly Handicapped: An International Perspective.* Springfield, IL: Charles C. Thomas, 1981.

HIGHER EDUCATION

Liscio, Mary Ann ed. *A Guide to Colleges for Hearing-Impaired Students.* San Diego: Academic Press, 1986.

Liscio, Mary Ann, ed. *A Guide to Colleges for Learning Disabled Students.* Rev. ed. San Diego: Academic Press, 1986.

Liscio, Mary Ann, ed. *A Guide to Colleges for Mobility Impaired Students,* San Diego: Academic Press, 1986.

Liscio, Mary Ann, ed. *A Guide to Colleges for Visually Impaired Students,* San Diego: Academic Press, 1986.

Thomas, Carol H., and James Thomas, eds. *Directory of College Facilities and Services for the Disabled.* 2nd ed. Phoenix, AZ: Oryx Press, 1986.

LIBRARY SERVICE

Baskin, Barbara H., and Karen H. Harris. *More Notes from a Different Drummer: A Guide to Juvenile Fiction Portraying the Disabled.* New York: Bowker, 1984.
An update of *Notes from a Different Drummer*, reviews 348 fiction titles published from 1976 through 1981, including picture books, novels, foreign titles distributed in the US, and some titles now out of print.

Dalton, Phyllis. *Library Service to the Deaf and Hearing Impaired.* Phoenix, AZ: Oryx Press, 1985.
Contains information and suggestions for developing library programs for deaf and hard-of-hearing people, parents of hearing-impaired children, and professionals in all fields of service to the deaf.

Friedberg, Joan B., June B. Mullins, and Adelaide Sukiennik. *Accept Me As I Am.* New York: Bowker, 1985.
A guide to juvenile non-fiction about individuals with impairments and disabilities. Complements *More Notes from a Different Drummer.*

Lucas, Linda, and Marilyn H. Karenbrock. *The Disabled Child in the Library: Moving into the Mainstream.* Littleton, CO: Libraries Unlimited, 1983.
Stating that each child must be educated in the least restrictive environment for that child, this book deals with attitudes and definitions of major disabilities, outlines library and information needs, and suggests materials, equipment, and programming.

PERIODICALS: A PARTIAL LISTING

A comprehensive, up-to-date periodical listing may be obtained from The National Rehabilitation Information Center at 8455 Colesville Rd., Suite 935, Silver Spring, MD 20910-3319. Print and disk versions of a listing of educational journals and newsletters that includes many in special education and related areas may be obtained from LINC Resources Inc., 3857 N. High St., Columbus, OH 43214. Disks are available in both Apple and IBM compatible. Specify version when requesting.

Accent on Living
Cheever Publishing
PO Box 700
Bloomington, IL 61701

Advocate
National Society for Children and Adults with Autism
1234 Massachusetts Ave. NW, Suite 1017
Washington, DC 20005

American Annals of the Deaf
814 Thayer Ave.
Silver Spring, MD 20910

American Archives of Rehabilitation Therapy
American Association for Rehabilitation Therapy
West 32 Ferndale Rd.
Paramus, NJ 07652

American Journal of Diseases of Children
American Medical Association
535 N. Dearborn St.
Chicago, IL 60610

American Journal of Mental Deficiency
American Association of Mental Deficiency
1719 Kalorama Rd., NW
Washington, DC 20009

American Journal of Occupational Therapy
American Occupational Therapy Association
1383 Piccard Dr.
Rockville, MD 20850

American Journal of Physical Medicine and Rehabilitation
Williams and Wilkins
428 E. Preston St.
Baltimore, MD 21202

American Rehabilitation
US Department of Education
Rehabilitation Services Administration
330 C St. SW
Washington, DC 20201

*Archives of Physical Medicine and
Rehabilitation*
78 E. Adams
Chicago, IL 60603

*Augmentative and Alternative
Communication*
International Society for Augmentative
and Alternative Communication
Williams and Wilkins
428 E. Preston St.
Baltimore, MD 21202

Braille Monitor
National Federation of the Blind
1800 Johnson St.
Baltimore, MD 21230

Canadian Journal of Rehabilitation
Canadian Association for Research in
Rehabilitation
13325 St. Albert Trail
Edmonton, Alberta
Canada T5L 4R3

Careers and the Handicapped
Equal Opportunity Publications, Inc.
44 Broadway
Greenlawn, NY 11740

Deaf American
National Association of the Deaf
814 Thayer Ave.
Silver Spring, MD 20910

Disabled Outdoors
5223 S. Lorel Ave.
Chicago, IL 60638

Exceptional Children
Council for Exceptional Children
1920 Association Dr.
Reston, VA 22091

Exceptional Parent
Psy-Ed
805 Commonwealth Ave.
Boston, MA 02215

Gallaudet Today
Gallaudet University
Kendall Green NE
Washington, DC 20002

*Independent Living and Health Care
Today*
Equal Opportunity Publications, Inc.
44 Broadway
Greenlawn, NY 11740

*International Journal of Rehabilitation
Research*
G. Schindele Verlag International
Publishers
Hugo-Stotz-Str. 14
D06900 Heidelberg 1
Federal Republic of Germany

*JAMA: Journal of the American Medical
Association*
535 N. Dearborn St.
Chicago, IL 60610

*Journal of Applied Rehabilitation
Counseling*
National Rehabilitation Counseling
Association
National Rehabilitation Association
633 S. Washington St.
Alexandria, VA 22314

*Journal of the Association for Persons with
Severe Handicaps*
Association for Persons with Severe
Handicaps
7010 Roosevelt Way NE
Seattle, WA 98115

Journal of Learning Disabilities
5341 Industrial Oaks Blvd.
Austin, TX 78735-8809

Journal of Learning Disabilities Focus
Division for Learning Disabilities
Council for Exceptional Children
1920 Association Dr.
Reston, VA 22091

Journal of Learning Disabilities Research
Division for Learning Disabilities
Council for Exceptional Children
1920 Association Dr.
Reston, VA 22091

Journal of the Multi-Handicapped Person
Plenum Publishing Corporation
233 Spring St.
New York, NY 10013

Journal of Occupational Medicine
American Occupational Medicine
Association
2340 S. Arlington Heights Rd., Suite 400
Arlington Heights, IL 60005

Journal of Private Sector Rehabilitation
National Association of Rehabilitation
Professionals in the Private Sector
PO Box 1945
Athens, GA 30603

Journal of Prosthetics and Orthotics
American Orthotics and Prosthetics
  Association
Academy of Orthotics and Prosthetics
717 Pendleton St.
Alexandria, VA 22314

Journal of Rehabilitation
National Rehabilitation Association
633 S. Washington St.
Alexandria, VA 22314

Journal of Rehabilitation Administration
National Rehabilitation Administration
  Association
Rehabilitation Services Program of
  DePaul University
25 E. Jackson Blvd.
Chicago, IL 60604

Journal of Rehabilitation of the Deaf
American Deafness and Rehabilitation
  Association
814 Thayer Ave.
Silver Spring, MD 20901

*Journal of Rehabilitation Research and
  Development*
Veterans Administration
Department of Medicine and Surgery
Washington, DC 20420

Journal of Special Education Technology
Association for Special Education
  Technology
Exceptional Child Center
Utah State University
Logan, UT 84322

Journal of Speech and Hearing Disorders
American Speech, Language and Hearing
  Association
10801 Rockville Pike
Rockville, MD 20852

Journal of Speech and Hearing Research
American Speech, Language and Hearing
  Association
10801 Rockville Pike
Rockville, MD 20852

*Journal of Visual Impairment and
  Blindness*
American Foundation for the Blind
15 W. 16th St.
New York, NY 10011

Mainstream
Able-Disabled Advocacy
861 Sixth Ave., Suite 610
San Diego, CA 92101

*Mental and Physical Disability Law
  Reporter*
American Bar Association
1800 M St. NW
Washington, DC 20036

Mental Retardation
Association of Mental Deficiency
1719 Kalorama Rd. NW
Washington, DC 20009-2684

Paraplegia News
Paralyzed Veterans of America
801 Eighteenth St., NW
Washington, DC 20006

Physical Therapy
American Physical Therapy Association
1111 N. Fairfax St.
Alexandria, VA 22314

The Pointer
Heldreg Publications
4000 Albemarle St. NW
Washington, DC 20016

A Positive Approach
1600 Malone St.
Municiple Airport
Millville, NJ 08332

Prosthetics and Orthotics International
International Society for Prosthetics and
  Orthotics
Borgervaenget 5
2100 Copenhagen
Denmark

*Psychiatric Aspects of Mental Retardation
  Reviews*
Psych-Media
PO Box 786
Brookline Village, MA 02147

Psychosocial Rehabilitation Journal
Boston University Center for Psychiatric
  Rehabilitation
730 Commonwealth Ave.
Boston, MA 02215

Rehabilitation Counseling Bulletin
American Rehabilitation Counseling
  Association
American Association for Counseling and
  Development
5999 Stevenson Ave.
Alexandria, VA 22304

Rehabilitation Digest
Canadian Rehabilitation Council for the
  Disabled
One Yonge St., Suite 2110
Toronto, ON
Canada M5E 9Z9

Rehabilitation Gazette
4502 Maryland Ave.
St. Louis, MO 63108

Rehabilitation Nursing
Association of Rehabilitation Nurses
2506 Gross Point Rd.
Evanston, IL 60201

Rehabilitation Psychology
American Psychological Association
Division of Rehabilitation Psychology
1200 Seventeenth St. NW
Washington, DC 20036

Sexuality and Disability
Human Sciences Press
72 Fifth Ave.
New York, NY 10011

Spinal Network Extra
Spinal Associates Ltd.
PO Box 4162
Boulder, CO 80306

Sports 'N Spokes
5201 N. 19th Ave., Suite 111
Phoenix, AZ 85015

Teaching Exceptional Children
Council for Exceptional Children
1920 Association Dr.
Reston, VA 22091

Volta Review
Alexander Graham Bell Association for
the Deaf
3417 Volta Pl. NW
Washington, DC 20007

Worklife
The President's Committee on
Employment of People with
Disabilities
1111 Twentieth St. NW, Suite 636
Washington, DC 20036

NEWSLETTERS

Many of the governors' committees for disabled people, state advocacy committees, and organizations devoted to specific disabilities publish newsletters, which are often free. They are too numerous to be listed here. For a listing of governors' committees, contact the President's Committee on Employment of People with Disabilities.

Advocate (Canada)
Ontario March of Dimes
60 Overlea Blvd.
Toronto, ON
Canada M4H 1B6

AFB News
15 W. 16th St.
New York, NY 10011

Aging
US Department of Health and Human
Services
Administration on Aging
330 Independence Ave. SW, Room 4245
Washington, DC 20201

ATA Newsletter
American Tinnitus Association
PO Box 5
Portland, OR 97207

"Can Do—Will Do" Bulletin for the
Disabled
2006 Iowa
Topeka, KS 66607

CARF Report
Commission on Accreditation of
Rehabilitation Facilities
101 N. Wilmot Rd.
Suite 500
Tucson, AZ 85711

Coalition Quarterly
Technical Assistance for Parent Programs
Network
Federation for Children with Special
Needs
312 Stuart St.
Boston, MA 02116

College "Helps"
College Handicapped and Exceptional
Learners Programs and Service
Partners in Publishing
1419 W. First St.
Tulsa, OK 74127

Communication Outlook
International Society for Augmentative
and Alternative Communication
Artificial Language Laboratory
Computer Science Department
Michigan State University
East Lansing, MI 48824

Computer-Disability News
National Easter Seal Society
70 E. Lake St.
Chicago, IL 60601

Computers: Closing the Gap
Closing the Gap
Route 2, Box 68
Henderson, MN 56044

COPH Bulletin
National Congress of Organizations of
the Physically Handicapped
2030 Irving Parr Rd.
Chicago, IL 60618

Disability and Chronic Disease Quarterly
c/o Department of Sociology
Brandeis University
Waltham, MA 02254

Disability Law Briefs
Commission on the Mentally Disabled
American Bar Association
1800 M St. NW, Suite 200
Washington, DC 20036

Easter Seal Communicator
National Easter Seal Society
70 E. Lake St.
Chicago, IL. 60601

Education of the Handicapped
Capitol Publications
1300 Seventeenth St.
Arlington, VA 22209

First Dibs
Disability Information Brokerage System
PO Box 1285
Tucson, AZ 85702

Focus
National Council on the Handicapped
800 Independence Ave. SW, Suite 814
Washington, DC 20591

ICTA Inform
Swedish Institute for the Handicapped
and Rehabilitation International
International Commission on Technical
Aids, Housing and Transportation
Box 303, S-161
26 Broma
Sweden

In the Mainstream
Mainstream
1200 Fifteenth St. NW
Washington, DC 20005

Independent Living Forum
University of Kansas Research and
Training Center on Independent
Living
348 Haworth
Lawrence, KS 66045

Information from HEATH
National Clearinghouse on Postsecondary
Education for Individuals with
Handicaps
One Dupont Circle NW, Suite 800
Washington, DC 20036-1193

International Rehab Review
Rehabilitation International
25 E. 21st St.
New York, NY 10010

Itinerary
Whole Person Tours
PO Box 1084
Bayonne, NJ 07002-1084

LINC Notes
Newsbriefs to the Publishing Industry
LINC Resources Inc.
4820 Indianola Ave.
Columbus, OH 43214

NARIC Quarterly
A Newsletter of Disability and
Rehabilitation
Research and Resources
National Rehabilitation Information
Center
8455 Colesville Rd.
Suite 935
Silver Spring, MD 20910-3319

*National Center for Law and the Deaf
Newsletter*
National Center for Law and the Deaf
800 Florida Ave. NE
Washington, DC 20002

NCHRTM Memo
National Clearinghouse of Rehabilitation
Training Materials
Oklahoma State University
115 Old USDA Bldg.
Stillwater, OK 74078

News
National Library Service for the Blind
and Physically Handicapped
Library of Congress
Washington, DC 20542

News Digest
National Information Center for
Handicapped Children and Youth
PO Box 1492
Washington, DC 20013

OSERS News in Print
Office of Special Education and
Rehabilitative Services
US Department of Education
Rm. 3018 Switzer Bldg.
330 C St. SW
Washington, DC 20202

Rehab Brief: Bringing Research into Effective Focus
National Institute on Disability and Rehabilitation Research
Office of Special Education and Rehabilitative Services
Department of Education
Washington, DC 20202

Rehabilitation Technology Review
Association for the Advancement of Rehabilitation Technology (RESNA)
1101 Connecticut Ave. NW, Suite 700
Washington, DC 20036

The Report
National Organization on Disability
2100 Pennsylvania Ave. NW, Suite 234
Washington, DC 20037

Report on Disability Programs (formerly *Handicapped Americans Report*)
Business Publishers Inc.
951 Pershing Dr.
Silver Spring, MD 20910-4464

SAINT (Special and Individual Needs Technology)
Leader's Digest, Inc.
6803 Whittier Ave.
Suite 200
McLean, VA 22101

SATH News
Society for the Advancement of Travel for the Handicapped
26 Court St.
Brooklyn, NY 11242

Sibling Information Network Newsletter
Connecticut's University affiliated program on developmental disabilities
991 Main St.
East Hartford, CT 06108

Talking Book Topics
National Library Service for the Blind and Physically Handicapped
Library of Congress
Washington, DC 20542

Tips and Trends
The President's Committee on Employment of People with Disabilities
1111 Twentieth St. NW, Suite 636
Washington, DC 20036-3470

Update
National Library Service for the Blind and Physically Handicapped
Library of Congress
Washington, DC 20542

Vocational Developmental Rehabilitation Review
National Association of Rehabilitation Facilities
PO Box 17675
Washington, DC 20041

Vocational Evaluation and Work Adjustment Bulletin
Rehabilitation Institute
Southern Illinois University
Carbondale, Il 62901

Word from Washington
United Cerebral Palsy Association
Chester Arthur Bldg., Suite 141
425 I St. NW
Washington, DC 20001

AUDIOVISUAL MATERIALS

Many university departments, associations for specific disabilities and commercial producers have such materials available. The following short list can only serve as a start for locating audiovisual materials.

American Foundation for the Blind
(see Phoenix Films)

Campbell Films, Inc.
Film Library
Guidance Information Center
Cory Hill
Saxton River, VT 05154
  This collection includes films produced by the Perkins School for the Blind, which are available for rental.

Captioned Films for the Deaf
Modern Talking Picture Service
5000 Park St. North
St. Petersburg, FL 33709
  Apply for an account number to borrow captioned films under the U.S. Department of Education's Educational Media program.

Florida Division of Blind Services
Bureau of Library Services for the Blind
and Physically Handicapped
PO Box 2299
Daytona Beach, FL 32015-2299

This media catalog, produced in March 1988, with supplement, lists basic films which are available for loan from the Bureau; also lists producers.

Harris County Center for the Retarded, Inc.
PO Box 130403
Houston, TX 77219

Offers an educational packet of audiovisual materials for sale.

Maryland Rehabilitation Center
Library Films
2301 Argonne Dr.
Baltimore, MD 21218

An annotated bibliography of films and videotapes compiled in 1986, with 1987 and 1988 updates. Topics include access, advocacy, disabilities, attitudes, attendants, employment, families, independent living, vocational rehabilitation, and computers and technology. Available for loan from the Center but must be picked up and returned. Producers are listed for direct rental or purchase of films and videotapes.

National Audiovisual Center
General Services Administration
8700 Edgeworth Dr.
Capitol Heights. MD 20743

A catalog of government films, many of them about disabled people.

National Technical Institute for the Deaf
PO Box 9887
Rochester, NY 14623-0887

A catalog of captioned educational videotapes that are available for free loan, rental or purchase.

Phoenix Films
468 Park Ave. South
New York, NY 10016

Phoenix Films now handles all films and videotapes produced by the American Foundation for the Blind. These are available for rental or purchase.

Appendices

Appendix A
US Department of Education, Office for Civil Rights, Regional Civil Rights Offices

Region I
Connecticut, Maine, Massachusetts, New
  Hampshire, Rhode Island
Post Office Square, Rm. 222
Boston, MA 02109

Region II
New Jersey, New York, Puerto Rico,
  Virgin Islands
26 Federal Plaza
Rm. 33-130
New York, NY 10278

Region III
Delaware, Maryland, Pennsylvania,
  Virginia, Washington, DC, West
  Virginia
Gateway Bldg., 3535 Market St.
PO Box 13716
Philadelphia, PA 19101

Region IV
Alabama, Florida, Georgia, Kentucky,
  Mississippi, North Carolina, South
  Carolina, Tennessee
PO Box 1705
101 Marietta St. Tower, 27th Fl.
Atlanta, GA 30301

Region V
Illinois, Indiana, Michigan, Minnesota,
  Ohio, Wisconsin
401 S. State St., 7th Fl.
Chicago, IL 60605

Region VI
Arkansas, Louisiana, New Mexico,
  Oklahoma, Texas
1200 Main Tower Bldg., Suite 2260
Dallas, TX 75202

Region VII
Iowa, Kansas, Missouri, Nebraska
10220 N. Executive Hills Blvd.
8th Fl.
PO Box 901381
Kansas City, MO 64190

Region VIII
Colorado, Montana, North Dakota, South
  Dakota, Utah, Wyoming
1961 Stout St., Rm. 342
Denver, CO 80294

Region IX
American Samoa, Arizona, California,
  Guam, Hawaii, Nevada, Trust
  Territories of Pacific Islands
221 Main St., 10th Fl.
San Francisco, CA 94105

Region X
Alaska, Idaho, Oregon, Washington
2901 Third Ave., Rm. 100
Seattle, WA 98121

Appendix B
Office of Special Education and Rehabilitative Services, Rehabilitation Services Administration Regional Offices

Region I
RSA Regional Commissioner
John F. Kennedy Federal Bldg.
Rm. E400 Government Center
Boston, MA 02203

Region II
RSA Regional Commissioner
26 Federal Plaza
Rm. 4104
New York, NY 10278

Region III
RSA Regional Commissioner
3535 Market St., Rm. 16120
Philadelphia, PA 19104

Region IV
RSA Regional Commissioner
101 Marietta St. NW, Suite 2210
PO Box 1691
Atlanta, GA 30301

Region V
RSA Regional Commissioner
401 S. State St., Suite 700E
Chicago, IL 60605

Region VI
RSA Regional Commissioner
1200 Main Tower Bldg.
Rm. 2140
Dallas, TX 75202

Region VII
RSA Regional Commissioner
PO Box 901381
Kansas City, MO 64190-1381

Region VIII
RSA Regional Commissioner
Federal Office Bldg.
Rm. 398
1961 Stout St.
Denver, CO 80294

Region IX
RSA Regional Commissioner
Federal Office Bldg.
Rm. 229
50 United Nations Plaza
San Francisco, CA 94102

Region X
RSA Regional Commissioner
915 Second Ave., Rm. 3390
Seattle, WA 98174-1099

Appendix C
State Vocational
Rehabilitation Agencies

General/Blind

Council of State Administrators of
  Vocational Rehabilitation
PO Box 3776
1055 Thomas Jefferson St. NW, Suite
  401
Washington, DC 20007

Alabama

Division of Rehabilitation and Crippled
  Children Service
PO Box 11586
Montgomery, AL 36111

Alaska

Division of Vocational Rehabilitation
Box F, MS 0581
Juneau, AK 99811

American Samoa

Office of Vocational Rehabilitation
Department of Human Resources
PO Box 3492
American Samoa Government
Pago Pago, American Samoa 96799

Arizona

Rehabilitation Services Administration
Department of Economic Security
1300 W. Washington St.
Phoenix, AZ 85007

Arkansas

Division of Rehabilitation Services
PO Box 3781
Arkansas Department of Human Services
Little Rock, AR 72203

Division of Services for the Blind
Department of Human Services
PO Box 3237
411 Victory St.
Little Rock, AR 72203

California

Department of Rehabilitation
830 K Street Mall
Sacramento, CA 95814

Colorado

Division of Rehabilitation
Department of Social Services
1575 Sherman St., 4th Fl.
Denver, CO 80203-1714

Commonwealth of Northern Mariana Islands

Vocational Rehabilitation Division
Saipan, Northern Mariana Islands 96950

Connecticut

Division of Rehabilitative Services
State Board of Education
600 Asylum Ave.
Hartford, CT 06105

Services for the Blind
Department of Human Resources
170 Ridge Rd.
Wethersfield, CT 06100

Delaware

Division for the Visually Impaired
Department of Health and Social
  Services
305 W. 8th St.
Wilmington, DE 19801

Division of Vocational Rehabilitation
Department of Labor
Elwyn Bldg.
321 E. 11th St.
Wilmington, DE 19801

District of Columbia

DC Rehabilitation Services
Administration, Commission on Social
  Services
Department of Human Services
605 G St. NW
Rm. 1111
Washington, DC 20007

Federated States of Micronesia

VRS Coordinator
Office of Education
Kolonia, Pehnpen
Eastern Caroline Island 96941

Florida

Division of Blind Services
Department of Education
2540 Executive Center Circle W.
Douglas Bldg.
Tallahassee, FL 32301

Division of Vocational Rehabilitation
Department of Labor and Employment
  Security
1709-A Mahan Dr.
Tallahassee, FL 32399-0696

Georgia

Division of Rehabilitation Services
Department of Human Services
878 Peachtree St. NW
Rm. 706
Atlanta, GA 30309

Guam

Department of Vocational Rehabilitation
Government of Guam
122 Harmon Plaza
Rm. B201
Harmon Industrial Park
GU 96911

Hawaii

Division of Vocational Rehabilitation
Department of Human Services
Bishop Trust Bldg.
1000 Bishop St., Rm. 615
Honolulu, HI 96813

Idaho

Division of Vocational Rehabilitation
Len B. Jordon Bldg.
Rm. 150
650 W. State
Boise, ID 83720

Idaho Commission for the Blind
341 W. Washington St.
Boise, ID 83702

Illinois

Department of Rehabilitation Services
623 E. Adams St.
PO Box 19429
Springfield, IL 62794-9429

Indiana

Department of Human Services
Capital Center
251 N. Illinois St.
PO Box 7983
Indianapolis, IN 46207-7083

Iowa

Department for the Blind
524 Fourth St.
Des Moines, IA 50309

Division of Vocational Rehabilitation
  Services
Department of Education
510 E. 12th St.
Des Moines, IA 50319

Kansas

Commissioner of Rehabilitation Services
Department of Social and Rehabilitation
   Services
300 SW Oakley St.
Biddle Bldg., 2nd Fl.
Topeka, KS 66606

Kentucky

Department for Blind Services
Education and Arts Cabinet
427 Versailles Rd.
Frankfort, KY 40601

Office of Vocational Rehabilitation
930 Capital Plaza Tower
Frankfort, KY 40601

Louisiana

Division of Rehabilitation Services
Office of Community Services
Department of Health and Hospitals
PO Box 94371
1755 Florida St.
Baton Rouge, LA 70804

Maine

Bureau of Rehabilitation
Department of Human Services
32 Winthrop St.
Augusta, ME 04330

Maryland

Division of Vocational Rehabilitation
State Department of Education
200 W. Baltimore St.
Baltimore, MD 21201-2595

Massachusetts

Commission for the Blind
110 Tremont St., 6th Fl.
Boston, MA. 02108

Massachusetts Rehabilitation
   Commission
Statler Office Bldg.
11th Fl.
20 Park Plaza
Boston, MA 02116

Michigan

Commission for the Blind
Department of Labor
309 N. Washington Sq.
Lansing, MI 48909

Michigan Rehabilitation Services
Department of Education
PO Box 30010
Lansing, MI 48909

Minnesota

State Services for the Blind
Division of Rehabilitation Services
Department of Jobs and Training
1745 University Ave.
St. Paul, MN 55104

Vocational Rehabilitation Division
Department of Jobs and Training
390 N. Robert St., 5th Fl.
St. Paul, MN 55101

Mississippi

Vocational Rehabilitation for the Blind
PO Box 4892
Jackson, MS 39215

Vocational Rehabilitation Services
PO Box 1698
Jackson, MS 39205

Missouri

Bureau for the Blind
Division of Family Services
619 E. Capitol
Jefferson City, MO 65101

Division of Vocational Rehabilitation
State Department of Education
2401 E. McCarty
Jefferson City, MO 65101

Montana

Rehabilitative Services Division
Department of Social and Rehabilitation
   Services
PO Box 4210
111 Sanders
Helena, MT 59604

Nebraska

Division of Rehabilitative Services
State Department of Education
301 Centennial Mall, 6th Fl.
Lincoln, NE 68509

Services for the Visually Impaired
Department of Public Institutions
4600 Valley Rd.
Lincoln, NE 68510-4844

Nevada

Rehabilitation Division
Department of Human Resources
Kinkead Bldg., 5th Fl.
505 E. King St.
Carson City, NV 89710

New Hampshire

Division of Vocational Rehabilitation
State Department of Education
78 Regional Dr.
Concord, NH 03301

New Jersey

Commission for the Blind and Visually
  Impaired
1100 Raymond Blvd.
Newark, NJ 07102

Division of Vocational Rehabilitation
  Services
New Jersey Department of Labor and
  Industry
John Fitch Plaza
Trenton, NJ 08625

New Mexico

Commission for the Blind
Pera Bldg., Rm. 205
Santa Fe, NM 87503

Division of Vocational Rehabilitation
State Department of Education
604 W. San Mateo
Sante Fe, NM 87503

New York

Commission for the Blind and Visually
  Handicapped
10 Eyck Office Bldg.
40 N. Pearl St.
Albany, NY 12243

Office of Vocational Rehabilitation
New York State Education Department
99 Washington Ave.
Rm. 1907
Albany, NY 12234

North Carolina

Division of Services for the Blind
North Carolina Department of Human
  Resources
309 Ashe Ave.
Raleigh, NC 27606

Division of Vocational Rehabilitation
  Services
Department of Human Resources
State Office
PO Box 26053
Raleigh, NC 27611

North Dakota

Office of Vocational Rehabilitation
Department of Human Services
State Capitol
Bismarck, ND 58505

Ohio

Rehabilitation Services Commission
400 E. Campus View Blvd.
Columbus, OH 43235-4604

Oklahoma

Division of Rehabilitation Services
Department of Human Services
PO Box 25352
2409 N. Kelly
Oklahoma City, OK 73125

Oregon

Commission for the Blind
535 SW 12th Ave.
Portland, OR 97214

Vocational Rehabilitation Division
Department of Human Resources
2045 Silverton Road NE
Salem, OR 97310

Pennsylvania

Bureau of Blindness and Visual Services
Department of Public Welfare
Capital Associates Bldg., Rm. 300
PO Box 2675
Harrisburg, PA 17105

Office of Vocational Rehabilitation
Department of Labor and Industry
1300 Labor and Industry Bldg.
7th and Forster St.
Harrisburg, PA 17120

Puerto Rico

Secretary for Vocational Rehabilitation
Department of Social Services
PO Box 1118
Hato Rey, PR 00910

Republic of the Marshall Islands

Vocational Rehabilitation Coordinator
Health Services Department
PO Box 832
Majuro, Marshall Islands 96960

Republic of Palau

Vocational Rehabilitation Coordinator
Bureau of Education
PO Box 189
Koror, Palau
Western Caroline Islands 96940

Rhode Island

Administrator, Vocational Rehabilitation
Department of Human Services
40 Fountain St.
Providence, RI 02903

State Services for the Blind and Visually
Impaired
Department of Human Services
46 Aborn St.
Providence, RI 02903

South Carolina

Commission for the Blind
1430 Confederate Ave.
Columbia, SC 29201

Vocational Rehabilitation Department
PO Box 15
1410 Boston Ave.
West Columbus, SC 29171-0015

South Dakota

Department of Vocational Rehabilitation
Richard F. Kneip Bldg.
700 Governors Dr.
Pierre, SD 57501

Tennessee

Division of Rehabilitation Services
Department of Human Services
Citizen Plaza Bldg., 15th Fl.
400 Deaderick St.
Nashville, TN 37219

Texas

Commission for the Blind
Administration Bldg.
4800 N. Lamar St.
PO Box 12886, Capitol Station
Austin, TX 78711

Texas Rehabilitation Commission
118 E. Riverside Dr.
Austin, TX 78704

Utah

Services for the Visually Handicapped
State Office of Education
309 E. First South
Salt Lake City, UT 84111

Vocational Rehabilitation Services
State Office of Education
250 E. 500 South
Salt Lake City, UT 84111

Vermont

Division for the Blind and Visually
Impaired
Agency of Human Services
Osgood Bldg.
Waterbury Complex
103 S. Main St.
Waterbury, VT 05676

Vocational Rehabilitation Division
Agency of Human Services
Osgood Bldg.
Waterbury Complex
103 S. Main St.
Waterbury, VT 05676

Virgin Islands

Division of Disabilities and
    Rehabilitation Services
c/o Department of Human Services
Barbel Plaza South
St. Thomas, VI 00802

Virginia

Department of Rehabilitative Services
4901 Fitzhugh Ave.
PO Box 11045
Richmond, VA 23230-1045

Department for the Visually
    Handicapped
397 Azalea Ave.
Richmond, VA 23227-3697

Washington

Department of Services for the Blind
521 East Legon Way, MS FD-11
Olympia, WA 98504-1422

Division of Vocational Rehabilitation
Department of Social and Health
    Services
OB 21 C
Olympia, WA 98504

West Virginia

Division of Rehabilitation Services
State Board of Rehabilitation
State Capitol
Charleston, WV 25305

Wisconsin

Division of Vocational Rehabilitation
Department of Health and Social
    Services
1 W. Wilson, 8th Fl.
PO Box 7852
Madison, WI 53702

Wyoming

Division of Vocational Rehabilitation
Department of Health and Social Service
347 Hathaway Bldg.
Cheyenne, WY 82002

Appendix D
US Department of Education, Office of Special Education, Regional Resource Centers (RRCs)

Region I

Connecticut, Maine, Massachusetts, New
Hampshire, New Jersey, New York,
Rhode Island, Vermont
Northest RRC
Trinity College
Colchester Ave.
Burlington, VT 05401
SPECIALNET: NERRC

Region II

Delaware, Kentucky, Maryland, North
Carolina, South Carolina, Tennessee,
Virginia, Washington, DC, West
Virginia
MidSouth RRC
University of Kentucky
128 Porter Bldg.
Lexington, KY 40506-0205
SPECIALNET: MSRRC

Region III

Alabama, Arkansas, Florida, Georgia,
Louisiana, Mississippi, New Mexico,
Oklahoma, Puerto Rico, Texas, Virgin
Islands
South Atlantic RRC
Florida Atlantic University
1236 N. University Dr.
Plantation, FL 33322
SPECIALNET: SARRC

Region IV

Illinois, Indiana, Michigan, Minnesota,
Ohio, Pennsylvania, Wisconsin
Great Lakes Area RRC
700 Ackerman Rd.
Suite 440
Columbus, OH 43202
SPECIALNET: GLARRC

Region V

Bureau of Indian Affairs, Colorado, Iowa,
Kansas, Missouri, Montana,
Nebraska, North Dakota, South
Dakota, Utah, Wyoming
Mountain Plains RRC
1780 N. Research Pkwy., Suite 112
Logan, UT 84321
SPECIALNET: UTAH. USU

Region VI

Alaska, American Samoa, Arizona,
California, Federated States of
Micronesia, Guam, Hawaii, Idaho,
Marshall Islands, Nevada, Northern
Mariana Islands, Oregon, Palau,
Washington
Western RRC
College of Education, Clinical Services
Bldg.
University of Oregon
Eugene, OR 97403
SPECIALNET: WRRC

NEC*TAS NETWORK

National Early Childhood Technical
  Assistance System
Coordinating Office:
Frank Porter Graham Child
  Development Center
The University of North Carolina at
  Chapel Hill
CB 8040
500 NCNB Plaza
Chapel Hill, NC 27599

Child Development Center
Georgetown University
3800 Reservoir Rd., NW
Washington, DC 20007-2197

Department of Special Education
University of Hawaii at Manoa
1776 University Ave.
208 Wist
Honolulu, HI 96822

National Association of State Directors of
  Special Education
2021 K St. NW
Suite 315
Washington, DC 20006

National Center for Clinical Infant
  Programs
733 Fifteenth St. NW
Suite 912
Washington, DC 20005

National Network of Parent Centers, Inc.
312 Stuart St., 2nd Fl.
Boston, MA 02116

Appendix E
US Department of Health and Human Services; Agency for Children, Youth and Families; Resource Access Projects (RAPs)

Region I

Massachusetts, New Hampshire, Rhode
    Island, Vermont
New England RAP
Educational Development Center
55 Chapel St.
Newton, MA 02160

Region II

New Jersey, New York, Puerto Rico,
    Virgin Islands
New York University RAP
Department of Human Services and
    Education
48 Cooper Square, Rm. 103
New York, NY 10003

Region III

Delaware, Washington, DC, Maryland,
    Pennsylvania, Virginia, West Virginia
University of Maryland RAP
Head Start Resource and Training Center
University of Maryland
University College
University Blvd. at Adelphi Rd.
College Park, MD 20742

Region IV

Alabama, Florida, Georgia, Kentucky,
    Mississippi, North Carolina, South
    Carolina, Tennessee
Chapel Hill RAP
Lincoln Center
Merritt Mill Rd.
Chapel Hill, NC 27514

Mississippi RAP
Friends of Children of Mississippi, Inc.
119 Mayes St.
Jackson, MS 39213

Region V

Illinois, Indiana, Michigan, Minnesota,
    Ohio, Wisconsin
Great Lakes RAP
Colonel Wolfe School
403 E. Healy
Champaign, IL 61820

Great Lakes RAP
Portage Subcontract—
CESA 5
626 E. Slifer St.
Portage, WI 53901

Region VI

Arkansas, Louisiana, New Mexico,
    Oklahoma, Texas
Texas Tech University RAP
PO Box 4170
Lubbock, TX 79409

Region VII

Iowa, Kansas, Missouri, Nebraska
Region VII Head Start RAP
CRU 26
University of Kansas Medical Center
39th & Rainbow Blvd.
Kansas City, KS 66103

Region VIII

Colorado, Montana, North Dakota, South
Dakota, Utah, Wyoming
The Denver RAP
Greenlee Metro Lab School
1150 Lipan St., Rm. 105
Denver, CO 80204

Region IX

American Samoa, Arizona, California,
Guam, Hawaii, Nevada
Southwest Human Development RAP
1366 E. Thomas Rd., Suite 100
Phoenix, AZ 85014

Region X

Alaska, Idaho, Oregon, Washington
Region X RAP
Portland State University
PO Box 14901
Portland, OR 97207

Native American Grantees

Montana, New Mexico, North Dakota,
Oklahoma, South Dakota
Native American Grantees
Three Feathers Associates Resource
Center
PO Box 5508
Norman, OK 73070

Index

Compiled by Linda Webster

RUTH A. VELLEMAN

Ruth A. Velleman managed the information services at Human Resources Center and served as children's librarian at Human Resources School in Albertson, New York, for 25 years. She now acts as consultant to the organization. Velleman has taught courses in Library and Information Services for People with Disabilities at the Palmer Graduate School of Library and Information Science and now is a visiting professor. She has published many articles in library and rehabilitation journals, has conducted workshops around the country for many years, and authored the award-winning book *Serving Physically Disabled People: An Information Handbook for All Libraries* (Bowker, 1979).